Advances
in COMPUTERS
VOLUME 48

Advances in
COMPUTERS

Distributed Information Resources

EDITED BY

MARVIN V. ZELKOWITZ

Department of Computer Science
and Institute for Advanced Studies
University of Maryland
College Park, Maryland

VOLUME 48

ACADEMIC PRESS
San Diego London Boston
New York Sydney Tokyo Toronto

This book is printed on acid-free paper.

Copyright © 1999 by ACADEMIC PRESS

All Rights Reserved.
No part of this publication may be reproduced or transmitted in any form or by any means electronic or mechanical, including photocopying, recording, or any information storage and retrieval system, without permission in writing from the publisher.

Academic Press
A Harcourt Science and Technology Company
525 B Street, Suite 1900, San Diego, California 92101-4495, USA
http://www.apnet.com

Academic Press
24–28 Oval Road, London NW1 7DX, UK
http://www.hbuk.co.uk/ap/

ISBN 0-12-012148-4

A catalogue for this book is available from the British Library

Typeset by Mathematical Composition Setters Ltd, Salisbury, UK
Printed in Great Britain by Redwood Books, Trowbridge, Wiltshire

99 00 01 02 03 04 RB 9 8 7 6 5 4 3 2 1

Contents

CONTRIBUTORS ix
PREFACE xiii

Architectures and Patterns for Developing High-performance, Real-time ORB Endsystems

Douglas C. Schmidt, David L. Levine and Chris Cleeland

1. Introduction 2
2. Evaluating OMG CORBA for High-performance,
   Real-time Systems 3
3. Architectural Components and Features for High-performance,
   Real-time ORB Endsystems 13
4. Supporting Real-time Scheduling in CORBA 31
5. Designing a Real-time ORB Core 50
6. Using Patterns to Build TAO's Extensible ORB Software
   Architecture 82
7. Concluding Remarks 113
   References 114

Heterogeneous Data Access in a Mobile Environment – Issues and Solutions

J. B. Lim and A. R. Hurson

1. Introduction 120
2. Background 125
3. Multidatabase Systems 134
4. The MDAS Environment 139
5. Transaction Management and Concurrency Control 146
6. Evaluation of Proposed Algorithm 158
7. Conclusions and Future Directions 165
   Appendix: Related Projects 167
   Glossary 174
   References 175

The World Wide Web

Hal Berghel and Douglas Blank

1. Introduction	180
2. The Internet: Precursor to the Web	182
3. The Success of the Web	183
4. Perspectives	184
5. The Underlying Technologies	188
6. Dynamic Web Technologies	194
7. Security and Privacy	210
8. The Web as a Social Phenomenon	214
9. Conclusion	216
References	217

Progress in Internet Security

Randall J. Atkinson and J. Eric Klinker

1. Introduction	220
2. The Internet Protocol	222
3. Security for the Internet Protocol	224
4. Routing Protocols and Technology	227
5. Domain Name System	234
6. Dynamic Host Configuration Protocol (DHCP)	236
7. Key Management	237
8. Public Key Infrastructure	239
9. Network Management	241
10. Interactive Applications	243
11. Electronic Commerce	244
12. Electronic Mail	248
13. Other Considerations	250
14. Conclusions	251
References	251

Digital Libraries: Social Issues and Technological Advances

Hsinchun Chen and Andrea L. Houston

1. Introduction	258
2. Digital Libraries: Historical Overview	259

3. What Is a Digital Library?	261
4. Drives towards Digital Libraries	265
5. Digital Library Research Issues in the Social Context	268
6. Digital Library Research Activities: An Overview	276
7. Digital Library Research Issues in Semantic Interoperability	299
8. Conclusions and the Future	306
References	309

Architectures for Mobile Robot Control

Julio K. Rosenblatt and James A. Hendler

1. Introduction	316
2. Architectures for Mobile Robot Control	319
3. Command Arbitration	335
4. Conclusion	347
References	350

AUTHOR INDEX	355
SUBJECT INDEX	365
CONTENTS OF VOLUMES IN THIS SERIES	375

Contributors

Randall Atkinson is a Senior Scientist with @Home Network, where he performs research and development for new Internet services. He has been active in Internet R&D for many years, including participating in IETF standards. He has undergraduate and graduate degrees in Electrical Engineering and Computer Science from the University of Virginia, Charlottesville, VA.

Hal Berghel is a professor of Computer Science at the University of Arkansas and a frequent contributor to the literature on cyberspace. He has been an active researcher in computer science for several decades, most especially within the areas of information management and highly interactive and participatory systems. He is a Fellow of the ACM and received the ACM Distinguished Service Award in 1996 for his work in experimental computing and service to the ACM.

Douglas Blank is an assistant professor of Computer Science at the University of Arkansas. His research interests include connectionist networks and intelligent and interactive computer systems. He is currently experimenting with applications of his research to robotics.

Hsinchun Chen is a professor of Management Information Systems at the University of Arizona and head of the UA/MIS Artificial Intelligence Group. He is also a Visiting Senior Research Scientist at National Center for Supercomputing Applications (NCSA). He received the PhD degree in Information Systems from New York University in 1989. He is a Principal Investigator of the Illinois digital Library Initiative project, funded by NSF/ARPA/NASA, and has received several grants from NSF, DARPA, NASA, NIH, and NCSA.

Chris Cleeland is a member of the technical staff at Catalyst, Inc., in St Louis, Missouri. As a research associate at Washington University, Chris's research focused on design patterns and optimization strategies for real-time ORB endsystems, particularly the ORB Core component of TAO.

James Hendler is an associate professor and head of both the Mobile Robots Laboratory and the Advanced Information Technology Laboratory at the University of Maryland, where he has joint appointments in the Department of Computer Science, the Institute for Systems Research, the

Institute for Advanced Computer Studies and is also an affiliate of the Electrical Engineering Department. In 1985, he received his PhD in artificial intelligence working with Dr Eugene Charniak at Brown University. He is the author of the book *Integrating Marker-Passing and Problem Solving: An activation spreading approach to improved choice in planning* and is the editor of *Expert Systems: The User Interface*, *Readings in Planning* (with J. Allen and A. Tate), and *Massively Parallel AI* (with H. Kitano). Prof. Hendler was the recipient of a 1995 Fulbright Fellowship, is a member of the US Air Force Science Advisory Board, chairs the ACM doctoral dissertation awards committee, and will be Program Chair of the 16th National Conference on Artificial Intelligence (AAAI-99).

Andrea L. Houston worked in industry for 15 years before returning to academe and earning a PhD from the University of Arizona. Her BA is from the University of Pennsylvania, and her MBA is from the University of New Hampshire. She is currently an assistant professor at Louisiana State University. Her research interests include medical information systems, digital libraries, and information retrieval.

A. R. Hurson is a Computer Science and Engineering professor at The Pennsylvania State University. His research for the past 16 years has been directed toward the design and analysis of general as well as special purpose computer architectures. Professor Hurson has been active in various IEEE/ACM conferences and has given tutorials for various conferences on global information sharing, dataflow processing, database management systems, supercomputer technology, data/knowledge-based systems, scheduling and load balancing, and parallel computing. He served as a member of the IEEE Computer Society Press Editorial Board and as an IEEE Distinguished Speaker. Currently, he is serving in the IEEE/ACM Computer Sciences Accreditation Board, as the editor of IEEE transactions on computers, and as an ACM lecturer.

Eric Klinker is a Senior Network Engineer with @Home Network. He works on developing new Internet services and technologies for distribution over @Home's broadband network. Eric has been active in Internet research for several years, including work in scalable multicast routing algorithms and security. He has an undergraduate degree in Electrical Engineering from the University of Illinois at Urbana-Champaign (UIUC) and a master's degree in Electrical Engineering from the Naval Postgraduate School, Monterey, California.

David L. Levine is a Senior Research Associate in the Distributed Object Computing (DOC) Group at Washington University in St Louis, Missouri.

He received his PhD in Computer Science from the University of California, Irvine, in 1993. His research focuses on scheduling of ORB endsystem system resources like CPU and network bandwidth.

James B. Lim received the MS degree in 1995 and PhD degree in 1998 in computer engineering from The Pennsylvania State University. Research at Penn State included clustering in object-oriented databases, and transaction processing in mobile, heterogeneous environments. Dr. Lim is currently working at the Advanced Research Center at EMC Corporation. His is currently researching storage and backup techniques for large databases (100s of terabytes) in high availability and fault tolerant environments.

Julio Rosenblatt is a Senior Research Associate in the Department of Mechanical and Mechatronic Engineering at Sydney University. He has over 10 years' experience in autonomous vehicle navigation and planning research, with an emphasis on the development of behavioral approaches to vehicle navigation. As a Research Associate at the University of Maryland Institute for Advanced Computer Studies, he was Director of the Autonomous Mobile Robotics Laboratory. Dr Rosenblatt received the MS and PhD degrees in Robotics in 1991 and 1996, respectively, from Carnegie Mellon University. Dr Rosenblatt received the SB in Computer Science from the Massachusetts Institute of Technology in 1985. He is currently investigating the use of classical navigation methods such as Kalman filtering within the context of behavior-based approaches, and applying this research towards straddle-carrier docking and path control for subsea vehicles. Working in conjunction with a cognitive psychologist, Dr Rosenblatt is also developing intelligent agents for human-computer interaction based on cognitive models of users and of tasks in time-critical domains such as radar operation, air traffic control, and satellite operation.

Douglas C. Schmidt is an Associate Professor of Computer Science at Washington University in St Louis, Missouri. He received his PhD in Computer Science from the University of California, Irvine in 1994. His research focuses on design patterns, implementation, and experimental analysis of object-oriented techniques for developing high-performance distributed object computing middleware that run over high-speed ATM networks.

Preface

As we approach the twenty-first century, *Advances in Computers* remains the oldest continuously published anthology chronicling the evolution of the information technology field. Since 1960, this series has described the ever-changing nature of computing. In this volume, we will emphasize the major themes that have dominated computing in these latter days of the 1990s. Of course we mean the distributed nature of information technology.

The growth of networking, the Internet and the World Wide Web have greatly changed the role of the computer, and in turn, our lives as well. Starting as a computer science research topic in 1969, the ARPANET, funded by the US government's Advanced Research Projects Agency (ARPA), tied together university, research, and military computing centers. By the mid-1980s the ARPANET evolved into the Internet under funding by the US National Science Foundation (NSF). The computer experimenter, the so-called "computer geek," discovered the Internet and joined the fun. By the early 1990s, the World Wide Web (WWW) grew as a subnet of the Internet, and email and Web browsing became available to all. Today millions of "computer illiterate" individuals daily use these resources to send mail and search for online information. No longer is the Internet the domain of the serious computer researcher. In this volume we will describe some of the changes the Internet has brought us.

In the first paper, "Architectures and Patterns for Developing High-performance Real-time ORB Endsystems," Douglas Schmidt, David Levine, and Chris Cleeland describe the growing need for software called "middleware." As we build networks of computers, increased efficiency in solving problems can be achieved by having an application execute on several machines, each solving part of the problem. In order to do this, there has to be a standard way for the various computers to communicate among one another. Various communication channels have been proposed. One such proposal was the Common Object Request Broker Architecture (CORBA). In this paper Professor Schmidt and his co-authors describe several new contributions for using Object Request Brokers (ORBs) for applications with real-time and high-performance requirements.

Along with the Internet, another major innovation in the 1990s is the growth of cellular telephones and mobile communications. No longer are we tied to wires in order to communicate with anyone in the world. In the second paper, "Heterogeneous Data Access in a Mobile Environment—Issues and

Solutions," by J. B. Kim and A. R. Hurson, the authors show how the merging of computer and communication technologies leads to accessing data in such a mobile environment. A new hierarchical concurrent control algorithm is introduced that allows a large number of users to simultaneously access data available on the network.

The third paper, "The World Wide Web," by Hal Berghel and Douglas Blank, chronicles the growth of the Internet and the evolving World Wide Web. In particular, the paper discusses the various languages users resort to in order to communicate on the Web. By now, just about everyone has "surfed the Web" using a Web browser. In this paper, the authors describe some of the inner workings of Web browsers. In particular, they briefly describe the major language used by browsers, HTML (Hyper-Text Markup Language), and show how Web browsers read and execute HTML scripts in order to execute and display users' Web commands.

Of growing concern with the rise of the Internet is the security of the information that travels among computers. As electronic commerce grows in importance and individuals enter credit card numbers and other personal information, it is important that this information reaches its intended destination reliably and unseen by unauthorized individuals. Randall Atkinson and J. Eric Klinker discuss these problems in "Progress in Internet Security." They discuss the growth of various algorithms that are used to route information around the network and discuss the use of various key encryption algorithms so that if information is intercepted by unauthorized individuals, that information will be unreadable.

One of the major promises of these global networks is the ability to find information quickly, reliably, and cheaply. Rather than having individual libraries of information scattered worldwide, people needing such information will be able to use the network to access an appropriate central library. Fewer backup copies of any piece of information will be needed, and keeping information current will be easier since fewer repositories of such information will need to be updated with new information. Creators of such information will still need an economic incentive to collect such information, and ensuring the correctness of that information is necessary to give credibility to such repositories. These and other issues are discussed in "Digital Libraries: Social Issues and Technological Advances" by Hsinchun Chen and Andrea Houston.

The final chapter in this volume, "Architectures for Mobile Robot Control" by Julio Rosenblatt and James Hendler is a slight departure from the other papers in this volume. Here the authors discuss mobile robots and the problems of building autonomous mobile robots that can follow paths independent of human control. They discuss architectural frameworks for such robots in terms of system design issues—centralized versus distributed, reactive versus deliberative, and top-down versus bottom-up control.

At this time I would like to thank my two employers, the Department of Computer Science at the University of Maryland, College Park, Maryland and the Fraunhofer Center—Maryland in College Park Maryland, for the encouragement and time to work on these volumes. It takes a significant amount of time to get these volumes produced. I would also like to thank the authors of this volume for their efforts at producing their chapters. If you would like to see a topic covered that you believe I have not discussed recently, send me email to either `mvz@cs.umd.edu` or `mvz@fc-md.umd.edu`, and you will see it in a future volume.

MARVIN V. ZELKOWITZ
College Park, Maryland

Architectures and Patterns for Developing High-performance, Real-time ORB Endsystems

DOUGLAS C. SCHMIDT, DAVID L. LEVINE, CHRIS CLEELAND

Department of Computer Science
Washington University
St Louis, MO 63130*
USA
{schmidt,levine,cleeland,irfan}@cs.wustl.edu

Abstract

Many types of applications can benefit from flexible and open middleware. CORBA is an emerging middleware standard for Object Request Brokers (ORBs) that simplifies the development of distributed applications and services. Experience with CORBA demonstrates that it is suitable for traditional RPC-style applications. However, the lack of performance optimizations and quality of service (QoS) features in conventional CORBA implementations make them unsuited for high-performance and real-time applications.

This paper makes four contributions to the design of CORBA ORBs for applications with high-performance and real-time requirements. First, it describes the design of TAO, which is our high-performance, real-time CORBA-compliant ORB. Second, it presents TAO's real-time scheduling service, which provides QoS guarantees for deterministic real-time CORBA applications. Third, it empirically evaluates the effects of priority inversion and non-determinism in conventional ORBs and shows how these hazards are avoided in TAO. Fourth, it presents a case study of key patterns used to develop TAO and quantifies the impact of applying patterns to reduce the complexity of common ORB tasks.

1. Introduction 2
2. Evaluating OMG CORBA for High-performance, Real-time Systems 3
   2.1 Overview of the CORBA Reference Model 3
   2.2 Limitations of CORBA for Real-time Applications 6
   2.3 Overcoming CORBA Limitations for High-performance and Real-time
       Applications. 8

* This work was supported in part by NSF grant NCR-9628218, DARPA contracts 9701516 and S30602-98-C-0187, Boeing, Lucent, Motorola, SAIC, Siemens, and Sprint.

3. Architectural Components and Features for High-performance, Real-time ORB Endsystems.. 13
   3.1 High-performance, Real-time I/O Subsystem........................... 15
   3.2 Efficient and Predictable ORB Cores................................. 18
   3.3 Efficient and Predictable Object Adapters 25
   3.4 Efficient and Predictable Stubs and Skeletons 29
   3.5 Efficient and Predictable Memory Management......................... 30
4. Supporting Real-time Scheduling in CORBA................................ 31
   4.1 Synopsis of Application Quality of Service Requirements.............. 31
   4.2 Responsibilities of a Real-time Scheduling Service 32
   4.3 Specifying QoS Requirements in TAO using Real-time IDL Schemas 34
   4.4 Overview of TAO's Scheduling Model.................................. 39
   4.5 Overview of TAO's Off-line Scheduling Service 41
5. Designing a Real-time ORB Core 50
   5.1 Alternative ORB Core Connection Architectures....................... 51
   5.2 Alternative ORB Core Concurrency Architectures...................... 54
   5.3 Benchmarking Testbed 60
   5.4 Performance Results on Solaris...................................... 63
   5.5 Performance Results on Chorus ClassiX............................... 73
   5.6 Evaluation and Recommendations...................................... 79
6. Using Patterns to Build TAO's Extensible ORB Software Architecture...... 82
   6.1 Why We Need Dynamically Configurable Middleware 83
   6.2 Overview of Patterns that Improve ORB Extensibility................. 85
   6.3 How to Use Patterns to Resolve ORB Design Challenges 87
   6.4 Summary of Design Challenges and Patterns that Resolve Them 109
   6.5 Evaluating the Contribution of Patterns to ORB Middleware........... 109
7. Concluding Remarks 113
Acknowledgments 114
References 114

1. Introduction

Distributed computing helps improve application performance through multi-processing; reliability and availability through replication; scalability, extensibility, and portability through modularity; and cost effectiveness though resources sharing and open systems. An increasingly important class of distributed applications requires stringent quality of service (QoS) guarantees. These applications include telecommunication systems command and control systems, multimedia systems, and simulations.

In addition to requiring QoS guarantees, distributed applications must be flexible and reusable. Flexibility is needed to respond rapidly to evolving functional and QoS requirements of distributed applications. Reusability is needed to yield substantial improvements in productivity and to enhance the quality, performance, reliability, and interoperability of distributed application software.

The Common Object Request Broker Architecture (CORBA) [46] is an emerging standard for distributed object computing (DOC) middleware. DOC middleware resides between clients and servers. It simplifies application development by providing a uniform view of heterogeneous network and OS layers.

At the heart of DOC middleware are Object Request Brokers (ORBs), such as CORBA [46], DCOM [1], and Java RMI [76]. ORBs eliminate many tedious, error-prone, and non-portable aspects of developing and maintaining distributed applications using low-level network programming mechanisms like sockets [65]. In particular, ORBs automate common network programming tasks such as object location, object activation, parameter marshaling/demarshaling, socket and request demultiplexing, fault recovery, and security. Thus, ORBs facilitate the development of flexible distributed applications and reusable services in heterogeneous distributed environments.

The remainder of this paper is organized as follows: section 2 evaluates the suitability of CORBA for high-performance, real-time systems; section 3 outlines the real-time feature enhancements and performance optimizations supported by TAO, which is our high-performance, real-time ORB endsystem; section 4 describes the design of TAO's real-time scheduling service; section 5 qualitatively and quantitatively evaluates alternative ORB Core concurrency and connection architectures; section 6 qualitatively and quantitatively evaluates the patterns that resolve key design challenges we faced when developing TAO; and section 7 presents concluding remarks.

2. Evaluating OMG CORBA for High-performance, Real-time Systems

This section provides an overview of CORBA, explains why the current CORBA specification and conventional ORB implementations are currently inadequate for high-performance and real-time systems, and outlines the steps required to develop ORBs that can provide end-to-end QoS to applications.

2.1 Overview of the CORBA Reference Model

CORBA Object Request Brokers (ORBs) [46] allow clients to invoke operations on distributed objects without concern for the following issues [75]:

- *Object location.* CORBA objects can be collocated with the client or distributed on a remote server, without affecting their implementation or use.
- *Programming language.* The languages supported by CORBA include C, C++, Java, Ada95, COBOL, and Smalltalk, among others.

- *OS platform.* CORBA runs on many OS platforms, including Win32, UNIX, MVS, and real-time embedded systems like VxWorks, Chorus, and LynxOS.
- *Communication protocols and interconnects.* The communication protocols and interconnects that CORBA can run on include TCP/IP, IPX/SPX, FDDI, ATM, Ethernet, Fast Ethernet, embedded system back-planes, and shared memory.
- *Hardware.* CORBA shields applications from side-effects stemming from differences in hardware such as storage layout and data type sizes/ranges.

Figure 1 illustrates the components in the CORBA 2.x reference model, all of which collaborate to provide the portability, interoperability, and transparency outlined above.

Each component in the CORBA reference model is outlined below:

- *Client.* This program entity performs application tasks by obtaining object references to objects and invoking operations on them. Objects can be remote or collocated relative to the client. Ideally, accessing a remote object should be as simple as calling an operation on a local object, i.e. object → operation(args). Figure 1 shows the underlying components described below that ORBs use to transmit remote operation requests transparently from client to object.
- *Object.* In CORBA, an object is an instance of an Interface Definition Language (IDL) interface. The object is identified by an *object*

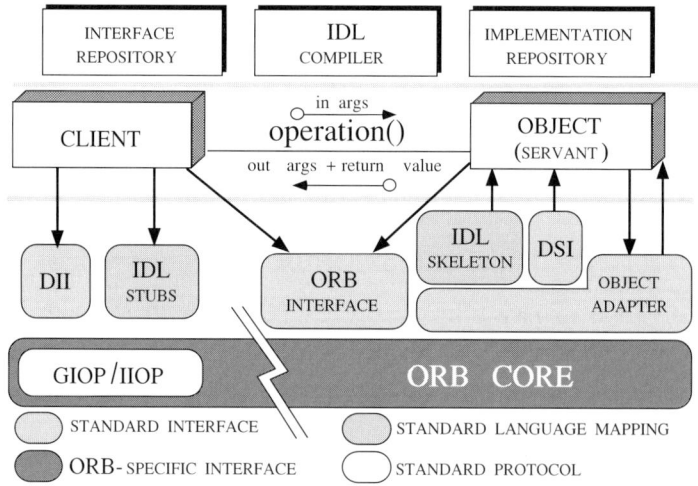

FIG. 1. Components in the CORBA 2.x reference model.

reference, which uniquely names that instance across servers. An *ObjectId* associates an object with its servant implementation, and is unique within the scope of an Object Adapter. Over its lifetime, an object has one or more servants associated with it that implement its interface.

- *Servant*. This component implements the operations defined by an OMG IDL interface. In languages like C++ and Java that support object-oriented (OO) programming, servants are implemented using one or more class instances. In non-OO languages, like C, servants are typically implemented using functions and `structs`. A client never interacts with a servant directly, but always through an object.

- *ORB Core*. When a client invokes an operation on an object, the ORB Core is responsible for delivering the request to the object and returning a response, if any, to the client. For objects executing remotely, a CORBA-compliant ORB Core communicates via a version of the General Inter-ORB Protocol (GIOP), most commonly the Internet Inter-ORB Protocol (IIOP), which runs atop the TCP transport protocol. An ORB Core is typically implemented as a run-time library linked into both client and server applications.

- *ORB interface*. An ORB is an abstraction that can be implemented various ways, e.g. one or more processes or a set of libraries. To decouple applications from implementation details, the CORBA specification defines an interface to an ORB. This ORB interface provides standard operations that (1) initialize and shutdown the ORB, (2) convert object references to strings and back, and (3) create argument lists for requests made through the dynamic invocation interface (DII).

- *OMG IDL stubs and skeletons*. IDL stubs and skeletons serve as a "glue" between the client and servants, respectively, and the ORB. Stubs provide a strongly-typed, static invocation interface (SII) that marshals application parameters into a common data-level representation. Conversely, skeletons demarshal the data-level representation back into typed parameters that are meaningful to an application.

- *IDL compiler*. An IDL compiler automatically transforms OMG IDL definitions into an application programming language like C++ or Java. In addition to providing programming language transparency, IDL compilers eliminate common sources of network programming errors and provide opportunities for automated compiler optimizations [11].

- *Dynamic invocation interface (DII)*. The DII allows clients to generate requests at run-time. This flexibility is useful when an application has no compile-time knowledge of the interface it accesses. The DII also allows clients to make *deferred synchronous* calls, which decouple the request and response portions of two-way operations to avoid blocking the client until the servant responds. In contrast, in CORBA 2.x, SII stubs only support *two-way*, i.e. request/response, and *one-way*, i.e. request-only operations.[1]

- *Dynamic skeleton interface (DSI)*. The DSI is the server's analogue to the client's DII. The DSI allows an ORB to deliver requests to servants that have no compile-time knowledge of the IDL interface they implement. Clients making requests need not know whether the server ORB uses static skeletons or dynamic skeletons. Likewise, servers need not know if clients use the DII or SII to invoke requests.
- *Object adapter*. An object adapter associates a servant with objects, demultiplexes incoming requests to the servant, and collaborates with the IDL skeleton to dispatch the appropriate operation upcall on that servant. CORBA 2.2 portability enhancements [46] define the Portable Object Adapter (POA), which supports multiple nested POAs per ORB. Object adapters enable ORBs to support various types of servants that possess similar requirements. This design results in a smaller and simpler ORB that can support a wide range of object granularities, lifetimes, policies, implementation styles, and other properties.
- *Interface Repository*. The Interface Repository provides run-time information about IDL interfaces. Using this information, it is possible for a program to encounter an object whose interface was not known when the program was compiled, yet, be able to determine what operations are valid on the object and make invocations on it. In addition, the Interface Repository provides a common location to store additional information associated with interfaces to CORBA objects, such as type libraries for stubs and skeletons.
- *Implementation Repository*. The Implementation Repository [28] contains information that allows an ORB to activate servers to process servants. Most of the information in the Implementation Repository is specific to an ORB or OS environment. In addition, the Implementation Repository provides a common location to store information associated with servers, such as administrative control, resource allocation, security, and activation modes.

2.2 Limitations of CORBA for Real-time Applications

Our experience using CORBA on telecommunication [59], avionics [27], and medical imaging projects [50] indicates that it is well-suited for

---

[1] The OMG has standardized an asynchronous method invocation interface in the Messaging specification [47], which will appear in CORBA 3.0.

conventional RPC-style applications that possess "best-effort" quality of service (QoS) requirements. However, conventional CORBA implementations are not yet suited for high-performance, real-time applications for the following reasons:

- *Lack of QoS specification interfaces.* The CORBA 2.x standard does not provide interfaces to specify end-to-end QoS requirements. For instance, there is no standard way for clients to indicate the relative priorities of their requests to an ORB. Likewise, there is no interface for clients to inform an ORB the rate at which to execute operations that have periodic processing deadlines.

    The CORBA standard also does not define interfaces that allow applications to specify admission control policies. For instance, a video server might prefer to use available network bandwidth to serve a limited number of clients and refuse service to additional clients, rather than admit all clients and provide poor video quality [43]. Conversely, a stock quote service might want to admit a large number of clients and distribute all available bandwidth and processing time equally among them.

- *Lack of QoS enforcement.* Conventional ORBs do not provide end-to-end QoS enforcement, i.e. from application-to-application across a network. For instance, most ORBs transmit, schedule, and dispatch client requests in FIFO order. However, FIFO strategies can yield unbounded priority inversions [52, 36], which occur when a lower priority request blocks the execution of a higher priority request for an indefinite period. Likewise, conventional ORBs do not allow applications to specify the priority of threads that process requests.

    Standard ORBs also do not provide fine-grained control of servant execution. For instance, they do not terminate servants that consume excess resources. Moreover, most ORBs use ad hoc resource allocation. Consequently, a single client can consume all available network bandwidth and a misbehaving servant can monopolize a server's CPU.

- *Lack of real-time programming features.* The CORBA 2.x specification does not define key features that are necessary to support real-time programming. For instance, the CORBA General Inter-ORB Protocol (GIOP) supports asynchronous messaging. However, no standard programming language mapping exists in CORBA 2.x to transmit client requests asynchronously, though the messaging specification in CORBA 3.0 will define this mapping. Likewise, the CORBA specification does not require an ORB to notify clients when transport layer flow control occurs, nor does it support timed operations [13]. As a result, it is hard to develop portable and efficient real-time applications that behave deterministically when ORB endsystem or network resources are unavailable temporarily.

- *Lack of performance optimizations.* Conventional ORB endsystems incur significant throughput [50] and latency [22] overhead, as well as exhibiting many priority inversions and sources of non-determinism [62], as shown in Fig. 2. These overheads stem from (1) non-optimized presentation layers that copy and touch data excessively [11] and overflow processor caches [21]; (2) internal buffering strategies that produce non-uniform behavior for different message sizes [17]; (3) inefficient demultiplexing and dispatching algorithms [20]; (4) long chains of intra-ORB virtual method calls [16]; and (5) lack of integration with underlying real-time OS and network QoS mechanisms [62, 64, 67].

2.3 Overcoming CORBA Limitations for High-performance and Real-time Applications

Meeting the QoS needs of next-generation distributed applications requires much more than defining IDL interfaces or adding pre-emptive real-time scheduling to an OS. Instead, it requires a vertically and horizontally integrated *ORB endsystem* that can deliver end-to-end QoS guarantees at multiple levels throughout a distributed system. The key components in an ORB

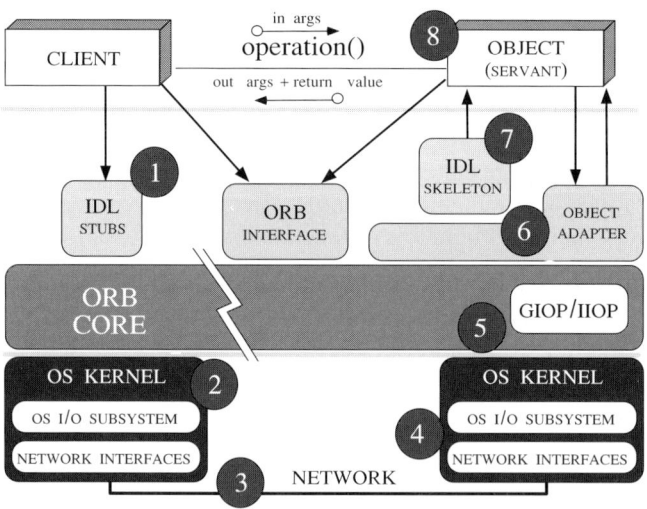

FIG. 2. Sources of latency and priority inversion in conventional ORBs. (1) Client marshaling; (2) Client protocol queueing; (3) Network delay; (4) Server protocol queueing; (5) Thread dispatching; (6) Request dispatching; (7) Server demarshaling; (8) Method execution.

endsystem include the network interfaces, operating system I/O subsystems, communication protocols, and common middleware object services.

Implementing an effective framework for real-time CORBA requires ORB endsystem developers to address two types of issues: *QoS specification* and *QoS enforcement*. First, real-time applications must meet certain timing constraints to ensure the usefulness of the applications. For instance, a video-conferencing application may require an upper bound on the propagation delay of video packets from the source to the destination. Such constraints are defined by the QoS specification of the system. Thus, providing effective OO middleware requires a real-time ORB endsystem that supports the mechanisms and semantics for applications to specify their QoS requirements. Second, the architecture of the ORB endsystem must be designed carefully to *enforce* the QoS parameters specified by applications.

Section 3 describes how we are developing such an integrated middleware framework called The ACE ORB (TAO) [64]. TAO is a high-performance, real-time CORBA-compliant ORB endsystem developed using the ACE framework [56], which is a highly portable OO middleware communication framework. ACE contains a rich set of C++ components that implement strategic design patterns [63] for high-performance and real-time communication systems. Since TAO is based on ACE it runs on a wide range of OS platforms including general-purpose operating systems, such as Solaris and Windows NT, as well as real-time operating systems such as VxWorks, Chorus, and LynxOS.

2.3.1 Synopsis of TAO

The TAO project focuses on the following topics related to real-time CORBA and ORB endsystems:

- Identifying enhancements to standard ORB specifications, particularly OMG CORBA, that will enable applications to specify their QoS requirements concisely and precisely to ORB endsystems [19].
- Empirically determining the features required to build real-time ORB endsystems that can enforce deterministic and statistical end-to-end application QoS guarantees [67].
- Integrating the strategies for I/O subsystem architectures and optimizations [62] with ORB middleware to provide end-to-end bandwidth, latency, and reliability guarantees to distributed applications.
- Capturing and documenting the key design patterns [63] necessary to develop, maintain, configure, and extend real-time ORB endsystems.

In addition to providing a real-time ORB, TAO is an integrated ORB endsystem that consists of a high-performance I/O subsystem [6, 25] and an

ATM Port Interconnect Controller (APIC) [9]. Figure 4 illustrates the main components in TAO's ORB endsystem architecture.

2.3.2 Requirements for High-performance and Real-time ORB Endsystems

The remainder of this section describes the requirements and features of ORB endsystems necessary to meet high-performance and real-time application QoS needs. It outlines key performance optimizations and provides a roadmap for the ORB features and optimizations presented in subsequent sections. Figure 3 summarizes the material covered below.

2.3.2.1 Policies and mechanisms for specifying end-to-end application QoS requirements
ORB endsystems must allow applications to specify the QoS requirements of their IDL operations using a small number of application-centric, rather than OS/network-centric parameters. Typical QoS parameters include computation time, execution period, and bandwidth/delay requirements. For instance, video-conferencing groupware [24, 43] may require high throughput and *statistical* real-time latency deadlines. In contrast, avionics mission control platforms [27] may require rate-based periodic processing with *deterministic* real-time deadlines.

QoS specification is not addressed by the CORBA 2.x specification, though there is an OMG special interest group (SIG) devoted to this topic. Section 4.3 explains how TAO allows applications to specify their QoS

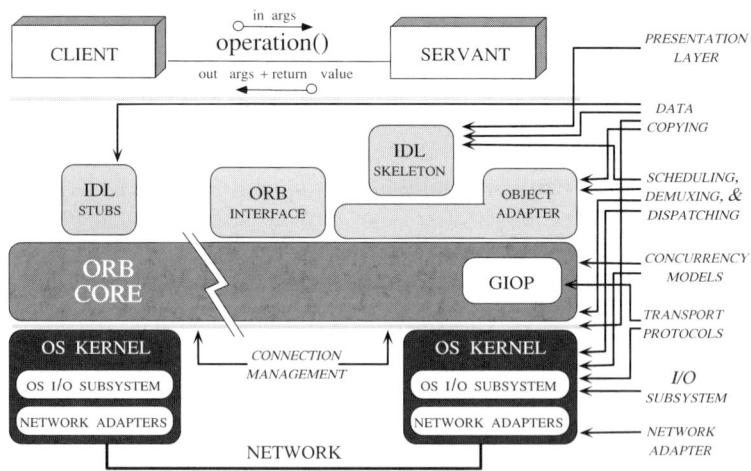

FIG. 3. Features and optimizations for real-time ORB endsystems.

requirements using a combination of standard OMG IDL and QoS-aware ORB services.

2.3.2.2 QoS enforcement from real-time operating systems and networks Regardless of the ability to *specify* application QoS requirements, an ORB endsystem cannot deliver end-to-end guarantees to applications without network and OS support for QoS *enforcement*. Therefore, ORB endsystems must be capable of scheduling resources such as CPUs, memory, and network connection bandwidth and latency. For instance, OS scheduling mechanisms must allow high-priority client requests to run to completion and prevent unbounded priority inversion.

Another OS requirement is pre-emptive dispatching. For example, a thread may become runnable that has a higher priority than one currently running a CORBA request on a CPU. In this case, the low-priority thread must be pre-empted by removing it from the CPU in favor of the high-priority thread.

Section 3.1 describes the OS I/O subsystem and network interface we are integrating with TAO. This infrastructure is designed to scale up to support performance-sensitive applications that require end-to-end gigabit data rates, predictable scheduling of I/O within an ORB endsystem, and low latency to CORBA applications.

2.3.2.3 Efficient and predictable real-time communication protocols and protocol engines The throughput, latency, and reliability requirements of multimedia applications like teleconferencing are more stringent and diverse than those found in traditional applications like remote login or file transfer. Likewise, the channel speed, bit-error rates, and services (such as isochronous and bounded-latency delivery guarantees) of networks like ATM exceed those offered by traditional networks like Ethernet. Therefore, ORB endsystems must provide a protocol engine that is efficient, predictable, and flexible enough to be customized for different application QoS requirements and network/endsystem environments.

Section 3.2.1 outlines TAO's protocol engine, which provides real-time enhancements and high-performance optimizations to the standard CORBA General InterORB Protocol (GIOP) [46]. The GIOP implementation in TAO's protocol engine specifies (1) a connection and concurrency architecture that minimizes priority inversion and (2) a transport protocol that enables efficient, predictable, and interoperable processing and communication among heterogeneous ORB endsystems.

2.3.2.4 Efficient and predictable request demultiplexing and dispatching ORB endsystems must demultiplex and dispatch incoming client requests to the appropriate operation of the target servant. In conventional ORBs, demultiplexing occurs at multiple layers, including the network interface, the protocol stack, the user/kernel boundary, and several levels in an ORB's object adapter. Demultiplexing client requests through all these layers is expensive, particularly when a large number of operations appear in an IDL interface and/or a large number of servants are managed by an ORB endsystem. To minimize this overhead, and to ensure predictable dispatching behavior, TAO applies the perfect hashing and active demultiplexing optimizations [20] described in section 3.3 to demultiplex requests in $O(1)$ time.

2.3.2.5 Efficient and predictable presentation layer ORB presentation layer conversions transform application-level data into a portable format that masks byte order, alignment, and word length differences. Many performance optimizations have been designed to reduce the cost of presentation layer conversions. For instance, [29] describes the tradeoffs between using compiled vs interpreted code for presentation layer conversions. Compiled marshaling code is efficient, but requires excessive amounts of memory. This can be problematic in many embedded real-time environments. In contrast, interpreted marshaling code is slower, but more compact and can often utilize processor caches more effectively.

Section 3.4 outlines how TAO supports predictable performance guarantees for both interpreted and compiled marshaling operations via its GIOP protocol engine. This protocol engine applies a number of innovative compiler techniques [11] and optimization principles [21]. These principles include optimizing for the common case; eliminating gratuitous waste; replacing general purpose operations with specialized, efficient ones; precomputing values, if possible; storing redundant state to speed up expensive operations; passing information between layers; and optimizing for the cache.

2.3.2.6 Efficient and predictable memory management On modern high-speed hardware platforms, data copying consumes a significant amount of CPU, memory, and I/O bus resources [10]. Likewise, dynamic memory management incurs a significant performance penalty due to locking overhead and non-determinism due to heap fragmentation. Minimizing data copying and dynamic memory allocation requires the collaboration of multiple layers in an ORB endsystem, i.e. the network interfaces, I/O subsystem protocol stacks, ORB Core and object adapter, presentation layer, and application-specific servants.

Section 3.5 outlines TAO's vertically integrated memory management scheme that minimizes data copying and lock contention throughout its ORB endsystem.

2.3.3 Real-time vs High-performance Tradeoffs

There is a common misconception [72] that applications with "real-time" requirements are equivalent to application with "high-performance" requirements. This is not necessarily the case. For instance, an Internet audioconferencing system may not require high bandwidth, but it does require predictably low latency to provide adequate QoS to users in real-time.

Other multimedia applications, such as teleconferencing, have both real-time and high-performance requirements. Applications in other domains, such as avionics and process control, have stringent periodic processing deadline requirements in the worst case. In these domains, achieving predictability in the worst case is often more important than high performance in the average case.

It is important to recognize that high-performance requirements may conflict with real-time requirements. For instance, real-time scheduling policies often rely on the predictability of endsystem operations like thread scheduling, demultiplexing, and message buffering. However, certain optimizations can improve performance at the expense of predictability. For instance, using a self-organizing search structure to demultiplex client requests in an ORB's object adapter can increase the average-case performance of operations, which decreases the predictability of any given operation in the worst case.

To allow applications to select the appropriate tradeoffs between average-case and worst-case performance, TAO is designed with an extensible software architecture based on key communication patterns [63]. When appropriate, TAO employs algorithms and data structures that can optimize for both performance and predictability. For instance, the de-layered active demultiplexing scheme described in Section 3.3 can increase ORB performance *and* predictability by eliminating excessive searching and avoiding priority inversions across demultiplexing layers [20].

3. Architectural Components and Features for High-performance, Real-time ORB Endsystems

TAO's ORB endsystem contains the network interface, I/O subsystem, communication protocol, and CORBA middleware components shown in Fig. 4. These components include the following.

(1) *I/O subsystem*: which send/receives requests to/from clients in real-time across a network (such as ATM) or backplane (such as VME or compactPCI).

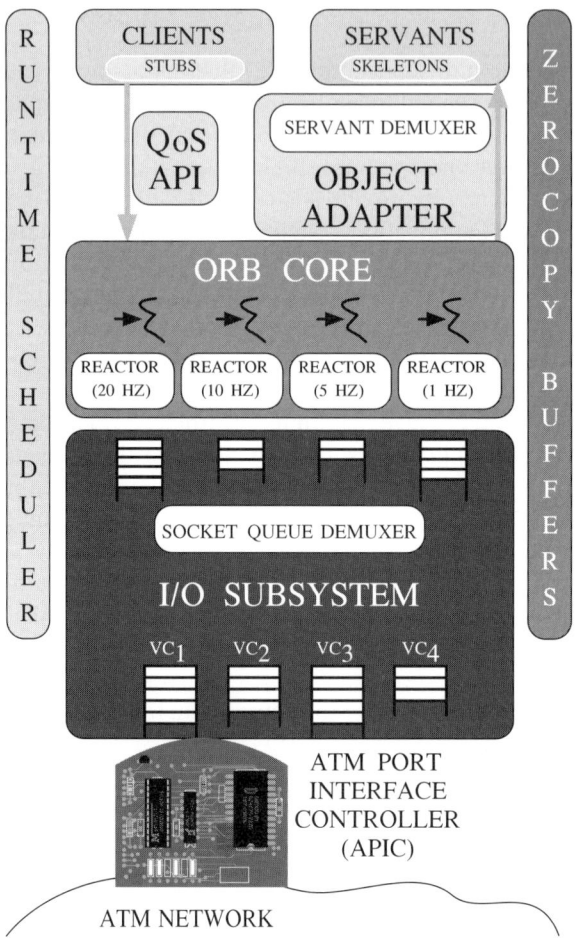

FIG. 4. Architectural components in the TAO real-time ORB endsystem.

(2) *Run-time scheduler*: which determines the priority at which requests are processed by clients and servers in an ORB endsystem.
(3) *ORB Core*: which provides a highly flexible, portable, efficient, and predictable CORBA inter-ORB protocol engine that delivers client requests to the Object Adapter and returns responses (if any) to clients.
(4) *Object adapter*: which demultiplexes and dispatches client requests optimally to servants using perfect hashing and active demultiplexing.
(5) *Stubs and skeletons*: which optimize key sources of marshaling and demarshaling overhead in the code generated automatically by TAO's IDL compiler.

(6) *Memory manager*: which minimizes sources of dynamic memory allocation and data copying throughout the ORB endsystem.
(7) *QoS API*: which allows applications and higher-level CORBA services to specify their QoS parameters using an OO programming model.

TAO's I/O subsystem and portions of its run-time scheduler and memory manager run in the kernel. Conversely, TAO's ORB Core, object adapter, stubs/skeletons, and portions of its run-time scheduler and memory manager run in user-space.

The remainder of this section describes components 1, 3, 4, 5, and 6 and explains how they are implemented in TAO to meet the requirements of high-performance, real-time ORB endsystems described in Section 2.3. Section 4 focuses on components 2 and 7, which allow applications to specify QoS requirements for real-time servant operations. This paper discusses both high-performance and real-time features in TAO since it is designed to support applications with a wide range of QoS requirements.

3.1 High-performance, Real-time I/O Subsystem

An I/O subsystem is responsible for mediating ORB and application access to low-level network and OS resources such as device drivers, protocol stacks, and CPU(s). The key challenges in building a high-performance, real-time I/O subsystem are to (1) make it convenient for applications to specify their QoS requirements, (2) enforce QoS specifications and minimize priority inversion and non-determinism, and (3) enable ORB middleware to leverage QoS features provided by the underlying network and OS resources.

To meet these challenges, we have developed a high-performance, real-time network I/O subsystem that is customized for TAO [62]. The components in this subsystem are shown in Fig. 5. They include (1) a high-speed ATM network interface, (2) a high-performance, real-time I/O subsystem, (3) a real-time scheduling service and run-time scheduler, and (4) an admission controller, as described below.

- *High-speed network interface*. At the bottom of TAO's I/O subsystem is a "daisy-chained" interconnect containing one or more ATM Port Interconnect Controller (APIC) chips [9]. APIC can be used both as an endsystem/network interface and as an I/O interface chip. It sustains an aggregate bi-directional data rate of 2.4 Gbps.

  Although TAO is optimized for the APIC I/O subsystem, it is designed using a layered architecture that can run on conventional OS platforms, as well. For instance, TAO has been ported to real-time

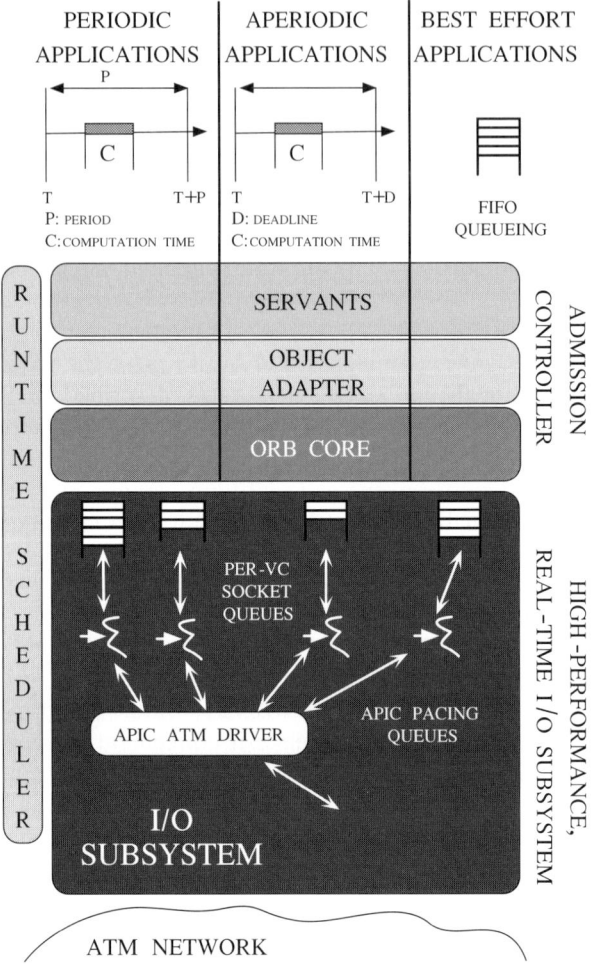

FIG. 5. Components in TAO's high-performance, real-time I/O subsystem.

interconnects, such as VME and compactPCI backplanes [62] and multiprocessor shared memory environments, and QoS-enabled networks, such as IPv6 with RSVP [2].

- *Real-time I/O subsystem.* Some general-purpose operating systems like Solaris and Windows NT now support real-time scheduling. For example, Solaris 2.x provides a real-time scheduling class [36] that attempts to bound the time required to dispatch threads in this thread class. However, general-purpose operating systems do not provide real-time I/O subsystems. For instance, the Solaris STREAMS [54] implementation does not support QoS guarantees since STREAMS processing is performed at system thread priority, which is lower than all real-time threads [62]. Therefore, the Solaris I/O subsystem is prone to priority inversion since low-priority real-time threads can pre-empt the I/O operations of high-priority threads. Unbounded priority inversion is highly undesirable in many real-time environments.

TAO enhances the STREAMS model provided by Solaris and real-time operating systems like VxWorks and LynxOS. TAO's real-time I/O (RIO) subsystem minimizes priority inversion and hidden scheduling[2] that arise during protocol processing. TAO minimizes priority inversion by pre-allocating a pool of kernel threads dedicated to protocol processing. These kernel threads are co-scheduled with a pool of application threads. The kernel threads run at the same priority as the application threads, which prevents the real-time scheduling hazards outlined above.

To ensure predictable performance, the kernel threads belong to a *real-time I/O* scheduling class. This scheduling class uses rate monotonic scheduling (RMS) [40, 37] to support real-time applications with periodic processing behavior. Once a real-time I/O thread is admitted by the OS kernel, TAO's RIO subsystem is responsible for (1) computing its priority relative to other threads in the class and (2) dispatching the thread periodically so that its deadlines are met.

- *Real-time scheduling service and run-time scheduler.* The scheduling abstractions defined by real-time operating systems like VxWorks, LynxOS, and POSIX 1003.1c [32] implementations are relatively low level. For instance, they require developers to map their high-level application QoS requirements into lower-level OS mechanisms, such as thread priorities and virtual circuit bandwidth/latency parameters. This manual mapping step is non-intuitive for many application developers, who prefer to design in terms of objects and operations on objects.

  To allow applications to specify their scheduling requirements in a higher-level, more intuitive manner, TAO provides a real-time scheduling service. This service is a CORBA object that is responsible for allocating system resources to meet the QoS needs of the applications that share the ORB endsystem.

---

[2] Hidden scheduling occurs when the kernel performs work asynchronously without regard to its priority. STREAMS processing in Solaris is an example of hidden scheduling since the computation time is not accounted for by the application or OS scheduler. To avoid hidden scheduling, the kernel should perform its work at the priority of the thread that requested the work.

Applications can use TAO's real-time scheduling service to specify the processing requirements of their operations in terms of various parameters, such as computation time C, period P, or deadline D. If all operations can be scheduled, the Scheduling Service assigns a priority to each request. At run-time, these priority assignments are then used by TAO's run-time scheduler. The run-time scheduler maps client requests for particular servant operations into priorities that are understood by the local endsystem's OS thread dispatcher. The dispatcher then grants priorities to real-time I/O threads and performs preemption so that schedulability is enforced at run-time. Section 4.2 describe the run-time scheduler and real-time scheduling service in detail.

- *Admission controller.* To ensure that application QoS requirements can be met, TAO performs admission control for its real-time I/O scheduling class. Admission control allows the OS to either guarantee the specified computation time or to refuse to admit the thread. Admission control is useful for real-time systems with deterministic and/or statistical QoS requirements.

This paper focuses primarily on admission control for ORB endsystems. Admission control is also important at higher-levels in a distributed system, as well. For instance, admission control can be used for global resource managers [35, 77] that map applications onto computational, storage, and network resources in a large-scale distributed system, such as a ship-board computing environment.

3.2 Efficient and Predictable ORB Cores

The ORB Core is the component in the CORBA architecture that manages transport connections, delivers client requests to an Object Adapter, and returns responses (if any) to clients. The ORB Core typically implements the ORB's transport endpoint demultiplexing and concurrency model, as well.

The key challenges to developing a real-time ORB Core are (1) implementing an efficient protocol engine for CORBA inter-ORB protocols like GIOP and IIOP, (2) determining a suitable connection and concurrency model that can share the aggregate processing capacity of ORB endsystem components predictably among operations in one or more threads of control, and (3) designing an ORB Core that can be adapted easily to new endsystem/network environments and application QoS requirements. The following describes how TAO's ORB Core is designed to meet these challenges.

3.2.1 TAO's Inter-ORB Protocol Engine

TAO's protocol engine is a highly optimized, real-time version of the SunSoft IIOP reference implementation [21] that is integrated with the high-performance I/O subsystem described in section 3.1. Thus, TAO's ORB Core on the client, server, and any intermediate nodes can collaborate to process requests in accordance with their QoS attributes. This design allows clients to indicate the relative priorities of their requests and allows TAO to enforce client QoS requirements end-to-end.

To increase portability across OS/network platforms, TAO's protocol engine is designed as a separate layer in TAO's ORB Core. Therefore, it can either be tightly integrated with the high-performance, real-time I/O subsystem described in section 3.1 or run on conventional embedded platforms linked together via interconnects like VME or shared memory.

Below, we outline the existing CORBA interoperability protocols and describe how TAO implements these protocols in an efficient and predictable manner.

3.2.1.1 Overview of GIOP and IIOP CORBA is designed to run over multiple transport protocols. The standard ORB interoperability protocol is known as the general inter-ORB protocol (GIOP) [46]. GIOP provides a standard end-to-end interoperability protocol between potentially heterogeneous ORBs. GIOP specifies an abstract interface that can be mapped onto transport protocols that meet certain requirements, i.e. connection-oriented, reliable message delivery, and untyped bytestream. An ORB supports GIOP if applications can use the ORB to send and receive standard GIOP messages.

The GIOP specification consists of the following elements:

- *Common Data Representation (CDR) definition*. The GIOP specification defines a common data representation (CDR). CDR is a transfer syntax that maps OMG IDL types from the native endsystem format to a bi-canonical format, which supports both little-endian and big-endian binary data formats. Data is transferred over the network in CDR encodings.
- *GIOP Message Formats*. The GIOP specification defines messages for sending requests, receiving replies, locating objects, and managing communication channels.
- *GIOP Transport Assumptions*. The GIOP specification describes what types of transport protocols can carry GIOP messages. In addition, the GIOP specification describes how connections are managed and defines constraints on message ordering.

The CORBA inter-ORB protocol (IIOP) is a mapping of GIOP onto the TCP/IP protocols. ORBs that use IIOP are able to communicate with other ORBs that publish their locations in an interoperable object reference (IOR) format.

3.2.1.2 Implementing GIOP/IIOP efficiently and predictably

In Corba 2.x, neither GIOP nor IIOP provide support for specifying or enforcing the end-to-end QoS requirements of applications.[3] This makes GIOP/IIOP unsuitable for real-time applications that cannot tolerate the latency overhead and jitter of TCP/IP transport protocols. For instance, TCP functionality like adaptive retransmissions, deferred transmissions, and delayed acknowledgments can cause excessive overhead and latency for real-time applications. Likewise, routing protocols like IPv4 lack functionality like packet admission policies and rate control, which can lead to excessive congestion and missed deadlines in networks and endsystems.

To address these shortcomings, TAO's ORB Core supports a priority-based concurrency architecture, a priority-based connection architecture, and a real-time inter-ORB protocol (RIOP), as described below.

- *TAO's priority-based concurrency architecture.* TAO's ORB Core can be configured to allocate a real-time thread[4] for each application-designated priority level. Every thread in TAO's ORB Core can be associated with a Reactor, which implements the Reactor pattern [57] to provide flexible and efficient endpoint demultiplexing and event handler dispatching.

  When playing the role of a server, TAO's Reactor(s) demultiplex incoming client requests to connection handlers that perform GIOP processing. These handlers collaborate with TAO's object adapter to dispatch requests to application-level servant operations. Operations can either execute at (1) the priority of the client that invoked the operation or (2) at the priority of the real-time ORB Core thread that received the operation. The latter design is well-suited for deterministic real-time applications since it minimizes priority inversion and non-determinism in TAO's ORB Core [68]. In addition, it reduces context switching and synchronization overhead since servant state must be locked only if servants interact across different thread priorities.

  TAO's priority-based concurrency architecture is optimized for statically configured, fixed priority real-time applications. In addition, it is well suited for scheduling and analysis techniques that associate priority with *rate*, such as rate monotonic scheduling (RMS) and rate monotonic analysis (RMA) [40, 37]. For instance, avionic mission computing systems commonly execute their tasks in *rates groups*. A rate group assembles all periodic processing operations that occur at

---
[3] The Real-time CORBA specification [45] supports this capability.
[4] In addition, TAO's ORB Core can be configured to support thread pool, thread-per-connection, and single-threaded reactive dispatching [61].

particular rates (e.g. 20 Hz, 10 Hz, 5 Hz, and 1 Hz) and assigns them to a pool of threads using fixed-priority scheduling.

- *TAO's priority-based connection architecture*. Figure 6 illustrates how TAO can be configured with a priority-based connection architecture. In this model, each client thread maintains a Connector [60] in thread-specific storage. Each Connector manages a map of pre-established connections to servers. A separate connection is maintained for each thread priority in the server ORB. This design enables clients to preserve end-to-end priorities as requests traverse through ORB endsystems and communication links [68].

Figure 6 also shows how the Reactor in each thread priority in a server ORB can be configured to use an Acceptor [60]. The Acceptor is a socket endpoint factory that listens on a specific port number for clients to connect to the ORB instance running at a particular thread priority. TAO can be configured so that each priority level has its own Acceptor port. For instance, in statically scheduled, rate-based avionics mission computing systems [39], ports 10020, 10010, 10005, 10001 could be mapped to the 20 Hz, 10 Hz, 5 Hz, and 1 Hz rate groups, respectively. Requests arriving at these socket ports can then be processed by the appropriate fixed-priority real-time threads.

Once a client connects, the Acceptor in the server ORB creates a new socket queue and a GIOP connection handler to service that queue. TAO's I/O subsystem uses the port number contained in arriving requests as a demultiplexing key to associate requests with the appropriate socket queue. This design minimizes priority inversion through

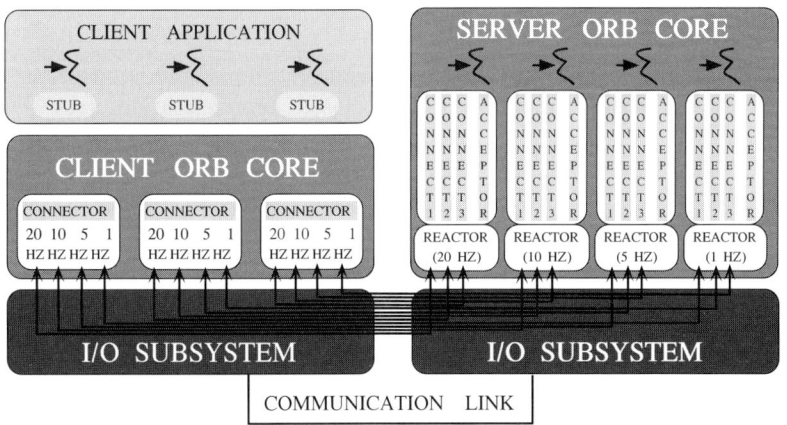

FIG. 6. TAO's priority-based connection and concurrency architectures.

the ORB endsystem via *early demultiplexing* [6, 25, 9], which associates requests arriving on network interfaces with the appropriate real-time thread that services the target servant. As described in section 8, early demultiplexing is used in TAO to vertically integrate the ORB endsystem's QoS support from the network interface up to the application servants.

- *TAO's real-time inter-ORB protocol (RIOP).* TAO's connection-per-priority scheme described above is optimized for fixed-priority applications that transfer their requests at particular rates through statically allocated connections serviced at the priority of real-time server threads. Applications that possess dynamic QoS characteristics, or that propagate the priority of a client to the server, require a more flexible protocol, however. Therefore, TAO supports a real-time inter-ORB protocol (RIOP).

RIOP is an implementation of GIOP that allows ORB endsystems to transfer their QoS attributes end-to-end from clients to servants. For instance, TAO's RIOP mapping can transfer the *importance* of an operation end-to-end with each GIOP message. The receiving ORB endsystem uses this QoS attribute to set the priority of a thread that processes an operation in the server.

To maintain compatibility with existing IIOP-based ORBs, TAO's RIOP protocol implementation transfers QoS information in the `service_context` member of the `GIOP::requestHeader`. ORBs that do not support TAO's RIOP extensions can transparently ignore the `service_context` member. Incidentally, the RIOP feature will be standardized as a QoS property in the asynchronous messaging portion of the CORBA 3.0 specification.

The TAO RIOP `service_context` passed with each client invocation contains attributes that describe the operation's QoS parameters. Attributes supported by TAO's RIOP extensions include priority, execution period, and communication class. Communication classes supported by TAO include Isochronous for continuous media, Burst for bulk data, Message for small messages with low delay requirements, and Message_Stream for message sequences that must be processed at a certain rate [25].

In addition to transporting client QoS attributes, TAO's RIOP is designed to map CORBA GIOP on a variety of networks including high-speed networks like ATM LANs and ATM/IP WANs [48]. RIOP also can be customized for specific application requirements. To support applications that do not require complete reliability, TAO's RIOP mapping can selectively omit transport layer functionality and run directly atop ATM virtual circuits. For instance, teleconferencing or certain types of imaging may not require retransmissions or bit-level error detection.

3.2.2 Enhancing the Extensibility and Portability of TAO's ORB Core

Although most conventional ORBs interoperate via IIOP over TCP/IP, an ORB is not limited to running over these transports. For instance, while TCP can transfer GIOP requests reliably, its flow control and congestion control algorithms may preclude its use as a real-time protocol. Likewise, shared memory may be a more effective transport mechanism when clients and servants are co-located on the same endsystem. Therefore, a key design challenge is to make an ORB Core extensible and portable to multiple transport mechanisms and OS platforms.

To increase extensibility and portability, TAO's ORB Core is based on patterns in the ACE framework [56]. Section 6 describes the patterns used in TAO in detail. The following outlines the patterns that are used in TAO's ORB Core.

TAO's ORB Core uses the Strategy and Abstract Factory patterns [14] to allow the configuration of multiple scheduling algorithms, such as earliest deadline first or maximum urgency first [73]. Likewise, the Bridge pattern [14] shields TAO's ORB Core from the choice of scheduling algorithm. TAO uses ACE components based on the Service Configurator pattern [34] to allow new algorithms for scheduling, demultiplexing, concurrency, and dispatching to be configured dynamically, i.e. at run-time. On platforms with C++ compilers that optimize virtual function calls, the overhead of this extensibility is negligible [27].

Other patterns are used in TAO's ORB Core to simplify its connection and concurrency architectures. For instance, the Acceptor-Connector pattern [60] defines ACE components used in TAO to decouple the task of connection establishment from the GIOP processing tasks performed after connection establishment. TAO uses the Reactor pattern [57], which defines an ACE component that simplifies the event-driven portions of the ORB core by integrating socket demultiplexing and the dispatching of the corresponding GIOP connection handlers. Likewise, the Active Object pattern [38] defines an ACE component used in TAO to configure multiple concurrency architectures by decoupling operation invocation from operation execution.

TAO ports easily to many OS platforms since it is built using ACE components based on the patterns described above. Currently, ACE and TAO have been ported to a wide range of OS platforms including Win32 (i.e. WinNT 3.5.x/4.x, Win95, and WinCE), most versions of UNIX (e.g. SunOS

4.x and 5.x, SGI IRIX 5.x and 6.x, HP-UX 9.x, 10.x, and 11.x, DEC UNIX 4.x, AIX 4.x, Linux, SCO, UnixWare, NetBSD, and FreeBSD), real-time operating systems (e.g. VxWorks, Chorus, LynxOS, and pSoS), and MVS OpenEdition.

Figure 7 illustrates the components in the client-side and server-side of TAO's ORB Core. The client-side uses a `Strategy_Connector` to create and cache `Connection_Handlers` that are bound to each server. These connections can be pre-allocated during ORB initialization. Pre-allocation minimizes the latency between client invocation and servant operation execution since connections can be established *a priori* using TAO's explicit binding operation.

On the server-side, the `Reactor` detects new incoming connections and notifies the `Strategy_Acceptor`. The `Strategy_Acceptor` accepts the new connection and associates it with a `Connection_Handler` that executes in a thread with an appropriate real-time priority. The client's `Connection_Handler` can pass GIOP requests (described in

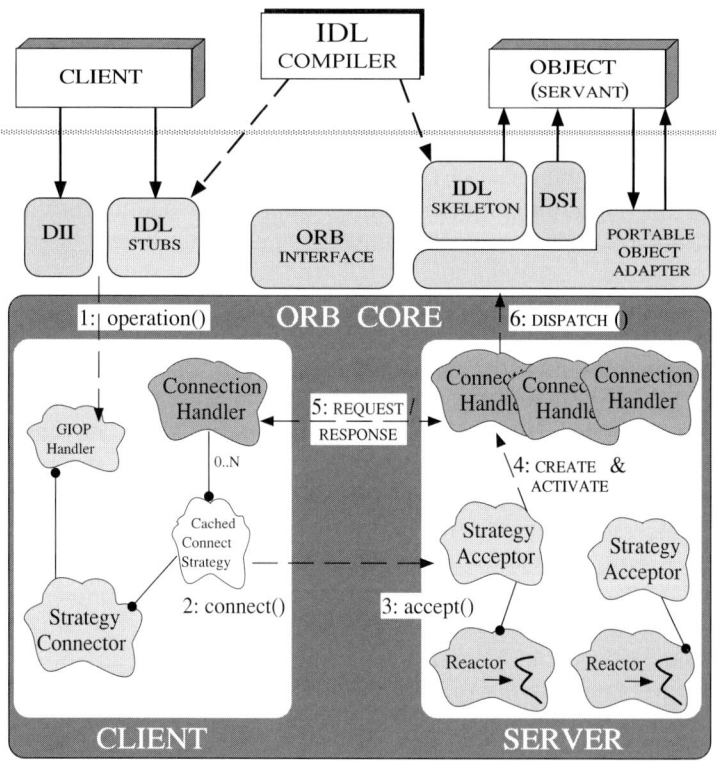

FIG. 7. Components in the TAO's ORB Core.

section 3.2.1) to the server's `Connection_Handler`. This handler upcalls TAO's object adapter, which dispatches the requests to the appropriate servant operation.

3.2.3 Real-time Scheduling and Dispatching of Client Requests

TAO's ORB Core can be configured to implement custom mechanisms that process client requests according to application-specific real-time scheduling policies. To provide a guaranteed share of the CPU among application operations [25, 27], TAO's ORB Core uses the real-time scheduling service described in section 4. One of the strategies provided by TAO's ORB Core is variant of periodic rate monotonic scheduling implemented with real-time threads and real-time upcalls (RTUs) [25].

TAO's ORB Core contains an object reference to its run-time scheduler shown in Fig. 4. This scheduler dispatches client requests in accordance with a real-time scheduling policy configured into the ORB endsystem. The run-time scheduler maps client requests to real-time thread priorities and connectors.

TAO's initial implementation supports deterministic real-time applications [62]. In this case, TAO's run-time scheduler consults a table of request priorities generated off-line. At run-time, TAO's ORB Core dispatches threads to the CPU(s) according to its dispatching mechanism. We have extended TAO to support dynamically scheduling and applications with statistical QoS requirements [39].

3.3 Efficient and Predictable Object Adapters

The object adapter is the component in the CORBA architecture that associates a servant with an ORB, de-multiplexes incoming client requests to the servant, and dispatches the appropriate operation of that servant. The key challenges associated with designing an object adapter for real-time ORBs are determining how to demultiplex client requests efficiently, scalably, and predictably.

TAO is the first CORBA ORB whose object adapter implements the OMG POA (portable object adapter) specification [46]. The POA specification defines a wide range of features, including: user- or system-supplied Object Ids, persistent and transient objects, explicit and on-demand activation, multiple servant → CORBA object mappings, total application control over object behavior and existence, and static and DSI servants [70, 71].

The demultiplexing and dispatching policies in TAO's object adapter are instrumental in ensuring its predictability and efficiency. This subsection describes how TAO's object adapter can be configured to use perfect hashing or active demultiplexing to map client requests directly to servant/operation tuples in $O(1)$ time.

3.3.1 Conventional ORB Demultiplexing Strategies

A standard GIOP-compliant client request contains the identity of its remote object and remote operation. A remote object is represented by an Object Key `octet sequence` and a remote operation is represented as a `string`. Conventional ORBs demultiplex client requests to the appropriate operation of the servant implementation using the *layered demultiplexing* architecture shown in Fig. 8. These steps perform the following tasks:

- *Steps 1 and 2*: The OS protocol stack demultiplexes the incoming client request multiple times, e.g. through the data link, network, and transport layers up to the user/kernel boundary and the ORB Core.

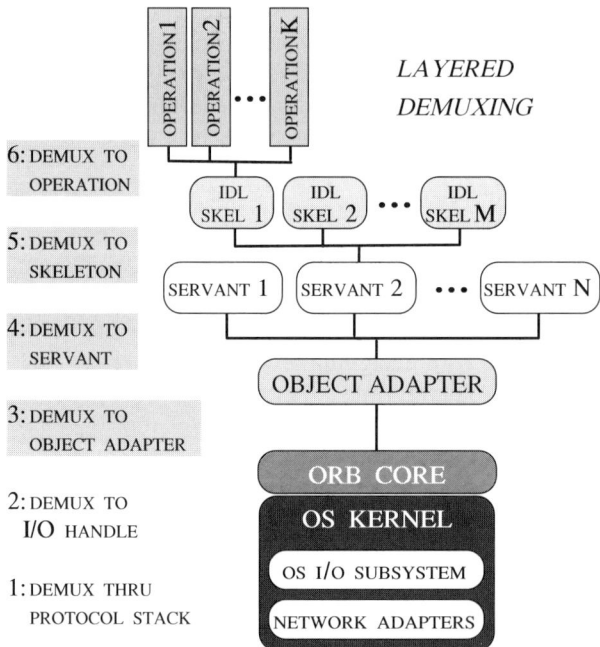

FIG. 8. Layered CORBA request demultiplexing.

- *Steps 3, 4, and 5*: The ORB Core uses the addressing information in the client's object key to locate the appropriate object adapter, servant, and the skeleton of the target IDL operation.
- *Step 6*: The IDL skeleton locates the appropriate operation, demarshals the request buffer into operation parameters, and performs the operation upcall. However, layered demultiplexing is generally inappropriate for high-performance and real-time applications for the following reasons [74]:
  - *Decreased efficiency*: Layered demultiplexing reduces performance by increasing the number of internal tables that must be searched as incoming client requests ascend through the processing layers in an ORB endsystem. Demultiplexing client requests through all these layers is expensive, particularly when a large number of operations appear in an IDL interface and/or a large number of servants are managed by an object adapter.
  - *Increased priority inversion and non-determinism*: Layered demultiplexing can cause priority inversions because servant-level quality of service (QoS) information is inaccessible to the lowest-level device drivers and protocol stacks in the I/O subsystem of an ORB endsystem. Therefore, an object adapter may demultiplex packets according to their FIFO order of arrival. FIFO demultiplexing can cause higher priority packets to wait for an indeterminate period of time while lower priority packets are demultiplexed and dispatched [62].

Conventional implementations of CORBA incur significant demultiplexing overhead. For instance, [16, 22] show that conventional ORBs spend ~ 17% of the total server time processing demultiplexing requests. Unless this overhead is reduced and demultiplexing is performed predictably, ORBs cannot provide uniform, scalable QoS guarantees to real-time applications.

3.3.2 TAO's Optimized ORB Demultiplexing Strategies

To address the limitations with conventional ORBs, TAO provides the demultiplexing strategies shown in Fig. 9. TAO's optimized demultiplexing strategies include the following:

- *Perfect hashing*: The perfect hashing strategy shown in Fig. 9(a) is a two-step layered demultiplexing strategy. This strategy uses an automatically-generated perfect hashing function to locate the servant. A second perfect hashing function is then used to locate the operation.

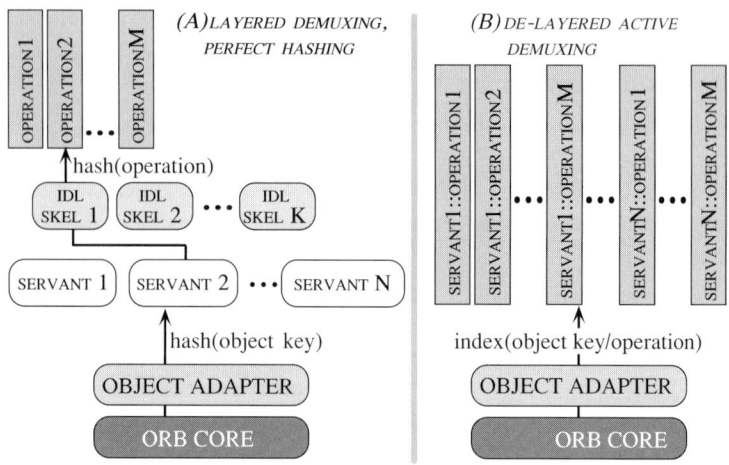

FIG. 9. Optimized CORBA request demultiplexing strategies.

The primary benefit of this strategy is that servant and operation lookups require $O(1)$ time in the worst case.

TAO uses the GNU gperf [55] tool to generate perfect hash functions for object keys and operation names. This perfect hashing scheme is applicable when the keys to be hashed are known *a priori*. In many deterministic real-time systems, such as avionic mission control systems [27, 39], the servants and operations can be configured statically. For these applications, it is possible to use perfect hashing to locate servants and operations.

- *Active demultiplexing*: TAO also provides a more dynamic demultiplexing strategy called *active demultiplexing*, shown in Fig. 9(b). In this strategy, the client passes an object key that directly identifies the servant and operation in $O(1)$ time in the worst case. The client obtains this object key when it obtains a servant's object reference, e.g. via a naming service or trading service. Once the request arrives at the server ORB, the object adapter uses the object key the CORBA request header to locate the servant and its associated operation in a single step.

  Unlike perfect hashing, TAO's active demultiplexing strategy does not require that all Object Ids be known *a priori*. This makes it more suitable for applications that incarnate and etherealize CORBA objects dynamically.

Both perfect hashing and active demultiplexing can demultiplex client requests efficiently and predictably. Moreover, these strategies perform optimally regardless of the number of active connections, application-level servant implementations, and operations defined in IDL interfaces. [20] presents a detailed study of these and other request demultiplexing strategies for a range of target objects and operations.

TAO's object adapter uses the Service Configurator pattern [34] to select perfect hashing or active demultiplexing dynamically during ORB installation [63]. Both strategies improve request demultiplexing performance and predictability *above* the ORB Core.

To improve efficiency and predictability *below* the ORB Core, TAO uses the ATM Port Interconnect Controller (APIC) described in section 3.1 to directly dispatch client requests associated with ATM virtual circuits [62]. This vertically integrated, optimized ORB endsystem architecture reduces demultiplexing latency and supports end-to-end QoS on either a per-request or per-connection basis.

3.4 Efficient and Predictable Stubs and Skeletons

Stubs and skeletons are the components in the CORBA architecture responsible for transforming typed operation parameters from higher-level representations to lower-level representations (marshaling) and vice versa (demarshaling). Marshaling and demarshaling are major bottlenecks in high-performance communication subsystems [5] due to the significant amount of CPU, memory, and I/O bus resources they consume while accessing and copying data. Therefore, key challenges for a high-performance, real-time ORB are to design an efficient presentation layer that performs marshaling and demarshaling predictably, while minimizing the use of costly operations like dynamic memory allocation and data copying.

In TAO, presentation layer processing is performed by client-side stubs and server-side skeletons that are generated automatically by a highly-optimizing IDL compiler [11]. In addition to reducing the potential for inconsistencies between client stubs and server skeletons, TAO's IDL compiler supports the following optimizations:

- *Reduced use of dynamic memory*: TAO's IDL compiler analyzes the storage requirements for all the messages exchanged between the client and the server. This enables the compiler to allocate sufficient storage *a priori* to avoid repeated run-time tests that determine if sufficient storage is available. In addition, the IDL compiler uses the run-time stack to allocate storage for unmarshaled parameters.
- *Reduced data copying*: TAO's IDL compiler analyzes when it is possible to perform block copies for atomic data types rather than copying them individually. This reduces excessive data access since it minimizes the number of load and store instructions.

- *Reduced function call overhead*: TAO's IDL compiler can selectively optimize small stubs via *inlining*, thereby reducing the overhead of function calls that would otherwise be incurred by invoking these small stubs.

TAO's IDL compiler supports multiple strategies for marshaling and demarshaling IDL types. For instance, TAO's IDL compiler can generate either compiled and/or interpreted IDL stubs and skeletons. This design allows applications to select between (1) *interpreted* stubs/skeletons, which can be somewhat slower, but more compact in size and (2) *compiled* stubs/skeletons, which can be faster, but larger in size [29].

Likewise, TAO can cache premarshaled application data units (ADUs) that are used repeatedly. Caching improves performance when ADUs are transferred sequentially in "request chains" and each ADU varies only slightly from one transmission to the other. In such cases, it is not necessary to marshal the entire request every time. This optimization requires that the real-time ORB perform flow analysis [4, 8] of application code to determine what request fields can be cached.

Although these techniques can significantly reduce marshaling overhead for the common case, applications with strict real-time service requirements often consider only worst-case execution. As a result, the flow analysis optimizations described above can only be employed under certain circumstances, e.g. for applications that can accept statistical real-time service or when the worst-case scenarios are still sufficient to meet deadlines.

3.5 Efficient and Predictable Memory Management

Conventional ORB endsystems suffer from excessive dynamic memory management and data copying overhead [16]. For instance, many I/O subsystems and ORB Cores allocate a memory buffer for each incoming client request and the I/O subsystem typically copies its buffer to the buffer allocated by the ORB Core. In addition, standard GIOP/IIOP demarshaling code allocates memory to hold the decoded request parameters. Likewise, IDL skeletons dynamically allocate and delete copies of client request parameters before and after upcalls, respectively.

In general, dynamic memory management is problematic for real-time systems. For instance, heap fragmentation can yield non-uniform behavior for different message sizes and different workloads. Likewise, in multi-threaded ORBs, the locks required to protect the heap from race conditions increase the potential for priority inversion [68]. In general, excessive data copying throughout an ORB endsystem can significantly lower throughput and increase latency and jitter.

TAO is designed to minimize and eliminate data copying at multiple layers in its ORB endsystem. For instance, TAO's buffer management system uses the APIC network interface to enhance conventional operating systems with a *zero-copy* buffer management system [9]. At the device level, the APIC interacts directly with the main system bus and other I/O devices. Therefore, it can transfer client requests between endsystem buffer pools and ATM virtual circuits with no additional data copying.

The APIC buffer pools for I/O devices described in section 3.1 can be configured to support *early demultiplexing* of periodic and aperiodic client requests into memory shared among user- and kernel-resident threads. These APIs allow client requests to be sent/received to/from the network without incurring any data copying overhead. Moreover, these buffers can be preallocated and passed between various processing stages in the ORB, thereby minimizing costly dynamic memory management.

In addition, TAO uses the Thread-Specific Storage pattern [66] to minimize lock contention resulting from memory allocation. TAO can be configured to allocate its memory from thread-specific storage. In this case, when the ORB requires memory it is retrieved from a thread-specific heap. Thus, no locks are required for the ORB to dynamically allocate this memory.

4. Supporting Real-time Scheduling in CORBA

Section 3 described the architectural components used in TAO to provide a high-performance ORB endsystem for real-time CORBA. TAO's architecture has been realized with minimal changes to CORBA. However, the CORBA 2.x specification does not yet address issues related to real-time scheduling. Therefore, this section provides in-depth coverage of the components TAO uses to implement a real-time scheduling service, based on standard CORBA features.

4.1 Synopsis of Application Quality of Service Requirements

The TAO ORB endsystem [67] is designed to support various classes of quality of service (QoS) requirements, including applications with deterministic and statistical real-time requirements. Deterministic real-time applications, such as avionics mission computing systems [27], must meet periodic deadlines. These types of applications commonly use static scheduling and analysis techniques, such as rate monotonic analysis (RMA) and rate monotonic scheduling (RMS).

Statistical real-time applications, such as teleconferencing and video-on-demand, can tolerate minor fluctuations in scheduling and reliability guarantees, but nonetheless require QoS guarantees. These types of applications commonly use dynamic scheduling techniques [39], such as earliest deadline first (EDF), minimum laxity first (MLF), or maximum urgency first (MUF).

Deterministic real-time systems have traditionally been more amenable to well-understood scheduling analysis techniques. Consequently, our research efforts were initially directed toward static scheduling of deterministic real-time systems. However, the architectural features and optimizations that we studied and developed are applicable to real-time systems with statistical QoS requirements, such as constrained latency multimedia systems or telecom call processing. This section describes the static scheduling service [67] that we developed to support scheduling for hard real-time systems with deterministic QoS requirements.

4.2 Responsibilities of a Real-time Scheduling Service

This subsection examines the analysis capabilities and scheduling policies provided by TAO's real-time scheduling service. This service is responsible for allocating CPU resources to meet the QoS needs of the applications that share the ORB endsystem. For real-time applications with deterministic QoS requirements, the scheduling service guarantees that all processing requirements will be met. For real-time applications with statistical QoS requirements, the scheduling service tries to meet system processing requirements within the desired tolerance, while also trying to maximize CPU utilization.

The initial design and implementation of TAO's real-time scheduling service [67] targeted deterministic real-time applications that require off-line, static scheduling on a single CPU. However, the scheduling service is also useful for dynamic and distributed real-time scheduling, as well [39]. Therefore, the scheduling service is defined as a CORBA object, i.e. as an implementation of an IDL interface. This design enables the scheduling service to be accessed either locally or remotely without having to reimplement clients that use it.

TAO's real-time scheduling service has the following off-line and on-line responsibilities:

- *Off-line scheduling feasibility analysis.* TAO's Scheduling Service performs off-line feasibility analysis of all IDL operations that register with it. This analysis results in a determination of whether there are sufficient CPU resources to perform all requested operations, as discussed in Section 4.5.
- *Request priority assignment.* Request priority is the relative priority of

a request[5] to any other. It is used by TAO to dispatch requests in order of their priority. Thread priority is the priority that corresponds to that of the thread that will invoke the request. During off-line analysis, the scheduling service (1) assigns a request priority to each request and (2) assigns each request to one of the preconfigured thread priorities. At run-time, the scheduling service provides an interface that allows TAO's real-time ORB endsystem to access these priorities. Priorities are the mechanism for interfacing with the local endsystem's OS dispatcher, as discussed in section 4.4.

A high-level depiction of the steps involved in the off-line and on-line roles of TAO's scheduling service is shown in Fig. 10. In step 1, the scheduling service constructs graphs of dependent operations using the QoS information registered with it by the application. This QoS information is stored in RT_Info structures described in section 4.3.3. In step 2, it identifies threads by looking at the terminal nodes of these dependency graphs and populates an RT_Info repository in step 3. In step 4 it assesses schedulability and assigns priorities, generating the priority tables as compilable C++ code in step 5. These five steps occur off-line during the (static) schedule configuration process. Finally, the priority tables generated in step 5 are used at run-time in step 6 by TAO's ORB endsystem.

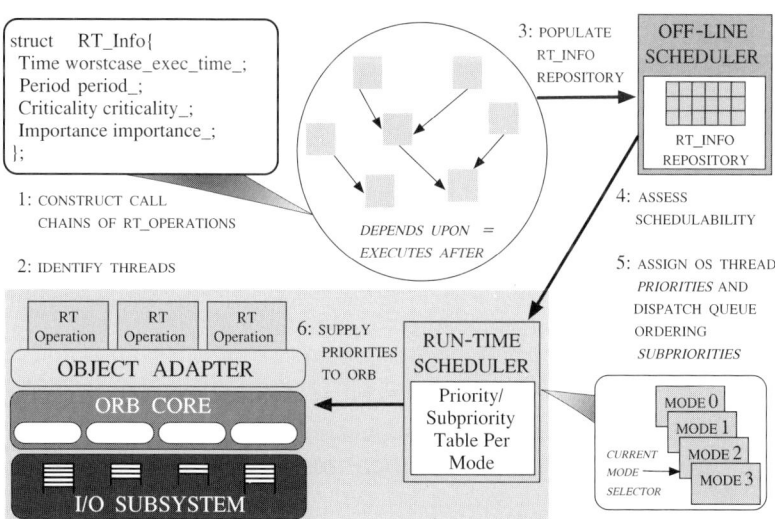

FIG. 10. Steps involved with off-line and on-line scheduling.

[5] A *request* is the run-time representation of an operation in an IDL interface that is passed between client and server.

TAO's real-time scheduling service guarantees that all `RT_Operations` in the system are dispatched with sufficient time to meet their deadlines. To accomplish this, the scheduling service can be implemented to perform various real-time scheduling policies. [67] Describes the rate monotonic scheduling implementation used by TAO's scheduling service.

Below, we outline the information that the service requires to build and execute a feasible system-wide schedule. A feasible schedule is one that is schedulable on the available system resources; in other words, it can be verified that none of the operations in the critical set will miss their deadlines. The *critical set* of operations is the subset of all system operations whose failure to execute before the respective deadline would compromise system integrity.

To simplify the presentation, we focus on ORB scheduling for a single CPU. The distributed scheduling problem is not addressed in this presentation. [39] Outlines the approaches we are investigating with TAO.

4.3 Specifying QoS Requirements in TAO using Real-time IDL Schemas

Invoking operations on objects is the primary collaboration mechanism between components in an OO system [13]. However, QoS research at the network and OS layers has not addressed key requirements and usage characteristics of OO middleware. For instance, research on QoS for ATM networks has focused largely on policies for allocating bandwidth on a per-connection basis [9]. Likewise, research on real-time operating systems has focused largely on avoiding priority inversion and non-determinism in synchronization and scheduling mechanisms for multi-threaded applications [52].

Determining how to map the insights and mechanisms produced by QoS work at the network and OS layers onto an OO programming model is a key challenge when adding QoS support to ORB middleware [13, 77]. This subsection describes the real-time OO programming model used by TAO. TAO supports the specification of QoS requirements on a per-operation basis using TAO's real-time IDL schemas.

4.3.1 Overview of QoS Specification in TAO

Several ORB endsystem resources are involved in satisfying application QoS requirements, including CPU cycles, memory, network connections, and storage devices. To support end-to-end scheduling and performance guarantees, real-time ORBs must allow applications to specify their QoS requirements so that an ORB subsystem can guarantee resource availability.

In non-distributed, deterministic real-time systems, CPU capacity is typically the scarcest resource. Therefore, the amount of computing time required to process client requests must be determined *a priori* so that CPU capacity can be allocated accordingly. To accomplish this, applications must specify their CPU capacity requirements to TAO's off-line scheduling service.

In general, scheduling research on real-time systems that consider resources other than CPU capacity relies upon on-line scheduling [53]. Therefore, we focus on the specification of CPU resource requirements. TAO's QoS mechanism for expressing CPU resource requirements can be readily extended to other shared resources, such as network and bus bandwidth, once scheduling and analysis capabilities have matured.

The remainder of this subsection explains how TAO supports QoS specifications for the purpose of CPU scheduling for IDL operations that implement real-time operations. We outline our real-time IDL (RIDL) schemas: `RT_Operation` interface and its `RT_Info struct`. These schemas convey QoS information, e.g. CPU requirements, to the ORB on a per-operation basis. We believe that this is an intuitive QoS specification model for developers since it maps directly onto the OO programming paradigm.

4.3.2 The `RT_Operation` Interface

The `RT_Operation` interface is the mechanism for conveying CPU requirements from processing tasks performed by application operations to TAO's scheduling service, as shown in the following CORBA IDL interface:[6]

```
module RT_Scheduler
{
  // Module TimeBase defines the OMG Time Service.
  typedef TimeBase::TimeT Time; // 100 nanoseconds
  typedef Time Quantum;
  typedef long Period; // 100 nanoseconds

  enum Importance
  // Defines the importance of the operation,
  // which can be used by the Scheduler as a
  // "tie-breaker" when other scheduling
  // parameters are equal.
  {
    VERY_LOW_IMPORTANCE,
    LOW_IMPORTANCE,
```

---

[6] The remainder of the `RT_Scheduler` module IDL description is shown in section 4.5.1.

```
  MEDIUM_IMPORTANCE,
  HIGH_IMPORTANCE,
  VERY_HIGH_IMPORTANCE
};

typedef long handle_t;
// RT_Info's are assigned per-application
// unique identifiers.

struct Dependency_Info
{
  long number_of_calls;
  handle_t rt_info;
  // Notice the reference to the RT_Info we
  // depend on.
};

typedef sequence<Dependency_Info> Dependency_Set;

typedef long OS_Priority;
typedef long Sub_Priority;
typedef long Preemption_Priority;

struct RT_Info
  // = TITLE
  // Describes the QoS for an "RT_Operation".
  //
  // = DESCRIPTION
  // The CPU requirements and QoS for each
  // "entity" implementing an application
  // operation is described by the following
  // information.
{
  // Application-defined string that uniquely
  // identifies the operation.
  string entry_point_;

  // The scheduler-defined unique identifier.
  handle_t handle_;

  // Execution times.
  Time worstcase_execution_time_;
  Time typical_execution_time_;

  // To account for server data caching.
  Time cached_execution_time_;
```

```
    // For rate-base operations, this expresses
    // the rate. 0 means "completely passive",
    // i.e., this operation only executes when
    // called.
    Period period_;

    // Operation importance, used to "break ties".
    Importance importance_;

    // For time-slicing (for BACKGROUND
    // operations only).
    Quantum quantum_;

    // The number of internal threads contained
    // by the operation.
    long threads_;

    // The following attributes are defined by
    // the Scheduler once the off-line schedule
    // is computed.

    // The operations we depend upon.
    Dependency_Set dependencies_;

    // The OS por processing the events generated
    // from this RT_Info.
    OS_Priority priority_;

    // For ordering RT_Info's with equal priority.
    Sub_Priority subpriority_;

    // The queue number for this RT_Info.
    Preemption_Priority preemption_priority_;
  };
};
```

As shown above, the `RT_Operation` interface contains type definitions and its key feature, the `RT_Info struct`, which is described below.

4.3.3 The `RT_Info` Struct

Applications that use TAO must specify all their scheduled resource requirements. This QoS information is currently provided to TAO before program execution. In the case of CPU scheduling, the QoS requirements are expressed using the following attributes of an `RT_Info` IDL `struct`:

- *Worst-case execution time.* The worst-case execution time, C, is the maximum execution time that the RT_Operation requires. It is used in conservative scheduling analysis for applications with strict real-time requirements.
- *Typical execution time.* The typical execution time is the execution time that the RT_Operation usually requires. The typical execution time may be useful with some scheduling policies, e.g. statistical real-time systems that can relax the conservative worst-case execution time assumption. However, it is not currently used in TAO's deterministic real-time scheduling service.
- *Cached execution time.* If an operation can provide a cached result in response to service requests, then the cached execution time is set to a non-zero value. During execution, for periodic functions, the worst-case execution cost is only incurred once per period if caching is enabled, i.e. if this field is non-zero. The scheduling analysis incorporates caching by only including one term with the worst-case execution time for the operation, per period, no matter how many times it is called, and by using the cached execution time for all other calls.
- *Period.* The period is the minimum time between successive iterations of the operation. If the operation executes as an active object [34] with multiple threads of control, then at least one of those threads must execute at least that often.

    A period of 0 indicates that the operation is totally *reactive*, i.e. it does not specify a period. Reactive operations are always called in response to requests by one or more clients. Although the run-time scheduler in TAO need not treat reactive operations as occurring periodically, it must account for their execution time.
- *Criticality.* The operation criticality is an enumeration value ranging from lowest criticality, i.e. VERY_LOW_CRITICALITY, up to highest criticality, i.e. VERY_HIGH_CRITICALITY. Certain scheduling strategies implemented in the scheduling service (notably maximum urgency first [73]) consider criticality as the primary distinction between operations when assigning priority.
- *Importance.* The operation importance is an enumeration value ranging from lowest importance, i.e. VERY_LOW_IMPORTANCE, up to highest importance, i.e. VERY_HIGH_IMPORTANCE. The scheduling service uses importance as a "tie-breaker" to order the execution of RT_Operations when data dependencies or other factors such as criticality do not impose an ordering.
- *Quantum.* Operations within a given priority may be time-sliced, i.e. preempted at any time by the ORB endsystem dispatcher resumed at a later time. If a time quantum is specified for an operation, then that is

the maximum time that it will be allowed to run before preemption, if there are any other runnable operations at that priority. This time-sliced scheduling is intended to provide fair access to the CPU for lowest priority operations. Quantum is not currently used in the scheduling service.

- *Dependency Info.* This is an array of handles to other RT_Info instances, one for each RT_Operation that this one directly depends on. The dependencies are used during scheduling analysis to identify threads in the system: each separate dependency graph indicates a thread. In addition, the number of times that the dependent operation is called is specified, for accurate execution time calculation.

The RIDL schemas outlined above can be used to specify the run-time execution characteristics of object operations to TAO's scheduling service. This information is used by TAO to (1) validate the feasibility of a schedule and (2) allocate ORB endsystem and network resources to process RT_Operations. A single RT_Info instance is required for each RT_Operation.

4.4 Overview of TAO's Scheduling Model

TAO's on-line scheduling model includes the following participants, as shown in Fig. 11:

- *Work_Operation.* A Work_Operation is a unit of work that encapsulates application-level processing or communication activity. For

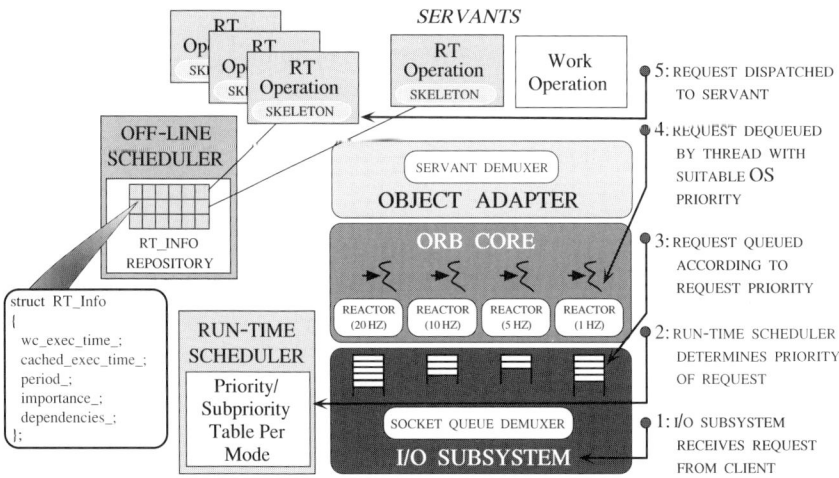

FIG. 11. TAO run-time scheduling participants.

example, utility functions that read input, print output, or convert physical units can be `Work_Operations`. In some real-time environments, a `Work_Operation` is called a *module* or *process*, but we avoid these terms because of their overloaded usage in OO and OS contexts.

- *RT_Operation.* An `RT_Operation` is a type of `Work_Operation` that has timing constraints. Each `RT_Operation` is considered to be an operation defined on a CORBA IDL interface, that has its own QoS information specified in terms of the attributes in its run-time information (`RT_Info`) descriptor. Thus, an application-level object with multiple operations may require multiple `RT_Operation` instances, one for each distinct class of QoS specifications.

- *Thread.* Threads are units of concurrent execution. A thread can be implemented with various threading APIs, e.g. a Solaris or POSIX thread, an Ada task, a VxWorks task, or a Windows NT thread. All threads are contained within `RT_Operations`. An `RT_Operation` containing one or more threads is an *active object* [38]. In contrast, an `RT_Operation` that contains zero threads is a *passive object*. Passive objects only execute in the context of another `RT_Operation`, i.e. they "borrow" the calling operation's thread of control to run.

- *OS dispatcher.* The OS dispatcher uses request priorities to select the next runnable thread that it will assign to a CPU. It removes a thread from a CPU when the thread blocks, and therefore is no longer runnable, or when the thread is *preempted* by a higher priority thread. With *preemptive dispatching*, any runnable thread with a priority higher than any running thread will preempt a lower priority thread. Then, the higher priority, runnable thread can be dispatched onto the available CPU.

  Our analysis assumes *fixed priority*, i.e. the OS does not unilaterally change the priority of a thread. TAO currently runs on a variety of platforms, including real-time operating systems, such as VxWorks and LynxOS, as well as general-purpose operating systems with real-time extensions, such as Solaris 2.x [36] and Windows NT. All these platforms provide fixed priority real-time scheduling. Thus, from the point of view of an OS dispatcher, the priority of each thread is constant. The fixed priority contrasts with the operation of time-shared OS schedulers, which typically *age* long-running processes by decreasing their priority over time [42].

- *RT_Info.* As described in section 4.3, an `RT_Info` structure specifies an `RT_Operation`'s scheduling characteristics such as computation time and execution period.

- *Run-time scheduler.* At run-time, the primary visible vestige of the scheduling service is the run-time scheduler. The run-time scheduler maps client requests for particular servant operations into priorities that are understood by the local OS dispatcher. Currently, these priorities are assigned statically prior to run-time and are accessed by TAO's ORB endsystem via an $O(1)$ time table lookup.

4.5 Overview of TAO's Off-line Scheduling Service

To meet the demands of statically scheduled, deterministic real-time systems, TAO's scheduling service uses *off-line scheduling*, which has the following two high-level goals:

(1) *Schedulability analysis.* If the operations cannot be scheduled because one or more deadlines could be missed, then the off-line scheduling service reports that prior to run-time.
(2) *Request priority assignment.* If the operations can be scheduled, the scheduling service assigns a priority to each request. This is the mechanism that the scheduling service uses to convey execution order requirements and constraints to TAO's ORB endsystem dispatcher.

4.5.1 Off-line Scheduling Service Interface

The key types and operations of the IDL interface for TAO's off-line scheduling service are defined below[7]:

```
module RT_Scheduler
{
 exception DUPLICATE_NAME {};
 // The application is trying to
 // register the same task again.

 exception UNKNOWN_TASK {};
 // The RT_Info handle was not valid.

 exception NOT_SCHEDULED {};
 // The application is trying to obtain
 // scheduling information, but none
 // is available.

 exception UTILIZATION_BOUND_EXCEEDED {};
 exception
   INSUFFICIENT_PRIORITY_LEVELS {};
 exception TASK_COUNT_MISMATCH {};
```

---
[7] The remainder of the `RT_Scheduler` module IDL description is shown in section 4.3.2.

```
// Problems while computing off-line
// scheduling.

typedef sequence<RT_Info> RT_Info_Set;

interface Scheduler
  // = DESCRIPTION
  // This class holds all the RT_Info's
  // for a single application.
{
  handle_t create (in string entry_point)
    raises (DUPLICATE_NAME);
  // Creates a new RT_Info entry for the
  // function identifier "entry_point",
  // it can be any string, but the fully
  // qualified name function name is suggested.
  // Returns a handle to the RT_Info.

  handle_t lookup (in string entry_point);
  // Lookups a handle for entry_point.

  RT_Info get (in handle_t handle)
  raises (UNKNOWN_TASK);
  // Retrieve information about an RT_Info.

  void set (in handle_t handle,
            in Time time,
            in Time typical_time,
            in Time cached_time,
            in Period period,
            in Importance importance,
            in Quantum quantum,
            in long threads)
  raises (UNKNOWN_TASK);
  // Set the attributes of an RT_Info.
  // Notice that some values may not
  // be modified (like priority).

  void add_dependency
       (in handle_t handle,
        in handle_t dependency,
        in long number_of_calls)
    raises (UNKNOWN_TASK);
  // Adds <dependency> to <handle>

  void priority
```

ARCHITECTURES AND PATTERNS FOR ORB ENDSYSTEMS

```
         (in handle_t handle,
           out OS_Priority priority,
           out Sub_Priority subpriority,
           out Preemption_Priority p_priority)
    raises (UNKNOWN_TASK, NOT_SCHEDULED);
  void entry_point_priority
          (in string entry_point,
           out OS_Priority priority,
           out Sub_Priority subpriority,
           out Preemption_Priority p_priority)
    raises (UNKNOWN_TASK, NOT_SCHEDULED);
  // Obtain the run time priorities.

  void compute_scheduling
         (in long minimum_priority,
          in long maximum_priority,
          out RT_Info_Set infos)
    raises (UTILIZATION_BOUND_EXCEEDED,
            INSUFFICIENT_PRIORITY_LEVELS,
            TASK_COUNT_MISMATCH);
  // Computes the scheduling priorities,
  // returns the RT_Info's with their
  // priorities properly filled. This info
  // can be cached by a Run_Time_Scheduler
  // service or dumped into a C++ file for
  // compilation and even faster (static)
  // lookup.
  };
};
```

Not shown are accessors to system configuration data that the scheduler contains, such as the number of operations and threads in the system. In general, the scheduling service interface need not be viewed by application programmers; the only interface they need to use is the `RT_Info` interface, described in section 4.3.3. This division of the scheduling service interface into application and privileged sections is shown in Fig. 12.

The privileged interface is only used by common TAO services, such as:

- the event channel in TAO's real-time event service [27], which registers its `RT_Operations` with the off-line scheduling service;
- application-level schedulable operations that do not use the event channel;
- TAO's real-time ORB endsystem, which accesses these interfaces to determine client request dispatch priorities.

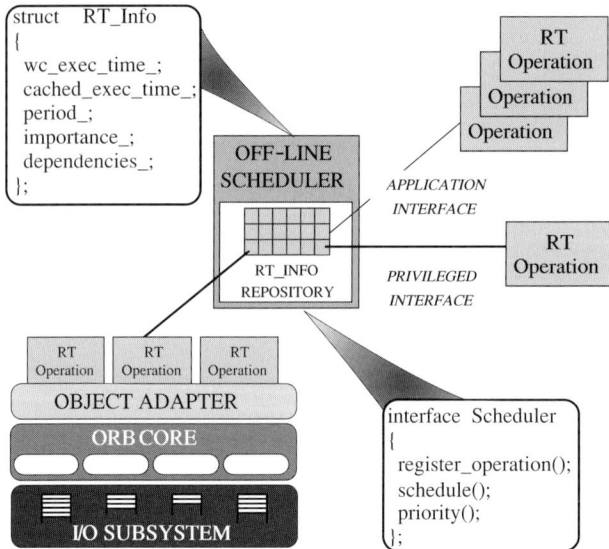

FIG. 12. TAO's two scheduling service interfaces.

The remainder of this subsection clarifies the operation of TAO's scheduling service, focusing on how it assigns request priorities, when it is invoked, and what is stored in its internal database.

4.5.2 RT_Operation *Priority Assignments*

The off-line scheduling service assigns priorities to each RT_Operation. Because the current implementation of the Scheduling Service utilizes a rate monotonic scheduling policy, priorities are assigned based on an operation's rate. For each RT_Operation in the repository, a priority is assigned based on the following rules:

(1) If the RT_Info::period of an operation is non-zero, TAO's off-line scheduling service uses this information to map the period to a thread priority. For instance, 100 msec periods may map to priority 0 (the highest), 200 msec periods may map to priority 1, and so on. With rate monotonic scheduling, for example, higher priorities are assigned to shorter periods.

(2) If the operation does not have a rate requirement, i.e. its RT_Info::period is 0, then its rate requirement must be implied from the operation_dependencies_ field stored in the RT_Info struct. The RT_Info struct with the smallest period, ie, with

the fastest rate, in the `RT_Info::operation_dependencies_` list will be treated as the operation's implied rate requirement, which is then mapped to a priority. The priority values computed by the off-line scheduling service are stored in the `RT_Info::priority_` field, which the run-time scheduler can query at run-time via the `priority` operation.

The final responsibility of TAO's off-line scheduling service is to verify the schedulability of a system configuration. This validation process provides a definitive answer to the question "given the current system resources, what is the lowest priority level whose operations all meet their deadlines?" The off-line scheduling service uses a repository of `RT_Info` structures shown in Fig. 14 to determine the utilization required by each operation in the system. By comparing the total required utilization for each priority level with the known resources, an assessment of schedulability can be calculated.

TAO's off-line scheduling service currently uses the `RT_Info` attributes of application `RT_Operations` to build the static schedule and assign priorities according to the following steps:

(1) *Extract RT_Infos.* Extract all `RT_Info` instances for all the `RT_Operations` in the system.
(2) *Identify real-time threads.* Determine all the real-time threads by building and traversing operation dependency graphs.
(3) *Determine schedulability and priorities.* Traverse the dependency graph for each thread to calculate its execution time and periods. Then, assess schedulability based on the thread properties and assign request priorities.
(4) *Generate request priority table.* Generate a table of request priority assignments. This table is subsequently integrated into TAO's run-time system and used to schedule application-level requests.

These steps are described further in the remainder of this section.

4.5.3 *Extract* `RT_Infos`

The scheduling service is a CORBA object that can be accessed by applications during *configuration runs*. To use the scheduling service, users must instantiate one `RT_Info` instantiation for each `RT_Operation` in the system. A configuration run is an execution of the application, TAO, and TAO services which is used to provide the services with any information needed for static configuration. The interactions between the applications and scheduling Service during a configuration run are shown in Fig. 13.

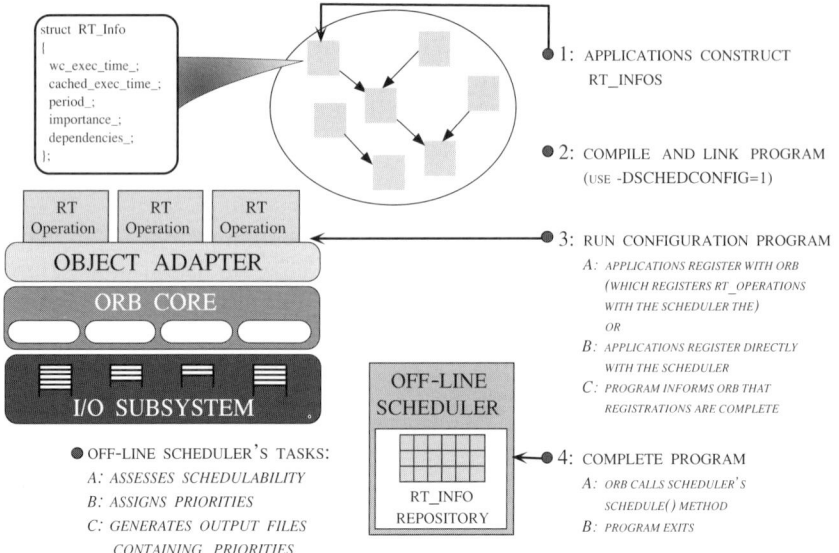

FIG. 13. Scheduling steps during a configuration run.

The RT_Info instantiations, Step 1, are compiled and linked into the main program, Step 2. The application is then executed, Step 3. It registers each RT_Operation with either TAO (currently, via TAO's real-time event service), Step 3A, or directly with the scheduling service, Step 3B, for operations that do not use TAO. The application notifies TAO, Step 3C, which in turn notifies the scheduling service, when all registrations have finished. TAO invokes the off-line scheduling process, Step 4A. Finally, the application exits, Step 4B.

With off-line scheduling, the RT_Infos are not needed at run-time. Therefore, one space-saving optimization would be to conditionally compile RT_Infos only during configuration runs.

The application should use the destroy operation to notify the scheduling service when the program is about to exit so that it can release any resources it holds. It is necessary to release memory during configuration runs in order to permit repeated runs on OS platforms, such as VxWorks, that do not release heap-allocated storage when a program terminates.

For consistency in application code, the scheduling service configuration and run-time interfaces are identical. The schedule operation is essentially a *no-op* in the run-time version; it merely performs a few checks to ensure that all operations are registered and that the number of priority values are reasonable.

4.5.4 Identify Real-time Threads

After collecting all of the RT_Info instances, the scheduling service identifies threads and performs its schedulability analysis. A *thread* is defined by a directed acyclic graph of RT_Operations. An RT_Info instance is associated with each RT_Operation by the application developer; RT_Info creation has been automated using the information available to TAO's real-time event service. RT_Infos contain dependency relationships and other information, e.g. *importance*, which determines possible run-time ordering of RT_Operation invocations. Thus, a *graph* of dependencies from each RT_Operation can be generated mechanically, using the following algorithm:

(1) Build a repository of RT_Info instances. This task consists of the following two steps:

   (a) Visit each RT_Info instance; if not already visited, add to repository, and
   (b) Visit the RT_Info of each dependent operation, depth first, and add a link to the dependent operation's internal (to the scheduling service) Dependency_Info array.

(2) Find terminal nodes of dependent operation graphs. As noted in section 4.5.2, identification of real-time threads involves building and traversing operation dependency graphs. The terminal nodes of separate dependent operation graphs indicate, and are used to identify, threads. The operation dependency graphs capture data dependency, e.g. if operation A calls operation B, then operation A needs some data that operation B produces, and therefore operation A depends on operation B. If the two operations execute in the context of a single thread, then operation B must execute before operation A. Therefore, the terminal nodes of the dependency graphs delineate threads.

(3) Traverse dependent operation graphs. After identifying the terminal nodes of dependent operation graphs, the graphs are traversed to identify the operations that compose each thread. Each traversal starts from a dependent operation graph terminal node, and continues towards the dependent operation's roots until termination. An operation may be part of more than one thread, indicating that each of the threads may call that operation.

The algorithm described above applies several restrictions on the arrangement of operation dependencies. First, a thread may be identified by only one operation; this corresponds directly to a thread having a single entry point. Many OS thread implementations support only a single entry point, i.e. a unique function which is called when the thread is started. This restriction imposes no additional constraints on those platforms.

The second restriction is that cycles are prohibited in dependency relationships. Again, this has a reasonable interpretation. If there was a cycle in a dependency graph, there would be no bound, known to the scheduler, on the number of times the cycle could repeat. To alleviate this restriction, the application can absorb dependency graph cycles into an operation that encapsulates them. Its RT_Info would reflect the (bounded) number of internal dependency graph cycles in its worst-case execution time.

The RT_Info repository that the Scheduling Service builds is depicted in Fig. 14.

The scheduling service's RT_Info repository includes the RT_Info reference and an array of the RT_Operations that it depends upon. These RT_Operation dependencies are depicted by blocks with arrows to the dependent operations. The Dependency_Info arrays are initialized while first traversing the RT_Info instances, to identify threads. Terminal nodes of the dependent operation graphs are identified; these form the starting point for thread identification.

Passive RT_Operations, i.e. those without any internal threads of their own, do not appear as terminal nodes of dependent operation graphs. They may appear further down a dependent operation graph, in which case their worst-case and typical execution times are added to the corresponding execution times of the calling thread. However, cached execution times may be added instead, for periodic functions, depending on whether result caching

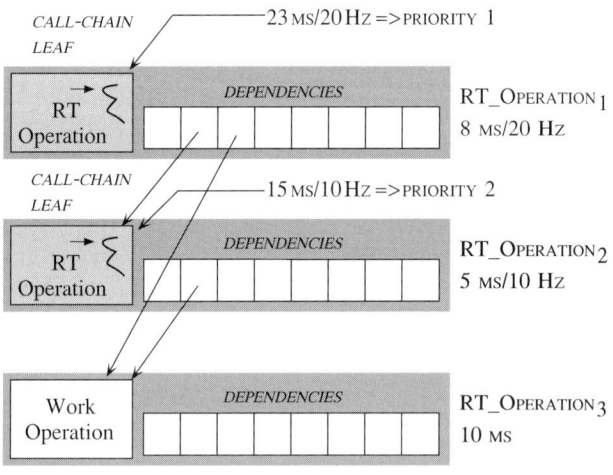

FIG. 14. The RT_Info repository.

is enabled and whether the operation has been visited already in the current period.

The algorithm for identifying real-time threads may appear to complicate the determination of operation execution times. For instance, instead of specifying a thread's execution time, an operation's execution time must be specified. However, this design is instrumental in supporting an OO programming abstraction that provides QoS specification and enforcement on a per-operation basis. The additional information is valuable for accurately analyzing the impact of object-level caching and to provide finer granularity for reusing RT_Infos. In addition, this approach makes it convenient to measure the execution times of operations; profiling tools typically provide that information directly.

4.5.5 Determine Schedulability and Priorities

Starting from terminal nodes that identify threads, the RT_Info dependency graphs are traversed to determine thread properties, as follows:

- *Traverse each graph*: summing the worst case and typical execution times along the traversal. To determine the period at which the thread must run, save the minimum period of all of the non-zero periods of all of the RT_Infos visited during the traversal.
- *Assign priorities*: depending on the scheduling strategy used, higher priority is assigned to higher criticality, higher rate, etc.

Based on the thread properties, and the scheduling strategy used, schedule feasibility is assessed. For example, with RMA, EDF, or MLF, if the total CPU utilization is below the utilization bound, then the schedule for the set of threads is feasible. With MUF, if utilization by all operations in the critical set is below the utilization bound, then the schedule is feasible, even though schedulability of operations outside the critical set may or may not be guaranteed. If the schedule is feasible, request priorities are assigned according to the scheduling strategy, i.e. for RMS requests with higher rates are assigned higher priorities, for MUF requests with higher criticality levels are assigned higher priorities, etc.

4.5.6 Generate Request Priority Table

The scheduling service generates a table of request priority assignments. Every thread is assigned a unique integer identifier. This identifier is used at run-time by TAO's ORB endsystem to index into the request priority assignment table. These priorities can be accessed in $O(1)$ time because all scheduling analysis is performed off-line.

Output from the scheduling service is produced in the form of an initialized static table that can be compiled and linked into the executable for runtime, i.e. other than configuration, runs. The scheduling service provides an interface for the TAO's ORB endsystem to access the request priorities contained in the table.

The initial configuration run may contain, at worst, initial estimates of `RT_Operation` execution times. Likewise, it may include some execution times based on code simulation or manual instruction counts. Successive iterations should include actual measured execution times. The more accurate the input, the more reliable the schedulability assessment.

Off-line configuration runs can be used to fill in the `Dependency_Info` arrays and calibrate the execution times of the `RT_Info` instances for each of the `RT_Operations`. The initial implementation of the scheduling service requires that this input be gathered manually. TAO's real-time event service [27] fills in the `Dependency_Info` arrays for its suppliers. Therefore, applications that manage all of their real-time activity through TAO's event service do not require manual collection of dependency information.

One user of the scheduling service has written a thin layer interface for calibrating the `RT_Info` execution times on VxWorks, which provides a system call for timing the execution of a function. During a configuration run, conditionally compiled code issues that system call for each `RT_Operation` and stores the result in the `RT_Info` structure.

5. Designing a Real-time ORB Core

Section 4 examined the components used by TAO to analyze and generate feasible real-time schedules based on abstract descriptions of CORBA operations. To ensure that these schedules operate correctly at run-time requires an ORB Core that executes operations efficiently and predictably end-to-end. This section describes alternative designs for ORB Core concurrency and connection architectures. Sections 5.1 and 5.2 qualitatively evaluate how the ORB Core connection and concurrency architectures manage the aggregate processing capacity of ORB endsystem components and application operations.

Sections 5.3, 5.4, and 5.5 then present quantitative results that illustrate empirically how the concurrency architectures used by CORBAplus, COOL, MT-Orbix, and TAO perform on Solaris, which is a general-purpose OS with real-time extensions, and Chorus Classix, which is a real-time operating system. CORBAplus and MT-Orbix were not designed to support applications with real-time requirements. The Chorus COOL ORB was designed for embedded systems with small memory footprints. TAO was designed to support real-time applications with deterministic and statistical quality of service requirements, as well as best-effort requirements, as described in section 3.

5.1 Alternative ORB Core Connection Architectures

There are two general strategies for structuring connection architecture in an ORB Core: *multiplexed* and *non-multiplexed*. We describe and evaluate various design alternatives for each approach below, focusing on client-side connection architectures in our examples.

5.1.1 Multiplexed Connection Architectures

Most conventional ORBs multiplex all client requests emanating from a single process through one TCP connection to their corresponding server process. This multiplexed connection architecture is commonly used to build scalable ORBs by minimizing the number of TCP connections open to each server. When multiplexing is used, however, a key challenge is to design an efficient ORB Core connection architecture that supports concurrent read and write operations.

TCP provides untyped bytestream data transfer semantics. Therefore, multiple threads cannot read or write from the same socket concurrently. Likewise, writes to a socket shared within an ORB process must be serialized. Serialization is typically implemented by having a client thread acquire a lock before writing to a shared socket.

For one-way operations, there is no need for additional locking or processing once a request is sent. Implementing two-way operations over a shared connection is more complicated, however. In this case, the ORB Core must allow multiple threads to concurrently "read" from a shared socket endpoint.

If server replies are multiplexed through a single TCP connection then multiple threads cannot read simultaneously from that socket endpoint. Instead, the ORB Core must demultiplex incoming replies to the appropriate client thread by using the GIOP sequence number sent with the original client request and returned with the servant's reply.

Several common ways of implementing connection multiplexing to allow concurrent read and write operations are described below.

- *Active connection architecture*. One approach is the active connection architecture shown in Fig. 15. An application thread (**1**) invokes a

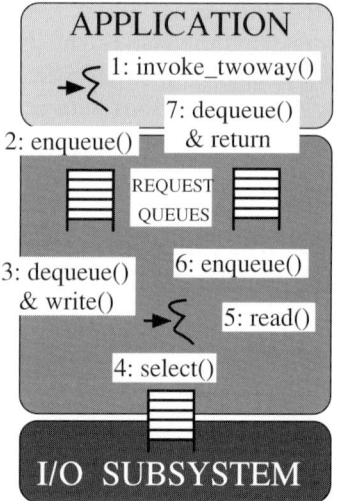

FIG. 15. Active connection architecture.

two-way operation, which enqueues the request in the ORB (**2**). A separate thread in the ORB Core services this queue (**3**) and performs a write operation on the multiplexed socket. The ORB thread selects[8] (**4**) on the socket waiting for the server to reply, reads the reply from the socket (**5**), and enqueues the reply in a message queue (**6**). Finally, the application thread retrieves the reply from this queue (**7**) and returns back to its caller.

The advantage of the active connection architecture is that it simplifies ORB implementations by using a uniform queueing mechanism. In addition, if every socket handles packets of the same priority level, i.e. packets of different priorities are not received on the same socket, the active connection can handle these packets in FIFO order without causing request-level priority inversion [62].

The disadvantage with this architecture, however, is that the active connection forces an extra context switch on all two-way operations. To minimize their overhead, many ORBs use a variant of the active connection architecture described next.

- *Leader/followers connection architecture.* An alternative to the active connection model is the leader/followers architecture shown in Fig. 16. As before, an application thread invokes a two-way operation call (**1**).

---

[8] The select call is typically used since a client may have multiple multiplexed connections to multiple servers.

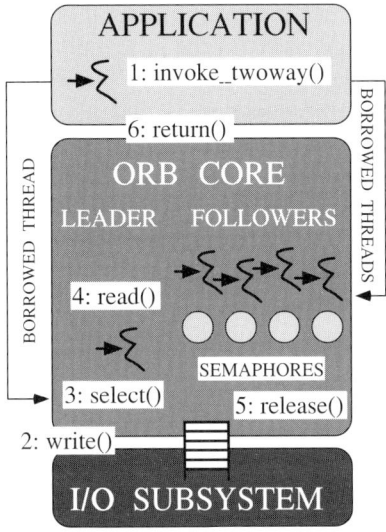

FIG. 16. Leader/follower connection architecture.

Rather than enqueueing the request in an ORB message queue, however, the request is sent across the socket immediately (**2**), using the thread of the application to perform the write. Moreover, no single thread in the ORB Core is dedicated to handling all the socket I/O in the leader/follower architecture. Instead, the first thread that attempts to wait for a reply on the multiplexed connection will block in select waiting for a reply (**3**). This thread is called the *leader*.

To avoid corrupting the socket bytestream, only the leader thread can select on the socket(s). Thus, all client threads that "follow the leader" to read replies from the shared socket will block on semaphores managed by the ORB Core. If replies return from the server in FIFO order this strategy is optimal since there is no unnecessary processing or context switching. However, replies may arrive in non-FIFO order. For instance, the next reply arriving from a server could be for any one of the client threads blocked on semaphores.

When the next reply arrives from the server, the leader reads the reply (**4**). It uses the sequence number returned in the GIOP reply header to identify the correct thread to receive the reply. If the reply is for the leader's own request, the leader releases the semaphore of the next follower (**5**) and returns to its caller (**6**). The next follower becomes the new leader and blocks on select.

If the reply is *not* for the leader, however, the leader must signal the semaphore of the appropriate thread. The signaled thread then wakes up, reads its reply, and returns to its caller. Meanwhile, the leader thread continues to select for the next reply.

Compared with active connections, the advantage of the leader/ follower connection architecture is that it minimizes the number of context switches incurred *if replies arrive in FIFO order*. The drawback, however, is that the complex implementation logic can yield significant locking overhead and priority inversion. The locking overhead stems from the need to acquire mutexes when sending requests and to block on the semaphores while waiting for replies. The priority inversion occurs if the priorities of the waiting threads are not respected by the leader thread when it demultiplexes replies to client threads.

5.1.2 Non-multiplexed Connection Architectures

One technique for minimizing ORB Core priority inversion is to use a non-multiplexed connection architecture, such as the one shown in Fig. 17. In this connection architecture, each client thread maintains a table of preestablished connections to servers in thread-specific storage [66]. A separate connection is maintained in each thread for every priority level, e.g. P_1, P_2, P_3, etc. As a result, when a two-way operation is invoked (**1**) it shares no socket endpoints with other threads. Therefore, the write, (**2**), select (**3**), read (**4**), and return (**5**) operations can occur without contending for ORB resources with other threads in the process.

The primary benefit of a non-multiplexed connection architecture is that it preserves end-to-end priorities and minimizes priority inversion while sending requests through ORB endsystems. In addition, since connections are not shared, this design incurs low synchronization overhead because no additional locks are required in the ORB Core when sending/receiving two-way requests.

The drawback with a non-multiplexed connection architecture is that it can use a larger number of socket endpoints than the multiplexed connection model, which may increase the ORB endsystem memory footprint. Therefore, it is most effective when used for statically configured real-time applications, such as avionics mission computing systems [62], which possess a small, fixed number of connections.

5.2 Alternative ORB Core Concurrency Architectures

There are a variety of strategies for structuring the multi-threading architecture in an ORB. Below, we describe a number of alternative ORB Core multi-threading architectures, focusing on server-side multi-threading. Thread pool is a common architecture for structuring ORB multi-threading,

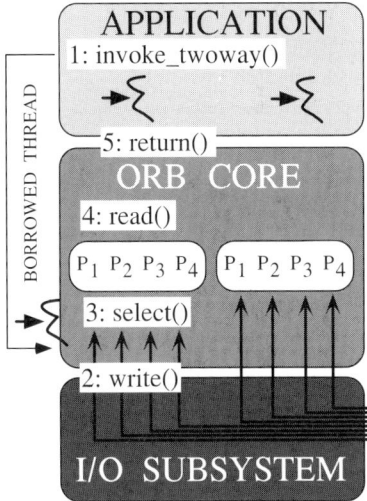

FIG. 17. Non-multiplexed connection architecture.

particularly for real-time ORBs [68]. Below, we describe and evaluate several common thread pool architectures.

5.2.1 The Worker Thread Pool Architecture

This ORB multi-threading architecture uses a design similar to the active connection architecture described in section 5.1.1. As shown in Fig. 18, the components in a worker thread pool include an I/O thread, a request queue, and a pool of worker threads. The I/O thread selects (**1**) on the socket endpoints, reads (**2**) new client requests, and (**3**) inserts them into the tail of the request queue. A worker thread in the pool dequeues (**4**) the next request from the head of the queue and dispatches it (**5**).

The chief advantage of the worker thread pool multi-threading architecture is its ease of implementation. In particular, the request queue provides a straightforward producer/consumer design. The disadvantages of this model stem from the excessive context switching and synchronization required to manage the request queue, as well as request-level priority inversion caused by connection multiplexing. Since different priority requests share the same transport connection, a high-priority request may wait until a low-priority request that arrived earlier is processed. Moreover, thread-level priority inversions can occur if the priority of the thread that originally reads the request is lower than the priority of the servant that processes the request.

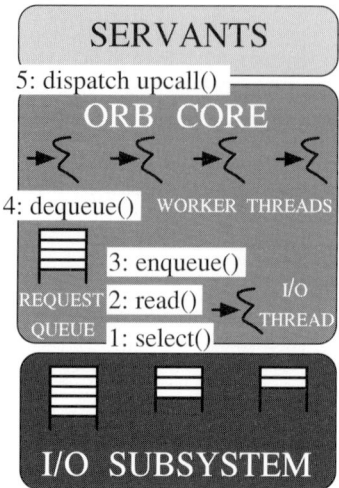

FIG. 18. Server-side worker thread pool multi-threading architecture.

5.2.2 The Leader/Follower Thread Pool Architecture

The leader/follower thread pool architecture is an optimization of the worker thread pool model. It is similar to the leader/follower connection architecture discussed in section 5.1.1. As shown in Fig. 19, a pool of threads is allocated and a leader thread is chosen to select (**1**) on connections for all servants in the server process. When a request arrives, this thread reads (**2**) it into an internal buffer. If this is a valid request for a servant, a follower thread in the pool is released to become the new leader (**3**) and the leader thread dispatches the upcall (**4**). After the upcall is dispatched, the original leader thread becomes a follower and returns to the thread pool. New requests are queued in socket endpoints until a thread in the pool is available to execute the requests.

Compared with the worker thread pool design, the chief advantage of the leader/follower thread pool architecture is that it minimizes context switching overhead incurred by incoming requests. Overhead is minimized since the request need not be transferred from the thread that read it to another thread in the pool that processes it. The disadvantages of the leader/follower architecture are largely the same as with the worker thread design. In addition, it is harder to implement the leader/follower model.

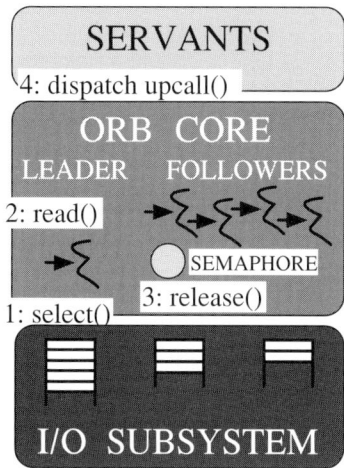

FIG. 19. Server-side leader/follower multi-threading architecture.

5.2.3 Threading Framework Architecture

A very flexible way to implement an ORB multi-threading architecture is to allow application developers to customize hook methods provided by a *threading framework*. One-way of structuring this framework is shown in Fig. 20. This design is based on the MT-Orbix thread filter framework, which is a variant of the Chain of Responsibility pattern [14].

In MT-Orbix, an application can install a thread filter at the top of a chain of filters. Filters are application-programmable hooks that can perform a number of tasks. Common tasks include intercepting, modifying, or examining each request sent to and from the ORB.

In the thread framework architecture, a connection thread in the ORB Core reads (**1**) a request from a socket endpoint and enqueues the request on a request queue in the ORB Core (**2**). Another thread then dequeues the request (**3**) and passes it through each filter in the chain successively. The topmost filter, i.e. the thread filter, determines the thread to handle this request. In the *thread-pool* model, the thread filter enqueues the request into a queue serviced by a thread with the appropriate priority. This thread then passes control back to the ORB, which performs operation demultiplexing and dispatches the upcall (**4**).

The main advantage of a threading framework is its flexibility. The thread filter mechanism can be programmed by server developers to support various multi-threading strategies. For instance, to implement a thread-per-request strategy, the filter can spawn a new thread and pass the request

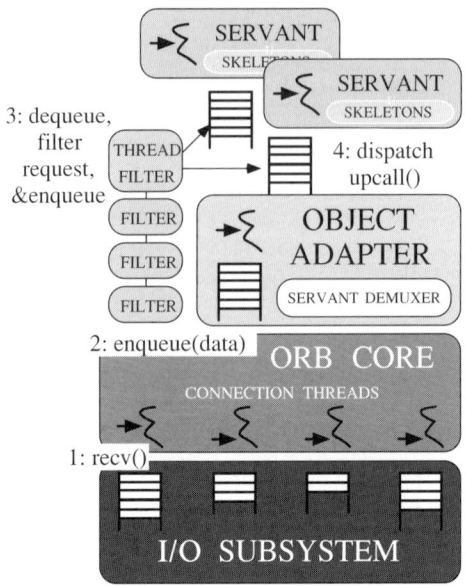

FIG. 20. Server-side thread framework multi-threading architecture.

to this new thread. Likewise, the MT-Orbix threading framework can be configured to implement other multi-threading architectures such as thread-per-servant and thread-per-connection.

There are several disadvantages with the thread framework design, however. First, since there is only a single chain of filters, priority inversion can occur because each request must traverse the filter chain in FIFO order. Second, there may be FIFO queueing at multiple levels in the ORB endsystem. Therefore, a high priority request may be processed only after several lower priority requests that arrived earlier. Third, the generality of the threading framework may increase locking overhead, e.g. locks must be acquired to insert requests into the queue of the appropriate thread.

5.2.4 The Reactor-per-Thread-Priority Architecture

The Reactor-per-thread-priority architecture is based on the Reactor pattern [57], which integrates transport end-point demultiplexing and the dispatching of the corresponding event handlers. This threading architecture associates a group of Reactors with a group of threads running at different priorities. As shown in Fig. 21, the components in the Reactor-per-thread-priority architecture include multiple pre-allocated Reactors, each of

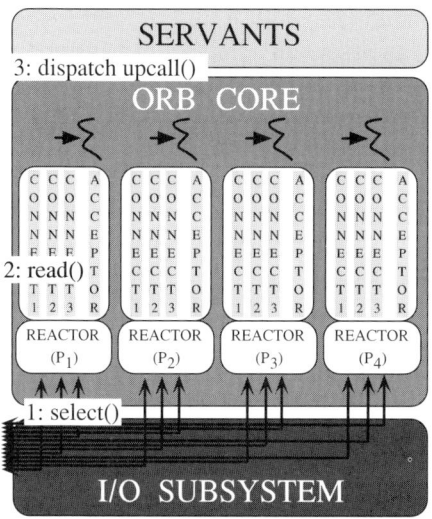

FIG. 21. Server-side Reactor-per-thread-priority multi-threading architecture.

which is associated with its own real-time thread of control for each priority level in the ORB. For instance, avionics mission computing systems [27] commonly execute their tasks in fixed priority threads corresponding to the *rates*, e.g. 20 Hz, 10 Hz, 5 Hz, and 1 Hz, at which operations are called by clients.

Within each thread, the Reactor demultiplexes (**1**) all incoming client requests to the appropriate connection handler, i.e. connect$_1$, connect$_2$, etc. The connection handler reads (**2**) the request and dispatches (**3**) it to a servant that executes the upcall at its thread priority.

Each Reactor in an ORB server thread is also associated with an Acceptor [60]. The Acceptor is a factory that listens on a particular port number for clients to connect to that thread and creates a connection handler to process the GIOP requests. In the example in Fig. 21, there is a listener port for each priority level.

The advantage of the Reactor-per-thread-priority architecture is that it minimizes priority inversion and non-determinism. Moreover, it reduces context switching and synchronization overhead by requiring the state of servants to be locked only if they interact across different thread priorities. In addition, this multi-threading architecture supports scheduling and analysis techniques that associate priority with rate, such as rate monotonic scheduling (RMS) and rate monotonic analysis (RMA) [40, 37].

The disadvantage with the Reactor-per-thread-priority architecture is that it serializes all client requests for each Reactor within a single thread of control, which can reduce parallelism. To alleviate this problem, a variant of this architecture can associate a *pool* of threads with each priority level. Though this will increase potential parallelism, it can incur greater context switching overhead and non-determinism, which may be unacceptable for certain types of real-time applications.

The `Reactor`-per-thread-priority architecture can be integrated seamlessly with the non-multiplexed connection model described in section 5.1.2. to provide end-to-end priority preservation in real-time ORB endsystems, as shown in Fig. 6. As shown in this diagram, the `Acceptors` listen on ports that correspond to the 20 Hz, 10 Hz, 5 Hz, and 1 Hz rate group thread priorities, respectively. Once a client connects, its `Acceptor` creates a new socket queue and connection handler to service that queue. The I/O subsystem uses the port number contained in arriving requests as a demultiplexing key to associate requests with the appropriate socket queue.

The `Reactor`-per-thread-priority architecture minimizes priority inversion through the entire distributed ORB endsystem by eagerly demultiplexing incoming requests onto the appropriate real-time thread that services the priority level of the target servant. As shown in section 5.4, this design is well suited for real-time applications with deterministic QoS requirements.

5.3 Benchmarking Testbed

This section describes the experimental testbed we designed to systematically measure sources of latency and throughput overhead, priority inversion, and non-determinism in ORB endsystems. The architecture of our testbed is depicted in Fig. 22. The hardware and software components used in the experiments are outlined in section 5.3.1.

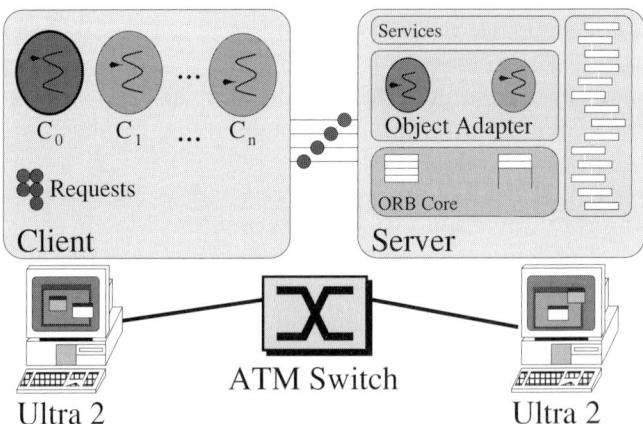

FIG. 22. ORB endsystem benchmarking testbed.

5.3.1 Hardware Configuration

The experiments in this section were conducted using a FORE systems ASX-1000 ATM switch connected to two dual-processor UltraSPARC-2s running Solaris 2.5.1. The ASX-1000 is a 96 Port, OC12 622 Mbs/port switch. Each UltraSPARC-2 contains two 168 MHz Super SPARC CPUs with a 1 Megabyte cache per-CPU. The Solaris 2.5.1 TCP/IP protocol stack is implemented using the STREAMS communication framework [54].

Each UltraSPARC-2 has 256 Mbytes of RAM and an ENI-155s-MF ATM adaptor card, which supports 155 Mbps SONET multimode fiber. The maximum transmission unit (MTU) on the ENI ATM adaptor is 9180 bytes. Each ENI card has 512 Kbytes of on-board memory. A maximum of 32 Kbytes is allotted per ATM virtual circuit connection for receiving and transmitting frames (for a total of 64 Kbytes). This allows up to eight switched virtual connections per card. The CORBA/ATM hardware platform is shown in Fig. 23.

5.3.2 Client/Server Configuration and Benchmarking Methodology

5.3.2.1 Server benchmarking configuration
As shown in Fig. 22, our testbed server consists of two servants within an ORB's Object Adapter.

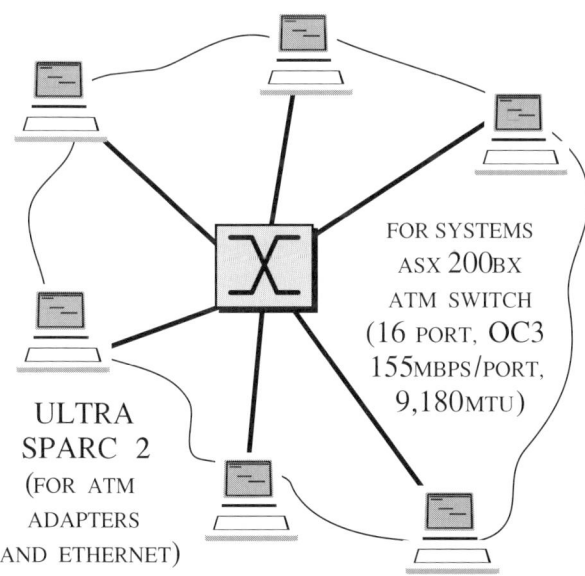

FIG. 23. Hardware for the CORBA/ATM testbed.

One servant runs in a higher priority thread than the other. Each thread processes requests that are sent to its servant by client threads on the other UltraSPARC-2.

Solaris real-time threads [36] are used to implement servant priorities. The high-priority servant thread has the *highest* real-time priority available on Solaris and the low-priority servant has the *lowest* real-time priority.

The server benchmarking configuration is implemented in the various ORBs as follows:

- *CORBAplus*: which uses the worker thread pool architecture described in section 5.2.1. In version 2.1.1 of CORBAplus, multi-threaded applications have an event dispatcher thread and a pool of worker threads. The dispatcher thread receives the requests and passes them to application worker threads, which process the requests. In the simplest configuration, an application can choose to create no additional threads and rely upon the main thread to process all requests.

- *miniCOOL*: which uses the leader/follower thread pool architecture described in section 5.2.2. Version 4.3 of miniCOOL allows application-level concurrency control. The application developer can choose between thread-per-request or thread-pool. The thread-pool concurrency architecture was used for our benchmarks since it is better suited than thread-per-request for deterministic real-time applications. In the thread-pool concurrency architecture, the application initially spawns a fixed number of threads. In addition, when the initial thread pool size is insufficient, miniCOOL can be configured to dynamically spawn threads on behalf of server applications to handle requests, up to a maximum limit.

- *MT-Orbix*: which uses the thread pool framework architecture based on the Chain of Responsibility pattern described in section 5.2.3. Version 2.2 of MT-Orbix is used to create two real-time servant threads at startup. The high-priority thread is associated with the high-priority servant and the low-priority thread is associated with the low-priority servant. Incoming requests are assigned to these threads using the Orbix thread filter mechanism, as shown in Fig. 20. Each priority has its own queue of requests to avoid priority inversion within the queue. This inversion could otherwise occur if a high-priority servant and a low-priority servant dequeue requests from the same queue.

- *TAO*: which uses the Reactor-per-thread-priority concurrency architecture described in section 5.2.4. Version 1.0 of TAO integrates the Reactor-per-thread-priority concurrency architecture with a non-multiplexed connection architecture, as shown in Fig. 21. In contrast, the other three ORBs multiplex all requests from client threads in each process over a single connection to the server process.

5.3.2.2 Client benchmarking configuration

Figure 22 shows how the benchmarking test used one high-priority client C_0 and n low-priority clients, $C_1 \ldots C_n$. The high-priority client runs in a high-priority real-time OS thread and invokes operations at 20 Hz, i.e. it invokes 20 CORBA two-way calls per second. All low-priority clients have the same lower priority OS thread priority and invoke operations at 10 Hz, i.e. they invoke 10 CORBA two-way calls per second. In each call, the client sends a value of type `CORBA::Octet` to the servant. The servant cubes the number and returns it to the client.

When the test program creates the client threads, they block on a barrier lock so that no client begins work until the others are created and ready to run. When all threads inform the main thread they are ready to begin; the main thread unblocks all client threads. These threads execute in an order determined by the Solaris real-time thread dispatcher. Each client invokes 4,000 CORBA two-way requests at its prescribed rate.

5.4 Performance Results on Solaris

Two categories of tests were used in our benchmarking experiments: *blackbox* and *whitebox*.

- *Blackbox benchmarks*. We computed the average two-way response time incurred by various clients. In addition, we computed two-way operation jitter, which is the standard deviation from the average two-way response time. High levels of latency and jitter are undesirable for real-time applications since they degrade worst-case execution time and reduce CPU utilization. Section 5.4.1 explains the blackbox results.

- *Whitebox benchmarks*. To precisely pinpoint the *sources* of priority inversion and performance non-determinism, we employed whitebox benchmarks. These benchmarks used profiling tools such as UNIX truss and Quantify [49]. These tools trace and log the activities of the ORBs and measure the time spent on various tasks, as explained in section 5.4.2.

Together, the blackbox and whitebox benchmarks indicate the end-to-end latency/jitter incurred by CORBA clients and help explain the reason for these results. In general, the results reveal why ORBs like MT-Orbix, CORBAplus, and miniCOOL are not yet suited for applications with real-time performance requirements. Likewise, the results illustrate empirically how and why the non-multiplexed, priority-based ORB Core architecture used by TAO is more suited for many types of real-time applications.

5.4.1 Blackbox Results

As the number of low-priority clients increases, the number of low-priority requests sent to the server also increases. Ideally, a real-time ORB endsystem should exhibit no variance in the latency observed by the high-priority client, irrespective of the number of low-priority clients. Our measurements of end-to-end two-way ORB latency yielded the results in Fig. 24.

Figure 24 shows that as the number of low-priority clients increases, MT-Orbix and CORBAplus incur significantly higher latencies for their high-priority client thread. Compared with TAO, MT-Orbix's latency is 7 times higher and CORBAplus' latency is 25 times higher. Note the irregular behavior of the average latency that miniCOOL displays, i.e. from 10 msec latency running 20 low-priority clients down to 2 msec with 25 low-priority clients. Such non-determinism is clearly undesirable for real-time applications.

The low-priority clients for MT-Orbix, CORBAplus and miniCOOL also exhibit very high levels of jitter. Compared with TAO, CORBAplus incurs 300 times as much jitter and MT-Orbix 25 times as much jitter in the worst case, as shown in Fig. 25. Likewise, miniCOOL's low-priority clients

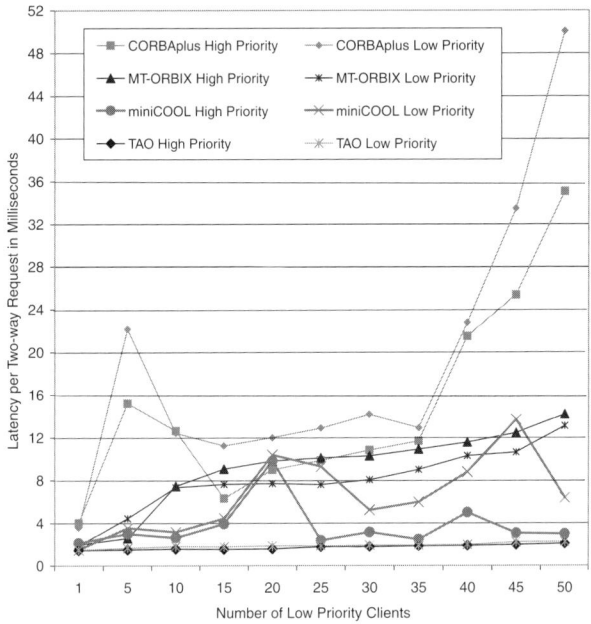

FIG. 24. Comparative latency for CORBAplus, MT-Orbix, miniCOOL, and TAO.

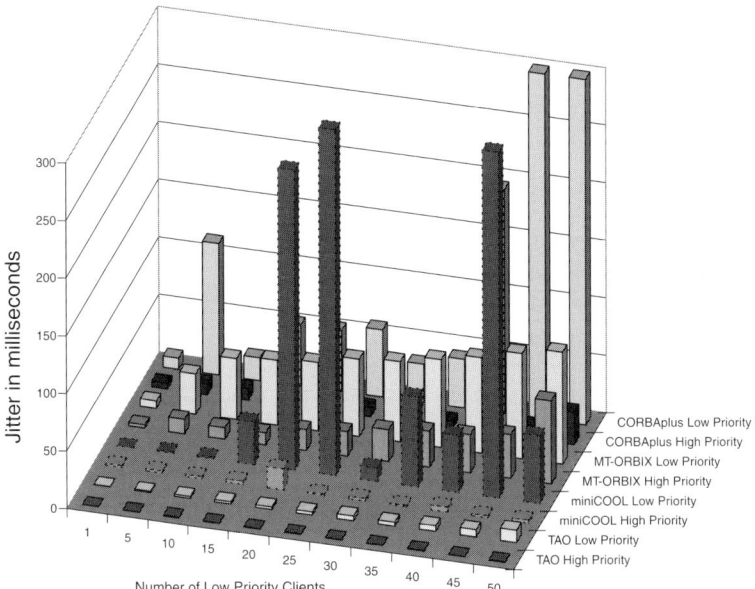

FIG. 25. Comparative jitter for CORBAplus, MT-Orbix, miniCOOL and TAO.

display an erratic behavior with several high bursts of jitter, which makes it undesirable for deterministic real-time applications.

The blackbox results for each ORB are explained below.

- *CORBAplus results.* CORBAplus incurs priority inversion at various points in the graph shown in Fig. 24. After displaying a high amount of latency for a small number of low-priority clients, the latency drops suddenly at 10 clients, then eventually rises again. Clearly, this behavior is not suitable for deterministic real-time applications. Section 5.4.2 reveals how the poor performance and priority inversions stem largely from CORBAplus' concurrency architecture. Figure 25 shows that CORBAplus generates high levels of jitter, particularly when tested with 40, 45, and 50 low-priority clients. These results show an erratic and undesirable behavior for applications that require real-time guarantees.

- *MT-Orbix results.* MT-Orbix incurs substantial priority inversion as the number of low-priority clients increase. After the number of clients exceeds 10, the high-priority client performs increasingly worse than the low-priority clients. This behavior is not conducive to deterministic real-time applications. Section 5.4.2 reveals how these inversions stem largely from the MT-Orbix's concurrency architecture on the server. In addition, MT-Orbix produces high levels of jitter, as shown in Fig. 25. This behavior is caused by priority inversions in its ORB Core, as explained in section 5.4.2.

- *miniCOOL results*. As the number of low-priority clients increase, the latency observed by the high-priority client also increases, reaching ~ 10 msec, at 20 clients, at which point it decreases suddenly to 2.5 msec with 25 clients. This erratic behavior becomes more evident as more low-priority clients are run. Although the latency of the high-priority client is smaller than the low-priority clients, the non-linear behavior of the clients makes miniCOOL problematic for deterministic real-time applications.

  The difference in latency between the high- and the low-priority client is also unpredictable. For instance, it ranges from 0.55 msec to 10 msec. Section 5.4.2 reveals how this behavior stems largely from the connection architecture used by the miniCOOL client and server.

  The jitter incurred by miniCOOL is also fairly high, as shown in Fig. 25. This jitter is similar to that observed by the CORBAplus ORB since both spend approximately the same percentage of time executing locking operation. Section 5.4.2 evaluates ORB locking behavior.

- *TAO results*. Figure 24 reveals that as the number of low-priority clients increase from 1 to 50, the latency observed by TAO's high-priority client grows by ~ 0.7 msecs. However, the difference between the low-priority and high-priority clients starts at 0.05 msec and ends at 0.27 msec. In contrast, in miniCOOL, it evolves from 0.55 msec to 10 msec, and in CORBAplus it evolves from 0.42 msec to 15 msec. Moreover, the rate of increase of latency with TAO is significantly lower than MT-Orbix, Sun miniCOOL, and CORBAplus. In particular, when there are 50 low-priority clients competing for the CPU and network bandwidth, the low-priority client latency observed with MT-Orbix is more than 7 times that of TAO, the miniCOOL latency is ~ 3 times that of TAO, and CORBAplus is ~ 25 times that of TAO.

  In contrast to the other ORBs, TAO's high-priority client always performs better than its low-priority clients. This demonstrates that the connection and concurrency architectures in TAO's ORB Core can maintain real-time request priorities end-to-end. The key difference between TAO and other ORBs is that its GIOP protocol processing is performed on a dedicated connection by a dedicated real-time thread with a suitable end-to-end real-time priority. Thus, TAO shares the minimal amount of ORB endsystem resources, which substantially reduces opportunities for priority inversion and locking overhead.

  The TAO ORB produces very low jitter (less than 11 msecs) for the low-priority requests and lower jitter (less than 1 msec) for the high-priority requests. The stability of TAO's latency is clearly desirable for applications that require predictable end-to-end performance.

In general, the blackbox results described above demonstrate that improper choice of ORB Core concurrency and connection software architectures can play a significant role in exacerbating priority inversion and non-determinism. The fact that TAO achieves such low levels of latency and jitter when run over the non-real-time Solaris I/O subsystem further demonstrates the feasibility of using standard OO middleware like CORBA to support real-time applications.

5.4.2 Whitebox Results

For the whitebox tests, we used a configuration of ten concurrent clients similar to the one described in section 5.3. Nine clients were low-priority and one was high-priority. Each client sent 4000 two-way requests to the server, which had a low-priority servant and high-priority servant thread.

Our previous experience using CORBA for real-time avionics mission computing [27] indicated that locks constitute a significant source of overhead, non-determinism and potential priority inversion for real-time ORBs. Using `Quantify` and `truss`, we measured the time the ORBs consumed performing tasks like synchronization, I/O, and protocol processing.

In addition, we computed a metric that records the number of calls made to user-level locks (`mutex_lock` and `mutex_unlock`) and kernel-level locks (`_lwp_mutex_lock`, `_lwp_mutex_unlock`, `_lwp_sema_post`, and `_lwp_sema_wait`). This metric computes the average number of lock operations per-request. In general, kernel-level locks are considerably more expensive since they incur kernel/user mode switching overhead.

The whitebox results from our experiments are presented below.

5.4.2.1 CORBAplus whitebox results
Our whitebox analysis of CORBAplus reveals high levels of synchronization overhead from mutex and semaphore operations at the user-level for each two-way request, as shown in Fig. 30. Synchronization overhead arises from locking operations that implement the connection and concurrency architecture used by CORBAplus.

As shown in Fig. 26, CORBAplus exhibits high synchronization overhead (52%) using kernel-level locks in the client and the server incurs high levels of processing overhead (45%) due to kernel-level lock operations.

For each CORBA request/response, CORBAplus's client ORB performs 199 lock operations, whereas the server performs 216 user-level lock operations, as shown in Fig. 30. This locking overhead stems largely from excessive dynamic memory allocation, as described in section 5.6. Each dynamic

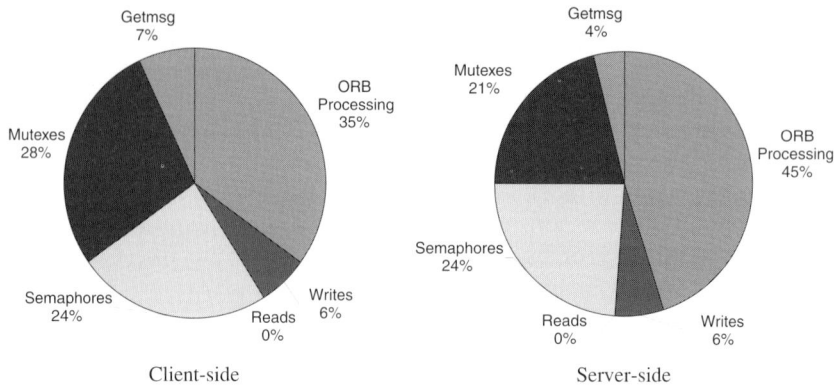

FIG. 26. Whitebox results for CORBAplus.

allocation causes two user-level lock operations, i.e. one acquire and one release.

The CORBAplus connection and concurrency architectures are outlined briefly below.

- *CORBAplus connection architecture.* The CORBAplus ORB connection architecture uses the active connection model described in section 5.1.1 and depicted in Fig. 18. This design multiplexes all requests to the same server through one active connection thread, which simplifies ORB implementations by using a uniform queueing mechanism.
- *CORBAplus concurrency architecture.* The CORBAplus ORB concurrency architecture uses the thread pool architecture described in section 5.2.1 and depicted in Fig. 18. This architecture uses a single I/O thread to `accept` and `read` requests from socket end-points. This thread inserts the request on a queue that is serviced by a pool of worker threads.

The CORBAplus connection architecture and the server concurrency architecture help reduce the number of simultaneous open connections and simplify the ORB implementation. However, concurrent requests to the shared connection incur high overhead because each send operation incurs a context switch. In addition, on the client-side, threads of different priorities can share the same transport connection, which can cause priority inversion. For instance, a high-priority thread may be blocked until a low-priority thread finishes sending its request. Likewise, the priority of the thread that blocks on the semaphore to receive a reply from a two-way connection may not reflect the priority of the *request* that arrives from the server, thereby causing additional priority inversion.

5.4.2.2 miniCOOL whitebox results

Our whitebox analysis of miniCOOL reveals that synchronization overhead from mutex and semaphore operations consume a large percentage of the total miniCOOL ORB processing time. As with CORBAplus, synchronization overhead in miniCOOL arises from locking operations that implement its connection and concurrency architecture. Locking overhead accounted for ~ 50% on the client-side and more than 40% on the server-side, as shown in Fig. 27.

For each CORBA request/response, miniCOOL's client ORB performs 94 lock operations at the user level, whereas the server performs 231 lock operations, as shown in Fig. 30. As with CORBAplus, this locking overhead stems largely from excessive dynamic memory allocation. Each dynamic allocation causes two user-level lock operations, i.e. one acquire and one release.

The number of calls per-request to kernel-level locking mechanisms at the server (shown in Fig. 31) are unusually high. This overhead stems from the fact that miniCOOL uses "system scoped" threads on Solaris, which require kernel intervention for all synchronization operations [12].

The miniCOOL connection and concurrency architectures are outlined briefly below.

- *miniCOOL connection architecture.* The miniCOOL ORB connection architecture uses a variant of the leader/followers model described in section 5.1.1. This architecture allows the leader thread to block in `select` on the shared socket. All following threads block on semaphores waiting for one of two conditions: (1) the leader thread will `read` their reply message and signal their semaphore or (2) the leader thread will `read` its own reply and signal another thread to enter and block in `select`, thereby becoming the new leader.

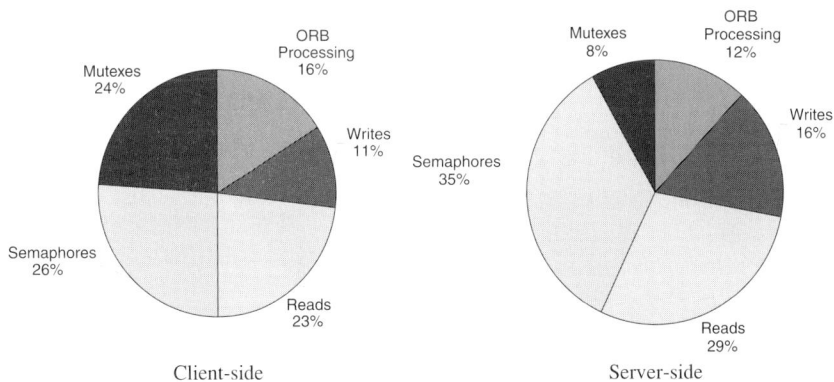

FIG. 27. Whitebox results for miniCOOL.

- *miniCOOL concurrency architecture.* The Sun miniCOOL ORB concurrency architecture uses the leader/followers thread pool architecture described in section 5.2.2. This architecture waits for connections in a single thread. Whenever a request arrives and validation of the request is complete, the leader thread (1) signals a follower thread in the pool to wait for incoming requests and (2) services the request.

The miniCOOL connection architecture and the server concurrency architecture help reduce the number of simultaneous open connections and the amount of context switching when replies arrive in FIFO order. As with CORBAplus, however, this design yields high levels of priority inversion. For instance, threads of different priorities can share the same transport connection on the client-side. Therefore, a high-priority thread may block until a low-priority thread finishes sending its request. In addition, the priority of the thread that blocks on the semaphore to access a connection may not reflect the priority of the *response* that arrives from the server, which yields additional priority inversion.

5.4.2.3 MT-Orbix whitebox results

Figure 28 shows the whitebox results for the client-side and server-side of MT-Orbix.

- *MT-Orbix connection architecture.* Like miniCOOL, MT-Orbix uses the leader/follower multiplexed connection architecture. Although this model minimizes context switching overhead, it causes intensive priority inversions.
- *MT-Orbix concurrency architecture.* In the MT-Orbix implementation of our benchmarking testbed, multiple servant threads were created,

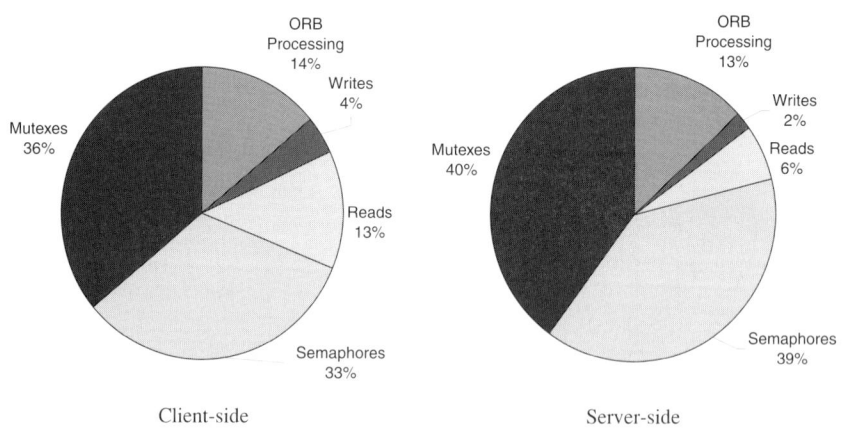

FIG. 28. Whitebox results for MT-Orbix.

each with the appropriate priority, i.e. the high-priority servant had the highest priority thread. A thread filter was then installed to look at each request, determine the priority of the request (by examining the target object), and pass the request to the thread with the correct priority. The thread filter mechanism is implemented by a high-priority realtime thread to minimize dispatch latency.

The thread pool instantiation of the MT-Orbix mechanism described in section 5.2.3 is flexible and easy to use. However, it suffers from high levels of priority inversion and synchronization overhead. MT-Orbix provides only *one* filter chain. Thus, all incoming requests must be processed sequentially by the filters before they are passed to the servant thread with an appropriate real-time priority. As a result, if a high-priority request arrives after a low-priority request, it must wait until the low-priority request has been dispatched before the ORB processes it.

In addition, a filter can only be called after (1) GIOP processing has completed and (2) the object adapter has determined the target object for this request. This processing is serialized since the MT-Orbix ORB Core is unaware of the request priority. Thus, a higher priority request that arrived after a low-priority request must wait until the lower priority request has been processed by MT-Orbix.

MT-Orbix's concurrency architecture is chiefly responsible for its substantial priority inversion shown in Fig. 24. This figure shows how the latency observed by the high-priority client increases rapidly, growing from ~ 2 msecs to ~ 14 msecs as the number of low-priority clients increase from 1 to 50.

The MT-Orbix filter mechanism also causes an increase in synchronization overhead. Because there is just one filter chain, concurrent requests must acquire and release locks to be processed by the filter. The MT-Orbix client-side performs 175 user-level lock operations per-request, while the server-side performs 599 user-level lock operations per-request, as shown in Fig. 30. Moreover, MT-Orbix displays a high number of kernel-level locks per-request, as shown in Fig. 31.

5.4.2.4 TAO whitebox results

As shown in Fig. 29, TAO exhibits negligible synchronization overhead. TAO performs 40 user-level lock operations per-request on the client-side, and 32 user-level lock operations per-request on the server-side. This low amount of synchronization results from the design of TAO's ORB Core, which allocates a separate connection for each priority, as shown in Fig. 6. Therefore, TAO's ORB Core minimizes additional user-level locking operations per-request and uses no kernel-level locks in its ORB Core.

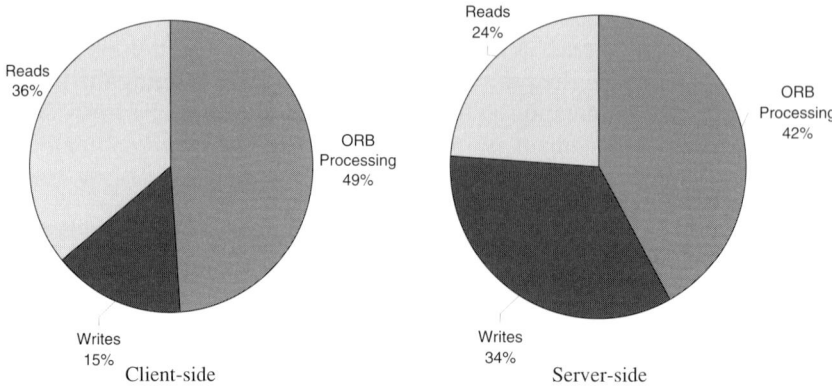

FIG. 29. Whitebox results for TAO.

- *TAO connection architecture*. TAO uses a non-multiplexed connection architecture, which preestablishes connections to servants, as described in section 5.1.2. One connection is preestablished for each priority level, thereby avoiding the non-deterministic delay involved in dynamic connection setup. In addition, different priority levels have their own connection. This design avoids request-level priority inversion, which would otherwise occur from FIFO queueing *across* client threads with different priorities.
- *TAO concurrency architecture*. TAO supports several concurrency architectures, as described in [62]. The `Reactor`-per-thread-priority architecture described in section 5.2.4 was used for the benchmarks in this paper. In this concurrency architecture, a separate thread is created for each priority level, i.e. each rate group. Thus, the low-priority client issues CORBA requests at a lower rate than the high-priority client (10 Hz vs 20 Hz, respectively).

On the server-side, client requests sent to the high-priority servant are processed by a high-priority real-time thread. Likewise, client requests sent to the low-priority servant are handled by the low-priority real-time thread. Locking overhead is minimized since these two servant threads share minimal ORB resources, i.e. they have separate `Reactors`, `Acceptors`, object adapters, etc. In addition, the two threads service separate client connections, thereby eliminating the priority inversion that would otherwise arises from connection multiplexing, as exhibited by the other ORBs we tested.

5.4.2.5 Locking overhead

Our whitebox tests measured user-level locking overhead (shown in Fig. 30) and kernel-level locking overhead

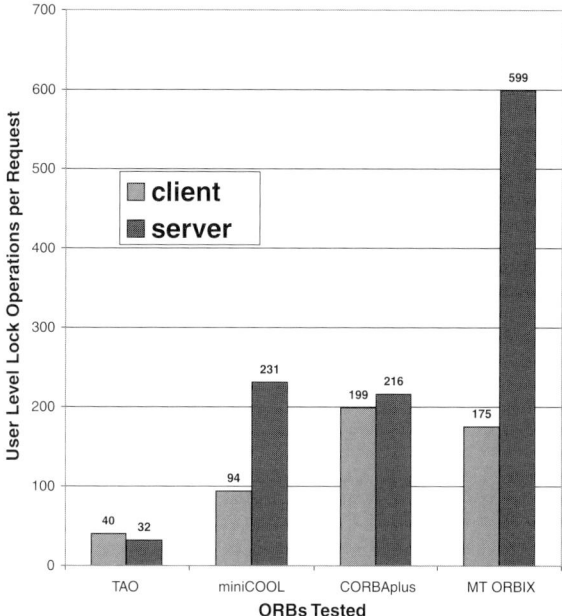

FIG. 30. User-level locking overhead in ORBs.

(shown in Fig. 31) in the CORBAplus, MT-Orbix, miniCOOL, and TAO ORBs. User-level locks are typically used to protect shared resources within a process. A common example is dynamic memory allocation using global C++ operators `new` and `delete`. These operators allocate memory from a globally managed heap in each process.

Kernel-level locks are more expensive since they typically require mode switches between the user level and the kernel. The semaphore and mutex operations depicted in the whitebox results for the ORBs evaluated above arise from kernel-level lock operations.

TAO limits user-level locking by using buffers that are pre-allocated off the run-time stack. This buffer is subdivided to accommodate the various fields of the request. Kernel-level locking is minimized since TAO can be configured so that ORB resources are not shared between its threads.

5.5 Performance Results on Chorus ClassiX

The performance results in section 5.4 were obtained on Solaris 2.5.1, which provides real-time scheduling but not real-time I/O [36]. Therefore, Solaris cannot guarantee the availability of resources like I/O buffers and network bandwidth [62]. Moreover, the scheduling performed by the Solaris

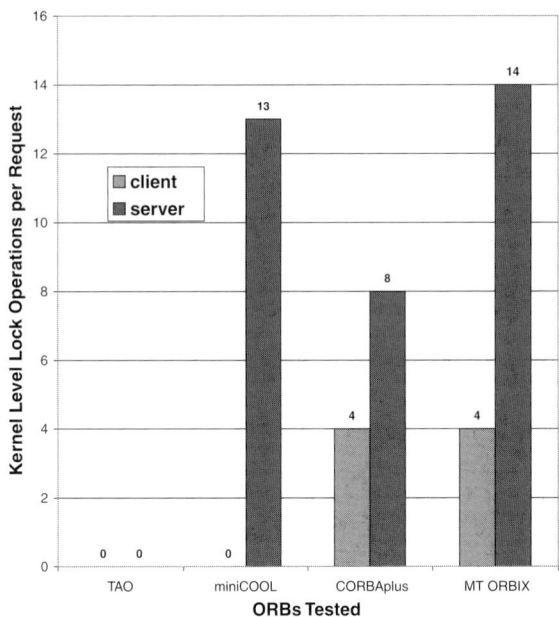

FIG. 31. Kernel-level locking overhead in ORBs.

I/O subsystem is not integrated with the rest of its resource management strategies.

So-called real-time operating systems (RTOS)s typically provide mechanisms for priority-controlled access to OS resources. This allows applications to ensure that QoS requirements are met. RTOS QoS mechanisms typically include real-time scheduling classes that enforce QoS usage policies, as well as real-time I/O to specify processing requirements and operation periods.

Chorus[9] ClassiX is a real-time OS that can scale down to small embedded configurations, as well as scale up to distributed POSIX-compliant platforms [26]. ClassiX provides a real-time scheduler that supports several scheduling algorithms, including priority-based FIFO preemptive scheduling. It supports real-time applications and general-purpose applications.

The IPC mechanism used on ClassiX, Chorus IPC, provides an efficient, location-transparent message-based communication facility on a single board and between multiple interconnected boards. In addition, ClassiX has a TCP/IP protocol stack, accessible via the Socket API, that enables internetworking connectivity with other OS platforms.

---

[9] Chorus has been purchased by Sun Microsystems.

To determine the impact of a real-time OS on ORB performance, this subsection presents blackbox results for TAO and miniCOOL using ClassiX.

5.5.1 Hardware Configuration

The following experiments were conducted using two MVME177 VMEbus single-board computers. The MVME177 contains a 60 MHz MC68060 processor and 64 Mbytes of RAM. The MVME177 boards are mounted on a MVME954A 6-slot, 32-bit, VME-compatible backplane. In addition, each MVME177 module has an 82596CA Ethernet transceiver interface.

5.5.2 Software Configuration

The experiments were run on version 3.1 of ClassiX. The ORBs benchmarked were miniCOOL 4.3 and TAO 1.0. The client/server configurations run were (1) locally, i.e. client and server on one board and (2) remotely, i.e. between two MVME177 boards on the same backplane.

The client/server benchmarking configuration implemented is the same[10] as the one run on Solaris 2.5.1 that is described in Section 5.3.2. MiniCOOL was configured to use the Chorus IPC communication facility to send messages on one board or across boards. This is more efficient than the TCP/IP protocol stack. In addition, we conducted benchmarks of miniCOOL and TAO using the TCP protocol. In general, miniCOOL performs more predictably using Chorus IPC as its transport mechanism.

5.5.3 Blackbox Results

We computed the average two-way response time incurred by various clients. In addition, we computed two-way operation jitter. High levels of latency and jitter are undesirable for real-time applications since they complicate the computation of worst-case execution time and reduce CPU utilization.

5.5.3.1 miniCOOL using Chorus IPC
As the number of low-priority clients increase, the latency observed by the remote high- and low-priority client also increases. It reaches ~ 34 msec, increasing linearly, when the client and the server are on different processor boards (remote) as shown in Fig. 32.

---

[10] Note the number of low-priority clients used was 5 rather than 50 due to a bug in ClassiX that caused `select` to fail if used to wait for events on more than 16 sockets.

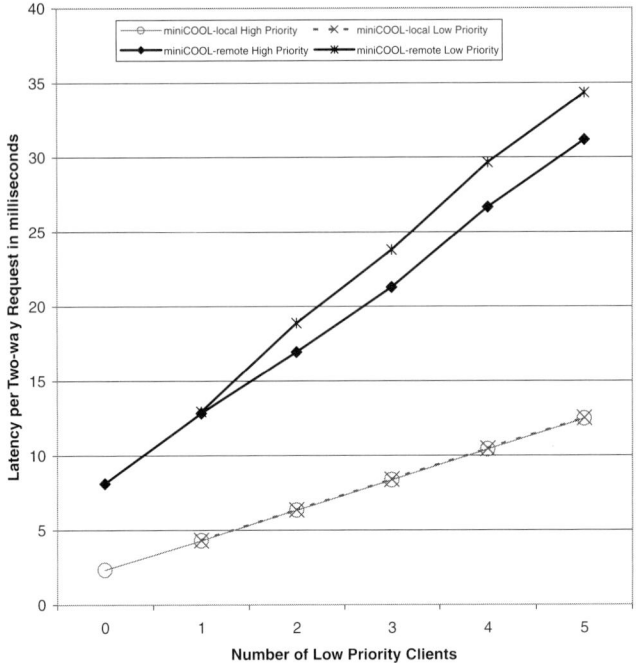

FIG. 32. Latency for miniCOOL with Chorus IPC on ClassiX.

When the client and server are collocated, the behavior is more stable on both the high and low-priority client, i.e. they are essentially identical since their lines in Fig. 32 overlap. The latencies start at ~ 2.5 msec of latency and reaches ~ 12.5 msecs. Both high- and low-priority clients incur approximately the same average latency.

In all cases, the latency for the high-priority client is always lower than the latency for the low-priority client. Thus, there is no significant priority inversion, which is expected for a real-time system. However, there is still variance in the latency observed by the high-priority client, in both, the remote and local configurations.

In general, miniCOOL performs more predictably on ClassiX than its version for Solaris. This is due to the use of TCP on Solaris versus Chorus IPC on ClassiX. The Solaris latency and jitter results were relatively erratic, as shown in the blackbox results from Solaris described in section 5.4.1.

Figure 33 shows that as the number of low-priority clients increases, the jitter increases in a progressive manner, for remote high- and low-priority clients. In addition, Fig. 33 illustrates that the jitter incurred by miniCOOL's remote clients is fairly high. The unpredictable behavior of high- and

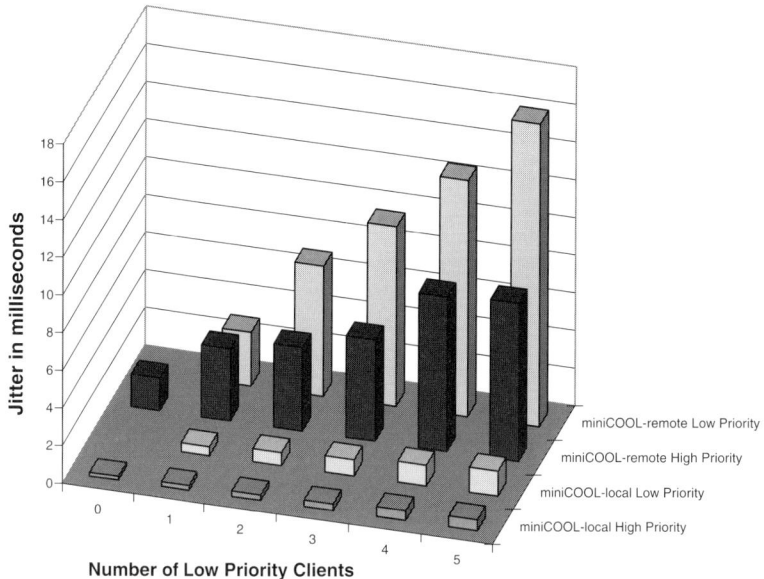

FIG. 33. Jitter for miniCOOL with Chorus IPC on ClassiX.

low-priority clients is more evident when the client and the server run on separate processor boards, as shown in Fig. 32. Moreover, Fig. 32 illustrates the difference in latency between the local and remote configurations, which appears to stem from the latency incurred by the network I/O driver.

5.5.3.2 miniCOOL using TCP

We also configured the miniCOOL client/server benchmark to use the Chorus TCP/IP protocol stack. The TCP/IP implementation on ClassiX is not as efficient as Chorus IPC. However, it provided a base for comparison between miniCOOL and TAO (which uses TCP as its transport protocol).

The results we obtained for miniCOOL over TCP show that as the number of low-priority clients increase, the latency observed by the remote high- and low-priority client also increased linearly. The maximum latency was ~ 59 msec, when the client and the server are on the same processor board (local) as shown in Fig. 34.

The increase in latency for the local configuration is unusual since one would expect the ORB to perform best when client and server are collocated on the same processor. However, when client and server reside in different processor boards, illustrated in Fig. 35, the average latency was more stable. This appears to be due to the implementation of the TCP/IP protocol stack, which may not to be optimized for local IPC.

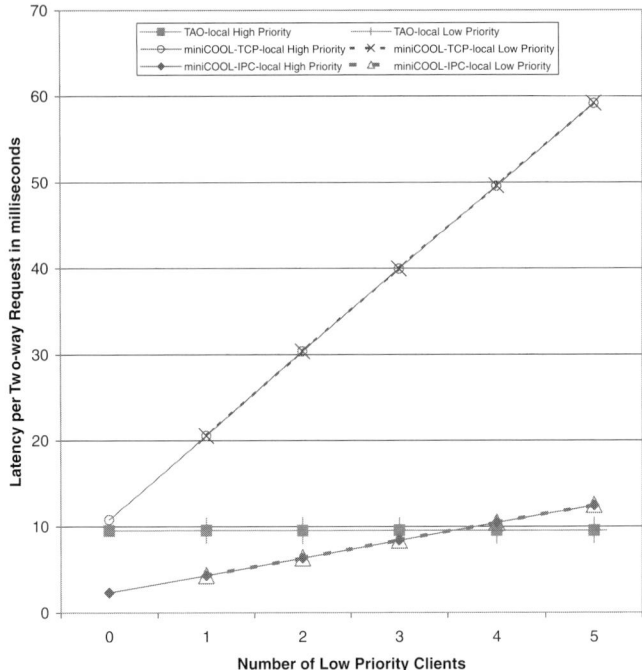

FIG. 34. Latency for miniCOOL-TCP, miniCOOL-IPC, and TAO-TCP on ClassiX, local configuration.

When the client and server are on separate boards, the behavior is similar to the remote clients using Chorus IPC. This indicates that at some of the bottlenecks reside in the Ethernet driver.

In all cases, the latency for the high-priority client is always lower than the latency for the low-priority client, i.e. there appears to be no significant priority inversion, which is expected for a real-time system. However, there is still variance in the latency observed by the high-priority client, in both the remote and local configurations, as shown in Fig. 36. The remote configurations incurred the highest variance, with the exception of TAO's remote high-priority clients, whose jitter remained fairly stable. This stability stems from TAO's `Reactor`-per-thread-priority concurrency architecture described in section 5.2.4.

5.5.3.3 *TAO using TCP*

Figure 34 reveals that as the number of low-priority clients increase from 0 to 5, the latency observed by TAO's high-priority client grows by ~0.005 msecs for the local configuration and Fig. 35 shows ~1.022 msecs for the remote one. Although the remote high-priority client performs as well as the local one, the difference between the low-priority and high-priority remote clients evolves from 0 msec to

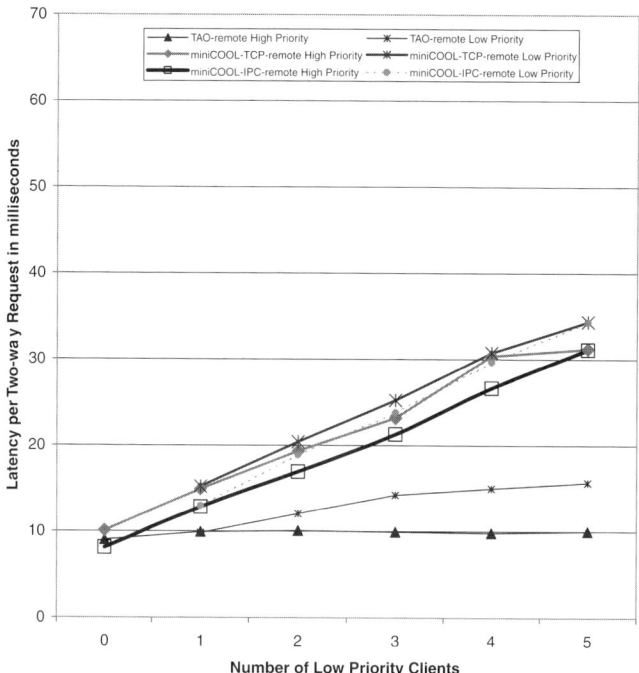

FIG. 35. Latency for miniCOOL-TCP, miniCOOL-IPC, and TAO-TCP on ClassiX, remote configuration.

6 msec. This increase is unusual and appears to stem from factors external to the ORB such as the scheduling algorithm and network latency. In general, TAO performs more predictably in other platforms tested with higher bandwidth, e.g. 155 Mbps ATM networks. The local client/server tests, in contrast, perform very predictably and have little increase in latency.

The TAO ORB produces very low jitter, less than 2 msecs, for the low-priority requests and lower jitter (less than 1 msec) for the high-priority requests. On this platform, the exception is the remote low-priority client, which may be attributed to the starvation of the low-priority clients by the high-priority one, and the latency incurred by the network. The stability of TAO's latency is clearly desirable for applications that require predictable end-to-end performance.

5.6 Evaluation and Recommendations

The results of our benchmarks illustrate the non-deterministic performance incurred by applications running atop conventional ORBs. In addition, the results show that priority inversion and non-determinism are significant problems in conventional ORBs. As a result, these ORBs are not

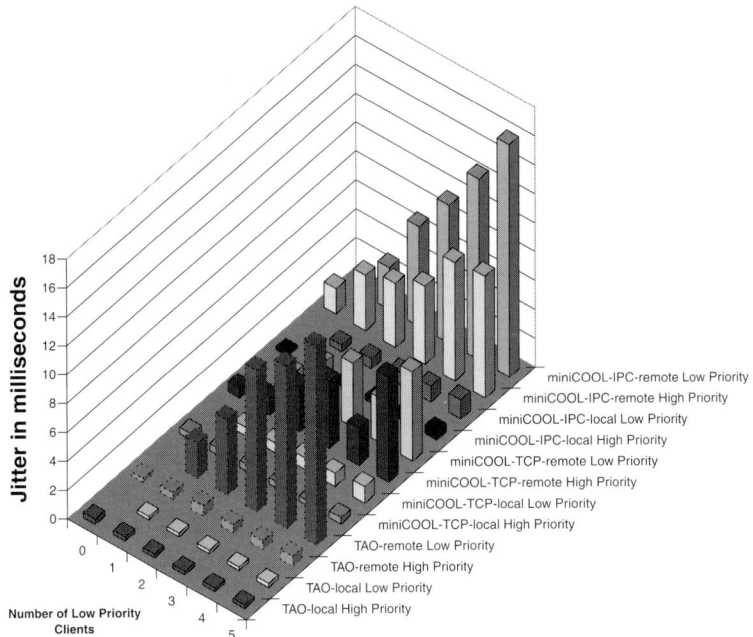

FIG. 36. Jitter for miniCOOL-TCP, miniCOOL-IPC and TAO-TCP on ClassiX.

currently suitable for applications with deterministic real-time requirements. Based on our results, and our prior experience [20, 16, 17, 22] measuring the performance of CORBA ORB endsystems, we suggest the following recommendations to decrease non-determinism and limit priority inversion in real-time ORB endsystems.

(1) *Real-time ORBs should avoid dynamic connection establishment.* ORBs that establish connections dynamically suffer from high jitter. Thus, performance seen by individual clients can vary significantly from the average. Neither CORBAplus, miniCOOL, nor MT-Orbix provide APIs for pre-establishing connections; TAO provides these APIs as extensions to CORBA.

We recommend that APIs to control the pre-establishment of connections should be defined as an OMG standard for real-time CORBA [44, 45].

(2) *Real-time ORBs should minimize dynamic memory management.* Thread-safe implementations of dynamic memory allocators require user-level locking. For instance, the C++ new operator allocates memory from a global pool shared by all threads in a process.

Likewise, the C++ `delete` operation, which releases allocated memory, also requires user-level locking to update the global shared pool. This lock sharing contributes to the overhead shown in Fig. 30. In addition, locking also increases non-determinism due to contention and queueing.

We recommend that real-time ORBs avoid excessive sharing of dynamic memory locks via the use of mechanisms such as thread-specific storage [66], which allocates memory from separate heaps that are unique to each thread.

(3) *Real-time ORBs should avoid multiplexing requests of different priorities over a shared connection.* Sharing connections among multiple threads requires synchronization. Not only does this increase locking overhead, but it also increases opportunities for priority inversion. For instance, high-priority requests can be blocked until low-priority threads release the shared connection lock. Priority inversion can be further exacerbated if multiple threads with multiple levels of thread priorities share common locks. For instance, medium priority threads can preempt a low-priority thread that is holding a lock required by a high-priority thread, which can lead to unbounded priority inversion [52].

We recommend that real-time ORBs allow application developers to determine whether requests with different priorities are multiplexed over shared connections. Currently, neither miniCOOL, CORBAplus, nor MT-Orbix support this level of control, though TAO provides this model by default.

(4) *Real-time ORB concurrency architectures should be flexible, efficient, and predictable.* Many ORBs, such as miniCOOL and CORBAplus, create threads on behalf of server applications. This design is inflexible since it prevents application developers from customizing ORB performance via a different concurrency architecture. Conversely, other ORB concurrency architectures are flexible, but inefficient and unpredictable, as shown by section 5.4.2's explanation of the MT-Orbix performance results. Thus, a balance is needed between flexibility and efficiency.

We recommend that real-time ORBs provide APIs that allow application developers to select concurrency architectures that are flexible, efficient, *and* predictable. For instance, TAO offers a range of concurrency architectures, such as `Reactor`-per-thread-priority, thread pool, and thread-per-connection. Developers can configure TAO [63] to minimize unnecessary sharing of ORB resources by using thread-specific storage.

(5) *Real-time ORBs should avoid reimplementing OS mechanisms.* Conventional ORBs incur substantial performance overhead because

they reimplement native OS mechanisms for endpoint demultiplexing, queueing, and concurrency control. For instance, much of the priority inversion and non-determinism miniCOOL, CORBAplus, and MT-Orbix stem from the complexity of their ORB Core mechanisms for multiplexing multiple client threads through a single connection to a server. These mechanism reimplement the connection management and demultiplexing features in the OS in a manner that (1) increases overhead and (2) does not consider the priority of the threads that make the requests for two-way operations.

We recommend that real-time ORB developers attempt to use the native OS mechanisms as much as possible, e.g. designing the ORB Core to work in concert with the underlying mechanisms rather than reimplementing them at a higher level. A major reason that TAO performs predictably and efficiently is because the connection management and concurrency model used in its ORB Core is closely integrated with the underlying OS features.

(6) *The design of real-time ORB endsystem architectures should be guided by empirical performance benchmarks.* Our prior research on pinpointing performance bottlenecks and optimizing middleware like Web servers [31, 30] and CORBA ORBs [16, 20, 22, 17] demonstrates the efficacy of a measurement-driven research methodology.

We recommend that the OMG adopt standard real-time CORBA benchmarking techniques and metrics. These benchmarks will simplify communication between researchers and developers. In addition, they will facilitate the comparison of performance results and real-time ORB behavior patterns between different ORBs and different OS/hardware platforms. The real-time ORB benchmarking test suite described in this section is available at `www.cs.wustl.edu/~schmidt/TAO.html`.

6. Using Patterns to Build TAO's Extensible ORB Software Architecture

The preceding sections in this paper focused largely on the QoS requirements for real-time ORB endsystems and described how TAO's scheduling, connection, and concurrency architectures are structured to meet these requirements. This section delves deeper into TAO's software architecture by exploring the *patterns* it uses to create *dynamically configurable* real-time ORB middleware.

A pattern represents a recurring solution to a software development problem within a particular context [14, 3]. Patterns help to alleviate the continual re-discovery and re-invention of software concepts and components by capturing solutions to standard software development problems [58]. For instance, patterns are useful for documenting the structure and participants in common communication software micro-architectures like Reactors [57], Active Objects [38], and Brokers [3]. These patterns are generalizations of object-structures that have proven useful to build flexible and efficient event-driven and concurrent communication software such as ORBs.

To focus the discussion, this section illustrates how we have applied patterns to develop TAO. A novel aspect of TAO is its extensible ORB design, which can be customized dynamically to meet specific application QoS requirements and network/endsystem characteristics. As a result, TAO can be extended and maintained more easily than conventional *statically configured* ORBs.

6.1 Why We Need Dynamically Configurable Middleware

A key motivation for ORB middleware is to offload complex distributed system infrastructure tasks from application developers to ORB developers. ORB developers are responsible for implementing reusable middleware components that handle common tasks, such as interprocess communication, concurrency, transport endpoint demultiplexing, scheduling, and dispatching. These components are typically compiled into a run-time ORB library, linked with application objects that use the ORB components, and executed in one or more OS processes.

Although this separation of concerns can simplify application development, it can also yield inflexible and inefficient applications and middleware architectures. The primary reason is that many conventional ORBs are configured *statically* at compile-time and link-time by ORB developers, rather than *dynamically* at installation-time or run-time by application developers. Statically configured ORBs have the following drawbacks [69, 34]:

- *Inflexibility*. Statically-configured ORBs tightly couple each component's *implementation* with the *configuration* of internal ORB components, i.e. which components work together and how they work together. As a result, extending statically-configured ORBs requires modifications to existing source code, which may not be accessible to application developers.

    Even if source code is available, extending statically configured ORBs requires recompilation and relinking. Moreover, any currently executing ORBs and their associated objects must be shutdown and restarted. This static reconfiguration process is not well-suited for application domains like telecom call processing that require 7×24 availability.

- *Inefficiency*. Statically configured ORBs can be inefficient, both in terms of space and time. Space inefficiency can occur if unnecessary components are always statically configured into an ORB. This can increase the ORB's memory footprint, forcing applications to pay a space penalty for features they do not require. Overly large memory footprints are particularly problematic for embedded systems, such as cellular phones or telecom switch line cards.

    Time inefficiency can stem from restricting an ORB to use statically configured algorithms or data structures for key processing tasks. This can make it hard for application developers to customize an ORB to handle new user-cases. For instance, real-time avionics systems [27] often can instantiate all their servants off-line. These systems can benefit from an ORB that uses perfect hashing or active demultiplexing [22] to demultiplex incoming requests to servants. However, ORBs that are configured statically to use a general-purpose, "one-size-fits-all" demultiplex strategy will not perform as well for mission-critical systems.

In theory, the drawbacks with static configuration described above are *internal* to ORBs and should not affect application developers directly. In practice, however, application developers are inevitably affected since the quality, portability, usability, and performance of the ORB middleware is reduced. Therefore, an effective way to improve ORB extensibility is to develop ORB middleware that can be *dynamically configured*.

Dynamic configuration enables the selective integration of customized implementations for key ORB strategies, such as communication, concurrency, demultiplexing, scheduling, and dispatching. This allows ORB developers to concentrate on the *functionality* of ORB components, without committing themselves prematurely to a specific *configuration* of these components. Moreover, dynamic configuration enables application developers and ORB developers to make these decisions very late in the design lifecycle, i.e. at installation-time or run-time.

Figure 37 illustrates the following key dimensions of ORB extensibility:

(1) *Extensibility to retargeting on new platforms*: which requires that the ORB be implemented using modular components that shield it from non-portable system mechanisms, such as those for threading, communication, and event demultiplexing. OS platforms like POSIX, Win32, VxWorks, and MVS provide a wide variety of system mechanisms.

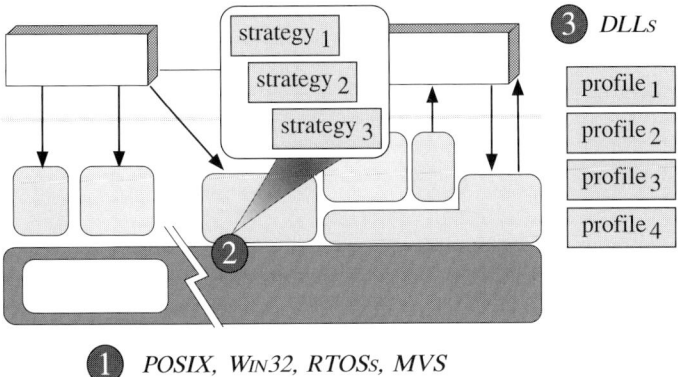

FIG. 37. Dimensions of ORB extensibility.

(2) *Extensibility via custom implementation strategies*: which can be tailored to specific application requirements. For instance, ORB components can be customized to meet periodic deadlines in real-time systems [27]. Likewise, ORB components can be customized to account for particular system characteristics, such as the availability of asynchronous I/O [22] or high-speed ATM networks [18].

(3) *Extensibility via dynamic configuration of custom strategies*: which takes customization to the next level by dynamically linking only those strategies that are necessary for a specific ORB "personality." For example, different application domains, such as medical systems or telecom call processing, may require custom combinations of concurrency, scheduling, or dispatch strategies. Configuring these strategies at run-time from dynamically linked libraries (DLLs) can (1) reduce the memory footprint of an ORB and (2) make it possible for application developers to extend the ORB without requiring access or changes to the original source code.

Below, we describe the patterns applied to enhance the extensibility of TAO along each dimension outlined above.

6.2 Overview of Patterns that Improve ORB Extensibility

This section uses TAO as a case study to illustrate how patterns can help application developers and ORB developers build, maintain, and extend communication software by reducing the coupling between components. Figure 38 illustrates the patterns used to develop an extensible ORB architecture for TAO. It is beyond the scope of this section to describe each

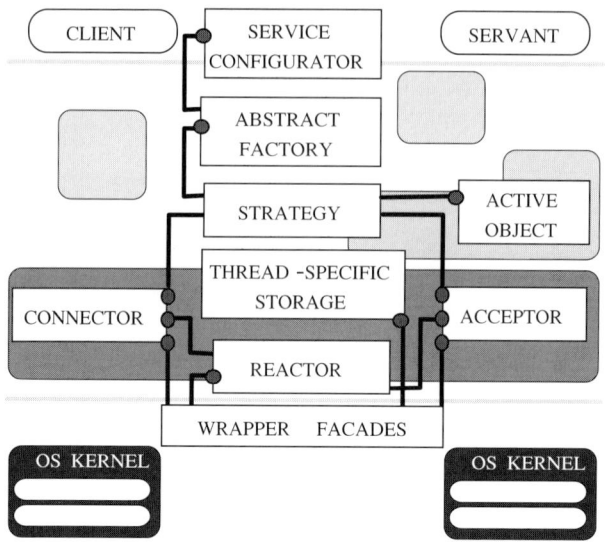

FIG. 38. Relationships among patterns used in TAO.

pattern in detail or to discuss all the patterns used within TAO. Instead, our goal is to focus on key patterns and show how they can improve the extensibility, maintainability, and performance of real-time ORB middleware. The references contain additional material on each pattern.

The intent and usage of these patterns are outlined below:

- *The Wrapper Facade pattern*: which simplifies the OS system programming interface by combining multiple related OS system mechanisms like the socket API or POSIX threads into cohesive OO abstractions [14]. TAO uses this pattern to avoid tedious, non-portable, and non-typesafe programming of low-level, OS-specific system calls.
- *The Reactor pattern*: which provides flexible event demultiplexing and event handler dispatching [57]. TAO uses this pattern to notify ORB-specific handlers synchronously when I/O events occur in the OS. The Reactor pattern drives the main event loop in TAO's ORB Core, which accepts connections and receives/sends client requests/responses.
- *The Acceptor-Connector pattern*: which decouples GIOP protocol handler initialization from the ORB processing tasks performed once initialization is complete [60]. TAO uses this pattern in the ORB Core on servers and clients to passively and actively establish GIOP connections that are independent of the underlying transport mechanisms.
- *The Active Object pattern*: which supports flexible concurrency architectures by decoupling request reception from request execution [38].

TAO uses this pattern to facilitate the use of multiple concurrency strategies that can be configured flexibly into its ORB Core at run-time.

- *The Thread-specific Storage pattern*: which allows multiple threads to use one logically global access point to retrieve thread-specific data without incurring locking overhead for each access [66]. TAO uses this pattern to minimize lock contention and priority inversion for real-time applications.

- *The Strategy pattern*: which provides an abstraction for selecting one of several candidate algorithms and packaging it into an object [14]. This pattern is the foundation of TAO's extensible software architecture and makes it possible to configure custom ORB strategies for concurrency, communication, scheduling, and demultiplexing.

- *The Abstract Factory pattern*: which provides a single factory that builds related objects. TAO uses this pattern to consolidate its dozens of Strategy objects into a manageable number of abstract factories that can be reconfigured *en masse* into clients and servers conveniently and consistently. TAO components use these factories to access related strategies without explicitly specifying their subclass name [14].

- *The Service Configurator pattern*: which permits dynamic run-time configuration of abstract factories and strategies in an ORB [34]. TAO uses this pattern to dynamically interchange abstract factory implementations in order to customize ORB personalities at run-time.

It is important to note that the patterns described in this section are not limited to ORBs or communication middleware. They have been applied in many other communication application domains, including telecom call processing and switching, avionics flight control systems, multimedia teleconferencing, and distributed interactive simulations.

6.3 How to Use Patterns to Resolve ORB Design Challenges

In the following discussion, we outline the forces that underlie the key design challenges that arise when developing extensible real-time ORBs. We also describe which pattern(s) resolve these forces and explain how these patterns are used in TAO. In addition, we show how the absence of these patterns in an ORB leaves these forces unresolved. To illustrate this latter point concretely, we compare TAO with SunSoft IIOP, which is a freely available[11] reference implementation of the Internet Inter-ORB Protocol (IIOP) written in C++. TAO evolved from the SunSoft IIOP

---

[11] See ftp://ftp.omg.org/pub/interop/ for the SunSoft IIOP source code.

release, so it provides an ideal baseline to evaluate the impact of patterns on the software qualities of ORB middleware.

6.3.1 Encapsulate Low-level System Mechanisms with the Wrapper Facade Pattern

6.3.1.1 Context One role of an ORB is to shield application-specific clients and servants from the details of low-level systems programming. Thus, ORB developers, rather than application developers, are responsible for tedious, low-level tasks like demultiplexing events, sending and receiving requests from the network, and spawning threads to execute client requests concurrently. Figure 39 illustrates a common approach used by SunSoft IIOP, which is programmed internally using system mechanisms like sockets, `select`, and POSIX threads directly.

6.3.1.2 Problem Developing an ORB is hard. It is even harder if developers must wrestle with low-level system mechanisms written in languages like C, which often yield the following problems:

- *ORB developers must have intimate knowledge of many OS platforms.* Implementing an ORB using system-level C APIs forces developers to deal with non-portable, tedious, and error-prone OS idiosyncrasies, such as using untyped socket handles to identify transport endpoints. Moreover, these APIs are not portable across OS platforms. For example, Win32 lacks POSIX threads and has subtly different semantics for sockets and `select`.
- *Increased maintenance effort.* One-way to build an ORB is to handle portability variations via explicit conditional compilation directives in ORB source code. Using conditional compilation to address platform-specific variations *at all points of use* increases the complexity of the source code, as shown in section 6.5. It is hard to maintain and extend

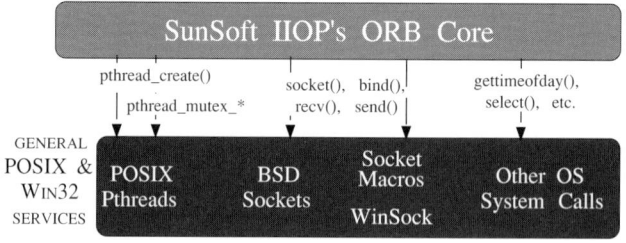

FIG. 39. SunSoft IIOP operating system interaction.

such ORBs since platform-specific details are scattered throughout the implementation source code files.

- *Inconsistent programming paradigms.* System mechanisms are accessed through C-style function calls, which cause an "impedance mismatch" with the OO programming style supported by C++, the language used to implement TAO.

How can we avoid accessing low-level system mechanisms when implementing an ORB?

6.3.1.3 Solution: The Wrapper Facade Pattern

An effective way to avoid accessing system mechanisms directly is to use the Wrapper Facade pattern. This pattern is a variant of the Facade pattern [14]. The intent of the Facade pattern is to simplify the interface for a subsystem. The intent of the Wrapper Facade pattern is more specific: it provides typesafe, modular, and portable class interfaces that encapsulate lower-level, stand-alone system mechanisms, such as sockets, `select`, and POSIX threads. In general, the Wrapper Facade pattern should be applied when existing system-level APIs are non-portable and non-typesafe.

6.3.1.4 Using the Wrapper Facade Pattern in TAO

TAO accesses all system mechanisms via the wrapper facades provided by ACE [56]. ACE is an OO framework that implements core concurrency and distribution patterns for communication software. It provides reusable C++ wrapper facades and framework components that are targeted to developers of high-performance, real-time applications and services across a wide range of OS platforms, including Win32, most versions of UNIX, and real-time operating systems like VxWorks, Chorus, and LynxOS.

Figure 40 illustrates how the ACE C++ wrapper facades improve TAO's robustness and portability by encapsulating and enhancing native OS concurrency, communication, memory management, event demultiplexing, and dynamic linking mechanisms with typesafe OO interfaces. The OO encapsulation provided by ACE alleviates the need for TAO to access the weakly-typed system APIs directly. Therefore, C++ compilers can detect type system violations at compile-time rather than at run-time.

The ACE wrapper facades use C++ features to eliminate performance penalties that would otherwise be incurred from its additional type safety and layer of abstraction. For instance, inlining is used to avoid the overhead of calling short methods. Likewise, static methods are used to avoid the overhead of passing a C++ `this` pointer to each invocation.

Although the ACE wrapper facades solve a common development problem, they are just the first step towards developing an extensible and

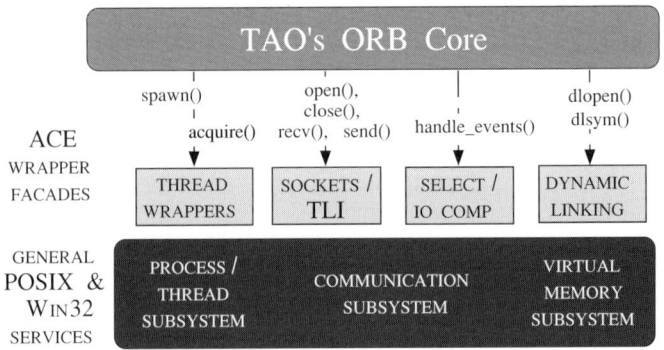

FIG. 40. TAO's wrapper facade encapsulation.

maintainable ORB. The remaining patterns described in this section build on the encapsulation provided by the ACE wrapper facades to address more challenging ORB design issues.

6.3.2 Demultiplexing ORB Core Events using the Reactor Pattern

6.3.2.1 Context An ORB Core is responsible for demultiplexing I/O events from multiple clients and dispatching their associated event handlers. For instance, a server-side ORB Core listens for new client connections and reads/writes GIOP requests/responses from/to connected clients. To ensure responsiveness to multiple clients, an ORB Core uses OS event demultiplexing mechanisms to wait for Connection, Read, and Write events to occur on *multiple* socket handles. Common event demultiplexing mechanisms include select, WaitForMultipleObjects, I/O completion ports, and threads.

Figure 41 illustrates a typical event demultiplexing sequence for SunSoft IIOP. In (**1**), the server enters its event loop by (**2**) calling get_request on the object adapter. The get_request method then (**3**) calls the static method block_for_connection on the server_endpoint. This method manages all aspects of server-side connection management, ranging from connection establishment to GIOP protocol handling. The ORB remains blocked (**4**) on select until the occurrence of I/O event, such as a connection event or a request event. When a request event occurs, block_for_connection demultiplexes that request to a specific server_endpoint and (**5**) dispatches the event to that endpoint. The GIOP engine in the ORB Core then (**6**) retrieves data from the socket and passes it to the object adapter, which demultiplexes it, demarshals it, and (**7**) dispatches the appropriate method upcall to the user-supplied servant.

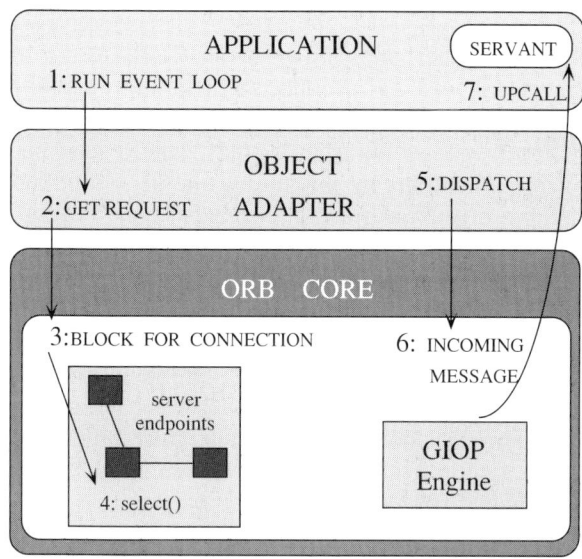

FIG. 41. SunSoft IIOP event loop.

6.3.2.2 Problem One-way to develop an ORB Core is to hardcode it to use one event demultiplexing mechanism, such as `select`. Relying on just one mechanism is undesirable, however, since no single scheme is efficient on all platforms or for all application requirements. For instance, asynchronous I/O completion ports are very efficient on Windows NT [31], whereas synchronous threads are the most efficient demultiplexing mechanism on Solaris [30].

Another way to develop an ORB Core is to tightly couple its event demultiplexing code with the code that performs GIOP protocol processing. For instance, the event demultiplexing logic of SunSoft IIOP is not a self-contained component. Instead, it is closely intertwined with subsequent processing of client request events by the Object Adapter and IDL skeletons. In this case, the demultiplexing code cannot be reused as a blackbox component by similar communication middleware applications, such as HTTP servers [31] or video-on-demand applications. Moreover, if new ORB strategies for threading or Object Adapter request scheduling algorithms are introduced, substantial portions of the ORB Core must be rewritten.

How then can an ORB implementation decouple itself from a specific event demultiplexing mechanism and decouple its demultiplexing code from its handling code?

6.3.2.3 Solution: The Reactor Pattern

An effective way to reduce coupling and increase the extensibility of an ORB Core is to apply the Reactor pattern [57]. This pattern supports synchronous demultiplexing and dispatching of multiple *event handlers*, which are triggered by events that can arrive concurrently from multiple sources. The Reactor pattern simplifies event-driven applications by integrating the demultiplexing of events and the dispatching of their corresponding event handlers. In general, the Reactor pattern should be applied when applications or components like an ORB Core must handle events from multiple clients concurrently, without becoming tightly coupled to a single low-level mechanism like `select`.

It is important to note that applying the Wrapper Facade pattern is not sufficient to resolve the event demultiplexing problems outlined above. A wrapper facade for `select` may improve ORB Core portability somewhat. However, this pattern does not resolve the need to completely decouple the low-level event demultiplexing logic from the higher-level client request processing logic in an ORB Core.

6.3.2.4 Using the Reactor Pattern in TAO

TAO uses the Reactor pattern to drive the main event loop within its ORB Core, as shown in Fig. 42. A TAO server (**1**) initiates an event loop in the ORB Core's `Reactor`, where it (**2**) remains blocked on `select` until an I/O event occurs. When a GIOP request event occurs, the `Reactor` demultiplexes

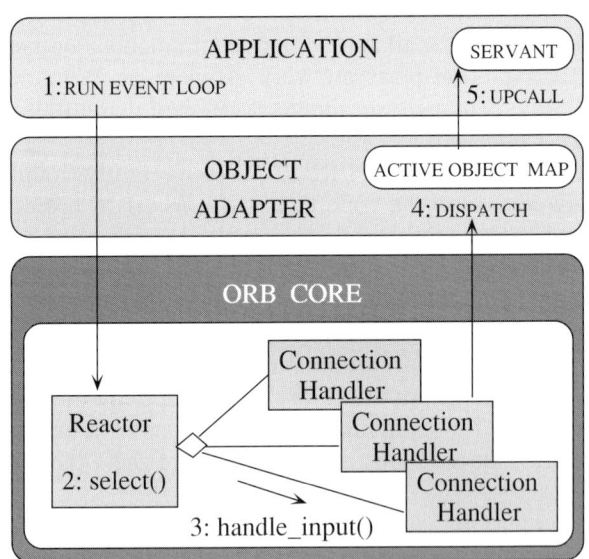

FIG. 42. Using the reactor pattern in TAO's event loop.

the request to the appropriate event handler, which is the GIOP `Connection_Handler` that is associated with each connected socket. The Reactor (**3**) then calls `Connection_Handler::handle_input`, which (**4**) dispatches the request to TAO's Object Adapter. The Object Adapter demultiplexes the request to the appropriate upcall method on the servant and (**5**) dispatches the upcall.

The Reactor pattern enhances the extensibility of TAO by decoupling the event handling portions of its ORB Core from the underlying OS event demultiplexing mechanisms. For example, the `WaitForMultipleObjects` event demultiplexing system call can be used on Windows NT, whereas `select` can be used on UNIX platforms. Moreover, the Reactor pattern simplifies the configuration of new event handlers. For instance, adding a new `Secure_Connection_Handler` that performs encryption/decryption of all network traffic does not affect the Reactor's implementation. Finally, unlike the event demultiplexing code in SunSoft IIOP, which is tightly coupled to one use-case, the ACE implementation of the Reactor pattern [58] used by TAO has been applied in many other OO event-driven applications ranging from HTTP servers [31] to real-time avionics infrastructure [27].

6.3.3 Managing Connections in an ORB Using Acceptor-Connector Pattern

6.3.3.1 Context Connection management is another key responsibility of an ORB Core. For instance, an ORB Core that implements the IIOP protocol must establish TCP connections and initialize the protocol handlers for each IIOP `server_endpoint`. By localizing connection management logic in the ORB Core, application-specific servants can focus solely on processing client requests, rather than dealing with low-level network programming tasks.

An ORB Core is not *limited* to running over IIOP and TCP transports, however. For instance, while TCP can transfer GIOP requests reliably, its flow control and congestion control algorithms can preclude its use as a real-time protocol [67]. Likewise, it may be more efficient to use a shared memory transport mechanism when clients and servants are collocated on the same endsystem. Ideally, an ORB Core should be flexible enough to support multiple transport mechanisms.

6.3.3.2 Problem The CORBA architecture explicitly decouples (1) the connection management tasks performed by an ORB Core from (2) the request processing performed by application-specific servants. A common way to implement an ORB's *internal* connection management activities, however, is to use low-level network APIs like sockets. Likewise, the ORB's connection establishment protocol is often tightly coupled with the communication protocol.

Figure 43 illustrates the connection management structure of SunSoft IIOP. The client-side of SunSoft IIOP implements a hard-coded connection caching strategy that uses a linked-list of client_endpoint objects. As shown in Fig. 43, this list is traversed to find an unused endpoint whenever (**1**) client_endpoint::lookup is called. If no unused client_endpoint to the server is in the cache, a new connection (**2**) is initiated; otherwise an existing connection is reused. Likewise, the server-side uses a linked list of server_endpoint objects to generate the read/write bitmasks required by the (**3**) select event demultiplexing mechanism. This list maintains passive transport endpoints that (**4**) accept connections and (**5**) receive requests from clients connected to the server.

The problem with this design is that it tightly couples (1) the ORB's connection management implementation with the socket network programming API and (2) the TCP/IP connection establishment protocol with the GIOP communication protocol, yielding the following drawbacks:

(1) *Too inflexible*: If an ORB's connection management data structures and algorithms are too closely intertwined, substantial effort is required to modify the ORB Core. For instance, tightly coupling the ORB to use the socket API makes it hard to change the underlying transport mechanism, e.g. to use shared memory rather than sockets. Thus, it can be hard to port such a tightly coupled ORB Core to

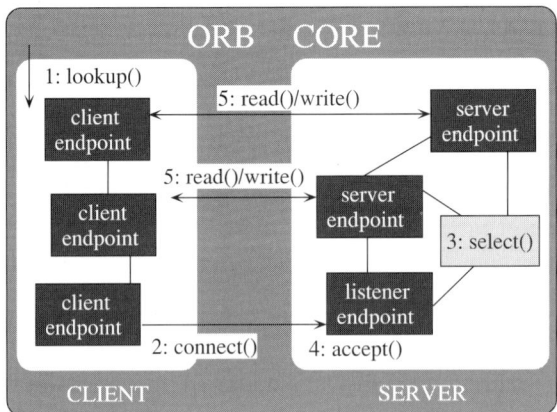

FIG. 43. Connection management in SunSoft IIOP.

new networks, such as ATM or Fibrechannel, or different network programming APIs, such as TLI or Win32 Named Pipes.

(2) *Too inefficient*: Many internal ORB strategies can be optimized by allowing both ORB developers and application developers to select appropriate implementations late in the software development cycle, e.g. after systematic performance profiling. For example, to reduce lock contention and overhead, a multi-threaded, real-time ORB client may need to store transport endpoints in thread-specific storage [66].

Similarly, the concurrency strategy for a CORBA server might require that each connection run in its own thread to eliminate per-request locking overhead. However, it is hard to accommodate efficient new strategies if connection management mechanisms are hard-coded and tightly bound with other internal ORB strategies.

How then can an ORB Core's connection management components support multiple transports and allow connection-related behaviors to be (re)configured flexibly late in the development cycle?

6.3.3.3 Solution: The Acceptor-Connector Pattern
An effective way to increase the flexibility of ORB Core connection management and initialization is to apply the Acceptor-Connector pattern [60]. This pattern decouples connection initialization from the processing performed once a connection endpoint is initialized. The Acceptor component in the pattern is responsible for *passive* initialization, i.e. the server-side of the ORB Core. Conversely, the Connector component in the pattern is responsible for *active* initialization, i.e. the client-side of the ORB Core. In general, the Acceptor-Connector pattern should be applied when client/server middleware must allow flexible configuration of network programming APIs and must maintain proper separation of initialization roles.

6.3.3.4 Using the Acceptor-Connector Pattern in TAO
TAO uses the Acceptor-Connector pattern in conjunction with the Reactor pattern to handle connection establishment for GIOP/IIOP communication. Within TAO's client-side ORB Core, a Connector initiates connections to servers in response to an operation invocation or explicit binding to a remote object. Within TAO's server-side ORB Core, an Acceptor creates a GIOP Connection_Handler to service each new client connection. Acceptors and Connection_Handlers both derive from an Event_Handler, which enable them to be dispatched automatically by a Reactor.

TAO's Acceptors and Connectors can be configured with any transport mechanisms, such as sockets or TLI, provided by the ACE wrapper facades. In addition, TAO's `Acceptor` and `Connector` can be imbued with custom strategies to select an appropriate concurrency mechanism, as described in section 6.3.4.

Figure 44 illustrates the use of Acceptor-Connector strategies in TAO's ORB Core. When a client (**1**) invokes a remote operation, it makes a `connect` call through the `Strategy_Connector`. The `Strategy_Connector` (**2**) consults its *connection strategy* to obtain a connection. In this example the client uses a "caching connection strategy" that recycles connections to the server and only creates new connections when all existing connections are busy. This caching strategy minimizes connection setup time, thereby reducing end-to-end request latency.

In the server-side ORB Core, the `Reactor` notifies TAO's `Strategy_Acceptor` to (**3**) accept newly connected clients and create `Connection_Handlers`. The `Strategy_Acceptor` delegates the choice of concurrency mechanism to one of TAO's *concurrency* strategies, e.g. reactive, thread-per-connection, thread-per-priority, etc., described in section 6.3.4. Once a `Connection_Handler` is activated (**4**) within the ORB Core, it performs the requisite GIOP protocol processing (**5**) on a connection and ultimately dispatches (**6**) the request to the appropriate servant via TAO's object adapter.

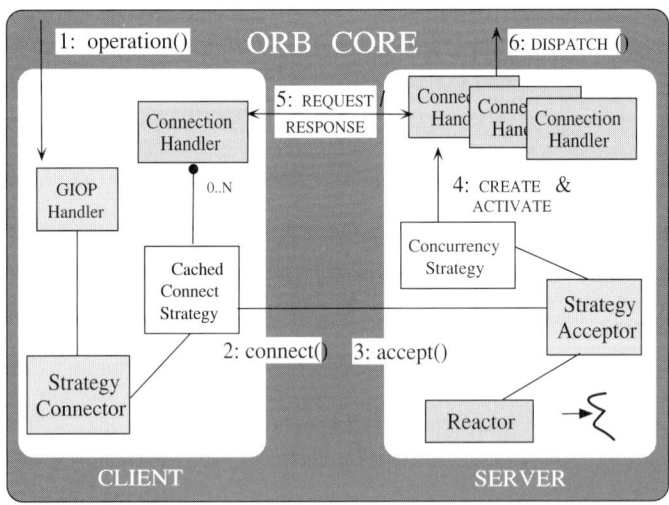

FIG. 44. Using the Acceptor-Connector pattern in TAO's connection management.

6.3.4 Simplifying ORB Concurrency using the Active Object Pattern

6.3.4.1 Context Once the object adapter has dispatched a client request to the appropriate servant, the servant executes the request. Execution may occur in the same thread of control as the `Connection_Handler` that received it. Conversely, execution may occur in a different thread, concurrent with other request executions.

The CORBA specification does not directly address the issue of concurrency within an ORB or a servant. Instead, it defines an interface on the POA for an application to specify that all requests be handled by a single thread or be handled using the ORB's internal multi-threading policy. In particular, the POA specification does not allow applications to specify concurrency models, such as thread-per-request or thread pools, which makes it inflexible for certain types of applications [70].

To meet application QoS requirements, it is important to develop ORBs that manage concurrent processing efficiently [61]. Concurrency allows long-running operations to execute simultaneously without impeding the progress of other operations. Likewise, preemptive multi-threading is crucial to minimize the dispatch latency of real-time systems [27].

Concurrency is often implemented via the multi-threading capabilities available on OS platforms. For instance, SunSoft IIOP supports the two concurrency architectures shown in Fig. 45: a single-threaded reactive architecture and a thread-per-connection architecture.

SunSoft IIOP's reactive concurrency architecture uses `select` within a single thread to dispatch each arriving request to an individual `server_endpoint` object, which subsequently reads the request from the appropriate OS kernel queue. In (**1**), a request arrives and is queued by the OS. Then, `select` fires, (**2**) notifying the associated `server_endpoint` of a waiting request. The `server_endpoint` finally (**3**) reads the request from the queue and processes it.

In contrast, SunSoft IIOP's thread-per-connection architecture executes each `server_endpoint` in its own thread of control, servicing all requests arriving on that connection within its thread. After a connection is established, `select` waits for events on the connection's descriptor. When (**1**) requests are received by the OS, the thread performing `select` (**2**) reads one from the queue and (**3**) hands it off to a `server_endpoint` for processing.

6.3.4.2 Problem: In many ORBs, the concurrency architecture is programmed directly using the OS platform's multi-threading API, such as the POSIX threads API [33]. However, there are several drawbacks to

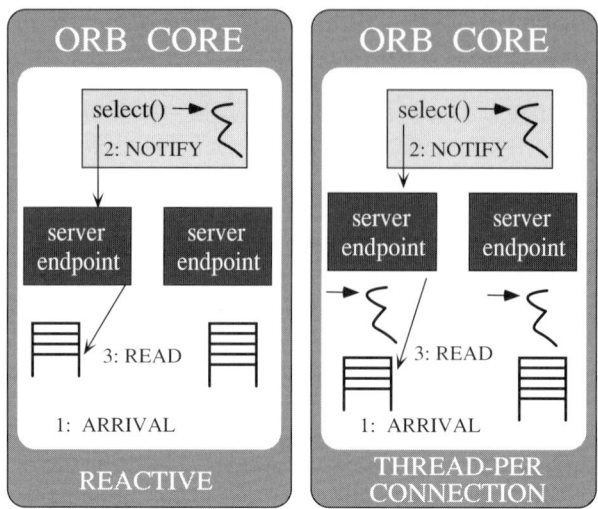

FIG. 45. SunSoft IIOP concurrency architectures.

this approach:

- *Non-portable*: Threading APIs are highly platform-specific. Even industry standards, such as POSIX threads, are not available on many widely used OS platforms, including Win32, VxWorks, and pSoS. Not only is there no direct syntactic mapping between APIs, but there is no clear mapping of semantic functionality either. For instance, POSIX threads supports deferred thread cancellation, whereas Win32 threads do not. Moreover, although Win32 has a thread termination API, the Win32 documentation strongly recommends *not* using it since it does not release all thread resources on exit. Moreover, even POSIX pthread implementations are non-portable since many UNIX vendors support different drafts of the pthreads specification.
- *Hard to program correctly*: Programming a multi-threaded ORB is hard since application and ORB developers must ensure that access to shared data is serialized properly in the ORB and servants. In addition, the techniques required to robustly terminate servants executing concurrently in multiple threads are complicated, non-portable, and non-intuitive.
- *Non-extensible*: The choice of an ORB concurrency strategy depends largely on external factors like application requirements and network/endsystem characteristics. For instance, reactive single-threading [57] is an appropriate strategy for short duration, compute-bound requests on a uni-processor. If these external factors change, however, an ORB's

design should be extensible enough to handle alternative concurrency strategies, such as thread pool or thread-per-priority.

When ORBs are developed using low-level threading APIs, however, they are hard to extend with new concurrency strategies *without* affecting other ORB components. For example, adding a thread-per-request architecture to SunSoft IIOP would require extensive changes in order to (1) store the request in a thread-specific storage (TSS) variable during protocol processing, (2) pass the key to the TSS variable through the scheduling and demarshaling steps in the object adapter, and (3) access the request stored in TSS before dispatching the operation on the servant. Therefore, there is no easy way to modify SunSoft IIOP's concurrency architecture without drastically changing its internal structure.

How then can an ORB support a simple, extensible, and portable concurrency mechanism?

6.3.4.3 Solution: The Active Object Pattern An effective way to increase the portability, correctness, and extensibility of ORB concurrency strategies is to apply the Active Object pattern [38]. This pattern provides a higher-level concurrency architecture that decouples (1) the thread that initially receives and processes a client request from (2) the thread that ultimately executes this request and/or subsequent requests.

While *Wrapper Facades* provide the basis for portability, they are simply a thin syntactic veneer over the low-level system APIs. Moreover, a facade's semantic behavior may still vary across platforms. Therefore, the Active Object pattern defines a higher-level concurrency abstraction that shields TAO from the complexity of low-level thread facades. By raising the level of abstraction for ORB developers, the Active Object pattern makes it easier to define more portable, flexible, and easy to program ORB concurrency strategies.

In general, the Active Object pattern should be used when an application can be simplified by centralizing the point where concurrency decisions are made. This pattern gives developers the flexibility to insert decision points between each request's initial reception and its ultimate execution. For instance, developers could decide whether or not to spawn a thread-per-connection or a thread-per-request.

6.3.4.4 Using the Active Object Pattern in TAO TAO uses the Active Object pattern to transparently allow a GIOP `Connection_Handler` to execute requests either *reactively* by borrowing the Reactor's thread of control or *actively* by running in its own thread of control. The sequence of steps is shown in Fig. 46.

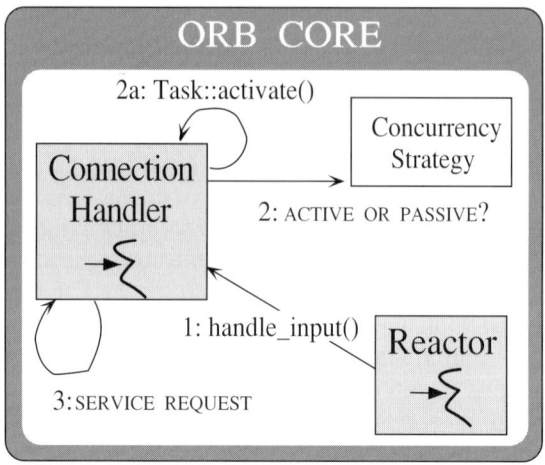

FIG. 46. Using the Active Object pattern to structure TAO's concurrency strategies.

The processing shown in Fig. 46 is triggered when (**1**) a Reactor notifies the Connection_Handler that an I/O event is pending. Based on the currently configured strategy, e.g. reactive single-threading, thread-per-connection, or thread pool, the handler (**2**) determines if it should be active or passive and acts accordingly. This flexibility is achieved by inheriting TAO's ORB Core connection handling classes from an ACE class called Task. To process a request concurrently, therefore, the handler simply (**2a**) invokes the Task::activate method. This method spawns a new thread and invokes a standard hook method. Whether active or passive, the handler ultimately (**3**) processes the request.

6.3.5 Reducing Lock Contention and Priority Inversions with the Thread-specific Storage Pattern

6.3.5.1 Context The Active Object pattern allows applications and components in the ORB to operate using a variety of concurrency strategies, rather than one enforced by the ORB itself. The primary drawback to concurrency, however, is the need to *serialize* access to shared resources. In an ORB, common shared resources include the dynamic memory heap, an object reference created by the CORBA::ORB_init ORB initialization factory, the Active Object Map in a POA [51], and the Acceptor, Connector, and Reactor components described earlier.

A common way to achieve serialization is to use mutual-exclusion locks on each resource shared by multiple threads. However, acquiring and releasing these locks can be expensive. Often, locking overhead negates the performance benefits of concurrency.

6.3.5.2 Problem In theory, multi-threading an ORB can improve performance by executing multiple instruction streams simultaneously. In addition, multi-threading can simplify internal ORB design by allowing each thread to execute synchronously rather than reactively or asynchronously. In practice, multi-threaded ORBs often perform no better, or even worse, than single-threaded ORBs due to (1) the cost of acquiring/releasing locks and (2) priority inversions that arise when high- and low-priority threads contend for the same locks [68]. In addition, multi-threaded ORBs are hard to program due to complex concurrency control protocols required to avoid race conditions and deadlocks.

6.3.5.3 Solution: The Thread-Specific Storage Pattern An effective way to minimize the amount of locking required to serialize access to resources shared within an ORB is to use the Thread-Specific Storage pattern [66]. This pattern allows multiple threads in an ORB to use one logically global access point to retrieve thread-specific data *without* incurring locking overhead for each access.

6.3.5.4 Using the Thread-Specific Storage Pattern in TAO TAO uses the Thread-Specific Storage pattern to minimize lock contention and priority inversion for real-time applications. Internally, each thread in the TAO uses thread-specific storage to store its ORB Core and object adapter components, e.g. Reactor, Acceptor, Connector, and POA. When a thread accesses any of these components, they are retrieved by using a key as an index into the thread's internal thread-specific state, as shown in Fig. 47. Thus, no additional locking is required to access ORB state.

6.3.6 Support Interchangeable ORB Behaviors with the Strategy Pattern

6.3.6.1 Context The alternative concurrency architectures described in section 6.3.4 are just one of the many strategies that an extensible ORB may need to support. In general, extensible ORBs must support multiple request demultiplexing and scheduling strategies in their object adapters. Likewise, they must support multiple connection establishment, request transfer, and concurrent request processing strategies in their ORB Cores.

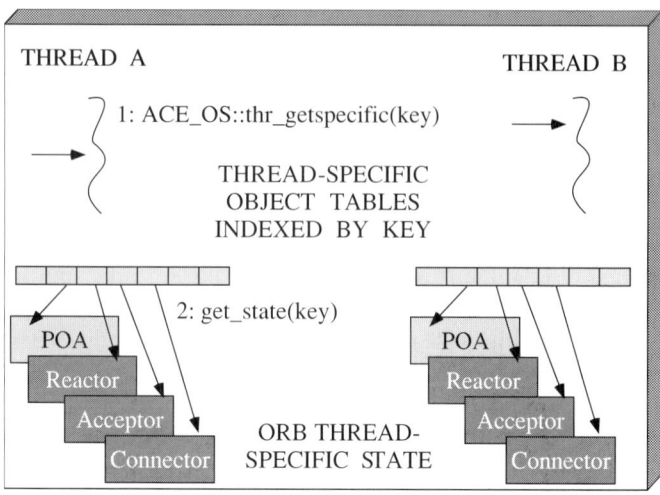

Fig. 47. Using the thread-specific storage pattern TAO.

6.3.6.2 Problem

One-way to develop an ORB is to provide only static, non-extensible strategies, which are typically configured in the following ways:

- *Preprocessor macros*: Some strategies are determined by the value of preprocessor macros. For example, since threading is not available on all OS platforms, conditional compilation is often used to select a feasible concurrency architecture.
- *Command-line options*: Other strategies are controlled by the presence or absence of flags on the command-line. For instance, command-line options can be used to enable various ORB concurrency strategies for platforms that support multi-threading [61].

While these two configuration approaches are widely used, they are inflexible. For instance, preprocessor macros only support compile-time strategy selection, whereas command-line options convey a limited amount of information to an ORB. Moreover, these hard-coded configuration strategies are completely divorced from any code they might affect. Thus, ORB components that want to use these options must (1) know of their existence, (2) understand their range of values, and (3) provide an appropriate implementation for each value. Such restrictions make it hard to develop highly extensible ORBs composed from transparently configurable strategies.

How then does an ORB (1) permit replacement of subsets of component strategies in a manner orthogonal and transparent to other ORB components and (2) encapsulate the state and behavior of each strategy so that changes to one component do not permeate throughout an ORB haphazardly?

6.3.6.3 Solution: The Strategy Pattern An effective way to support multiple transparently "pluggable" ORB strategies is to apply the *Strategy pattern* [14]. This pattern factors out similarity among algorithmic alternatives and explicitly associates the name of a strategy with its algorithm and state. Moreover, the Strategy pattern removes lexical dependencies on strategy implementations since applications access specialized behaviors only through common base class interfaces. In general, the Strategy pattern should be used when an application's behavior can be configured via multiple strategies that can be interchanged seamlessly.

6.3.6.4 Using the Strategy Pattern in TAO TAO uses a variety of strategies to factor out behaviors that are typically hard-coded in conventional ORBs. Several of these strategies are illustrated in Fig. 48. For instance, TAO supports multiple request demultiplexing strategies (e.g. perfect hashing vs active demultiplexing [22]) and scheduling strategies (i.e. FIFO vs rate monotonic vs maximal urgency first [39]) in its object adapter,

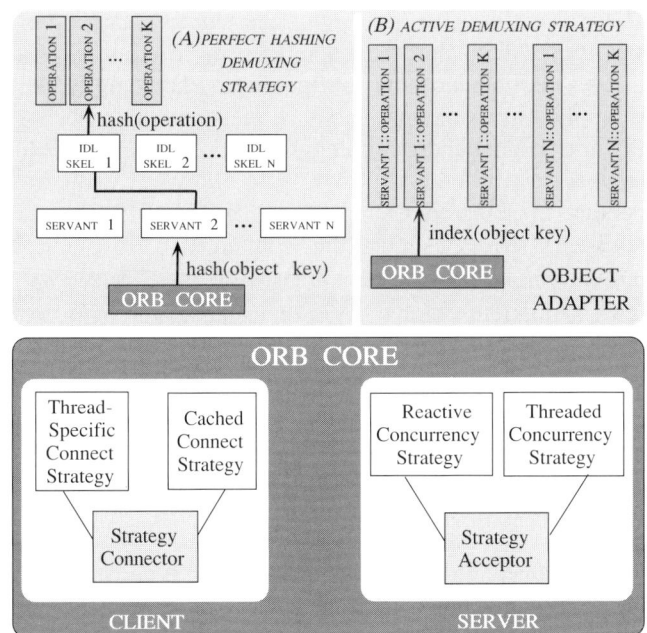

FIG. 48. Strategies in TAO.

as well as connection management strategies (e.g. process-wide cached connections vs thread-specific cached connections) and handler concurrency strategies (e.g. Reactive vs variations of Active Objects) in its ORB Core.

6.3.7 Consolidate ORB Strategies Using the Abstract Factory Pattern

6.3.7.1 Context There are many potential strategy variants supported by TAO. Table I shows a simple example of the strategies used to create two configurations of TAO. Configuration 1 is an avionics application with deterministic real-time requirements [27]. Configuration 2 is an electronic medical imaging application [50] with high throughput requirements. In general, the forces that must be resolved to compose all ORB strategies correctly are the need to (1) ensure the configuration of semantically compatible strategies and (2) simplify the management of a large number of individual strategies.

6.3.7.2 Problem: An undesirable side-effect of using the Strategy pattern extensively in complex software like ORBs is that extensibility becomes hard to manage for the following reasons:

- *Complicated maintenance and configuration*: ORB source code can become littered with hard-coded references to strategy types, which complicates maintenance and configuration. For example, within a particular application domain, such as real-time avionics or medical imaging, many independent strategies must act in harmony. Identifying these strategies individually by name, however, requires tedious replacement of selected strategies in one domain with a potentially different set of strategies in another domain.
- *Semantic incompatibilities*: It is not always possible for certain ORB strategies to interact compatibly. For instance, the FIFO strategy for

TABLE I

EXAMPLE APPLICATIONS AND THEIR ORB STRATEGY CONFIGURATIONS

Application	Strategy Configuration			
	Concurrency	Scheduling	Demultiplexing	Protocol
1. Avionics	Thread-per-priority	Rate-based	Perfect hashing	VME backplane
2. Medical Imaging	Thread-per-connection	FIFO	Active demultiplexing	TCP/IP

scheduling requests shown in Table I may not work with the thread-per-priority concurrency architecture. The problem stems from semantic incompatibilities between scheduling requests in their order of arrival, i.e. FIFO queueing vs dispatching requests based on their relative priorities, i.e. preemptive priority-based thread dispatching. Moreover, some strategies are only useful when certain preconditions are met. For instance, the perfect hashing demultiplexing strategy is generally feasible only for systems that statically configure all servants off-line [20].

How can a highly-configurable ORB reduce the complexities required in managing its myriad of strategies, as well as enforce semantic consistency when combining discrete strategies?

6.3.7.3 Solution: The Abstract Factory Pattern An effective way to consolidate multiple ORB strategies into semantically compatible configurations is to apply the Abstract Factory pattern [14]. This pattern provides a single access point that integrates all strategies used to configure an ORB. Concrete subclasses then aggregate semantically compatible application-specific or domain-specific strategies, which can be replaced *en masse* in semantically meaningful ways. In general, the Abstract Factory pattern should be used when an application must consolidate the configuration of many strategies, each having multiple alternatives that must vary together.

6.3.7.4 Using the Abstract Factory Pattern in TAO All of TAO's ORB strategies are consolidated into two abstract factories that are implemented as Singletons [14]. One factory encapsulates client-specific strategies, the other factory encapsulates server-specific strategies, as shown in Fig. 49. These abstract factories encapsulate request demultiplexing, scheduling, and dispatch strategies in the server, as well as concurrency strategies in both client and server. By using the Abstract Factory pattern, TAO can configure different ORB personalities conveniently and consistently.

6.3.8 Dynamically Configure ORBs with the Service Configurator Pattern

6.3.8.1 Context The cost of many computing resources, such as memory and CPUs, continue to drop. However, ORBs must still avoid excessive consumption of finite system resources. This parsimony is particularly essential for embedded real-time systems that require small memory footprints and predictable CPU processing overhead [23]. Likewise, many

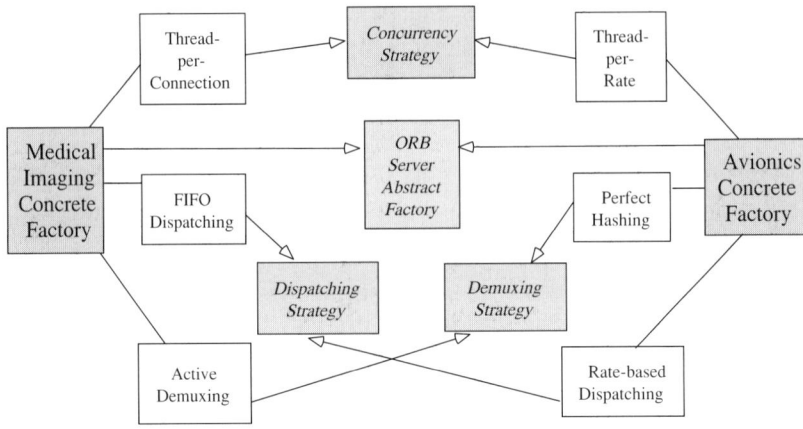

FIG. 49. Factories used in TAO.

applications can benefit from the ability to extend ORBs *dynamically*, i.e. by allowing their strategies to be configured at run-time.

6.3.8.2 Problem Although the Strategy and Abstract Factory patterns simplify the customization of ORBs for specific application requirements and system characteristics, these patterns can cause the following problems for extensible ORBs:

- *High resource utilization.* Widespread use of the Strategy pattern can substantially increase the number of strategies configured into an ORB, which can increase the system resources required to run an ORB.
- *Unavoidable system downtime.* If strategies are configured statically at compile-time or static link-time using abstract factories, it is hard to enhance existing strategies or add new strategies without (1) changing the existing source code for the consumer of the strategy or the abstract factory, (2) recompiling and relinking an ORB, and (3) restarting running ORBs and their application servants.

Although it does not use the Strategy pattern explicitly, SunSoft IIOP does permit applications to vary certain ORB strategies at run-time. However, the different strategies must be configured statically into SunSoft IIOP at compile-time. Moreover, as the number of alternatives increases, so does the amount of code required to implement them. For instance, Fig. 50 illustrates SunSoft IIOP's approach to varying the concurrency strategy.

Each area of code that might be affected by the choice of concurrency strategy is trusted to act independently of other areas. This proliferation of decision points adversely increases the complexity of the code, complicating

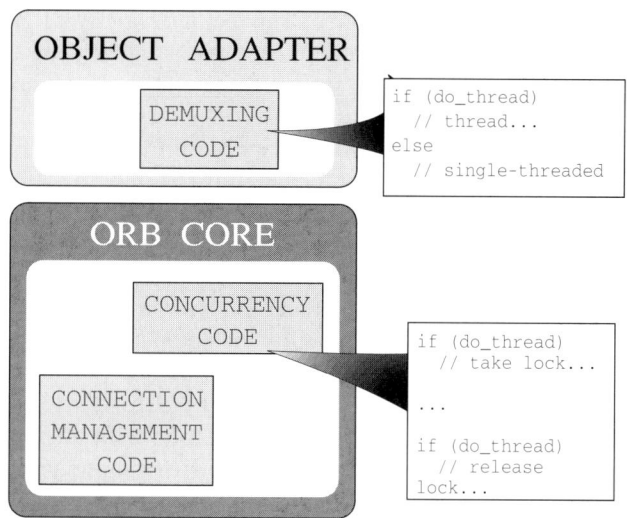

FIG. 50. SunSoft IIOP hard-coded strategy usage.

future enhancement and maintenance. Moreover, the selection of the data type specifying the strategy complicates integration of new concurrency architectures because the type (bool) would have to change, as well as the programmatic structure, if (do_thread) then...else..., that decodes the strategy specifier into actions.

In general, static configuration is only feasible for a small, fixed number of strategies. However, using this technique to configure complex middleware like ORBs complicates maintenance, increases system resource utilization, and leads to unavoidable system downtime to add or change existing components.

How then does an ORB implementation reduce the "overly-large, overly-static" side-effect of pervasive use of the Strategy and Abstract Factory patterns?

6.3.8.3 Solution: The Service Configurator Pattern

An effective way to enhance the dynamism of an ORB is to apply the Service Configurator pattern [34]. This pattern uses explicit dynamic linking [69] mechanisms to obtain, utilize, and/or remove the run-time address bindings of custom Strategy and Abstract Factory objects into an ORB at installation-time and/or run-time. Widely available explicit dynamic linking mechanisms include the dlopen/dlsym/dlclose functions in SVR4 UNIX [15] and the LoadLibrary/GetProcAddress functions in the WIN32 subsystem of Windows NT [7]. The ACE wrapper facades portably encapsulate these OS APIs.

By using the Service Configurator pattern, the *behavior* of ORB strategies are decoupled from *when* implementations of these strategies are configured into an ORB. For instance, ORB strategies can be linked into an ORB from DLLs at compile-time, installation-time, or even during run-time. Moreover, this pattern can reduce the memory footprint of an ORB by allowing application developers and/or system administrators to dynamically link only those strategies that are necessary for a specific ORB personality.

In general, the Service Configurator pattern should be used when (1) an application wants to configure its constituent components dynamically and (2) conventional techniques, such as command-line options, are insufficient due to the number of possibilities or the inability to anticipate the range of values.

6.3.8.4 Using the Service Configurator Pattern in TAO

TAO uses the Service Configurator pattern in conjunction with the Strategy and Abstract Factory patterns to dynamically install the strategies it requires without (1) recompiling or statically relinking existing code or (2) terminating and restarting an existing ORB and its application servants. This design allows the behavior of TAO to be tailored for specific platforms and application requirements without requiring access to, or modification of, ORB source code.

In addition, the Service Configurator pattern allows applications to customize the personality of TAO at run-time. For instance, during TAO's ORB initialization phase, it uses the dynamic linking mechanisms provided by the OS, and encapsulated by the ACE wrapper facades, to link in the appropriate concrete factory for a particular use-case. Figure 51 shows two factories tuned for different application domains supported by TAO: avionics and medical imaging.

In the particular configuration shown in Fig. 51, the avionics concrete factory has been installed in the process. Applications using this ORB

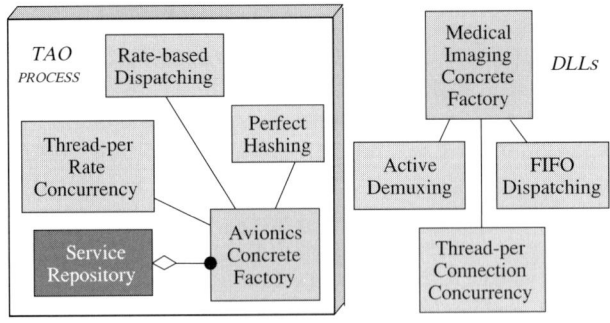

FIG. 51. Using the Service Configurator pattern in TAO.

personality will be configured with a particular set of ORB concurrency, demultiplexing, and dispatching strategies. The medical imaging concrete factory resides in a DLL outside of the existing ORB process. To configure a different ORB personality, this factory could be installed dynamically during the ORB server's initialization phase.

6.4 Summary of Design Challenges and Patterns that Resolve Them

Table II summarizes the mapping between ORB design challenges and the patterns we applied to resolve these challenges in TAO. This table focuses on the forces resolved by individual patterns. However, TAO also benefits from the collaborations among *multiple* patterns (shown in Fig. 38). For example, the Acceptor and Connector patterns utilize the Reactor pattern to notify them when connection events occur at the OS level.

Moreover, patterns often must collaborate to alleviate drawbacks that arise from applying them in isolation. For instance, the reason the Abstract Factory pattern is used in TAO is to avoid the complexity caused by its extensive use of the Strategy pattern. Although the Strategy pattern simplifies the effort required to customize an ORB for specific application requirements and network/endsystem characteristics, it is tedious and error-prone to manage a large number of strategy interactions manually.

6.5 Evaluating the Contribution of Patterns to ORB Middleware

Section 6.3 described the key patterns used in TAO and qualitatively evaluated how these patterns helped to alleviate limitations with the design of SunSoft IIOP. The discussion below goes one step further and quantitatively evaluates the benefits of applying patterns to ORB middleware.

TABLE II

SUMMARY OF FORCES AND THEIR RESOLVING PATTERNS

Forces	Resolving pattern(s)
Abstracting low-level system calls	Wrapper facade
ORB event demultiplexing	Reactor
ORB connection management	Acceptor-Connector
Efficient concurrency models	Active Object
Pluggable strategies	Strategy
Group similar initializations	Abstract Factory
Dynamic run-time configuration	Service Configurator

6.5.1 Where's the Proof?

Implementing TAO using patterns yielded significant quantifiable improvements in software reusability and maintainability. The results are summarized in Table III. This table compares the following metrics for TAO and SunSoft IIOP:

(1) The number of methods required to implement key ORB tasks (such as connection management, request transfer, socket and request demultiplexing, marshaling, and dispatching).
(2) The total non-comment lines of code (LOC) for these methods.
(3) The average McCabe Cyclometric Complexity metric $v(G)$ [41] of the methods. The $v(G)$ metric uses graph theory to correlate code complexity with the number of possible basic paths that can be taken through a code module. In C++, a module is defined as a method.

The use of patterns in TAO significantly reduced the amount of ad hoc code and the complexity of certain operations. For instance, the total lines of code in the client-side *Connection Management* operations were reduced by a factor of 5. Moreover, the complexity for this component was substantially reduced by a factor of 16. These reductions in LOC and complexity stem

TABLE III
CODE STATISTICS FOR TAO VS SUNSOFT IIOP.

ORB task	TAO			SunSoft IIOP		
	# methods	Total LOC	Avg. $v(G)$	# Methods	Total LOC	Avg. $v(G)$
Connection Management (Server)	2	43	7	3	190	14
Connection Management (client)	3	11	1	1	64	16
GIOP Message Send (client/Server)	1	46	12	1	43	12
GIOP Message Read (client/Server)	1	67	19	1	56	18
GIOP Invocation (client)	2	205	26	2	188	27
GIOP Message Processing (client/Server)	3	41	2	1	151	24
Object Adapter Message Dispatch (Server)	2	79	6	1	61	10

from the following factors:

- These ORB tasks were the focus of our initial work when developing TAO.
- Many of the details of connection management and socket demultiplexing were subsumed by patterns and components in the ACE framework, in particular, the Acceptor, Connector, and Reactor.

Other areas did not yield as much improvement. In particular, *GIOP Invocation* tasks actually increased in size and maintained a consistent $v(G)$. There were two reasons for this increase:

(1) The primary pattern applied in these cases was the Wrapper Facade, which replaced the low-level system calls with ACE wrappers but did not factor out common strategies; and
(2) SunSoft IIOP did not trap all the error conditions, which TAO addressed much more completely. Therefore, the additional code in TAO is necessary to provide a more robust ORB.

The most compelling evidence that the systematic application of patterns can positively contribute to the maintainability of complex software is shown in Fig. 52. This figure illustrates the distribution of $v(G)$ over the percentage of affected methods in TAO. As shown in the figure, most of TAO's code is structured in a straightforward manner, with almost 70% of the methods' $v(G)$ falling into the range of 1–5.

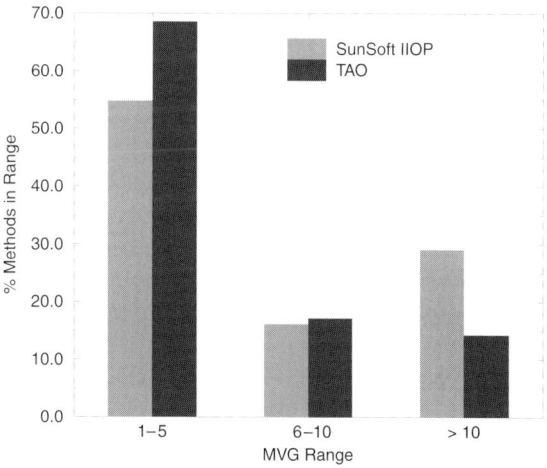

FIG. 52. Distribution of $v(G)$ over ORB methods.

In contrast, while SunSoft IIOP has a substantial percentage (55%) of its methods in that range, many of the remaining methods (29%) have $v(G)$ greater than 10. The reason for the difference is that SunSoft IIOP uses a monolithic coding style with long methods. For example, the average length of methods with $v(G)$ over 10 is over 80 LOC. This yields overly-complex code that is hard to debug and understand.

In TAO, most of the monolithic SunSoft IIOP methods were decomposed into smaller methods when integrating the patterns. The majority (86%) of TAO's methods have $v(G)$ under 10. Of that number, nearly 70% have a $v(G)$ between 1 and 5. The relatively few (14%) methods in TAO with $v(G)$ greater than 10 are largely unchanged from the original SunSoft IIOP TypeCode interpreter.

The use of monolithic methods not only increases the effort of maintaining TAO, it also degrades its performance due to reduced processor cache hits [21]. Therefore, we plan to experiment with the application of other patterns, such as *Command* and *Template Method* [14], to simplify and optimize these monolithic methods into smaller, more cohesive methods. There are a few methods with $v(G)$ greater than 10 which are not part of the TypeCode interpreter, and they will likely remain that way. Sometimes solving complex problems involves writing complex code; at such times, localizing complexity is a reasonable recourse.

6.5.2 What Are the Benefits?

In general, the use of patterns in TAO provided the following benefits:

- *Increased extensibility*. Patterns like Abstract Factory, Strategy, and Service Configurator simplify the configure of TAO for a particular application domain by allowing extensibility to be "designed into" the ORB. In contrast, middleware that lacks these patterns is significantly harder to extend. This article illustrated how patterns were applied to make the TAO ORB more extensible.

- *Enhanced design clarity*. By applying patterns to TAO, not only did we develop a more flexible ORB, we also devised a richer vocabulary for expressing ORB middleware designs. In particular, patterns capture and articulate the design rationale for complex object-structures in an ORB. Moreover, patterns help to demystify and motivate the structure of an ORB by describing its architecture in terms of design forces that recur in many types of software systems. The expressive power of patterns enabled us to concisely convey the design of complex software systems like TAO. As we continue to learn about ORBs and the patterns of which they are composed, we expect our pattern vocabulary to grow and evolve.

Thus, the patterns presented in this article help to improve the maintainability of ORB middleware by reducing software complexity, as shown in Fig. 52.

- *Increased portability and reuse.* TAO is built atop the ACE framework, which provides implementations of many key communication software patterns [59]. Using ACE simplified the porting of TAO to numerous OS platforms since most of the porting effort was absorbed by the ACE framework maintainers. In addition, since the ACE framework is rich with configurable high-performance, real-time network-oriented components, we were able to achieve considerable code reuse by leveraging the framework. This is indicated by the consistent decrease in lines of code (LOC) in Table III.

6.5.3 What Are the Liabilities?

The use of patterns can also incur some liabilities. We summarize these liabilities below and discuss how we minimize them in TAO.

- *Abstraction penalty.* Many patterns use indirection to increase component decoupling. For instance, the Reactor pattern uses virtual methods to separate the application-specific Event Handler logic from the general-purpose event demultiplexing and dispatching logic. The extra indirection introduced by using these pattern implementations can potentially decrease performance. To alleviate these liabilities, we carefully applied C++ programming language features (such as inline functions and templates) and other optimizations (such as eliminating demarshaling overhead [21] and demultiplexing overhead [22]) to minimize performance overhead. As a result, TAO is substantially faster than the original hard-coded SunSoft IIOP [21].

- *Additional external dependencies.* Whereas SunSoft IIOP only depends on system-level interfaces and libraries, TAO depends on the ACE framework. Since ACE encapsulates a wide range of low-level OS mechanisms, the effort required to port it to a new platform could potentially be higher than porting SunSoft IIOP, which only uses a subset of the OS's APIs. However, since ACE has been ported to many platforms already, the effort to port to new platforms is relatively low. Most sources of platform variation have been isolated to a few modules in ACE.

7. Concluding Remarks

Advances in distributed object computing technology are occurring at a time when deregulation and global competition are motivating the need for increased software productivity and quality. Distributed object computing is a promising paradigm to control costs through open systems and client/server computing. Likewise, OO design and programming are widely touted as an effective means to reduce software cost and improve software quality through reuse, extensibility, and modularity.

Meeting the QoS requirements of high-performance and real-time applications requires more than OO design and programming techniques, however. It requires an integrated architecture that delivers end-to-end QoS guarantees at multiple levels of a distributed system. The TAO ORB endsystem described in this paper addresses this need with policies and mechanisms that span network adapters, operating systems, communication protocols, and ORB middleware.

We believe the future of real-time ORBs is very promising. Real-time system development strategies will migrate towards those used for "mainstream" systems to achieve lower development cost and faster time to market. We have observed real-time embedded software development projects that have lagged in terms of design and development methodologies (and languages) by *decades*. These projects are extremely costly to evolve and maintain. Moreover, they are so specialized that they cannot be adapted to meet new market opportunities.

The flexibility and adaptability offered by CORBA make it very attractive for use in real-time systems. If the real-time challenges can be overcome, and the progress reported in this paper indicates that they can, then the use of real-time CORBA is compelling. Moreover, the solutions to these challenges will be sufficiently complex, yet general, that it will be well worth re-applying them to other projects in domains with stringent QoS requirements.

The C++ source code for TAO and ACE is freely available at www.cs.wustl.edu/~schmidt/TAO.html. This release also contains the real-time ORB benchmarking test suite described in section 5.3.

ACKNOWLEDGMENTS

We gratefully acknowledge Expersoft, IONA, and Sun for providing us with their ORB software for the benchmarking testbed. We would also like to thank Frank Buschmann for his extensive comments on this paper. Finally, we are deeply appreciative of the efforts Chris Gill, Andy Gokhale, Irfan Pyarali, Carlos O'Ryan, and Nanbor Wang put into developing and optimizing TAO's real-time ORB Core and Scheduling Service.

REFERENCES

[1] Box, D. (1997). *Essential COM*. Addison-Wesley, Reading, MA.
[2] Braden, R. *et al.* (1997). Resource ReSerVation Protocol (RSVP) version 1 functional specification. Internet Draft, May. ftp://ietf.org/internet-drafts/draft-ietf-rsvp-spec-15.txt.

[3] Buschmann, F., Meunier, R., Rohnert, H., Sommerlad, P., and Stal, M. (1996). *Pattern-Oriented Software Architecture—A System of Patterns*. Wiley and Sons.
[4] Choi, J.-D., Cytron, R., and Ferrante, J. (1991). Automatic construction of sparse data flow evaluation graphs. *Conference Record of the Eighteenth Annual ACE Symposium on Principles of Programming Languages*, ACM, January.
[5] Clark, D. D., and Tennenhouse, D. L. (1990). Architectural considerations for a new generation of protocols. *Proceedings of the Symposium on Communications Architectures and Protocols (SIGCOMM)*, Philadelphia, PA, pp. 200–208, ACM, September.
[6] Cranor, C., and Parulkar, G. (1995). Design of universal continuous media I/O. *Proceedings of the 5th International Workshop on Network and Operating Systems Support for Digital Audio and Video (NOSSDAV '95)*, Durham, New Hampshire, pp. 83–86, April.
[7] Custer, H. (1993). *Inside Windows NT*. Redmond, Washington: Microsoft Press.
[8] Cytron, R., Ferrante, J., Rosen, B. K., Wegman, M. N., and Zadeck, F. K. (1991). Efficiently computing static single assignment form and the control dependence graph. *ACM Transactions on Programming Languages and Systems*, ACM, October.
[9] Dittia, Z. D., Parulkar, G. M., and Cox, J. J. R. (1997). The APIC approach to high performance network interface design: Protected DMA and other techniques. *Proceedings of INFOCOM '97*, Kobe, Japan, IEEE, April.
[10] Druschel, P., Abbott, M. B., Pagels, M., and Peterson, L. L. (1993). Network subsystem design. *IEEE Network (Special Issue on End-System Support for High Speed Networks)*, **7**, July.
[11] Eide, E., Frei, K., Ford, B., Lepreau, J., and Lindstrom, G. (1997). Flick: A flexible, optimizing IDL compiler. *Proceedings of ACM SIGPLAN '97 Conference on Programming Language Design and Implementation (PLDI)*, Las Vegas, NV, ACM, June.
[12] Eykholt, J., Kleiman, S., Barton, S., Faulkner, R., Shivalingiah, A., Smith, M., Stein, D., Voll, J., Weeks, M., and Williams, D. (1992). Beyond multiprocessing... multithreading the SunOS kernel. *Proceedings of the Summer USENIX Conference*, San Antonio, Texas, June.
[13] Fay-Wolfe, V., Black, J. K., Thuraisingham, B., and Krupp, P. (1995). Real-time method invocations in distributed environments. Tech. Rep. 95-244, University of Rhode Island, Department of Computer Science and Statistics.
[14] Gamma, E., Helm, R., Johnson, R., and Vlissides, J. (1995). *Design Patterns: Elements of Reusable Object-Oriented Software*. Reading, MA: Addison-Wesley.
[15] Gingell, R., Lee, M., Dang, X., and Weeks, M. (1987). Shared libraries in SunOS. *Proceedings of the Summer 1987 USENIX Technical Conference*, Phoenix, Arizona.
[16] Gokhale, A., and Schmidt, D. C. (1996). Measuring the performance of communication middleware on high-speed networks. *Proceedings of SIGCOMM '96*, Stanford, CA, pp. 306–317, ACM, August.
[17] Gokhale, A., and Schmidt, D. C. (1996). The performance of the CORBA dynamic invocation interface and dynamic skeleton interface over high-speed ATM networks. *Proceedings of GLOBECOM '96*, London, England, pp. 50–56, IEEE, November.
[18] Gokhale, A., and Schmidt, D. C. (1997). Evaluating latency and scalability of CORBA over high-speed ATM networks. *Proceedings of the International Conference on Distributed Computing Systems*, Baltimore, Maryland, IEEE, May.
[19] Gokhale, A., and Schmidt, D. C. (1997). Design principles and optimizations for high-performance ORBs. 12th OOPSLA Conference, poster session, Atlanta, Georgia, ACM, October.
[20] Gokhale, A., and Schmidt, D. C. (1997). Evaluating the performance of demultiplexing strategies for real-time CORBA. *Proceedings of GLOBECOM '97*, Phoenix, AZ, IEEE, November.

[21] Gokhale, A., and Schmidt, D. C. (1998). Principles for optimizing CORBA internet inter-ORB protocol performance. *Hawaiian International Conference on System Sciences*, January.
[22] Gokhale, A., and Schmidt, D. C. (1998). Measuring and optimizing CORBA latency and scalability over high-speed networks. *Transactions on Computing*, **47**, no. (4).
[23] Gokhale, A., and Schmidt, D. C. (1999). Techniques for optimizing CORBA middleware for distributed embedded systems. *Proceedings of INFOCOM '99*, March.
[24] Gopalakrishnan, R., and Parulkar, G. M. (1996). Efficient user space protocol implementations with QoS guarantees using real-time upcalls. *Technical Report 96-11*, Washington University Department of Computer Science, March.
[25] Gopalakrishnan, R., and Parulkar, G. (1996). Bringing real-time scheduling theory and practice closer for multimedia computing. *SIGMETRICS Conference*, Philadelphia, PA, ACM, May.
[26] Guillemont, M. (1997). CHORUS/ClassiX r3 technical overview. *Technical Report #CS/TR6-96-119.13*, Chorus Systems, May.
[27] Harrison, T. H., Levine, D. L., and Schmidt, D. C. (1997). The design and performance of a real-time CORBA event service. *Proceedings of OOPSLA '97*, Atlanta, GA, ACM, October.
[28] Henning, M. (1998). Binding, migration, and scalability in CORBA. *Communications of the ACM Special Issue on CORBA*, **41**, October.
[29] Hoschka, P. (1996). Automating performance optimization by heuristic analysis of a formal specification. *Proceedings of Joint Conference for Formal Description Techniques (FORTE) and Protocol Specification, Testing and Verification (PSTV)*, Kaiserslautern.
[30] Hu, J., Mungee, S., and Schmidt, D. C. (1998). Principles for developing and measuring high-performance web servers over ATM. *Proceeedings of INFOCOM '98*, March/April.
[31] Hu, J., Pyarali, I., and Schmidt, D. C. (1997). Measuring the impact of event dispatching and concurrency models on web server performance over high-speed networks. *Proceedings of the 2nd Global Internet Conference*, IEEE, November.
[32] Information technology—Portable Operating System Interface (POSIX)—Part 1: System application: Program Interface (API) [C Language], 1995.
[33] IEEE (1996). *Threads Extension for Portable Operating Systems (Draft 10)*, February.
[34] Jain, P., and Schmidt, D. C. (1997). Service configurator: A pattern for dynamic configuration of services. *Proceedings of the 3rd Conference on Object-Oriented Technologies and Systems*, USENIX, June.
[35] Kalogeraki, V., Melliar-Smith, P., and Moser, L. (1997). Soft real-time resource management in CORBA distributed systems. *Proceedings of the Workshop on Middleware for Real-Time Systems and Services*, San Francisco, CA, IEEE, December.
[36] Khanna, S. *et al.* (1992). Realtime scheduling in SunOS 5.0. *Proceedings of the USENIX Winter Conference*, pp. 375–390, USENIX Association.
[37] Klein, M. H., Ralya, T., Pollak, B., Obenza, R., and Harbour, M. G. (1993). *A practitioner's handbook for real-time analysis: Guide to rate monotonic analysis for real-time systems*. Norwell, Massachusetts: Kluwer Academic Publishers.
[38] Lavender, R. G., and Schmidt, D. C. (1996). Active object: An object behavioral pattern for concurrent programming. *Pattern Languages of Program Design* (eds J. O. Coplien, J. Vlissides, and N. Kerth), Reading, MA: Addison-Wesley.
[39] Gill, C. D., Levine, D. L., and Schmidt, D. C. (1999). The design and performance of a Real-Time CORBA scheduling service, *The International Journal of Time-Critical Computing Systems*, (*Special Issue on Real-Time Middleware*, (ed W. Zhao)), Kluwer Academic Publishers, to appear.

[40] Liu, C., and Layland, J. (1973). Scheduling algorithms for multiprogramming in a hard-real-time environment. *Journal of the ACM*, **20**, 46–61, January.
[41] McCabe, T. J. (1976). A complexity measure. *IEEE Transactions on Software Engineering*, **SE-2**, December.
[42] McKusick, M. K., Bostic, K., Karels, M. J., and Quarterman, J. S. (1996). *The Design and Implementation of the 4.4BSD Operating System*. Addison-Wesley.
[43] Mungee, S., Surendran, N., and Schmidt, D. C. (1999). The design and performance of a CORBA audio/video streaming service. *Proceedings of the Hawaiian International Conference on System Sciences*, January.
[44] Object Management Group (1997). *Minimum CORBA—Request for Proposal*, OMG Document orbos/97-06-14 edn, June.
[45] Object Management Group (1999). *Realtime CORBA Joint Revised Submission*, OMG Document orbos/99-02-12 edn, March.
[46] Object Management Group (1998). *The Common Object Request Broker: Architecture and Specification*, 2.2 edn, February.
[47] Object Management Group (1998). *Messaging Service Specification*, OMG Document orbos/98-05-05 edn, May.
[48] Parulkar, G., Schmidt, D. C., and Turner, J. S. (1995). a^It^Pm: A Strategy for integrating IP with ATM. *Proceedings of the Symposium on Communications Architectures and Protocols (SIGCOMM)*, ACM, September.
[49] Inc., P. S. (1996). *Quantify User's Guide*. PureAtria Software Inc.
[50] Pyarali, I., Harrison, T. H., and Schmidt, D. C. (1996). Design and performance of an object-oriented framework for high-performance electronic medical imaging. *USENIX Computing Systems*, **9**, November/December.
[51] Pyarali, I., and Schmidt, D. C. (1998). An overview of the CORBA portable object adapter. *ACM Standard-View*, **6**, March.
[52] Rajkumar, R., Sha, L., and Lehoczky, J. P. (1988). Real-time Synchronization protocols for multiprocessors. *Proceedings of the Real-Time Systems Symposium*, Huntsville, Alabama, December.
[53] Ramamritham, K., Stankovic, J. A., and Zhao, W. (1989). Distributed scheduling of tasks with deadlines and resource requirements. *IEEE Transactions on Computers*, **38**, 1110–1123, August.
[54] Ritchie, D. (1984). A stream input–output system. *AT&T Bell Labs Technical Journal*, **63**, 311–324, October.
[55] Schmidt, D. C. (1990). GPERF: A perfect hash function generator. *Proceedings of the 2nd C++ Conference*, San Francisco, California, pp. 87–102, USENIX, April.
[56] Schmidt, D. C. (1994). ACE: An object-oriented framework for developing distributed applications. *Proceedings of the 6th USENIX C++ Technical Conference*, Cambridge, Massachusetts, USENIX Association, April.
[57] Schmidt, D. C. (1995). Reactor: An object behavioral pattern for concurrent event demultiplexing and event handler dispatching. *Pattern Languages of Program Design* (eds J. O. Coplien and D. C. Schmidt), pp. 529–545, Reading, MA: Addison-Wesley.
[58] Schmidt, D. C. (1995). Experience using design patterns to develop reuseable object-oriented communication software. *Communications of the ACM (Special Issue on Object-Oriented Experiences)*, **38**, October.
[59] Schmidt, D. C. (1996). A family of design patterns for application-level gateways. *The Theory and Practice of Object Systems (Special Issue on Patterns and Pattern Languages)*, **2**, no. (1).
[60] Schmidt, D. C. (1997). Acceptor and connector: Design patterns for initializing commu-

nication services. *Pattern Languages of Program Design* (eds R. Martin, F. Buschmann, and D. Riehle), Reading, MA: Addison-Wesley.

[61] Schmidt, D. C. (1998). Evaluating architectures for multi-threaded CORBA object request brokers. *Communications of the ACM Special Issue on CORBA*, **41**, October.

[62] Kuhns, F., Schmidt, D. C., and Levine, D. L. (1999). The design and performance of a Real-Time I/O subsystem, *Proceedings of the 5th IEEE Real-Time Technology and Applications Symposium*, IEEE, Vancouver, British Columbia, Canada, June.

[63] Schmidt, D. C., and Cleeland, C. (1999). Applying patterns to develop extensible ORB middleware. *IEEE Communications Magazine*, **37**, no. (4), April.

[64] Schmidt, D. C., Gokhale, A., Harrison, T., and Parulkar, G. (1997). A high-performance endsystem architecture for real-time CORBA. *IEEE Communications Magazine*, **14**, February.

[65] Schmidt, D. C., Harrison, T. H., and Al-Shaer, E. (1995). Object-oriented components for high-speed network programming. *Proceedings of the 1st Conference on Object-Oriented Technologies and Systems*, Monterey, CA, USENIX, June.

[66] Schmidt, D. C., Harrison, T., and Pryce, N. (1997). Thread-specific storage—An object behavioral pattern for accessing per-thread state efficiently. *C++ report*, **9** no. (10), November/December.

[67] Schmidt, D. C., Levine, D. L., and Mungee, S. (1998). The design and performance of real-time object request brokers. *Computer Communications*, **21**, 294–324, April.

[68] Schmidt, D. C., Mungee, S., Flores-Gaitan, S., and Gokhale, A. (1999). Software architectures for reducing priority inversion and non-determinism in Real-time object request brokers, *Journal of Real-time systems*, Kluwer Academic Publishers, to appear.

[69] Schmidt, D. C., and Suda, T. (1994). An object-oriented framework for dynamically configuring extensible distributed communication systems. *IEE/BCS Distributed Systems Engineering Journal (Special Issue on Configurable Distributed Systems)*, **2**, 280–293, December.

[70] Schmidt, D. C., and Vinoski, S. (1997). Object adapters: concepts and terminology. *C++ Report*, **9**, November/December.

[71] Schmidt, D. C., and Vinoski, S. (1998). Using the portable object adapter for transient and persistent CORBA objects. *C++ Report*, **10**, April.

[72] Stankovic, J. A. (1988). Misconceptions about real-time computing. *IEEE Computer*, **21**, 10–19, October.

[73] Stewart, D. B., and Khosla, P. K. (1992). Real-time scheduling of sensor-based control systems. *Real-Time Programming* (eds W. Halang and K. Ramamritham), Tarrytown, NY: Pergamon Press.

[74] Tennenhouse, D. L. (1989). Layered multiplexing considered harmful. *Proceedings of the 1st International Workshop on High-Speed Networks*, May.

[75] Vinoski, S. (1997). CORBA: Integrating diverse applications within distributed heterogeneous environments. *IEEE Communications Magazine*, **14**, February.

[76] Wollrath, A., Riggs, R., and Waldo, J. (1996). A distributed object model for the Java system. *USENIX Computing Systems*, **9**, November/December.

[77] Zinky, J. A., Bakken, D. E., and Schantz, R. (1997). Architectural support for quality of service for CORBA objects. *Theory and Practice of Object Systems*, **3**, no. (1).

Heterogeneous Data Access in a Mobile Environment – Issues and Solutions

J. B. LIM AND A. R. HURSON

Department of Computer Science and Engineering
220 Pond Lab.
The Pennsylvania State University
University Park, PA 16802
hurson@cse.psu.edu

Abstract

A mobile computing environment involves accessing information through a wireless network connection. The mobile unit may be stationary, in motion, and/or intermittently connected to a fixed (wired) network. As technology advances are made in software and hardware, the feasibility of accessing information "anytime, anywhere" is becoming a reality. Furthermore, the diversity and amount of information available to a given user is increasing at a rapid rate. Current distributed and multidatabase systems are designed to allow timely and reliable access to large amounts of data from different data sources. Issues such as autonomy, heterogeneity, transaction management, concurrency control, transparency, and query resolution have been addressed by researchers for multidatabase systems. These issues are similar to many of the issues involved in accessing information in a mobile environment. However, in a mobile environment, additional complexities are introduced due to network bandwidth, processing power, energy, and display restrictions inherent in mobile devices.

This chapter discusses the fundamental issues involved with mobile data access, the physical environment of mobile systems, and currently implemented mobile solutions. Furthermore, the issues involved in accessing information in a multidatabase environment and mobile computing environment share similarities. Therefore, we propose to superimpose a wireless-mobile computing environment on a multidatabase system in order to realize a system capable of effectively accessing a large amount of data over a wireless medium. We show how one can easily map solutions from one environment to another. This new system is called a mobile data access system (MDAS), which is capable of accessing heterogeneous data sources through both fixed and wireless connections. We will show the feasibility of mapping solutions from one environment to another.

Within the scope of this new environment, a new hierarchical concurrency control algorithm is introduced that allows a potentially large number of users to simultaneously access the available data. Current multidatabase concurrency control schemes do not efficiently manage these accesses because they do not address the limited bandwidth and frequent disconnection associated with wireless networks. The proposed concurrency control algorithm—v-lock—uses global locking tables created with semantic information contained within the hierarchy. The locking tables are subsequently used to serialize global transactions, and detect and remove global deadlocks. The performance of the new algorithm is simulated and the results are presented.

1. Introduction 120
2. Background 125
    2.1 Physical Environment 125
    2.2 Mobility 131
3. Multidatabase Systems... 134
    3.1 Site Autonomy and Heterogeneity.............................. 134
    3.2 Multidatabase Issues 136
4. The MDAS Environment.. 139
    4.1 Summary Schemas Model for Multidatabase Systems 144
5. Transaction Management and Concurrency Control 146
    5.1 Multidatabase and MDAS Transaction Processing Model 147
    5.2 MDBMS Serializability Solutions.............................. 150
    5.3 Concurrency Control for an MDAS.............................. 152
6. Evaluation of Proposed Algorithm 158
    6.1 V-Locking Concurrency Control Scheme 158
7. Conclusions and Future Directions 165
    7.1 Conclusion... 165
    7.2 Future Directions.. 166
Appendix: Related Projects 167
    7.3 Mobile-Transparent Projects.................................. 167
    7.4 Mobile-Aware Projects 171
Glossary 174
References 175

1. Introduction

The traditional notion of timely and reliable access to global information in a distributed or multidatabase system must be expanded. Users have become much more demanding in that they desire and sometimes even require access to information "anytime, anywhere." The extensive diversity in the range of information that is accessible to a user at any given time is also growing at a rapid rate. This information can include data from legacy systems, database systems, data warehouses, information services (i.e. stock quotes, news, airline information, weather information, etc.), and the almost limitless information on the Internet and the World Wide Web. Furthermore, rapidly expanding technology is making available a wide breadth of devices through which access to this enormous amount of diverse data is possible. For example, the user may access information from a desktop workstation connected to a LAN (Local Area Network), or from a laptop computer via a modem, or from a hand-held device via a wireless connection. All of these devices have different memory, storage, network, power, and display requirements.

Remote access to data is a rapidly expanding and increasingly important aspect of computing. Remote access to data refers to both mobile nodes and fixed nodes accessing a wide variety of data via a network connection characterized by (1) lower bandwidth, (2) frequent disconnection, and (3) higher error rates. Whereas both fixed and mobile node remote connections to the network are made through land-based lines, e.g. a modem and telephone lines, mobile nodes also access data through a wireless medium. This wireless connection results in even more of a severe degradation in the network connection. Furthermore, a mobile node introduces additional complexities such as location dependence, system configuration variations, data placement issues, and long-lived transactions. However, regardless of the hardware device, connection medium, and type of data accessed, all users share the same requirements: timely and reliable access to various types of data. These data types are classified as follows:

(1) Private data—i.e. personal schedules, phone numbers, etc. The reader of this type of data is the sole owner/writer of the data.
(2) Public data—i.e. news, weather, traffic information, flight information, etc. This type of data is maintained by one source, and shared by many.
(3) Shared data—i.e. group data, replicated or fragmented data of a database. A node actually may contribute to maintaining consistency, and participates in distributed decision making with this type of data [3].

Access to various types of data (i.e. private, public, and shared) is not an entirely new concept. Traditional databases have addressed many of the issues involved in accessing these types of data in the form of relational, object-oriented, distributed, federated, and multidatabase management systems (MDBMS). These traditional systems are based upon fixed clients and servers connected over a reliable network infrastructure. However, the concept of mobility, where a user accesses data through a remote connection with a portable device, has introduced several disadvantages for traditional database management systems (DBMS). These include: (1) a reduced capacity network connection, (2) processing and resource restrictions, and (3) effectively locating and accessing information from a multitude of sources.

In order to overcome these shortcomings effectively, a suitable solution must address the following issues:

(1) *Isolation.* A method to deal with the degraded network connection. The solution should also include a means to work offline such that a user can effectively operate if an intentional/unintentional disconnection has occurred. Furthermore, if the connection is too slow or unreliable to work fully online the user may intentionally choose to work offline due to bandwidth restrictions.

(2) *Data integration.* A method to work with a subset of the global data set. This is particularly important for devices with limited resources and capabilities. With a very large amount of data available to the user, the entire set of data cannot be kept locally. Therefore, the user requires a method to choose data from the global set, and use it at local speeds.

(3) *Browsing.* Since there may be an enormous amount of information available to the user, the user should be able to search and look at the available data in an efficient manner. In other words, an efficient method to browse the data.

(4) *Distribution transparency.* The placement of the data and the topology of the network should be designed transparently and to maximize the performance for the overall system. This is particularly important for wireless devices, which have the largest communication cost.

(5) *Limited resources.* The system should be able to accommodate computing devices with limited capabilities. This includes memory, storage, and display deficiencies.

(6) *Data heterogeneity.* With a large amount of data available to the user, name and type differences, and semantic differences/similarities need to be resolved. There are additional difficulties when accessing data in a non-native language. The system should provide a means to address these issues.

(7) *Location transparency.* A higher degree of mobility argues for a higher degree of heterogeneous data access. In particular, a mobile user can potentially access a much wider variety of systems in different locations and can also receive broadcast-type data from various locations due to mobility. Therefore, heterogeneous remote access to data (HRAD) sources is required for a remote access system.

The literature has individually addressed some of the above issues [3, 10, 11, 23, 43, 44]. Current multidatabase systems can effectively handle heterogeneous data access to autonomous systems [10]. Moreover, there are existing mobile applications, which address some of the limited bandwidth issues involved with mobility [15, 17, 22, 23, 26, 27, 28, 44, 46]. However, a solution does not currently exist that provides an effective means to cope with the issues involved while accessing a massively diverse amount of data over a remote connection. This is particularly true for devices with limited processing capacity and resources.

This chapter is intended to address fundamental issues of mobile data access, the physical environment of mobile systems, and currently implemented mobile solutions. It will compare and contrast the characteristics of multidatabase systems against the characteristics of a wireless-mobile computing environment. In addition, by superimposing a multidatabase system on a wireless-mobile environment it proposes a computational paradigm for effectively accessing heterogeneous data.

In a distributed environment, concurrency is used as a means to increase the throughput and to reduce the response time. Data access in an MDBMS is accomplished through transactions. Concurrency control involves coordinating the operations of multiple transactions that operate in parallel and access shared data. By interleaving the operations in such a manner, the potential of interference between transactions arises. The concurrent execution of transactions is considered correct when the following properties (called ACID properties) hold for each individual transaction [20]:

- *Atomicity*. The operations of a transaction are considered to be atomic; either all operations occur, or none occur.
- *Consistency*. The actions of a transaction taken as a group do not violate any integrity constraints of the database.
- *Isolation*. Although transactions may execute concurrently, each transaction assumes that it is executing alone in the system. In other words, the system hides all intermediate results of a transaction from other concurrently executing transactions.
- *Durability*. Successful completion of a transaction (commit), should guarantee that the effects of the transaction survive failure.

Concurrency control in a mobile data access system (MDAS) involves global transactions under the control of a global transaction manager (GTM) that are correctly serialized to guarantee proper execution. A global transaction is decomposed into sub-transactions and executed as a local transaction at local sites under the control of the local database management system. Proper concurrent execution of transactions should be coordinated such that the interference does not violate the ACID properties. Furthermore, the concurrent execution of transactions should offer a higher throughput than the serial execution of transactions [20]. In an MDAS environment, the concurrent execution of transactions is a more difficult task to control properly. This is mainly due to the inferences among global transactions, inferences among global and local transactions, local autonomy of each site, and frequent network disconnection.

There has been extensive research performed to maintain the ACID properties in centralized and tightly coupled distributed systems [3, 20]. A primary feature of an MDAS or MDBMS that distinguishes it from a conventional distributed DBMS is the notion of local autonomy. In a conventional, tightly coupled distributed system, each site has limited or no local autonomy. In contrast, local sites in an MDAS operate autonomously, with little or no knowledge of other local DBMSs or the MDAS system.

The degree of autonomy of each local site in an MDAS varies considerably depending upon local and global conditions. Full autonomy refers to the condition where the local site retains full control, and may unilaterally abort a transaction (any local or global sub-transactions). Full autonomy introduces extremely difficult problems for global transaction management in a MDAS. Achieving a high degree of concurrency under full autonomy is not practically possible. However, if local autonomy is somewhat compromised, methods such as locking, time-stamp ordering, ticketing, and serialization graph testing may be used. In general, as the degree of local autonomy decreases, the ability to effectively process transactions in a MDAS becomes easier. Figure 1 illustrates this concept.

Within the scope of this new environment, this chapter will introduce a new hierarchical concurrency control algorithm that is designed to reduce the required communication overhead. The proposed scheme allows for a higher overall throughput and faster response times to users—timely access to data. The concurrency control for global transactions are performed at the global level in a hierarchical, distributed manner. A hierarchical structure was chosen for several reasons:

(1) A hierarchical organization offers potentially higher performance, in that processing and data structures can be easily distributed.
(2) The reliability of the system is increased by eliminating a single point of failure for the MDBS involved in a global transaction.

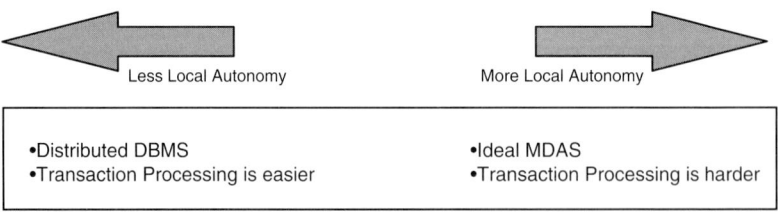

FIG. 1. Degree of mobile support.

(3) The algorithm is designed to work with the summary schemas model (SSM), which is a distributed, hierarchical, multidatabase environment [11]. The proposed algorithm is easily integrated into the SSM.

Concurrent execution of transactions is accomplished by creating global locking tables using semantic information within the hierarchy of the SSM.

Section 2 addresses the necessary background material on mobile systems, while section 3 covers multidatabase systems. Section 4 discusses a new computing environment in which a wireless-mobile computing environment is superimposed on a multidatabase system. The characteristics and issues of this new environment are discussed in this section. Furthermore, the details of a proposed multidatabase system, the summary schemas model (SSM), are discussed. Chapter 5 covers additional background material on concurrency control and a simulation of the proposed concurrency control scheme is introduced. A simulation model is developed to test the effectiveness of the proposed schemes. Subsequently, the results are presented and analyzed. Section 6 concludes the chapter, and discusses future solutions and research directions. Finally, section 7 contains references, a glossary of terms, and an appendix of current wireless/mobile systems.

2. Background

Accessing a large amount of data over a limited capability network connection involves two general aspects: (1) the mobile networking environment and (2) mobility issues. The mobile environment includes the physical network architecture and access devices. Mobility issues include adaptability to a mobile environment, autonomy, and heterogeneity. This section will introduce and discuss these topics in detail.

2.1 Physical Environment

2.1.1 Network Architecture

A remote access network consists of a variety of network connections and access devices with varying characteristics as shown in Fig. 2 [3, 16].

- *Fixed, land-based LAN connection.* This type of network connection ranges in speed from 10 Mbps to gigabits per second and usually does not impose any type of restriction on the system. Common fixed LAN connections include ethernet, fast ethernet, gigabit ethernet, and

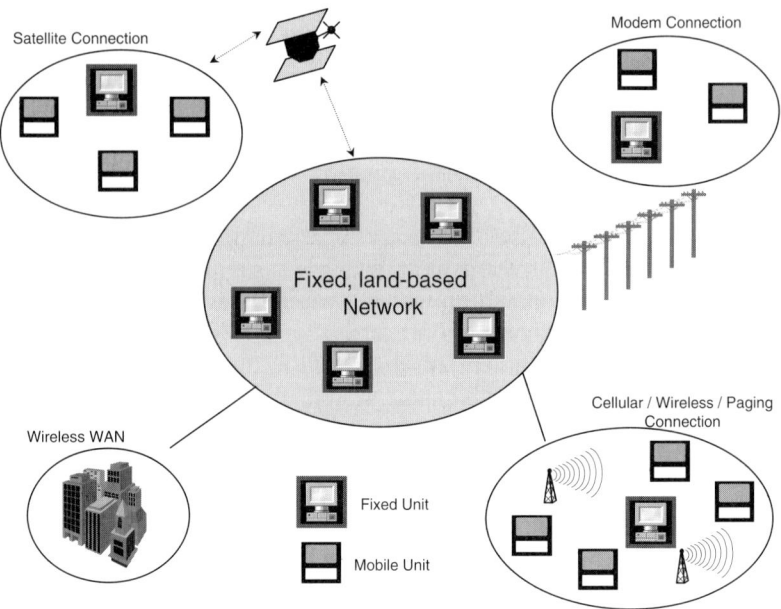

FIG. 2. Network architecture.

asynchronous transfer mode (ATM) [12, 47]. A remote access connection is usually made *to* this type of network.
- *Modem connection.* This is typically what a home/telecommuting/ mobile user would use to make a connection. The connection is made directly to a server, or via the Internet through an Internet service provider (ISP). Currently, the majority of these connections are made from a fixed point, such as a home or office. The connection is made with data transfer speeds up to 57.6 kbps [42], and is usually carried over the telephone network. This type of network connection has a much lower bandwidth and is less reliable than a fixed LAN connection. However, with the exception of a fixed connection, it provides the highest performance compared to other network types.
- *Cellular.* A cellular network provides both data and voice services to a user. Traditionally, a cellular network is used with handheld telephones, more recently, it has been used to provide data services to mobile systems. Typical bandwidth ranges from 9.6–19.2 kbps [16]. The cost of using a cellular network is relatively high, and furthermore, existing networking support using cellular technology does not scale well to large numbers of mobile users. Moreover, the use of this technology for data transmission is still in the early stages [16]. Cellular

networks, however, do provide very wide coverage, i.e. international coverage is available.

The geographic area covered by a cellular network is divided into fixed *cells*. Cells are connected to a base station that is attached to a fixed network (e.g. telephone network, data network, etc.). A cell covers a geographical area ranging from one to several square miles. Pico-cells cover a much smaller area (tens to hundreds of meters) and are placed in areas of high traffic and usage. When a user moves from the coverage of one cell to another, a "hand-off" occurs where the connection and control moves to the newly entered cell. This "hand-off" may cause a temporary disconnection, further degrading the reliability of the cellular system.

- *Wireless LAN*. This is a traditional LAN augmented with a wireless interface to provide wireless services within a small geographical area (i.e. up to a few kilometers). The bandwidth of this type of network is limited, ranging from 200 bps to 20 Mbps [30]. There is currently no networking support for any type of wide-area moves.
- *Wide-area wireless network*. These are special mobile radio networks that provide wide coverage and low bandwidth. These types of networks are expensive, provide nationwide data services, and bandwidth is available up to 19.2 kbps. However, there is no support for ubiquitous network connectivity and it is not clear if the systems will scale well for a large number of users [3].
- *Satellite network*. These network systems have been initially designed to carry voice, television, data, messaging, and paging services. They provide very wide coverage (global) at a relatively high cost with a bandwidth ranging from 9.6 kbps to 3 Mbps [41]. Some systems also only operate in a receive-only mode. Currently, the only such operational system is the Hughes Network Systems' DirecPC (the same network used by the DirecTV satellite system for television). Other proposed satellite systems include Motorola's Iridium, Qualcomm's Globalstar, and TRW's Odyssey [33].
- *Paging network*. This network is typically a receive-only system with very low bandwidth. Coverage ranges from a local city to global. AT&T and Motorola currently have two-way paging network systems [32, 41, 49].

In comparison to traditional fixed LANs, remote access connections have lower bandwidths, have higher error rates, and disconnection is much more frequent. Furthermore, due to large variations in bandwidths, there are varying degrees of disconnection that can occur with these types of networks. Table I summarizes these different connection mediums.

TABLE I
PHYSICAL CONNECTION MEDIUMS

Network type	Bandwidth	Transmission	Converge	Availability	Usage cost
Fixed LAN [49, 12]	10 M-Gbps	Symmetrical/Asymmetrical	N/A	High	Low
Modem [42]	up to 57.6 kbps	Symmetrical/Asymmetrical	N/A	Medium	Low
Cellular [49, 16]	9.6–19.2 kbps	Symmetrical	National	Low	High
Wireless LAN [30]	200 bps–20 Mbps	Symmetrical	Several kilometers	Medium	Medium
Wide-area wireless [3]	19.2 kbps	Symmetrical	National	Medium	Medium
Satellite [41, 33]	9.6 k–3 Mbps	Asymmetrical	International	Medium	High
Paging network [49, 41, 32]	less than 9.6 kbps	Asymmetrical	National	Medium	Low

2.1.2 Access Devices

The connection to the network is made through desktop computing devices, portable computers, and portable hand-held devices. The requirements and limitations of these devices vary greatly in terms of computing power, memory capacity, storage space, size, display area, and energy consumption. These devices are summarized in Table II.

Desktop computing devices include workstations, personal computers, and network computing devices. A workstation or desktop personal computer does not have many resource restrictions when connected to a fixed network. These systems can have very large processing capabilities, large memories, large disk drives, and large display areas. The primary restriction pertaining to this type of computing device is due to the remote network connection—typically, a modem when the system is used from a fixed remote location (e.g. home, satellite office, etc.).

A network computing (NC) device is characterized by its low cost and maintenance. As a result, the computer does not have a hard disk, floppy disk, or CD-ROM drive. In order to reduce the cost, the processing power is more limited than a traditional desktop system and memory sizes range from 16MB–128MB. The system must be connected via a network to a server. The NC downloads the operating environment and applications that it runs locally. The prices of these systems range from $500–1500. Currently, Intel/Microsoft, IBM, Oracle, and Sun are manufacturing NCs [37].

Compared to a desktop computer, portable computers have a slightly restricted functionality, but in a smaller package. Memory sizes range anywhere from 8MB–128MB; disk drive capacity can be up to several gigabytes; and typically, they weigh from 4–10 pounds. The display, however, is limited in size (up to 14 inches). In addition, since the system is portable and may not be attached to a non-battery power source, it has a low power requirement. This type of device may use a fixed, modem, or wireless type of network connection.

Portable handheld devices represent the most restrictive and, thus, most challenging device for remote access. First-generation PDAs (personal digital assistant) were handheld messaging units using a wireless connection to send/receive e-mail, small messages and faxes. They had very limited processing capability (equivalent to an Intel 8086), and memory capacity (128K–1MB), small displays, and very strict energy requirements. The Apple Newton and AT&T EO were examples of these types of devices [22]. Due to their limited functionality, the first-generation PDA was not considered very successful. Technological advances have given second-generation PDAs better processing capabilities and larger memories (1MB–32MB). Due to their small size, they still have some of the same restrictions as the

TABLE II
REMOTE ACCESS DEVICES

Device type	Relative computing power	Memory	Storage	Weight	Display size	Energy requirement
Workstation, desktop PC [a,b]	Very high	Gigabytes	Gigabytes–Terabytes (disk based)	<500 lbs	up to 21 inches	None
Network computer (NC) [37]	High	<128 MB	None	<100 lbs	up to 21 inches	None
Portable computer [c,d]	High	<128 MB	<6 GB (disk or electronic)	4–15 lbs	up to 14 inches	Battery (NiCAD, lithium, NiMH)—typical usage is 1–16 hours per recharge
Portable hand-held computer [e,f]	Low–medium	<32 MB	<500 MB (disk)	4–16 oz	up to 6 inches (640 × 480 pixels)	Battery (alkaline, NiCAD, lithium)— typical usage is up to 8–48 hours per recharge/battery
Pager [g,h]	Very low/none	<16 K	None	1–8 oz	up to 3 inches	Battery (alkaline—typical usage is 30 days)

[a] Sun Microsystems, Technical Specification Sheet for Sun Enterprise 3000 Servers, 1998.
[b] Dell Computer Systems, Technical Specification Sheet for XPS, 1998.
[c] Toshiba Computer, Technical Specification Sheet for Tecra 780DVD, 1998.
[d] IBM Computer, Technical Specification Sheet for Thinkpad 600, 770ED, 1998.
[e] Sharp, Technical Specification Sheet for Mobilon, 1998.
[f] US Robotics, Technical Specification Sheet for Palm III, 1998.
[g] Motorola, Technical Specification Sheet for Advisor, Bravo, Director, PageWriter, 1997.
[h] Motorola, ReFLEX Fact Sheet, 1997.

first-generation PDAs. Second-generation PDAs are more general-purpose computers and are capable of running non-messaging applications (e.g. database, Internet access, etc.). Some examples of these types of devices include the USR PalmPilot, and Windows CE devices.

Finally, pagers represent the most basic form of a handheld remote access device. They have almost no processing power, very limited memory, and very small displays, and are mostly designed to receive telephone numbers, alphanumeric messages or information (e.g. weather, stock, news, etc.). Most pagers are passive devices in that they only receive data and are unable to transmit data [32, 41, 49].

2.2 Mobility

A mobile application must be able to adapt to changing conditions [4]. These changes include the network environment and resources available to the application. A balance between self-autonomy and dependence on a server for a mobile user is very critical. A resource-scarce mobile system is better served by relying upon a server. However, frequent network disconnection, limited network bandwidth, and power restrictions argue for some degree of autonomy. As the environment changes, the application must adapt to the level of support required from stationary systems (servers).

2.2.1 Mobile Support

A mobile support system can be classified, based upon the level of mobile awareness, into three categories as shown in Fig. 3: mobile-transparent systems, mobile-aware systems, and non-supportive systems. A mobile-transparent system is one where the application is unaware of the environment, and the mobile aspects of the system are hidden from the application. These systems offer backward compatibility with existing applications, and existing applications run without any modifications. However, the major drawback of these systems is the lack of flexibility because they can not adequately adapt to the changing environment of the mobile system. Thus, the result is a degradation of the overall functionality and performance. Furthermore, these systems often require the cooperation of both the user and application [23].

On the other hand, a non-supportive approach offers no system support for mobile applications. The application must handle all of the restrictions imposed by mobility. Although this approach eliminates the need for system support, applications are more difficult to write, incompatibility issues arise, and the software becomes less reusable [3].

The middle ground between these two approaches is the mobile-aware

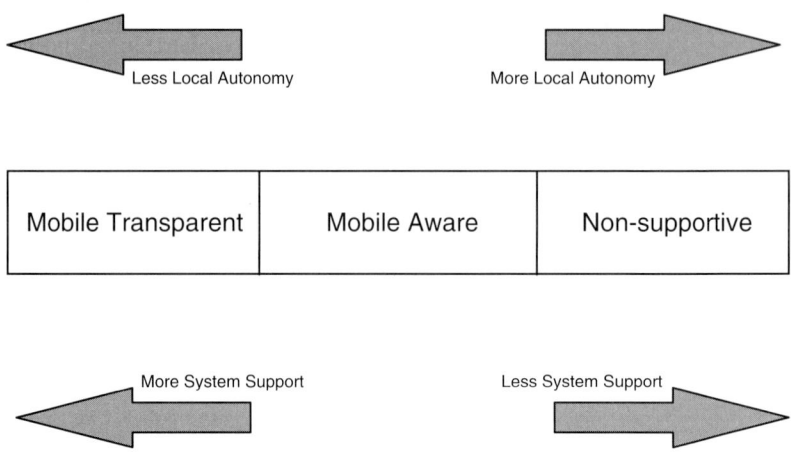

FIG. 3. Degree of mobile support.

environment. Instead of the system masking the environmental conditions from the application, this information is exposed to the applications, enabling them to actually participate in the decision-making process [23]. This approach allows for the system to support an application, as well as for the application to remain autonomous, depending upon environmental conditions, i.e. network, performance, reliability, power, etc.

2.2.2 Autonomy

The level of autonomy required in a mobile system varies with different systems. For mobile-transparent and non-supportive applications, the level of autonomy is fixed. In other words, the level of server dependence and self-reliance is unchanging. However, the level of autonomy required by a mobile-aware system is highly dependent upon the available network bandwidth, the reliability of the connection, available resources in the mobile unit, and the power limitations of the access unit. The application is alert to any changes to these resource restrictions and dynamically adapts accordingly.

The network connection has the largest impact upon the degree of autonomy required by the mobile system. If the system is connected to a land-based network, then the mobile system can rely heavily upon a server. However, as the network connection degrades (in terms of bandwidth and reliability), then the degree of autonomy required by the mobile system increases. The extreme case is when the mobile system is disconnected, and hence full autonomy is required.

2.2.3 Heterogeneous data

The level of access to heterogeneous data increases with mobile systems. A mobile system uses a wireless link as a network connection (albeit with degraded performance). However, because of mobility, there is a high chance for a system to be connected to different host units. This argues for support to access data, which is more heterogeneous than a stationary system. Furthermore, data can be broadcast to mobile users over a wireless medium. As a mobile user moves from one location to another, there is a wider range of broadcast data available to the user. Therefore, a higher

TABLE III
SUMMARY OF MOBILE ENVIRONMENT ISSUES

Mobile environment issue	Description
Site autonomy	Local control over resources and data. The degree of autonomy required depends upon the degree of mobile support offered by the system.
Heterogeneous interoperability	Hardware and software heterogeneity.
Disconnect and weak connection support	A mobile system should provide a means to provide access to data while faced with a disconnection or weak connection.
Support for resource scarce systems	A mobile system should address the inherent limitations of various resource scarce access devices. These include processing, storage, power, and display limitations.
Transaction management and concurrency control	Correct transaction management should satisfy the ACID properties (Atomicity, Consistency, Isolation, and Durability).
Distribution transparency	Distribution of data is transparent to the user.
Location transparency	The location of the data is transparent to the user
Location dependency	The content of the data is physically dependent upon the location of the user.
System transparency	The user should be able to access the desired data irrespective of the system.
Representation transparency	Representation transparency includes naming differences, format differences, structural differences, and missing or conflicting data.
Intelligent search and browsing or data	The system should provide a means for the user to efficiently search and browse the data.
Intelligent query resolution	The system should be able to efficiently process and optimize a query submitted by the user.

degree of mobility implies that there is a requirement to access a higher degree of heterogeneous data.

Mobile computing is a rapidly expanding technology. A remote access connection introduces many challenges, making the use of mobile devices more difficult. Furthermore, the concept of mobility implies a much more diverse range and amount of accessible data. Subsequently, a remote access system must provide access to a large set of heterogeneous data. Moreover, it must be able to facilitate the bandwidth, resource, and power restrictions of mobile systems. The various issues in accessing data in a mobile computing environment are summarized in Table III.

Multidatabase systems share many of the same characteristics of mobile systems. In the next section, we discuss these characteristics.

3. Multidatabase Systems

Multidatabase systems (MDBMS) are used to maintain, manage, and access a large amount of information. An MDBMS is a global system layer that allows distributed access to multiple pre-existing local database systems. The global layer provides full database functionality and interacts with the local DBMSs at their external user interface. Both the hardware and software intricacies of the different local systems are transparent to the user, and access to different local systems appears to the user as a single, uniform system. The term multidatabase includes federated databases, global schema multidatabases, multidatabase language systems, and homogeneous multidatabase language systems. The typical architecture of an MDBMS is shown in Fig. 4. This section will discuss the various issues involved in order to provide multidatabase functionality to a mobile user, and will show the similarities and differences between the two computational environments. Furthermore, the summary schemas model (SSM) as the underlying heterogeneous multidatabase environment [10] is introduced, and its concepts and structure are discussed.

3.1 Site Autonomy and Heterogeneity

One of the essential features of a multidatabase system is local site autonomy, meaning that each local database management system (DBMS) maintains complete control over local data and resources. Modifications to the global system should not impact the operation of the local system. There are two different classes of operations, global and local. A global operation is performed through the MDBMS on the entire system, and should not affect

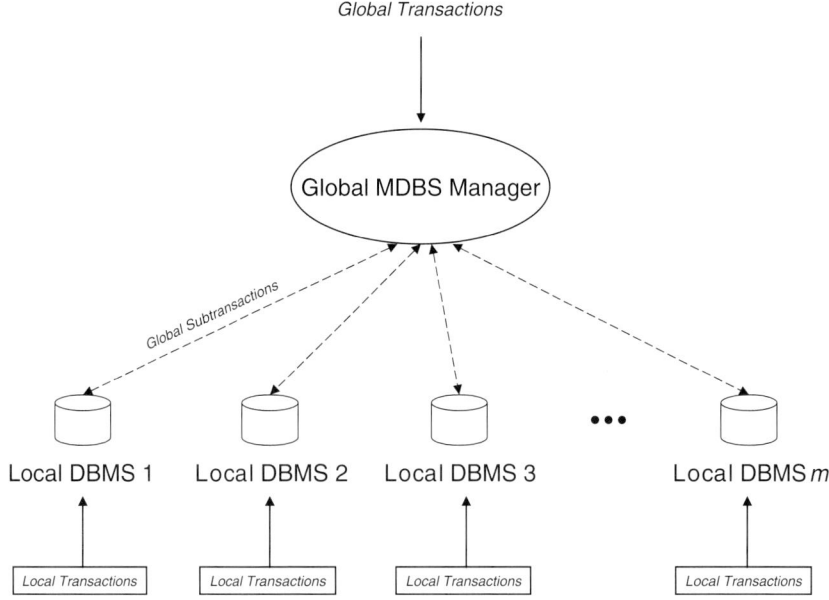

FIG. 4. Architecture of an MDBMS.

the operation of any single, local DBMS. There are three different forms of autonomy [18]:

- *Design autonomy.* When joining an MDBMS, a local DBMS should not require any software or hardware changes. The global MDBMS software should form a "wrapper" around an existing local system, allowing for easy integration into the existing MDBMS. Changes that impact the local system are undesirable, particularly for legacy systems, in which there may be a significant amount of capital invested in existing software, hardware, and user training.
- *Communication autonomy.* During integration into an MDBMS, the local DBMS decides exactly which local data should be available globally. There are two consequences of communication autonomy: (1) the local DBMS may or may not inform the global user about local operations, and (2) a local DBMS is not responsible for synchronization of global operations.
- *Execution autonomy.* A local DBMS executes operations at its site (global or local) in any manner it desires. In other words, a global operation is executed as any "normal" local operation executing at the local site. This implies that the local DBMS has the option of refusing or aborting any operation (global or local).

In addition to autonomy, heterogeneous data access is an important aspect of a multidatabase system. Multidatabase systems are designed to access a multitude of data, irrespective of the system, data type, or particular local access method. Heterogeneity occurs in the form of software or hardware. Support for heterogeneity is a tradeoff between developing and making changes in both hardware and software, and limiting participation. As a result, as the number of local systems and the degree of heterogeneity among these systems rises, the cost of integration into the global MDBMS increases. Furthermore, the global system software must also support any local deficiencies. Particularly with MDBMSs, autonomy and heterogeneity leads to issues in schema integration, query languages, query processing, and transaction management.

3.2 Multidatabase Issues

3.2.1 Schema Integration

When accessing a large amount of heterogeneous data, an MDBMS must address the schema issues related to data representation transparency, system transparency (interoperability), and location transparency. Local databases have their own schema, and the goal of an MDBMS is to provide an integrated schema that presents a logical, global view of the data.

There are many ways to model a given real-world object (or relationships to other objects). Local databases are developed independently with differing local requirements. Therefore, it is a reasonable assumption that a multidatabase system contains many different models or representations for similar objects. The differences in data representation which multidatabases address are [10]:

- *Naming differences.* Different information sources and services may have different conventions for naming data objects.
- *Format differences.* Differences in data type, domain, scale, and precision are types of format differences.
- *Structural differences.* Depending on how an object is used by a database, it may be structured differently throughout local databases.
- *Missing and conflicting data.* Databases that model the same real-world object may have conflicts in the actual data values recorded.

System transparency issues occur in the type of system, network connection, protocol, and data model (i.e. relational, object-oriented, network, hierarchical, etc.) used at the local level of a multidatabase system. The extent of system transparency in a multidatabase system is a tradeoff between writing translation code (in the form of a gateway or middleware), and limiting local system participation in the multidatabase [10]. Location transparency refers to both the distribution and location of the data. A multidatabase system usually provides location transparency such that a user can submit a query to access distributed objects without having to know the actual location of the object. In a large multidatabase system, a user could not be expected to remember or include the location of objects within a particular query. Distribution transparency hides the distribution of data from the user. In other words, the manner in which the data is distributed across the multidatabase is transparent to the user.

3.2.2 Query Languages and Processing

The basis of global query processing is similar across most MDBMSs. A global query is submitted to the system, and the query is decomposed into a set of subqueries—one for each local DBMS involved in the transaction. Query optimization is used to create an efficient access strategy that includes: (1) which local DBMSs are involved, (2) the operations to be performed at the local DBMSs, (3) integration of intermediate results from the local DBMSs, and (4) the location(s) of the global processing. During the actual execution of the query, the queries may require translation at several levels due to query language and data representational differences at the local DBMS. Furthermore, the distributed nature and execution autonomy of an MDBMS along with different processing capabilities at a local DBMS create additional challenges to an MDBMS. Additional considerations include communication bottlenecks, hot spots at servers, data fragmentation, and incomplete local information [20, 35, 39]. These issues place additional constraints on the query processor. However, despite these difficulties, the query processor must be able to efficiently handle the query processing as well as efficiently manage the global resources.

3.2.3 Transaction Management and Concurrency Control

An MDBMS transaction management scheme must guarantee correctness under all circumstances. By correctness, a transaction should satisfy the ACID properties [20]. Maintaining the ACID properties is desirable in any MDBMS, however, difficulties arise from the requirement to maintain the autonomy of a local DBMS in a multidatabase environment. Local autonomy states that each local DBMS retains complete control over its data. This implies that local operations are outside the control of the global system.

Therefore, the operations in a transaction can be subjected to large delays, frequent or unnecessary aborts, inconsistency, and deadlock.

Finally, concurrency control is an issue which requires consideration in a multidatabase system. Concurrency control in a multidatabase refers to the serializability of global and local transactions. The global system has information regarding global transactions; however, due to local autonomy, the local transactions are not seen at the global level. Therefore, direct or indirect conflicts may arise between local and global transactions. Concurrency control in multidatabase systems should address the issues involved with detecting and resolving these conflicts.

Many of the issues that are involved with accessing data in an MDBMS are summarized in Table IV. Comparing these characteristics to those listed in Table III for a mobile computing environment, one can find many similarities between the two data processing environments. In the next section, we address these characteristics, and discuss the similarities and differences between an MDBMS and mobile computing environment.

TABLE IV
SUMMARY OF MULTIDATABASE ENVIRONMENT ISSUES

Multidatabase environment issues	Description
Site autonomy	Local control over resources and data. Three different forms of autonomy include design, communication and execution.
Heterogeneous interoperability	Hardware and software heterogeneity.
Transaction management and concurrency control	Correct transaction management should satisfy the ACID properties (Atomicity, Consistency, Isolation, and Durability).
Distribution transparency	Distribution of data in the MDBMS is transparent to the user.
Location transparency	The location of the data in the MDBMS is transparent to the user.
System transparency	The user should be able to access the desired data irrespective of the system.
Representation transparency	Representation transparency includes naming differences, format differences, structural differences, and missing or conflicting data.
Intelligent search and browsing of data	The MDBS should provide a means for the user to efficiently search and browse the data contained in the MDBMS.
Intelligent query resolution	An MDBMS should be able to efficiently process and optimize a query submitted to the system.

4. The MDAS Environment

There are similarities in the objectives of effectively accessing data in a multidatabase and a wireless-mobile computing environment. This chapter proposes to superimpose a wireless-mobile computing environment on an MDBMS to realize a system capable of effectively accessing data over a wireless medium. This new system is called a mobile data access system (MDAS). By superimposing an MDBMS onto a mobile computing environment, one should be able to map solutions easily from one environment to another. This section will discuss the issues needed to support this new computing environment. Furthermore, we will discuss the structure of the summary schemas model (SSM), a heterogeneous multidatabase environment [11], and show how the SSM is used as the underlying multidatabase environment in an MDAS.

A summary of the issues facing a multidatabase and those involved in a mobile system is given in Table V. Both systems have autonomy and heterogeneity requirements, where the mobility of a system introduces more complexity. The objective of either system is to provide access to data, where the clients and servers of an MDBMS are typically connected through fixed network connections, and the clients in a mobile environment are typically connected through a wireless connection. Both systems must address the data, software, and hardware heterogeneity issues as discussed in sections 2.2 and 2.3. The larger number of potential data sources, the mobility, and the resource constraints in a mobile environment further complicates

TABLE V
MULTIDATABASE AND MOBILE SYSTEM COMPARISON

	Mobile system	Multidatabase system
Site autonomy	✓	✓
Heterogeneous interoperability	✓	✓
Transaction management and concurrency control	✓	✓
Disconnect and weak connection support	✓	○
Support for resource scarce systems	✓	✗
Distribution transparency	●	○
Location transparency	●	○
Location dependency	●	✗
System transparency	●	○
Representation transparency	●	○
Intelligent search and browsing of data	●	●
Intelligent query resolution	●	●

Key: ✓ Required; ● Desirable; ○ Optional; ✗ Not required

access to the data. The literature has addressed the heterogeneity issues in an MDBMS [10, 11]. However, these issues have not been addressed in a wireless-mobile computing environment. Traditionally, wireless-mobile computing researchers have investigated and addressed wireless connection, mobility, and portability issues, but have been inclined to ignore many of the issues related to heterogeneity. Consequently, the combined solutions from an MBDMS and a wireless-mobile system should be developed to form an integral part of any MDAS.

Autonomy of a system implies that the system should have complete control over the local data and resources, and be able to operate independently. In a multidatabase system, this is referred to as site autonomy, where a local DBMS is autonomous with respect to other systems in the MDBMS. In a mobile system, autonomy refers to the mobile user/application, where the level of autonomy is a function of the available resources (network, processing, storage, etc.). The level of autonomy also varies depending upon the mobile awareness of a particular application, and the support provided by the system. The quality of the wireless/fixed network connection and the processing capacity of the hardware are the primary factors in determining the level of application-autonomy that is required. This type of variable autonomy is only possible if the system and application support this functionality. Some systems may only provide partial application autonomy, or may not even provide any support for this functionality. An MDAS should support both site-level and application-level autonomy.

Schema integration issues include data representation, system, and location transparency issues. As with heterogeneity, these issues have been extensively researched in multidatabase systems [10, 11]. A primary goal of an MDBMS is to present the user with an integrated, global schema of the data. However, in a wireless-mobile computing environment, researchers have overlooked the importance of schema integration in a data access system. Particularly since mobility tends to increase the degree of heterogeneous data available, an MDAS must address schema integration issues in order to present the user with a viable solution for accessing heterogeneous data. Furthermore, mobility introduces an additional challenge in that it may be desirable to have location *dependence* when accessing data. In such instances, the content and representation of the data could actually depend upon the location of the accessing the data.

Query processing issues are well understood in an MDBMS. A global query is submitted to the system, and the query is decomposed into a set of sub-queries, one for each local DBMS involved in the transaction. In a mobile environment, where the processing power, storage, and energy may be restricted, query processing is non-trivial. If a mobile unit has sufficient resources to perform the query processing, then the query in the MDAS could be processed and executed similar to a query in an MDBMS. However, if the resources are limited, then the processing should be performed by a fixed, more resourceful computing device in the MDAS. One of the disadvantages of this method is that there may be an increase in the network traffic, which poses a problem in a wireless connection. Different strategies to address these issues include object-oriented designs, dynamic adjustment to bandwidth changes, data distillation, and query processing on fixed network devices [10, 23, 44].

Effectively accessing the data in a heterogeneous environment may require an efficient means of searching/browsing the data, in addition to an efficient mechanism to resolve and process a user's query. In a mobile environment, this may be more difficult to realize due to network, storage, processing power, and energy restrictions. Similar to query processing, the processing could be performed by a fixed, more resourceful computing device in the MDAS if the local host does not have the resources to search/browse data. Furthermore, network traffic increases depending upon the storage capacity of the mobile unit. The lower the storage space the local unit contains, the more the likelihood increases of generating network traffic. In other words, if the local node could store more information and data about the global schema and data, additional local processing (and hence less network traffic) could be achieved.

Transaction processing and concurrency control is an important, yet extremely challenging aspect of data processing. MDBMS researchers have been faced with the problem of maintaining serializability for global transactions. The problem of maintaining serializability in a multidatabase is complicated by the presence of local transactions that are invisible at the global level. There are two methods used to maintain serializability in an MDBMS:

1. *Bottom-up approach.* The global serializability is verified by collecting local information from the local DBMSs and validating the serialization orders at the global level. The global scheduler is responsible for detecting and resolving incompatibilities between global transactions and local serialization orders. Optimistic concurrency control mechanisms are usually used with the bottom-up approach. This optimistic nature allows for a higher degree of concurrency among transactions. However, the higher throughput is achieved at the expense of lower resource utilization and more overhead due to rollbacks from failed transactions.
2. *Top-down approach.* The global scheduler is allowed to determine the serialization order of global transactions before they are submitted to the local sites. The local DBMS must then enforce this order at the

local site. This method is a pessimistic approach, and subsequently leads to a potentially lower degree of concurrency. It forces the global order on the local schedulers. Consequently, runtime decisions regarding the ordering of transactions is not needed.

In an MDAS environment, the system should be able to provide global serializability and local autonomy to a user using a wireless connection. The restrictions imposed by a wireless connection have led to the use of optimistic concurrency control schemes in mobile-wireless environments [22, 25, 36, 39]. In addition, an application in an MDAS may be required to use both weak and strong consistency rules, where the application is required to adapt to changing environmental conditions. An operation uses weak consistency guidelines when data in a write operation is updated or written without immediate confirmation, and data in a read operation is based upon an approximately accurate value. In MDBMSs, weak consistency is used to increase global transaction throughput. In an MDAS, weak consistency may be required due to disconnection and/or a weak network connection.

Mobility and some of its consequences—e.g. disconnection and weak connections (communication restrictions), processing, storage, display, and energy restrictions—introduce additional complexities when a user accesses data. A local cache and prefetching in a mobile unit has been extensively used to address the problems associated with disconnection and weak connections. The idea is that when a disconnection occurs, the mobile unit operates in an autonomous state while performing operations on the local cache. When the connection is re-established, a resynchronization between the cache in the local unit and the server occurs [4, 15, 47]. The use of various prefetch schemes has been used to ensure that the required data is available in the cache during a disconnection [4, 36, 44, 46, 51]. Additionally, some type of queuing mechanism is usually provided in order to perform operations on data that may not be contained in the cache [4]. Predictive schemes, where the system is actually able to anticipate a disconnection, are used to lessen the impact of a disconnection. Finally, broadcasting of data on wireless channels has been suggested in order to reduce network traffic [52].

Finally, processing power and display limitations in a mobile unit introduce additional challenges to an MDAS. Offloading the processing performed on the local unit to fixed hosts is commonly used in wireless-mobile environments. Data distillation is commonly used to address the display network limitations of a mobile unit. Many mobile units are not capable of displaying multimedia data (video, images, sound, etc.). Data distillation is a process where incoming data is "distilled," or processed, such that only

TABLE VI
SUMMARY OF ISSUES AND SOLUTIONS FOR AN MDAS

Characteristics	Issues	Solutions
Site autonomy	Autonomy is required in an MDAS system.	Provide both site-level and application-level autonomy.
Heterogeneous interoperability	Heterogeneous interoperability is required in an MDAS system.	Use traditional methods for heterogeneity from MDBMSs.
Transaction management and concurrency control	Provide global serializability to transactions.	Use a bottom-up approach with optimistic concurrency control.
Disconnect and weak connection support	A wireless medium results in lower bandwidth and disconnections.	Local cache, prefetching, and broadcasts.
Support for resource scarce systems	Limited processing power, storage, energy, and display.	Object-oriented design, multi-tiered architecture, offload processing to fixed hosts, data distillation, and broadcasting.
Distribution transparency Location transparency Location dependency System transparency Representation transparency	Schema integration issues, and greater impact due to mobility.	Use traditional methods for schema integration from MDBMSs.
Intelligent search and browsing of data	Limited processing power, storage, energy, and display.	Reduction of local data storage requirements, object-oriented design, multi-tiered architecture, and offload processing to fixed hosts.
Intelligent query resolution	Limited processing power, storage, energy, and display.	Object-oriented design, multi-tiered architecture, offload processing to fixed hosts, and data distillation.

portions of the data that the unit is capable of displaying are shown on the screen. Furthermore, if network bandwidth is limited, data distillation is used to reduce the network traffic by distilling video, images, or sound. In order to address the limitations inherent in a mobile unit, an MDAS should use some or all of these aforementioned methods. A summary of the issues and possible solutions in an MDAS are given in Table VI.

4.1 Summary Schemas Model for Multidatabase Systems

Accessing a heterogeneous multidatabase system is a challenging problem. Multidatabase language and global schema systems suffer from inefficiencies and scalability problems. The SSM has been proposed as an efficient means to access data in a heterogeneous multidatabase environment [11]. The SSM primarily acts as a backbone to a multidatabase for query resolution. It uses a hierarchical meta structure that provides an incrementally concise view of the data in the form of summary schemas. The hierarchical data structure of the SSM consists of leaf nodes and summary schema nodes. Each leaf node represents a portion of a local database that is globally shared. The summary schema nodes provide a more concise view

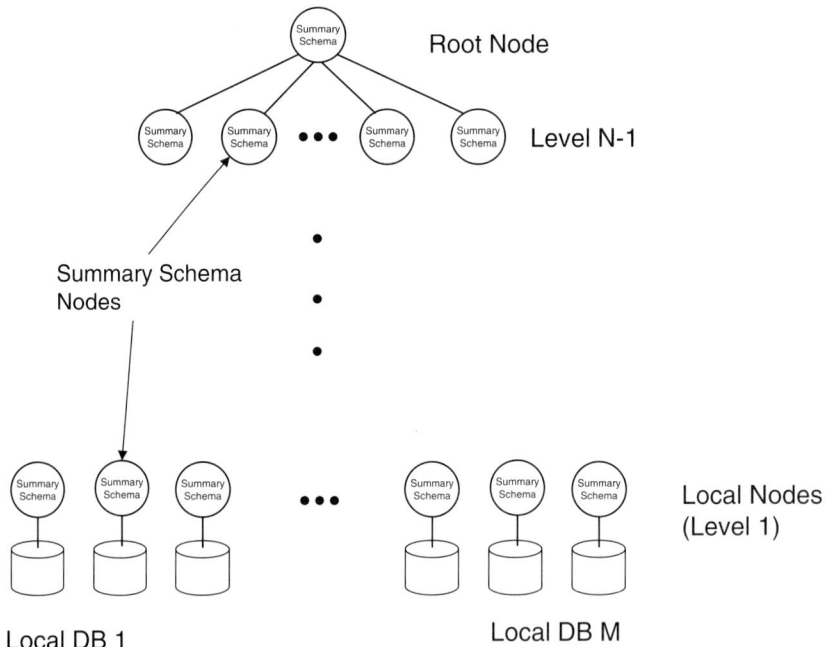

FIG. 5. Summary Schemas Model, N levels, and M local nodes.

of the data by summarizing the schema of each child node. Figure 5 depicts the architecture of the SSM. The terms in the schemas are related through synonym, hypernym and hyponym links [11]. Synonyms are words with a similar definition, and are used to link terms within the same level of the hierarchy. A hypernym is a word that has a more comprehensive and general definition, whereas a hyponym is a word that has a more precise definition. Hypernyms and hyponyms are used to establish links between terms of parent and child nodes.

The SSM intelligently resolves user queries [11]. When the user knows the precise access terms of a local database, the query is directly submitted to the corresponding local data source. However, when the precise access terms and/or location of the data not known to the user, the SSM processes the query in the user's own terms and submits a global query to the system. A simulation and benchmark of the SSM model was performed, and the benefits are shown in [10, 11, 14]. The simulator compared and contrasted the costs of querying a multidatabase system using precise queries (access terms and locations are known) against the intelligent query processing using the SSM for the imprecise queries (access terms and locations are unknown). The results showed that the intelligent query processing of the SSM and an exact query incurred very comparable costs (i.e. there were only small overhead costs to using the SSM) [11]. Interestingly, using intelligent SSM query processing actually outperformed an exact query in certain circumstances [14]. These results are very relevant to an MDAS in that a user would most likely require this functionality while accessing heterogeneous data sources.

The SSM provides several benefits to the user over traditional multidatabase systems, which can be directly applied to an MDAS. These include:

- The SSM provides global access to data without requiring precise knowledge of local access terms or local views. The system can intelligently process a user's query in his/her own terms.
- The SSM's hierarchical structure of hypernym/hyponym relationships produces incrementally concise views of the global data. The overall memory requirements for the SSM, compared to the requirements of a global schema, are drastically reduced by up to 94% [14]. Subsequently, the SSM could be kept in main memory, thus reducing the access time and query processing time. Furthermore, for very resource limited devices in an MDAS, only portions of the upper levels of the SSM meta data structure could be stored locally, which would still provide a global view (albeit less detailed) of the system.
- The SSM can be used to browse/view global data in the multidatabase system. The user can either (1) follow semantic links in a summary

schemas node, or (2) query the system for terms that are similar to the user's access terms. In either case, the SSM could be used to browse data by "stepping" through the hierarchy, or view semantically similar data through queries. Moreover, for resource limited devices in an MDAS, portions of the upper levels of the SSM could be used to provide a global view (albeit less detailed) of the system, which could be used for browsing/searching.

5. Transaction Management and Concurrency Control

A transaction is one of the fundamental concepts in a DBMS. A transaction is essentially a set of read and write operations performed on data items. It is atomic in that every operation in the transaction either completes, or does not complete. In other words, transactions comprise read and write operations terminated by either a commit operation, or an abort operation.

In order to increase the overall throughput, transactions are executed concurrently. The operations of different transactions can be interleaved as long as each transaction adheres to the ACID properties. The incorrect interaction of operations between two concurrent transactions is the only manner in which an inconsistency can occur in the system. Two read operations by different transactions, however, do not cause inconsistencies because the data values are not changed. The inconsistencies that occur are due to three anomalies [20]:

(1) *Lost update.* An update by one of two transactions is lost. For example, in a lost update, a write operation by transaction T1 is ignored by transaction T2. Transaction T2 writes based upon the original value of the data before transaction T1 altered the data.
(2) *Dirty read.* The final version of a read operation is inconsistent because it is not the final version of another transaction. For example, transaction T2 writes to a data item, then transaction T1 reads the data, and then transaction T2 makes further changes to the data.
(3) *Unrepeatable read.* Two read operations return different values. In this case, transaction T1 reads a data object, transaction T2 changes the data, followed by transaction T1 reading the altered value of the data.

These three anomalies are the basis of concurrency control; if they can be prevented, then the transactions may be interleaved in any manner [20]. This section introduces some additional background material for concurrency control. Subsequently, a new concurrency control algorithm is introduced and discussed.

5.1 Multidatabase and MDAS Transaction Processing Model

There are two basic transactions in an MDBMS:

- *Local transactions.* Transactions that are executed at the local site on local data. These transactions are managed only by the local system, outside the control of the MDBMS.
- *Global transactions.* Transactions that are submitted through a global interface executed under the control of the MDBMS. A global transaction consists of a number of potential sub-transactions executing at multiple local sites. Each sub-transaction, though, appears as a regular local transaction to the local DBMS.

The autonomy requirement of local databases in an MDAS introduces additional complexities in maintaining serializable histories because the local transactions are not seen at the global level. There are two types of conflicts that may arise due to the concurrent execution of transactions—*direct* and *indirect* conflicts. A direct conflict between two transactions T_a and T_b exists if, and only if, an operation of T_a on data item x (denoted $O(T_a(x))$) is followed by $O(T_b(x))$, where T_a does not commit or abort before $O(T_b(x))$, and either $O(T_a(x))$ or $O(T_b(x))$ is a write operation. An indirect conflict between the two transactions T_a and T_b exists if, and only if, there exists a sequence of transactions $T_1, T_2, \ldots T_n$ such that T_a is in direct conflict with T_1, T_1 is in direct conflict with T_2, ..., and T_n is in direct with T_b [8].

5.1.1 Indirect Conflict Example

Indirect conflicts are due to the execution of local transactions that can not be seen at the global level. The following example illustrates this problem. Suppose we have two sites and four transactions. Site 1 contains data items s and t; Site 2 contains data items x and y. There are two global transactions T_{G1} and T_{G2}, and two local transactions T_{L1} and T_{L2}. A w indicates a write operation, and an r indicates a read operation on a data item. The following operations represent the four transactions:

$$T_{G1}: w(G1,s), w_{G1}(G1,y)$$
$$T_{G2}: r(G2,x), r(G2,t)$$
$$T_{L1}: w(L1,t)\, r(L1,s)$$
$$T_{L2}: r(L2,y)\, w(L2,x)$$

Assume that a history is generated where T_{G1} has executed $w_{G1}(s)$ and T_{G2}

has executed $r_{G2}(x)$. Next, the two local transactions are executed. Finally, T_{G1} executes $w_{G1}(y)$ and T_{G2} executes $r_{G2}(t)$. This results in the following histories at site 1 and site 2:

$$\text{Site 1: } w(G1,s), w(L1,t), r(L1,s), r(G2,t)$$
$$\text{Site 2: } r(G2,x), r(L2,y), w(L2,x), w(G1,y)$$

The resulting local serialization graphs of each local site are both acyclic as shown in Figs 6 and 7. However, the resulting global serialization graph shown in Fig. 8 contains a cycle. Therefore, although there are no direct conflicts between global transactions, and each serialization graph at the local site is acyclic, a cycle is introduced in the global serialization graph due to the local operations. Since the GTM usually does not have any information regarding the transactions running at the local system, these types of indirect conflicts are very difficult to detect [8]. The reason that indirect conflicts do not occur in distributed database systems is that these solutions assume local sites are tightly coupled, homogeneous systems. Each site is also assumed to use the same concurrency control scheme along with the sharing of local control information, i.e. WFGs, serialization graphs, etc. It should also be noted that in the above example, if every site were to use a locking scheme for serialization, then a global deadlock would result.

5.1.2 Direct Conflict Example

The previous example illustrated the problem which arises with indirect conflicts from local transactions. It is possible for direct conflicts between global sub-transactions also to result in inconsistent data. The following

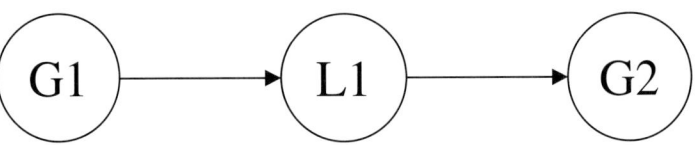

FIG. 6. Local conflict graph of site 1.

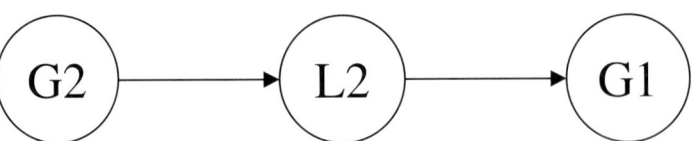

FIG. 7. Local conflict graph of local site 2.

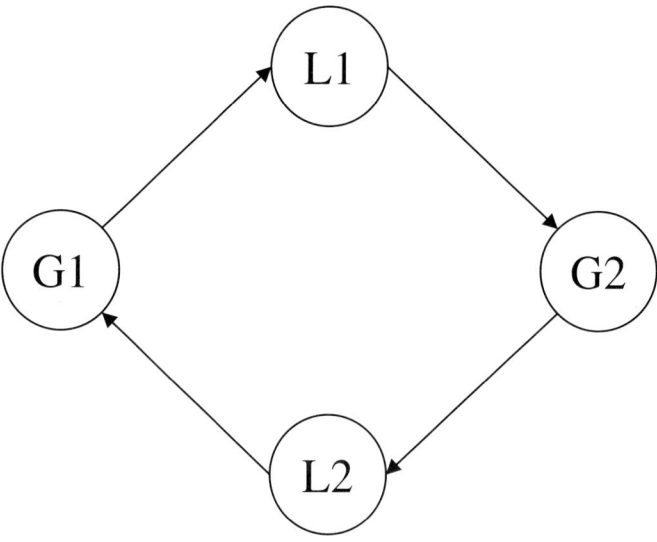

FIG. 8. Global conflict graph.

example of two global transactions illustrates this problem. Suppose we have two global transactions G1 and G2, operating at two sites. Site 1 contains the data item x, while site 2 contains data item y. The following operations represent the two transactions:

$$w(G1,x) \quad \text{and} \quad w(G2,x)$$
$$w(G1,y) \quad \text{and} \quad w(G2,y)$$

The following histories are generated at site 1 and site 2:

$$\text{Site 1: } w(G1,x) \quad \text{and} \quad w(G2,x)$$
$$\text{Site 2: } w(G2,y) \quad \text{and} \quad w(G1,y)$$

The local serialization graphs are acyclic for each local site as shown in Figs 9 and 10. Figure 11 shows that the global serialization graph contains a cycle. This cycle is due to a direct conflict between the two global transactions, G1 and G2.

FIG. 9. Local conflict graph of site 1.

FIG. 10. Local conflict graph of site 2.

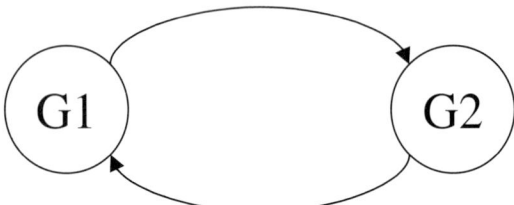

FIG. 11. Global conflict graph of a direct conflict.

5.2 MDBMS Serializability Solutions

An MDAS should maintain a globally serializable history for correct execution of concurrent transactions. This means that the global history should be conflict free while preserving as much local autonomy as possible. While the MDBMS is responsible for producing a globally serializable history, it is assumed that the local concurrency control system will produce a locally serializable history as well. It is important to note that the MDBMS needs to address both direct and indirect conflicts between global transactions. The remainder of this section describes several concurrency control algorithms that have been developed for an MDBMS.

5.2.1 Forced Conflicts under Full Autonomy

When a local site operates under full autonomy, there is no knowledge of the underlying concurrency control scheme used at the local DBMS. Furthermore, modifications to the local MDBMS to facilitate global concurrency control are not permitted under any conditions. This includes the use of the two-phase commit (2PC) or any other distributed commit protocol that requires a "prepared state."

The only known practical solution to multidatabase concurrency control that operates effectively under these stringent requirements is the forced conflict method [19]. Global serializability is achieved by forcing conflicts among global transactions through special data items called tickets. Global transactions at each site are required to read, increment, and subsequently write the new value of the ticket. The main disadvantage to this method is that the ticket operation may lead to numerous false aborts when using an aggressive policy, or lower concurrency when using a conservative policy [8].

5.2.2 Site Graph Algorithm

The site graph algorithm takes a conservative approach towards addressing MDBMS concurrency control [6]. This algorithm is somewhat similar to the lock-per-site algorithm [2]. The site graph algorithm maintains an undirected graph to execute concurrent transactions. Nodes in the graph represent transactions and sites that contain the data items accessed by a global transaction. The edges in the graph represent the sites spanned by a global transaction. For each global transaction, edges are added to the graph between the transaction and each site node in which the transaction participates. If a cycle in the site graph is detected, the transaction that caused the cycle is delayed until the graph becomes acyclic.

A transaction node and its associated edges can only be safely removed from the graph if the transaction aborts. Because conflicts may still occur after a transaction commits, a committed transaction node can only be safely removed from the graph if there are no paths to an uncommitted transaction [5]. This algorithm suffers from lower concurrency because a cycle in the graph does not necessarily imply an existing conflict, but it is used as a method to prevent possible conflicts.

5.2.3 Locking Schemes

When the local sites use locking schemes for concurrency control (i.e. most commercial systems), deadlocks resulting from either direct or indirect conflicts are the major challenge at the multidatabase level. A deadlocked global transaction could potentially block global as well as local transactions in *multiple sites* and, hence, will block resources and potentially reduce overall throughput at both global and local transaction levels.

It has been proven that if all local sites produce strict schedules and the transaction uses an atomic commit protocol then the resulting global schedule history is guaranteed to be serializable [7, 8]. It has been similarly shown that if all local sites produce at least recoverable schedules then it is sufficient to synchronize only the commit operations of the global transaction in order to ensure global serializability [6].

There are several multidatabase concurrency control schemes such as potential site graph locking [6], altruistic locking [8], site-graph method [6], ITM [54], and 2PC Agent [52] that use locking as the basis for concurrency control. When used in an environment where local sites produce strict histories, these algorithms result in serializable schedules by either preventing or detecting deadlocks arising between conflicts.

The information about the status of a local lock (pending or granted) of a data item is obtained from the acknowledgement of a transactional operation at the local site. Main disadvantages are that (1) there is no way to distinguish between direct conflicts and indirect conflicts, and (2) every operation that is sent to a local site, from a global coordinator, must be individually acknowledged.

As discussed before, a multidatabase transaction manager must process global transactions between loosely coupled, heterogeneous systems while preserving as much local autonomy as possible. Minimizing communication overhead in the system is also an important factor, particularly in a distributed environment consisting of mobile units and wireless communication. Furthermore, the cost of a multidatabase transaction processing is based upon parameters that are significantly different from the traditional distributed database systems and, hence, the tradeoffs between aggressive and conservative concurrency control schemes could be a determining factor. The proposed MDAS concurrency control algorithm, discussed in the next section, is intended to address these objectives.

5.3 Concurrency Control for an MDAS

The proposed v-locking algorithm uses a global locking scheme (GLS) in order to serialize conflicting operations of global transactions. Global locking tables are used to lock data items involved in a global transaction in accordance with the two-phase locking (2PL) rules. In typical multidatabase systems, maintaining a global locking table would require communication of information from the local site to the global transaction manager (GTM) regarding locked data items. This is impractical due to the delay and amount of communication overhead involved.

In the proposed algorithm, the MDAS is a collection of summary schema nodes and local databases distributed among local sites. A communication network as previously shown in Fig. 5 interconnects the SSM nodes and databases. The only difference in the MDAS model is that any communication link can be modeled as a wireless link. A transaction consists of a collection of read (r), write (w), commit (c), and abort (a) operations. The MDAS software is distributed in a hierarchical structure similar to the hierarchical structure of the SSM. Subsequently, transaction management is performed at the global level in a hierarchical, distributed manner.

The motivation behind using a hierarchical transaction management organization is due to the hierarchical structure of the SSM and the fact that such an organization offers higher performance and reliability [11, 31]. A global transaction is submitted at any node in the hierarchy—either at a local node or at a summary schema node. The transaction is resolved and mapped into sub-transactions by the SSM structure [11]. The resolution of the transaction also includes the determination of a coordinating node within the structure of the SSM—the coordinating node being the lowest summary schema node that semantically contains the information space manipulated by the global transaction. The concurrency control algorithm is based upon the following assumptions:

(1) There is no distinction between local and global transactions at the local level.
(2) A local site is completely isolated from other local sites.
(3) Each local system ensures local serializability and freedom from local deadlocks.
(4) A local database may abort any transaction at any time within the constraints of a distributed atomic commit protocol. The most widely supported distributed atomic commit protocol in commercial systems is the two-phase commit (2PC), and therefore our algorithm relies on the constraints of the 2PC. A distributed atomic commit protocol usually means that the local system will have to give up a certain degree of autonomy. In the case of the 2PC, once the "Yes" vote is given in response to a "Prepare to Commit" message, the local system may not subsequently abort any operation involved with the vote.
(5) Information pertaining to the type of concurrency control used at the local site will be available. In order for systems to provide robust concurrency and consistency, in most systems a *strict* history is produced through the use of a strict 2PL scheme. Therefore, the majority of local sites will use a strict 2PL scheme for local concurrency control.

As a result, the MDAS coordinates the execution of global transactions without the knowledge of any control information from any local DBMS. The only information (loss of local autonomy) required by the algorithm is the type of concurrency control performed at the local sites, i.e. locking, time stamp, unknown, etc.

5.3.1 Algorithm

The semantic information contained in the summary schemas is used to maintain global locking tables. Since each summary schema node contains the semantic contents of its children schemas, the "data" item being locked is reflected exactly or as a hypernym term in the summary schema of the

GTM. The locking tables can be used in an aggressive manner where the information is used only to detect potential global deadlocks. A more conservative approach can be used where the operations in a transaction are actually delayed at the GTM until a global lock request is granted. In either case, the global locking table is used to create a global wait-for-graph, which is subsequently used to detect and resolve potential global deadlocks. Higher reliability at the expense of lower throughput is the direct consequence of the application of semantic contents rather than an exact contents for an aggressive approach.

The accuracy of the "waiting information" contained in the graph is dependent upon the amount of communication overhead that is required. The proposed algorithm can dynamically adjust the frequency of the communications (acknowledgement signals) between the GTM and local sites, based on the network traffic and/or a threshold value. The number of acknowledgements that are performed varies from one per operation to only a single acknowledgement of the final commit/abort of the transaction. Naturally, the decrease in communication between the local and global systems comes at the expense of an increase in the number of potential false aborts. This effect is illustrated in Fig. 12. The extent of this incorrect detection of deadlocks is studied in the simulation.

The pseudo-code for the global locking algorithm is given in Figs 13 and 14. Figure 13 describes how the wait-for-graph is constructed based upon the available communication. Three cases are considered: (1) each operation in the transaction is individually acknowledged, (2) write operations are only acknowledged, and (3) only the commit or abort of the transaction is acknowledged. For the first case, based upon the semantic contents of the summary schema node, an edge inserted into the wait-for-graph is marked as being an exact or imprecise data item. For each acknowledgement signal received, the corresponding edge in the graph is marked as exact. In the second case, where each write operation generates an acknowledgement signal, for each signal only the edges preceding the last known acknowledgement are marked as being exact. Other edges that have been submitted but that have not been acknowledged are marked as pending. As in the pre-

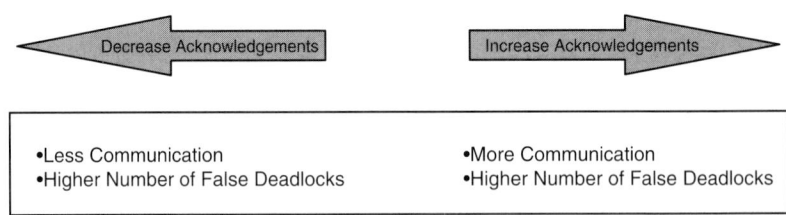

FIG. 12. Frequency of acknowledgements.

```
Repeat
Case 1, 2, and 3 are chosen based upon the available bandwidth:
Case 1: Acknowledge each operation
    Repeat until commit or abort
        For each operation in a global sub-transaction
            If the lock for the data item is free
                Acquire lock and add the entry into the lock table
                Mark as exact or imprecise
            Else
                Queue the data item into the locking table
                Enter edge into wait-for-graph and mark as acknowledged, exact or imprecise
                Wait for free lock
            Wait for acknowledgement
            Mark the acknowledgement
    End repeat
Case 2: Acknowledge write operations only
    Repeat until commit or abort
        Repeat until write
            For each operation in a global sub-transaction
                If the lock for the data item is free
                    Acquire lock and add the entry into the lock table
                    Mark as exact or imprecise
                Else
                    Queue the data item into the locking table
                    Enter pending edge into wait-for-graph
                    Mark as precise or imprecise
                    Wait for free lock
                Wait for acknowledgement of write
                Mark current and all proceeding read operations as acknowledged
        End repeat for write
    End repeat
Case 3: Acknowledge commit or abort only
    For each operation in a global sub-transaction
        If the lock for the data item is free
            Acquire lock and add the entry into the lock table
            Mark as exact or imprecise
        Else
            Queue the data item into the locking table
            Enter pending edge into wait-for-graph
            Mark as precise or imprecise
            Wait for free lock
    Wait for commit or abort
    Mark operations as acknowledged
```

FIG. 13. Global locking algorithm—insertion of edges.

vious two cases, in the third case, the edges are marked as representing exact or imprecise data. However, all edges are marked as pending until the commit or abort signal is received. Keeping the information about the data and status of the acknowledgement signals enables us to detect cycles in the wait-for-graph.

```
Repeat every chktime threshold
    Check for cycles /* depth first search (DFS) is used for cycle detection */
    For each cycle detected
        If all involved in cycle are exact data items AND acknowledged
            Choose victim and break deadlock /* victim is chosen based upon "progress" */
        /* else if the time threshold for imprecise data is reached */
        ElseIf time_elapsed > imprecise_data_time for all transactions in cycle AND
            All are acknowledged
                Choose victim and break deadlock
        /* if the ack passes a time threshold */
        Else time_elapsed > acktime for all non acknowledged transactions in cycle
                Choose victim and break deadlock
End repeat
```

FIG. 14. Global locking algorithm—detection of cycles.

Figure 14 shows how to detect cycles in the wait-for-graph based on the depth first search (DFS) policy [13]. The graph is checked for cycles after a time threshold for each transaction. For all of the transactions involved in a cycle, if the exact data items are known and all of the acknowledgements have been received, then a deadlock is precisely detected and broken. When imprecise data items are present within a cycle, the algorithm will consider the cycle a deadlock only after a longer time threshold has passed. Similarly, a pending acknowledgement of a transaction is only used to break a deadlock in a cycle after an even longer time threshold has passed. The time thresholds can be selected and adjusted dynamically to prevent as many false deadlocks as possible.

A potential deadlock situation may also occur due to the presence of indirect conflicts. By adding site information to the global locking tables, an implied wait-for-graph could be constructed using a technique similar to the potential conflict graph algorithm [9]. A potential wait-for-graph is a directed graph with transactions as nodes. The edges are inserted between two transactions for each site where there are both active and waiting transactions. The edges are then removed when a transaction aborts or commits. A cycle in the graph indicates the possibility that a deadlock has occurred.

The term "active" simply means that the transaction has begun execution at a site and is either actively processing, or waiting for a blocked resource. For the transactions that are waiting, it is much more difficult to determine exactly which resource is not available. In particular, indirect conflicts, where global transactions are waiting for some local transaction, are not exactly detected. Since the status of the locks at the local sites is not known, there is no way to accurately determine this information without severely violating the autonomy of the local DBMS. Therefore, the potential wait-for-graph is used to detect potential deadlocks. The actual deadlocks in the system are a subset of the deadlocks that are contained in the implied wait-for-graph. Thus, as is the case when detecting deadlocks using global locking, there is also the potential for false deadlock detection. To decrease the number of false deadlocks, the potential wait-for-graph is used in conjunction with a waiting period threshold. The waiting period threshold is longer than the maximum time threshold used in the global locking tables. This allows the global locking algorithm to "clear" as many deadlocks as possible, and hence reduces the possibility of detecting false cycles in the potential wait-for-graph. The pseudo-code for the extended algorithm is given in Fig. 15.

5.3.1.1 Handling Unknown Local Data Sources
Finally, the issue of handling the local "black box" site in which nothing is known about the local concurrency control scheme is addressed. This algorithm is extended to handle this case. Since nearly every commercial database system uses some form of 2PL, this case will only comprise a small percentage of local systems. Therefore, for this special case, the algorithm merely executes global transactions at that site in a serial order. This is done by requiring any transaction involving the "black box" to first obtain a site lock before executing any operations in the transaction. These types of locks will be managed by escalating any lock request to these sites to the highest level (site lock).

This section has examined some additional concurrency control issues in an MDAS environment. A new hierarchical concurrency control scheme was introduced and discussed. The scheme uses global locking scheme in order to serialize conflicting operations of global transactions. The semantic information in the summary schemas is used to maintain the global locking tables, and reduce the communication required by the GTM in order to serialize the global transactions.

```
Repeat every chktime threshold
        Check for cycles in implied wait-for-graph /* depth first search (DFS) used for cycle
            detection */
        For each cycle detected
            If time_elapsed > pcg_time for all transactions in cycle
                /* victim is chosen based upon "progress" */
                Choose victim and break deadlock
            Else
                Continue to wait
End repeat
```

FIG. 15. Global deadlock detection—potential graph algorithm.

6. Evaluation of Proposed Algorithm

The simulation models an MDAS environment and tests various aspects of the algorithms—v-locking and p-caching. Through the simulation, the proposed schemes are validated and the results are analyzed and discussed.

6.1 V-Locking Concurrency Control Scheme

6.1.1 Simulation

The performance of the proposed algorithm is evaluated through a simulator written in C++ using CSIM. The simulator for the v-locking algorithm measures performance in terms of global transaction throughput, response time, and CPU, disk I/O, and network utilization. In addition, the simulator was extended to compare and contrast the behavior of our algorithm against the site-graph, potential conflict graph, and the forced conflict algorithms.

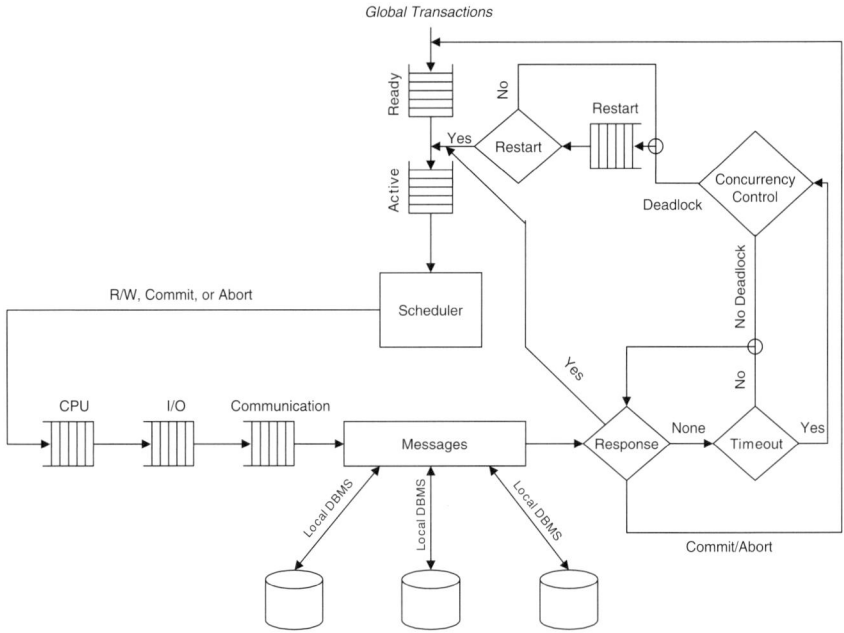

FIG. 16. Transaction flow at the global level.

The MDAS consists of both local and global components. The local component comprises local DBMS systems, each performing local transactions outside the control of the MDAS. The global component consists of the hierarchical global structure, performing global transactions executing under the control of the MDAS. Figure 16 depicts the global structure, whereas Fig. 17 shows the flow of operations in the local components.

There are a fixed number of active global transactions present in the system at any given time. An active transaction is defined as being in the active, CPU, I/O, communication, or restart queue. A global transaction is first generated, and subsequently enters the active queue. The global scheduler acquires the necessary global virtual locks, and processes the operation. The operation(s) then uses the CPU and I/O resources, and communicates the operation(s) to the local system based upon the available bandwidth. When acknowledgements or commit/abort signals are received from the local site, the algorithm determines if the transaction should proceed, commit, or abort. If a global commit is possible, then a new global transaction is generated and placed in the ready queue. However, if a deadlock is

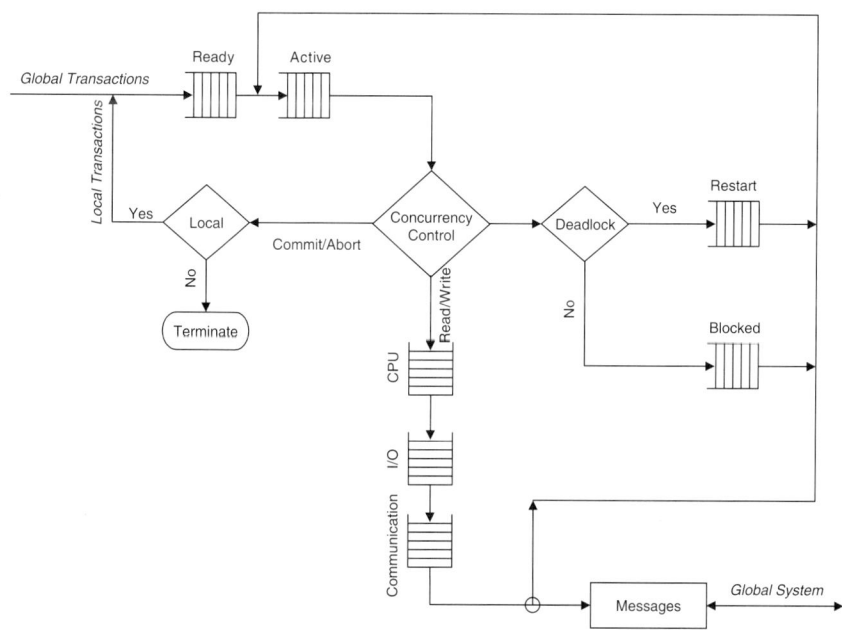

FIG. 17. Local transaction.

detected, or an abort message is received from a local site, then the transaction is aborted at all sites and the global transaction is placed in the restart queue. After a specified time has elapsed, the aborted transaction is again placed on the active queue.

At the local sites, there are a fixed number of active local transactions. The active transactions consist of both local transactions and global sub-transactions. The local system does not differentiate between the two types. An active transaction is defined as being in the active, CPU, I/O, communication, blocked, or restart queue. Transactions enter the active queue and are subsequently scheduled by acquiring the necessary lock on a data item. If the lock is granted, the operation proceeds through the CPU and I/O queue and, for global sub-transactions, is communicated back to the GLS. The acknowledgement for these transactions is communicated back based upon the available communication bandwidth. If a lock is not granted, the system checks for deadlocks and will either place the transaction in the blocked queue, or the restart queue. For local transactions, it goes into the restart queue if it is aborted, and subsequently it will be restarted later. Upon a commit, a new local transaction is generated and placed in the ready queue. For global sub-transactions, an abort or commit signal is communicated back to the GLS and sub-transaction terminates.

6.1.2 System parameters

The underlying global information sharing process is composed of 10 local sites. The size of the local databases at each site can be varied, and has a direct effect on the overall performance of the system. The simulation is run for 5000 time units, and the average of 10 runs is taken for the values presented. The global workload consists of randomly generated global queries, spanning over a random number of sites. Each operation of a sub-transaction (read, write, commit, or abort) may require data and/or acknowledgements to be sent from the local DBMS. The frequency of messages depends upon the quality of the network link. In order to determine the effectiveness of the proposed algorithm, several parameters are varied for different simulation runs. These parameters for the global system are given in Table VII, along with their default values.

The local systems perform two different types of transactions, local and global. Global sub-transactions are submitted to the local DBMS and appear as a local transaction. Local transactions are generated at the local sites and consist of a random number of read/write operations. The only difference between the two transactions is that a global sub-transaction will communicate with the global system, whereas the local transaction terminates upon a commit or abort. The number of local transactions, which can be varied,

TABLE VII
GLOBAL PARAMETERS

Global system parameters	Default value
The number of local sites in the system	10
The number of data items per local site	100
The maximum number of global transactions in the system. This number represents the global multiprogramming level	10
The maximum number of operations that a global transaction contains	8
The minimum number of operations that a global transaction contains	1
The service time for the CPU queue	0.005 sec
The service time for the I/O queue	0.010 sec
The service time for each communicated message to the local site	0.100 sec
The number of messages per operation (read/write)	2

affects the performance of the global system. In addition, the local system may abort a transaction, global or local, at any time. If a global sub-transaction is aborted locally, it is communicated to the global system and the global transaction is aborted at all sites. The various parameters for the local system are given in Table VIII along with their default values. Both the global and local systems are modeled similar to models used in [1, 9].

6.1.3 Performance Results

The performance of the algorithm (V-Lock) is evaluated relative to the number of completed global transactions, the average response time, as well as the communication utilization at each local site. In addition, the simulator compares and contrasts the proposed algorithm against the potential conflict graph method [7], site-graph method [2], and the forced conflict

TABLE VIII
LOCAL PARAMETERS

Local system parameters	Default value
The maximum number of local transactions per site. This number represents the local multiprogramming level	10
The maximum number of write operations per transaction	8
The maximum number of read operations per transaction	8
The minimum number of write operations per transaction	1
The minimum number of read operations per transaction	1
The service time for the local CPU queue	0.005 sec
The service time for the local I/O queue	0.010 sec
The service time for each communicated message to the MDAS	0.100 sec
The number of messages per operation (read/write)	2

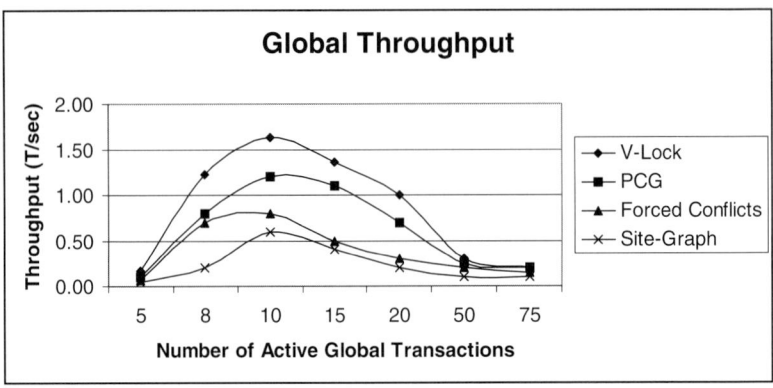

FIG. 18. Comparison of different concurrency control algorithms.

method [19]. Figure 18 shows the results. As can be concluded, the V-Lock algorithm has the highest throughput. This result is consistent with the fact that the V-Lock algorithm is better able to detect global conflicts and thus achieves higher concurrency than the other algorithms. As can be seen, the maximum occurs at a multi-programming level approximately equal to ten. As expected, as the number of concurrent global transactions increases, the number of completed global transactions decreases due to the increase in the number of conflicts.

Figure 19 shows the relationship between the global throughput and the number of sites in the MDAS. The number of sites was varied from 10 sites to 40 sites. The throughput decreases as the number of sites is increased. By fragmenting the data across more sites, the probability of a global transac-

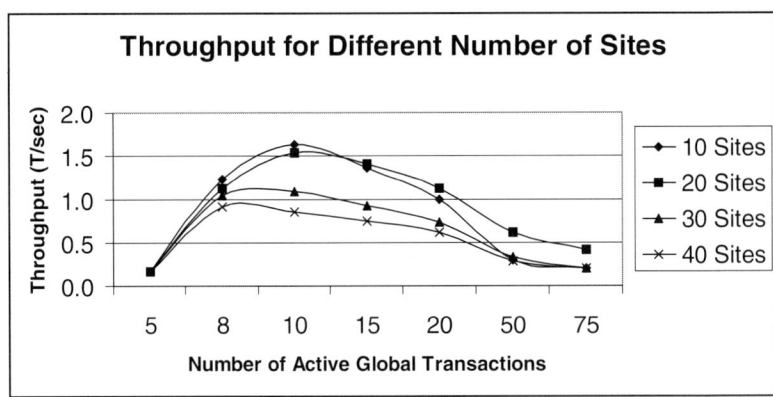

FIG. 19. Global throughput varying the number of local sites.

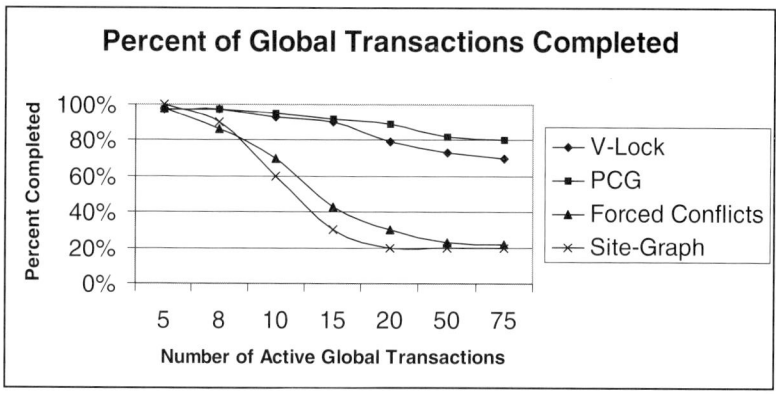

FIG. 20. Comparison of the percent of completed global transactions.

tion spanning over more sites also increases. This increases the likelihood of a conflict occurring and consequently, the lower throughput.

The simulator also measured the percentage of completed transactions during a certain period of time for the V-Lock, PCG, forced conflict, and site-graph schemes. Figure 20 shows the results. In general, for all schemes, the number of completed transactions decreases as the number of concurrent transactions increases, due to more conflicts among the transactions. However, the performance of both the forced conflict and site-graph algorithms decreases at a faster rate. This is due to the increase in the number of false aborts detected by these algorithms. On separate simulation runs, the simulator measured, compared, and contrasted the response time for various schemes. Figure 21 shows the results. The two locking algorithms have a

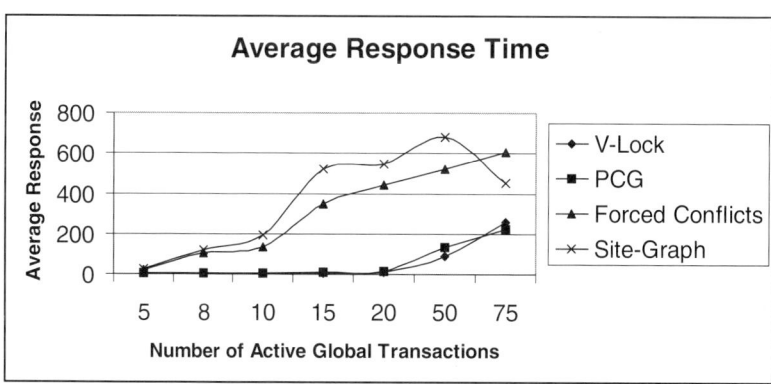

FIG. 21. Average response time.

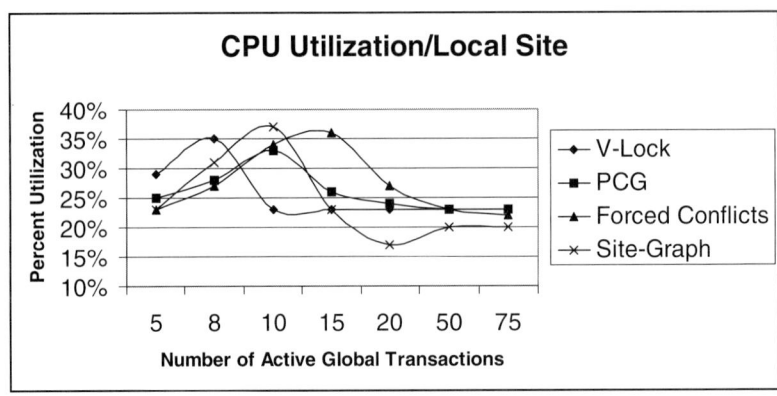

FIG. 22. CPU utilization for each local site.

much better response time than the forced-conflict and site-graph algorithms. The v-locking algorithm has the best response time, and performs better than PCG, particularly for a large number of users. As expected, as the number of concurrent users increases, the response time increases.

Finally, the resource utilization (communication, I/O, and CPU) is compared and contrasted. Figures 22, 23, and 24 show the results. From Fig. 22 it can be concluded that each scheme utilizes approximately 20–25% of the CPU time. Disk utilization generally follows the throughput of the system, with a range of 40–60% utilization under high concurrency (Fig. 23). Finally, the communication utilization is near 100% at peak throughput, and decreases slightly as the number of concurrent transactions increases

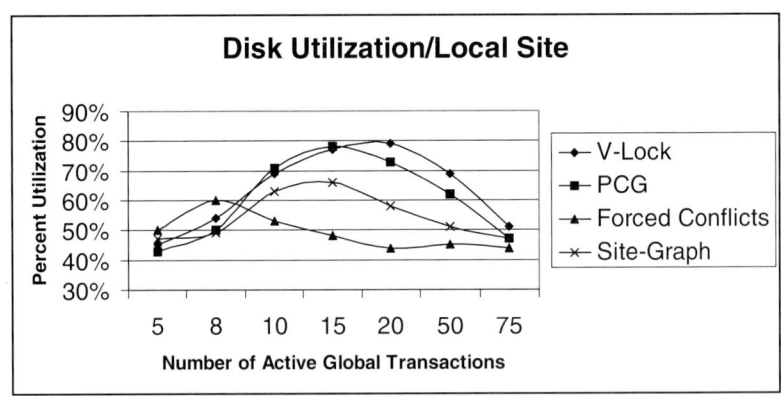

FIG. 23. Disk utilization for each local site.

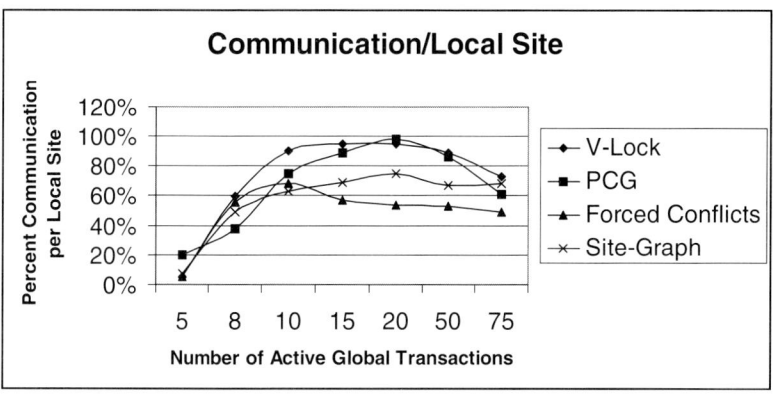

FIG. 24. Communication utilization for each local site.

(Fig. 24). It is easy to determine from this graph that the communication requirements for the v-locking algorithm represent the bottleneck of the system.

7. Conclusions and Future Directions

7.1 Conclusion

The requirements of an "anytime, anywhere" computing environment motivate new concepts that effectively allow a user to access information in a timely and reliable manner. An overview of the characteristics of a new computing environment—the MDAS—and the requirements and issues of this environment were introduced and discussed. With advances in technology, it is now possible to access globally shared data through wireless connections via a diverse number of access devices. These devices differ in computing, energy, display, and network requirements.

By superimposing a wireless-mobile computing environment on a multidatabase system, many of the objectives involved in accessing heterogeneous data sources through a wireless medium are addressed. This new class of computing environment is called an MDAS. Furthermore, the similarities and differences in the characteristics of both a mobile environment and a multidatabase system were individually discussed. The characteristics, issues, and subsequent solutions to an MDAS were discussed. Many of the issues in an MDAS can be addressed through work previously done by mobile system and multidatabase system researchers.

In an MDAS, a potentially large number of users may simultaneously access a rapidly increasing amount of aggregate, distributed data. In such an environment, a concurrency control algorithm must address important issues in the face of increased throughput and the limitations imposed by technology. A multidatabase transaction manager must process global transactions between loosely coupled, heterogeneous systems, while preserving as much local autonomy as possible as well as minimizing communication overhead in the system.

A new, distributed, hierarchically organized concurrency control algorithm has been presented and evaluated in this chapter. The advantage of this algorithm is that the global performance of the system is increased by dynamically adjusting the amount of communication required to detect and resolve conflicts. A simulator was developed in C++ using CSIM in order to evaluate the performance. The results verify that communication between the local and global systems is the bottleneck and thus the limiting factor in throughput and response time of the global system. Furthermore, it was shown how the proposed algorithm is used to decrease the communication requirements, resulting in higher global performance.

7.2 Future Directions

Although the results we have demonstrated are very promising, the work presented in this chapter can be extended in several ways:

- The impact of the Internet on data management is growing at a tremendous pace. Considerations of how this data (both structured and unstructured) can and should be integrated into MDAS systems is important.
- Support is needed to overcome disconnection and weak connection. Lower bandwidth and disconnection are common in an MDAS environment; local caches, prefetching, queueing, and data broadcasting have been suggested as ways of alleviating these restrictions. However, due to the local autonomy restrictions in the MDAS environment, a better method/protocol should be investigated to address this issue.
- The effect of changing the ratio of global to local transactions active in the system should be investigated. This is particularly important for systems that have a very high global transaction requirement. If the global sub-transactions were allowed to dominate the local systems, the overall global throughput would increase, while the throughput of local systems may decrease. It should be determine if an optimal ratio or even a range of the ratio can be found.
- As the architecture of the system is hierarchical, there may be several global coordinators active at any time. The current algorithm assumes that any conflicts between these coordinators are not communicated

directly between the coordinators, but that they manifest themselves in the form of an indirect conflict. If the coordinators were allowed to communicate information, would there be a significant impact on the global performance?
- The effect of various parameters upon the number of completed/aborted transactions is being investigated. An extensive study on the effects of changing the number of sites, distribution of data, processing, I/O, and communication is needed. Also, the impact of non-uniform communication requirements between the client and server as well as between servers should be investigated.

Appendix: Related Projects

There are several ongoing and completed projects which address the issues involved with mobile computing. Tables IX and X summarize the different mobile projects. These include various research/experimental projects along with a brief summary of their characteristics.

7.3 Mobile-Transparent Projects

Mobile-transparent systems include the Coda project [21, 34, 35], the Ficus project [40], the Little Work project [22], and the BNU project [50], which are summarized in Table IX. These projects all offer file system support for mobile clients.

7.3.1 Coda

Coda, developed at Carnegie Mellon University (CMU) as a descendant of the Andrew File System (AFS) [34], pioneered many of the distributed services for mobile clients. In particular, a cache and an operation log provides support for weak connectivity and disconnect operations [35]. Coda logs all transactions during periods of disconnection and replays the log upon reconnection. The cache manager, called *Venus*, is present in each client, and operates in one of three states: (1) hoarding, (2) emulating, and (3) reintegrating. The hoarding state is the "normal" state while connected to the server. The primary function of this state is to ensure that frequently used objects are cached during a connection [34]. When a disconnection occurs, the cache manager enters the emulating state and services all file system requests from the cache contents. If a cache miss occurs, it appears as a failure to the user. Upon reconnection, Venus resynchronizes the cache

TABLE IX
SUMMARY OF MOBILE-TRANSPARENT SYSTEMS

Project name	Location	Status	Brief summary of features	Cache/prefetching
BNU [50]	University of Washington	Research/ Experimental	RCP based proxy system providing access to data.	No/No
CODA [21, 34, 45]	Carnegie Mellon University	Experimental	Distributed file system that pioneered support for weak connectivity and the disconnect operation through the use of a cache, operation log, and rapid cache validation.	Yes/Yes
Ficus [40]	UCLA	Experimental	Distributed file system using replication and an optimistic concurrency control policy.	No/No
Little Work [22]	U. Michigan, Ann Arbor	Experimental	Cache based distributed file system.	Yes/Yes

HETEROGENEOUS DATA ACCESS IN A MOBILE ENVIRONMENT   169

TABLE X
SUMMARY OF MOBILE-AWARE SYSTEMS

Project name	Location	Status	Brief summary of features	Cache/Prefetching
Bayou [15]	Xerox PARC	Research/ Experimental	Data-sharing application using replication. Supports session guarantees and user selectable placement use of data.	Yes/Yes
Daedalus [47]	U.C. Berkeley	Research/ Experimental	Proxy-based system which distils data, transmitting only enough information which can be sent over a low bandwidth link.	No/No
GloMop [28]	U.C. Berkeley	Research/ Experimental	Closely related to the Daedalus project, this system primary focus is the connection between the proxy and the client.	No/No
InfoPad [17, 28, 36]	U.C. Berkeley	Research/ Experimental	Portable dumb-terminal capable of displaying text, video and graphics. All functionality is provided by computing nodes on a fixed network.	No/No
Rover [23, 24, 25]	M.I.T.	Research/ Experimental	RCP based toolkit which supports relocatable dynamic objects and queued remote procedure calls.	Yes/Yes
Wit [51]	University of Washington	Research/ Experimental	API based object-oriented proxy system.	Yes/Yes

with servers in the reintegrating state and returns to the hoarding state upon completion.

The use of volume validation (called rapid cache validation) and asynchronous data synchronization techniques are used to deal with weak connections. The resynchronization of the cache with weak connectivity may take a substantial amount of time. Rapid cache validation involves the use of version stamps for each volume and individual object on a server, which are incremented when objects are updated. Clients then store and use this information when reintegrating the cache. If volume stamp is still valid, then every object in the volume is valid, and the reintegration is complete. When a volume stamp is determined to be invalid, each object is validated individually. Finally, updates to the server are asynchronously propagated to the server in the background. Records must spend a minimal amount of time (called an aging window) in the operational log before reintegration is performed.

7.3.2 Ficus

Ficus is a research project at the University of California, Los Angeles (UCLA), which is a distributed file system that uses replication and optimistic concurrency control [40]. The system allows any replica of a file to be updated at any time, allowing for a very high degree of availability. Furthermore, replication of data to the local site is used to support disconnection. The tradeoff, however, is that conflicts result from this policy. Conflicts include: update/update conflicts, name conflicts, and remove/update conflicts. Ficus guarantees that conflicting updates are detected by using a version vector [40]. Each file replica has its own version vector, which keeps track of the history of updates to a file. Version vectors are compared in order to detect conflicts. When conflicts are detected, the file is marked as "in conflict," and normal operations to the file are suspended until the conflict is resolved. In some environments, up to two-thirds of the conflicts could be resolved automatically by Ficus without user intervention [40].

7.3.3 Little Work

Whereas the Ficus project uses replication to support the disconnect operation, the Little Work project is a file-based system which uses a cache [22]. The project is an experimental system from the University of Michigan, Ann Arbor. The cache manager services all requests whether connected or disconnected. While disconnected, if an operation requires the server, the cache manager logs the request. An optimistic control algorithm is used to detect conflicts. Upon reconnection, if no conflicts are detected, then a reconnect manager submits the operation to the server. If a conflict is detected, the user is notified. The Little Work project is similar to Coda, except that Little Work does not modify the servers in any way.

7.3.4 BNU

The BNU project uses proxy processes running on a fixed network which provide access to data in order to address mobility issues of handheld and limited capability processing devices [50]. The proxy processes run on workstations in the LAN. A remote procedure call (RPC) system provides the communication between a mobile system and the proxies. The proxies provide the transparency between the mobile system and application. A single RPC call can perform multiple operations, thus requiring less bandwidth. Furthermore, by using RPCs, the ability to load certain routines and data on the small device can be used to mask a disconnection. Non-blocking RPCs are queued by the proxy and immediately acknowledged, reducing latency and allowing for the delivery of the RPC to occur in parallel with application processing. Furthermore, queuing allows for multiple RPCs to the proxy to be unified into a single, equivalent RPC to the hand-held device.

7.4 Mobile-Aware Projects

Mobile-aware projects include the Rover project [23, 24, 25], Bayou project [15], the Wit project [51], the InfoPad [17, 28, 36] and the Daedalus/GloMop [28, 47]. These projects are summarized in Table X.

7.4.1 Rover Toolkit

The Rover project is a toolkit from the Massachusetts Institute of Technology (MIT) that supports relocatable dynamic objects and queued remote procedure calls (QRPC) [23]. The applications developed with this toolkit are object-based distributed client/server architecture. This system supports the development of mobile-aware as well as mobile-transparent applications.

A relocatable dynamic object is a well-defined object and interface that can be dynamically loaded to clients or servers. All application code and data are written as RDOs, and each RDO has a "home" server which maintains the primary copy. RDOs can be replicated and stored/prefetched in a client cache in order to improve bandwidth tolerance and provide a means to work during a disconnection. Furthermore, the relocatability of an RDO gives an application control over the location for computation, and is particularly useful for exporting computation to servers or for distilling data. RDOs can also use compression and decompression in order to reduce network and storage utilization.

A QRPC is a non-blocking RPC that allows operations to be performed while the client is either connected or disconnected. Clients fetch RDOs from servers with QRPCs. Subsequently, the QRPC is stored in a local stable log. While the client is connected to the network, the Rover scheduler forwards any QRPCs present in the log to the server. Cached copies of an RDO are lazily propagated to the server when there is sufficient bandwidth. QRPCs use split-phase communication, where the request and response pair of the communication is split. This allows the client to use separate channels for transmitting and receiving data, allowing the most efficient, available channel to be used while allowing a client to power down while waiting for a pending operation.

The Rover toolkit was used to implement both mobile-aware and mobile-transparent applications. Experimental results showed that for mobile-transparent applications improvements of up to 17%, while performance improvements for mobile-aware applications were shown to be up to 750%.

7.4.2 Wit

The Wit project is based upon the BNU project and is implemented in the form of an application-programming interface (API). The Wit designers define application partitioning as the assignment of functionality to both mobile and stationary devices through partitioning data and functions into hyperobjects. Hyperobjects are linked hierarchical objects, which are managed by the system and are migrated or replicated across the wireless connection. Links are directional and represent some type of relationship between hyperobjects. Data semantics (in the form of hyperobjects and links) and observation of access patterns are used in order to make informed policy decisions about resource allocation and usage [51].

Caching attributes of an object are specified by the application. Normally, an object is replicated on the mobile device, and the cache consistency is maintained by explicit synchronization. Prefetching is also performed based upon access patterns and the semantics contained in the hyperobject links. Finally, a form of data distillation is performed on the retrieved data in order to reduce the overall data which must be transferred. The system has only been proposed and has not been implemented.

7.4.3 Bayou

The Bayou project is from Xerox PARC and is designed to support data sharing among mobile users [15]. The design is a flexible client-server architecture. The architecture is designed such that "lightweight" servers will reside on portable machines. Similar to the Ficus project, the Bayou project uses replication to provide a high degree of availability of data, even while disconnected, to users. The policy used is a read-any/write-any replication scheme, where the user is able to read/write to any copy of the replicated data, and the data is only weakly consistent. Consistency is maintained by using a peer-to-peer anti-entropy policy for propagation of updates [15]. Anti-entropy ensures that all copies of the data are all converging towards the same state, where each server receives all write operations performed and correctly order the operations. And similar to Ficus, Bayou guarantees that conflicting updates are detected by using a version vector [15].

The system provides a client with a view of the replicated data, which is consistent with its own actions, through session guarantees. A session is an abstraction for the sequences of read and write operations performed on the data. Four types of guarantees are provided on a per-session basis to the user [15]:

- Read Your Writes—read operations reflect previous writes;
- Monotonic Reads—successive reads reflect a non-decreasing set of writes;
- Writes Follow Reads—writes are propagated after reads upon which they depend;
- Monotonic Writes—writes are propagated after writes that logically precede them.

7.4.4 Odyssey

Odyssey is a follow-up project to Coda that adds application-aware adaptation to the system. This system provides a fixed number of representations of data objects on a server, allowing for end-to-end bandwidth management. An API is provided for a client to track its current "environment" and negotiate for a representation that is appropriate for the current connectivity. It uses the concept of data fidelity, resource negotiation, and dynamic sets in order to effectively use and control system resources [45].

7.4.5 Daedalus/GloMop/Infopad

The Daedalus/GloMop project is a mobile computing project from the University of California, Berkeley. It runs processes on well-connected workstations that act as a proxy for a mobile client that is on the other side of a low-bandwidth connection. The proxy then distills and/or refines the data, transmitting only enough information to the client in a format that can be transmitted over the low-bandwidth link. The idea is to trade processing cycles for bandwidth. Datatype-specific distillation is a highly lossy, datatype-specific compression that preserves most of the semantic content of a data object while adhering to a particular set of constraints [47]. Three datatypes were mainly investigated: images, formatted text, and video streams. Datatype-specific refinement is the process of fetching some part of a source object at increased quality. The distillation and refinement occur on-demand in order to provide the best possible results to applications in a changing mobile environment.

The InfoPad [17, 28, 36] project uses a portable dumb-terminal, which is able to display text, video, and graphics. Computing nodes on a fixed network provide all of the functionality; the terminal (Pad) only displays the information. The Pad differs from other access devices in that it does not contain a general purpose processor. Applications and user-interfaces are currently under development, which use only pen and audio as inputs, allowing them to operate without a keyboard.

Glossary

ACID: (Atomicity, Consistency, Isolation, Durability). Four properties used to define the correctness of a transaction.

ATM: (Asynchronous transfer mode). A 53-byte, fixed communication protocol commonly used in high-speed networks.

Autonomy: Autonomy refers to the ability of a system to operate independently, without the help or resources of another system. There are three different forms of autonomy: design, communication, and execution.

Data distillation: Data distillation is a process where incoming data is processed such that only portions of the data are displayed. Data distillation may be performed in order to accommodate display restrictions, or to reduce bandwidth requirements of a system.

DBMS: (Database management system). An information storage and retrieval system.

HRAD: (Heterogeneous remote access to data).

ISP: (Internet service provider). An ISP provides internet access to a user. Typically the service is available though a modem connection.

LAN: (Local area network). A group of computers connected together which share resources.

Long-lived transaction: A transaction which is in an open or non-committed state for a long duration of time. These types transactions may last from several hours to days, and even weeks.

MDAS: (Mobile data access system). A term used to describe a new computational environment in which a wireless mobile computing environment is superimposed on a multidatabase environment providing efficient access heterogeneous data sources.

MDBMS: (Multidatabase management system). A global system layer that allows distributed access to multiple preexisting databases.

Mobile awareness: A system or application is alert to changes in the condition of its environment, and is able to adapt to those changes.

Mobility: The ability to physically move a computing device and use it in a different location or while actually moving.

NC: (Network computer). A low cost, low maintenance computer system connected to a network. These systems are usually diskless and rely heavily upon a server.

PDA: (Personal digital assistant). A hand held computing device.

Remote access: A fixed or mobile node that accesses data over a network connection characterized by lower bandwidth, frequent disconnection, and higher error rates.

SSM: (Summary schemas model). An adjunct to a multidatabase system used for query resolution.

REFERENCES

[1] Agrawal, R., Carey, M., and Livny, M. (1985). Models for studying concurrency control performance: alternatives and implications. *Proceedings of the ACM SIGMOD International Conference on Management of Data.*
[2] Alonso, R., Garcia-Molina, H., and Salem, K. (1987). Concurrency control and recovery for global procedures in federated database systems. *Data Engineering*, **10**(3), 5–11.
[3] Badrinath, B. R. (1996). Designing distributed algorithms for mobile computing networks. *Computer Communications*, **19**(4).
[4] Baker, M. G. (1994). Changing communication environments in MosquitoNet. *Proceedings of the 1994 IEEE Workshop on Mobile Computing Systems and Applications*, December.
[5] Bernstein, P., Hadzilacos, V., and Goodman, N. (1987). *Concurrency Control and Recovery in Database Systems*, Addison-Wesley Publishing Company.
[6] Breitbart, Y., Silberschatz, A., and Thompson, G. (1987). An update mechanism for multidatabase systems. *IEEE Data Engineering Bulletin*, **10**(3), 12–18.
[7] Breitbart, Y., Georgakopoulos, D., Rusinkiewicz, M., and Silberschatz, A. (1991). On rigorous transaction scheduling. *IEEE Transactions on Software Engineering*, **17**(9).
[8] Breitbart, Y., Garcia-Molina, H., and Silberschatz, A. (1992). Overview of multidatabase transaction management. *The VLDB Journal*, **1**(2), 181–239.
[9] Breitbart, Y., and Silberschatz, A. (1993). Performance evaluation of two multidatabase transaction management algorithms. *Computing Systems*, **6**(3).

[10] Bright, M., Hurson, A., and Pakzad, S. (1992). A taxonomy and current issues in multidatabase systems. *IEEE Computer*, **25**(3), 50–60.
[11] Bright, M. W., Hurson, A. R., and Pakzad, S. H. (1994). Automated resolution of semantic heterogeneity in multidatabases. *ACM Transactions on Database Systems*, **19**(2).
[12] Conover, J. (1997). Solutions for an ATM upgrade. *Network Computing*, 15 May.
[13] Cormen, T., Leiserson, C., and Rivest, R. (1990). *Introduction to Algorithms*, McGraw-Hill Book Company.
[14] Dash, K., Hurson, A., Phoha, S., and Chehadeh, C. (1994). Summary schemas model: a scheme for handling global information sharing. *Proceedings of the International Conference on Intelligent Information Management Systems*, pp. 47–51.
[15] Demers, A., Pertersen, K., Spreitzer, M., Terry, D., Theier, M., and Welch, B. (1994). The Bayou architecture: support for data sharing among mobile users. *IEEE Proceedings of the Workshop on Mobile Computing Systems and Applications*, December.
[16] Elmagarmid, A., Jing, J., and Furukawa, T. (1995). Wireless client/server computing for personal information services and applications. *ACM Sigmod Record*.
[17] Fox, A., Gribble, S. D., Brewer, E. A., and Amir, E. (1996). Adapting to network and client variability via on-demand dynamic distillation. *Proceedings of ASPLOS-VII*, Boston, MA, October.
[18] Garcia-Molina, H. (1988). Node autonomy in distributed systems. *IEEE Proceedings of the International Symposium on Databases and in Parallel and Distributed Systems*.
[19] Geogakopoulos, D., Rusinkiewicz, M., and Sheth, A. (1994). Using tickets to enforce the serializability of multidatabase transactions. *IEEE Transactions on Knowledge and Data Engineering*, **6**(1), 166–180, February.
[20] Gray, J., and Reuter, A. (1993). *Transaction Processing: Concepts and Techniques*, Morgan Kaufmann.
[21] Hills, A., and Johnson, D. B. (1996). Wireless data network infrastructure at Carnegie Mellon University. *IEEE Personal Communications*, **3**(1), February.
[22] Honeyman, P., Huston, L., Rees, J., and Bachmann, D. (1992). The LITTLE WORK Project. *Proceedings of the Third IEEE Workshop on Workstation Operating Systems*, April.
[23] Joseph, A. D., Tauber, J. A., and Kaashoek, M. F. (1997). Mobile computing with the Rover toolkit. *IEEE Transactions on Computers: Special Issue on Mobile Computing*, February.
[24] Joseph, A. D., and Kaashoek, M. F. (1996). Building reliable mobile-aware applications using the Rover toolkit. *Proceedings of the 2nd ACM International Conference on Mobile Computing and Networking*, November.
[25] Joseph, A. D., deLespinasse, A. F., Tauber, J. A., Gifford, D. K., and Kaashoek, M. F. (1995). Rover: A toolkit for mobile information access. *Proceedings of the Fifteenth Symposium on Operating Systems Principles*, December.
[26] Kaashoek, M. F., Pinckney, T., and Tauber, J. A. (1995). Dynamic documents: mobile wireless access to the WWW. *Proceedings of the IEEE Workshop on Mobile Computing Systems and Applications*, December.
[27] Lai, S. J., Zaslavsky, A. Z., Martin, G. P., and Yeo, L. H. (1995). Cost efficient adaptive protocol with buffering for advanced mobile database applications. *Proceedings of the Fourth International Conference on Database Systems for Advanced Applications*, April.
[28] Le, M. T., Burghardt, F., Seshan, S., and Rabaey, J. (1995). InfoNet: The networking infrastructure of InfoPad. *Proceedings of Compcon*, March.

[29] Lim, J. B., Hurson, A. R., and Chehadeh, C. (1997). *Heterogeneous Data Access in a Mobile Environment—Issues and Solutions.* Department of Computer Science and Engineering Technical Report CSE-97-010, September.
[30] Mayer, J. (1995). Wireless stretches LANs. *Computer Design*, February.
[31] Mehrotra, S., Korth, H., and Silberschatz, A. (1997). Concurrency control in hierarchical multidatabase systems. *The VLDB Journal*, **6**, 152–172.
[32] Motorola, ReFLEX Fact Sheet, 1997.
[33] Noble, B. B., and Helal, A. (1995). Mobile computing and databases: anything new? *Sigmod Record*, December.
[34] Noble, B. D., and Satyanarayanan, M. (1994). An empirical study of a highly available file system. *Proceedings of the 1994 ACM Sigmetrics Conference on Measurement and Modeling of Computer Systems.*
[35] Ortiz, R., and Dadam, P. (1995). Towards the boundary of concurrency. *2nd International Conference on Concurrent Engineering, Research and Applications.*
[36] Padmanabhan, V. N., and Mogul, J. C. (1996). Using predictive prefetching to improve World Wide Web latency. *ACM SIGCOMM Computer Communication review*, July.
[37] Perterson, T., and Yegyazarian, A. (1998). The New Networked Computers. *PC Magazine*, pp. 211–229, May.
[38] Pitoura, E., and Bhargava, B. (1995). Maintaining consistency of data in mobile distributed environments. *Proceedings of 15th International Conference on Distributed Computing Systems*, pp. 404–413.
[39] Prakash, R., and Singhal, M. (1996). Low-cost checkpointing and failure recovery in mobile computing systems. *IEEE Transactions on Parallel and Distributed Systems*, **7**(10), October.
[40] Reiher, P., Heidemann, J., Ratner, D., Skinner, G., and Popek, G. (1994). Resolving file conflicts in the Ficus file system. *Proceedings of the 1994 USENIX Conference.*
[41] Rogers, A. (1997). Networks in Space. *Communications Week*, February 17.
[42] Rogers, A. (1997). 56K on the way. *Communications Week*, February 3.
[43] Satyanarayanan, M. (1996). Mobile information access. *IEEE Personal Communications*, **3**(1), February.
[44] Satyanarayanan, M. (1996). Fundamental challenges in mobile computing. *15th ACM Symposium on Principles of Distributed Computing*, May.
[45] Satyanarayanan, M., Noble, B., Kumar, P., and Price, M. (1994). Application-Aware Adaptation for Mobile Computing, *Proceedings of the 6th ACM SIGOPS European Workshop*, September.
[46] Satyanarayanan, M., Kistler, J. J., and Mummert, L. B. (1993). Experience with disconnected operation in a mobile computing environment. *Proceedings of the 1993 USENIX Symposium on Mobile and Location-Independent Computing*, August.
[47] Seshan, S., Balakrishnan, H., and Katz, R. H. (1996). Handoffs in cellular wireless networks: The Daedalus implementation and experience. *Kluwer International Journal on Wireless Communications.*
[48] Sohn, K., and Moon, S. (1997). Achieving a high degree of concurrency in multidatabase transaction scheduling. *Proceedings of the 5th International Conference on Database Systems for Advanced Applications*, April 1–4.
[49] Stallings, W. (1994). *Data and Computer Communications*, 4th Edn, Macmillan Publishing Company, Englewood Cliffs, NJ.
[50] Watson, T., and Bershad, B. N. (1993). Local area mobile computing on stock hardware and mostly stock software. *Proceedings of the 1993 USENIX Symposium on Mobile and Location-Independent Computing.*

[51] Watson, T., Effective wireless communication through application partitioning. *Proceedings of the 5th Workshop on Hot Topics in Operating Systems.*
[52] Wolski, A., and Veijalainen, J. (1990). 2PC agent method: Achieving serializability in presence of failures in a heterogeneous multidatabase. *Proceedings of the International Conference on Databases, Parallel Architectures and Their Applications*, pp. 321–330.
[53] Zdonik, S., Alonso, R., Franklin, M., and Acharya, S. (1994). Are disks in the air just pie in the sky? *Proceedings of Workshop on Mobile Computing Systems and Applications*, pp. 1–8.
[54] Zhang, A., Bhargava, M., and Bukhres, O. (1994). Ensuring relaxed atomicity for flexible transactions in multidatabase systems, *Proceedings of ACM-SIGMOD International Conference on Management of Data.*

The World Wide Web

HAL BERGHEL AND DOUGLAS BLANK

Department of Computer Science
University of Arkansas
Fayetteville, AR 72701
USA

Abstract

This article provides a high-level overview of the World Wide Web in the context of a wide range of other Internet information access and delivery services. This overview will include client-side, server-side and "user-side" perspectives. Underlying Web technologies as well as current technology extensions to the Web will also be covered. Social implications of Web technology will also be addressed.

1.	Introduction	180
2.	The Internet: Precursor to the Web	182
3.	The Success of the Web	183
4.	Perspectives	184
	4.1 End Users' Perspective	184
	4.2 Historical Perspective	185
5.	The Underlying Technologies	188
	5.1 Hypertext Markup Language (HTML)	188
	5.2 Hypertext Transfer Protocol (HTTP)	192
6.	Dynamic Web Technologies	194
	6.1 Common Gateway Interface	194
	6.2 Forms	196
	6.3 Helper apps	198
	6.4 Plug-ins	199
	6.5 Executable Content	199
	6.6 Programming	202
	6.7 DHTML	203
	6.8 Server-Side Includes	204
	6.9 Push Technologies	206
	6.10 State Parameters	208
7.	Security and Privacy	210
	7.1 Secure Socket Layer	210
	7.2 Secure HTTP (S-HTTP)	210
	7.3 Cookies	211
8.	The Web as a Social Phenomenon	214
	8.1 Virtual Communities	215

9. Conclusion 216
Acknowledgments 217
References 217

1. Introduction

The World Wide Web, or "the Web," is a "finite but unbounded" collection of media-rich digital resources which are connected through high-speed digital networks. It relies upon an Internet protocol suite (see [9] [19]) which supports the cross-platform transmission and rendering of a wide variety of media types (i.e. multimedia). This cross-platform delivery environment represents an important departure from more traditional network communications protocols like email, Telnet and FTP because it is content-centric. It is also to be distinguished from earlier document acquisition systems such as Gopher and WAIS (Wide Area Information Systems) which accommodated a narrower range of media formats and failed to include hyperlinks within their network navigation protocols. Following Gopher, the Web quickly extended and enriched the metaphor of integrated browsing and navigation. This made it possible to navigate and peruse a wide variety of media types on the Web effortlessly, which in turn led to the Web's hegemony as an Internet protocol.

Thus, while earlier network protocols were special-purpose in terms of both function and media formats, the Web is highly versatile. It became the first convenient form of digital communication which had sufficient rendering and browsing utilities to allow any person or group with network access to share media-rich information with their peers. It also became the standard for hyper-linking cybermedia (cyberspace multimedia), connecting concept to source in manifold directions identified primarily by Uniform Resource Locators (URLs).

In a formal sense, the Web is a client-server model for packet-switched, networked computer systems defined by the protocol pair Hypertext Transfer Protocol (HTTP) and Hypertext Markup Language (HTML). HTTP is the primary transport protocol of the Web, while HTML defines the organization and structure of the Web documents to be exchanged. At this writing, the current HTTP standard is at version 1.0, and the current HTML version is 4.0.

HTTP and HTML are higher-order Internet protocols specifically created for the Web. In addition, the Web must also utilize the lower-level Internet protocols, Internet Protocol (IP) and Transmission Control Protocol (TCP). The basic Internet protocol suite is thus designated TCP/IP. IP determines how datagrams will be exchanged via packet-switched networks while TCP builds upon IP by adding control and reliability checking [9, 20].

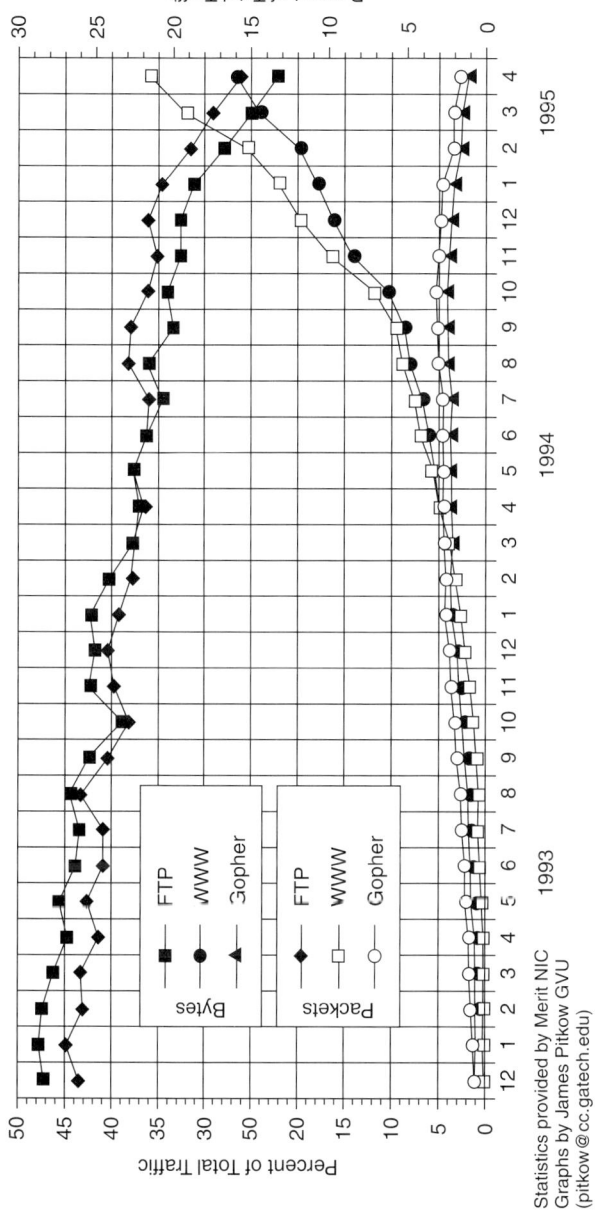

FIG. 1. Merit NIC Backbone statistics for the Web, Gopher and FTP from 1993–1995 in terms of both packet and byte counts (source: Merit NIC and Jim Pitkow [18], used with permission).

According to NSFNET Backbone statistics, the Web moved into first place both in terms of the percentage of total packets moved (21%) and percentage of total bytes moved (26%) along the NSF backbone in the first few months of 1995. This placed the Web well ahead of the traditional Internet activity leaders, FTP (14%/21%) and Telnet (7.5%/2.5%), as the most popular Internet service. A comparison of the evolutionary patterns of the Web, Gopher and FTP are graphically depicted in Fig. 1.

2. The Internet: Precursor to the Web

The Web evolution should be thought of as an extension of the digital computer network technology which began in the 1960s. Localized, platform-dependent, low-performance networks became prevalent in the 1970s. These LANS (local area networks) were largely independent of, and incompatible with, each other. In a quest for technology which could integrate these individual LANs, the US Department of Defense, through its Advanced Research Projects Agency (ARPA, nee DARPA), funded research in inter-networking—or inter-connecting LANS via a wide area network (WAN). The first national network which resulted from this project was called, not surprisingly, ARPANET. For most of the 1970s and 1980s ARPANET served as the primary network backbone in use for interconnecting LANs for both the research community and the US Government.

At least two factors considerably advanced the interest in the ARPANET project. First, and foremost, it was an "open" architecture: its underlying technological requirements, and software specifications were available for anyone to see. As a result, it became an attractive alternative to developers who bristled at the notion of developing software which would run on only a certain subset of available platforms.

Second, ARPANET was built upon a robust, highly versatile and enormously popular protocol suite: TCP/IP (Transmission Control Protocol/Internet Protocol). The success and stability of TCP/IP elevated it to the status of de facto standard for inter-networking. The US military began using ARPANET in earnest in the early 1980s, with the research community following suit. Since TCP/IP software was in essence in the public domain, a frenzy of activity in deploying TCP/IP soon resulted in both government and academe. One outgrowth was the NSF-sponsored CSNET which linked computer science departments together. By the end of the 1980s, virtually every one who wanted to be inter-networked could gain access through government or academic institutions. ARPANET gradually evolved into the Internet, and the rest, as they say, is history.

Not unexpectedly, the rapid (in fact, exponential) growth produced some problems. First and foremost was the problem of scalability. The original

ARPANET backbone was unable to carry the network traffic by the mid-1980s. It was replaced by a newer backbone supported by the NSF, a backbone operated by a consortium of IBM, MCI and Merit shortly thereafter, and finally by the privatized, not-for-profit corporation, Advanced Networks and Services (ANS), which consisted of the earlier NSFNET consortium members. In the mid-1990s, the MCI corporation deployed the high-speed Backbone Network System (vBNS) which completed the trend toward privatization of the digital backbone networks. The next stage of evolution for inter-network backbones is likely to be an outgrowth of the much-discussed Internet II project proposed to the US Congress in 1997. This "next generation" Internet is expected to increase the available bandwidth over the backbone by two orders of magnitude.

Of course, there were other network environments besides the Internet which have met with varying degrees of success. Bitnet was a popular alternative for IBM mainframe customers during the 1970s and early 1980s, as was UUCP for the Unix environment and the email-oriented FIDONET. Europeans, meanwhile, used an alternative network protocol, D.25, for several of their networks (Joint Academic Network—JANET, European Academic and Research Network—EARN). By 1991, however, the enormous popularity of the Internet drove even recalcitrant foreign network providers into the Internet camp. High-speed, reliable Internet connectivity was assured with the European Backbone (EBONE) project. At the time of writing all but a handful of developing countries have some form of Internet connectivity. For the definitive overview of the Internet, see [9].

3. The Success of the Web

It has been suggested [2] that the rapid deployment of the Web is a result of a unique combination of characteristics:

(1) *The Web is an enabling technology.* It was the first widespread network technology to extend the notion of "virtual network machine" to multimedia. While the ability to execute programs on, and retrieve content from, distributed computers was not new (e.g. Telnet and FTP were already in wide use by the time that the Web was conceived), the ability to produce and distribute media-rich documents via a common, platform-independent document structure, was new to the Web.
(2) *The Web is a unifying technology.* The unification came through the Web's accommodation of a wide range of multimedia formats. Since such audio (e.g. .WAV, .AU), graphics (e.g. .GIF, .JPG) and animation (e.g. MPEG) formats are all digital, they were already unified in desktop applications prior to the Web. The Web, however, unified

them for distributed, network applications. One Web "browser," as it later became called, would correctly render dozens of media formats regardless of network source. In addition, the Web unifies not only the access to many differing multimedia formats, but provides a platform-independent protocol which allows anyone, regardless of hardware or operating system, access to that media.

(3) *The Web is a social phenomenon.* The Web social experience evolved in three stages. Stage one was the phenomenon of Web "surfing". The richness and variety of Web documents and the novelty of the experience made Web surfing the de facto standard for curiosity-driven networking behavior in the 1990s. The second stage involved such Web interactive communication forums as Internet Relay Chat (IRC), which provided a new outlet for interpersonal but not-in-person communication. The third stage, which is in infancy at the time of writing, involves the notion of virtual community. The widespread popularity and social implications of such network-based, interactive communication is becoming an active area in computing research.

4. Perspectives

4.1 End User's Perspective

Extensive reporting on Web use and Web users may be found in a number of Web survey sites. Perhaps the most thorough of which is the biannual, self-selection World Wide Web Survey which began in January, 1994 (see reference, below). As this article is being written, the most current Web Survey is the ninth (April, 1998). Selected summary data appear in Table I.

Of course a major problem with self-selection surveys, where subjects determine whether, or to what degree, they wish to participate in the survey, is that the samples are likely to be biased. In the case of the Web survey, for example, the authors recommend that the readers assume biases towards the experienced users. As a consequence, they recommend that readers confirm the results through random sample surveys. Despite these limitations, however, the Web surveys are widely used and referenced and are among our best sources of information on Web use.

An interesting byproduct of these surveys will be an increased understanding of the difference between traditional and electronic surveying methodologies and a concern over possible population distortions under a new, digital lens. One may only conjecture at this point whether telephone respondents behave similarly to network respondents in survey settings. In

TABLE I

SUMMARY INFORMATION ON WEB USE

Average age of Web user	35.7 years
Male : female ratio of users	62 : 38
% users with college degrees	46.9
% in computing field	20.6
% in education	23.4
% in management	11.7
% of users from US	80.5 (and slowly decreasing)
% of users who connect via modems with transmission speeds of 33.5 kbps or less	55
% of respondents reported who use the Web for purchases exceeding $100	39
% of users for whom English is the primary language	93.1
% of users who have Internet bank accounts	5.5
% of Microsoft Windows platforms	64.5
% using Apple	25.6
% of users who plan to use Netscape	60
% who plan to use Internet Explorer	15

Source: GVU's WWW User Surveys, http://www.cc.gatech.edu/gvu/user_surveys/. Used with permission.

addition, Web surveyors will develop new techniques for non-biased sampling which avoids the biases inherent in self-selection. The science and technology behind such electronic sampling may well be indispensable for future generations of Internet marketers, communicators, and organizers.

4.2 Historical Perspective

The Web was conceived by Tim Berners-Lee and his colleagues at CERN (now called the European Laboratory for Particle Physics) in 1989 as a shared information space which would support collaborative work. Berners-Lee defined HTTP and HTML at that time. As a proof-of-concept prototype, he developed the first Web client navigator-browser in 1990 for the NeXTStep platform. Nicola Pellow developed the first cross-platform Web browser in 1991 while Berners-Lee and Bernd Pollerman developed the first server application—a phone book database. By 1992, the interest in the Web was sufficient to produce four additional browsers—Erwise, Midas, and Viola for X Windows, and Cello for Windows. The following year, Marc Andreessen of the National Center for Supercomputer Application (NCSA) wrote Mosaic for the X Windows System which soon became the browser standard against which all others would be compared. Andreessen went on to co-found Netscape Communications in 1994 whose current browser, Netscape Navigator, remains the current de facto standard Web browser, despite continuous loss of market share to Microsoft's Internet Explorer in recent years (see, Fig. 2). Netscape has also announced plans to license without cost the source code for version 5.0 to be released in Spring, 1998. At this point it is unclear what effect the move to "open sources" may have (see Figs 2 and 3).

Despite the original design goal of supporting collaborative work, Web use has become highly variegated. The Web has been extended into a wide range of products and services offered by individuals and organizations, for commerce, education, entertainment, "edutainment", and even propaganda. A partial list of popular Web applications includes:

- individual and organizational homepages;
- sales prospecting via interactive forms-based surveys;
- advertising and the distribution of product promotional material;
- new product information, product updates, product recall notices;
- product support—manuals, technical support, frequently asked questions (FAQs);
- corporate record-keeping—usually via local area networks (LANs) and intranets;
- electronic commerce made possible with the advent of several secure HTTP transmission protocols and electronic banking which can handle small charges (perhaps at the level of millicents);

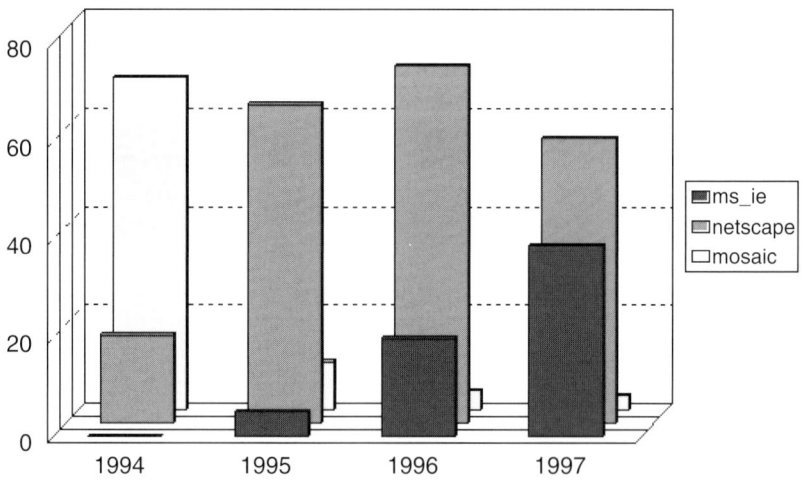

FIG. 2. Market share of the three dominant Web browsers from 1994 through 1997.

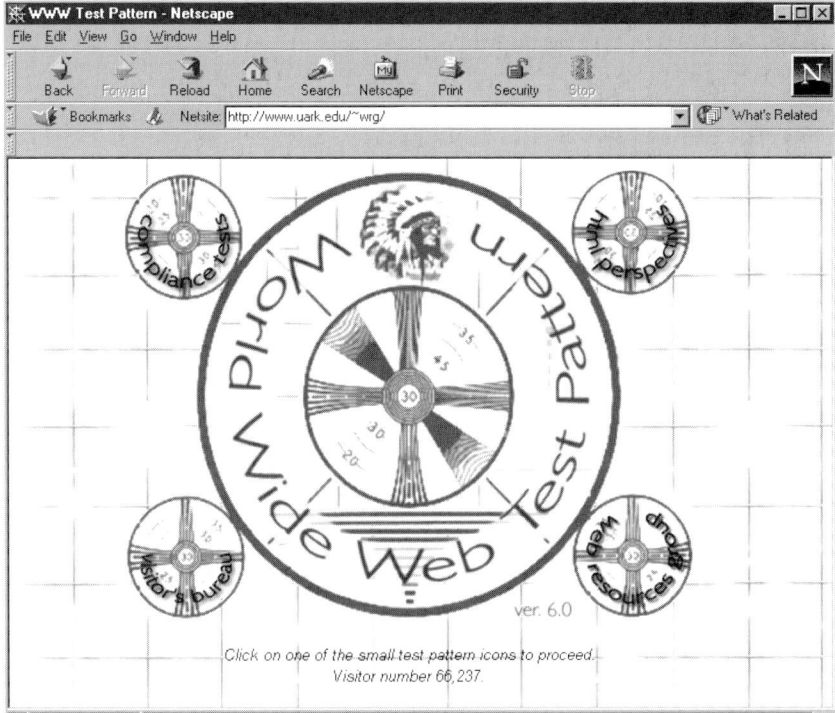

FIG. 3. Navigator 4.x is a recent generic "navigator/browser" from Netscape Corporation. Displayed is a vanilla "splash page" of the World Wide Web Test Pattern—a test bench for determining the level of HTML compliance of a browser.

- religious proselytizing;
- propagandizing;
- digital politics.

Most Web resources at this time are still set up for non-interactive, multimedia downloads (e.g. non-interactive Java [21] animation applets, movie clips, real-time audio transmissions, text with graphics). This will change in the next decade as software developers and Web content-providers shift their attention to the interactive and participatory capabilities of the Internet, the Web, and their successor technologies. Already, the Web is eating into television's audience and will probably continue to do so. Since it seems inevitable that some aspects of both television and the Web will merge in the 21st century, they are said to be convergent technologies. But as of this writing, the dominant Web theme seems to remain static HTML documents and non-interactive animations.

As mentioned above, the uniqueness of the Web as a network technology is a product of two protocols: HTML and HTTP. We elaborate on these protocols below.

5. The Underlying Technologies

5.1 Hypertext Markup Language (HTML)

HTML is the business part of document preparation for the Web. Two not-for-profit organizations play a major role in standardizing HTML: the World Wide Web Consortium (www.w3.org) and the Internet Engineering Task Force (www.ietf.org). Any document which conforms to the W3C/IETF HTML standards is called a Web message entity. HTML is about the business of defining Web message entities.

The hypertext orientation of HTML derives from the pioneering and independent visions of Vannevar Bush [8] in the mid-1940s, and Doug Englebart [10] and Ted Nelson [14] in the 1960s. Bush proposed mechanical and computational aids in support of associative memory, i.e. the linking together of concepts which shared certain properties. Englebart sought to integrate variegated documents and their references through a common core document in a project called Augment. Nelson, who coined the terms "hypertext" and "hypermedia," added to the work of Bush and Englebart the concept of non-linear document traversal, as his proposed project Xanadu (www.xanadu.net/the.project) attempted to "create, access and manipulate this literature of richly formatted and connected information cheaply, reliably and securely from anywhere in the world." Subsequently, Nelson has also defined the notions of "transclusion," or virtual copies of collections of documents, and "transcopyright" which enables the aggregation of information regardless of ownership by automating the procedure by means of which creators are paid for their intellectual property. We won't comment beyond saying that the Web is an ideal test bed for Nelson's ideas.

From technical perspective, HTML is a sequence of "extensions" to the original concept of Berners-Lee—which was text-oriented. By early 1993, when the NCSA Mosaic navigator-browser client was released for the X Windows System, HTML had been extended to include still-frame graphics. Soon audio and other forms of multimedia followed.

After 1993, however, HTML standards were a moving target. Marc Andreessen, the NCSA Mosaic project leader, left the NCSA to form what would become Netscape Corporation. Under his technical supervision, Netscape went its own way in offering new features which were not endorsed by W3C/IETF, and at times were inconsistent with the Standard

Generalized Markup Language (SGML) orientation intended by the designers of HTML. SGML is a document definition language which is independent of any particular structure—i.e. layout is defined by the presentation software based upon Under pressure to gain market share, navigator/browser developers attempted to add as many useful "extensions" to the HTML standards as could be practicably supported. This competition has been called the "Mosaic War," [3] which persists in altered form even to this day.

Although not complete, Table II provides a technical perspective of the evolution of HTML.

TABLE II

HTML EVOLUTION

GML (Generalized Markup Language)	Developed by IBM in 1969 to separate form from content in displaying documents
SGML (ISO 8879 Standard Generalized Markup Language)	Adopted 1986
HTML Version 1 (circa 1992–3)	basic HTML structure rudimentary graphics hypertext
HTML Version 2 (circa 1994)	forms lists
HTML Version 3.2 (circa 1996–7)	tables applets scripts advanced CGI programming security text flow around graphics
HTML Version 4.x (early 1998)	inline frames format via cascading style sheets (vs HTML tags) compound documents with hierarchy of alternate rendering strategies internationalization tty and braille support client-side image maps advanced forms/tables
XML (1998)	Extensible Markup Language. Subset of SGML

Note:

(1) Version 3.2 is actually a subset of Version 3.0, the latter of which failed to get endorsed by W3C/IETF.

(2) Dates are only approximate because of the time lag between the introduction of the technology and the subsequent endorsement as a standard. In some cases this delay is measured in years.

Among the many Netscape innovations are:

- typographical enhancements and fonts;
- alignment and colorization controls for text and graphics;
- dynamic updating (continuous refresh without reload);
- server push/client pull;
- frames;
- cookies;
- plug-ins;
- scripts;
- frames;
- Java applets;
- layers.

Many of these have become part of subsequent HTML standards. In addition to these formal standards, discussion is already underway for a radical extension of HTML called XML (www.w3.org/XML/Activity). In many ways, HTML evolved away from its nicely thought-out roots. GML, or Generalized Markup Language, was developed in the 1960s at IBM to describe many different kinds of documents. Standard Generalized Markup Language, or SGML, was based on GML and became an ISO standard years later in the 1980s. SGML still stands today as the mother of all markup languages. Its designers were very careful not to confuse form and content, and created a wonderfully rich language. HTML became a patchwork of ideas as it quickly evolved over the last few years, and muddied the difference between form and content. XML is an effort to reunite HTML with its SGML roots. The development of XML, which began in late 1996, deals with the non-extensibility of HTML to handle advanced page design and a full range of new multimedia. XML will accomplish this by using (1) a more SGML-like markup language (vs HTML), allowing "personal" or "group" -oriented tags, and (2) a low-level syntax for data definition.

To see how XML differs from HTML, we examine a page of HTML code:

```
<html>
<head>
    <title>Bibliography</title>
</head>
<body>
    <p>Smith, Aaron S. (1999). <i>Understanding the Web</i>.
       Web Books, Inc. </p>
</body>
</html>
```

This code, when rendered by an appropriate browser, would appear similar to the following:

Smith, Aaron S. (1999). *Understanding the Web*. Web Books, Inc.

Tags are special symbols in HTML and XML, and are indicated by the surrounding less-than and greater-than symbols. The majority of tags are paired—i.e. they surround the text that they affect. For example, <I> and </I> indicate that the italics should be turned on and off, respectively.

Now, contrast the HTML example with sample XML code:

```
<?XML version="1.0" ?>
<xmldoc>
<bibliography>
      <ref-name> Smith-1999b </ref-name>
      <name>
          <last> Smith </last>
          <first> Aaron </first>
          <mi> S </mi>
      </name>
      <title> Understanding the Web </title>
      <year> 1999 </year>
      <publisher> Web Books, Inc. </publisher>
      <type> Book </type>
</bibliography>
</xmldoc>
```

Like the HTML code, XML is made up of tags. However, XML does not describe how to render the data, it merely indicates the structure and content of the data. HTML does have some of these kinds of tags (for example, `<title>` in the above HTML example) but, for the most part, HTML has evolved completely away from its SGML roots.

XML was designed to be compatible with current HTML (and SGML, for that matter). Today's most common Web browsers (Microsoft's Internet Explorer and Netscape's Navigator) do not support XML directly. Instead, most XML processors have been implemented as Java applications or applets (see the Web Consortium's website for a list of XML processors at `www.w3.org`). Such a Java processor could be instructed to render the XML inside the browser exactly like the rendered HTML.

One of the nice properties of XML is the separation of content and format. This distinction will surely help tame the Wild Web as it will allow easier searching, better structuring, and greater assistance to software agents in general. However, this isn't XML's greatest virtue: what makes XML a great leap forward for the Web is its ability to create new tags. Much like a modern database management system can define new fields, XML can create a new tag. In addition, XML tags can also have structure like the name field above was composed of first, last, and middle initial. As long as client and server agree on the structure of the data, they can freely create and share new data fields, types, and content via XML.

Some have said that XML "does for data what Java does for programs." Examples of XML applications are the math-formula markup language, MathML (www.w3.org/TR/WD-math/), which combines the ability to define content with a less-powerful suite of features to define presentation. Another example is RDF, a resource description format for metadata (http://www.w3.org/RDF/Overview.html), which is used in both PICS, the Platform for Internet Content Selection (http://www.w3.org/PICS/) and SMIL, the Synchronized Multimedia Integration Language, which is a declarative language for synchronizing multimedia on the Web. The XML prototype client is Jumbo (www.venus.co.uk/omf/cml). Although XML will help make marking up Web pages easier, there is still a battle raging over which system should be responsible for the details of rendering pages. Current HTML coders must take responsibilty for exact placement over page layout, and getting a standard look across browsers is non-trivial. However, SGML leaves the page layout details up to the browser. Exactly how this important issue will play out remains to be seen.

5.2 Hypertext Transfer Protocol (HTTP)

HTTP is a platform-independent protocol based upon the client-server model of computing which runs on any TCP/IP, packet switched digital network—e.g. the Internet. HTTP stands for Hyper Text Transfer Protocol and is the communication protocol with which browsers request data, and servers provide it. This data can be of many types including video, sound, graphics, and text. In addition, HTTP is extensible in that it can be augmented to transfer types of data that do not yet exist.

HTTP is an application layer protocol, and sits directly on top of TCP (Transmission Control Protocol). It is similar in many ways to the File Transmission Protocol (FTP) and TELNET. HTTP follows the following logical flow:

(1) A connection from the client's browser is made to a server, typically by the user having clicked on a link.
(2) A request is made of the server. This request could be for data (i.e. a "GET") or could be a request to process data (i.e. "POST" or "PUT").
(3) The server attempts to fulfill the request. If successful, the client's

browser will receive additional data to render. Otherwise, an error occurs.
(4) The connection is then closed.

HTTP uses the same underlying communication protocols as do all the applications that sit on top of TCP. For this reason, one can use the TELNET application to make an HTTP request. Other TCP-based applications include FTP, TFTP (Trivial File Transfer Protocol), and SMTP (Simple Mail Transfer Protocol), to name just a few. Consider the following example:

```
% telnet www.uark.edu 80
GET / HTTP/1.0
Accept: text/html
Accept: text/plain
User-Agent: TELNET/1.0
```

This command made from any operating system with access to the TELNET program requests to talk to port 80, the standard HTTP port, of a machine running a web server (TELNET normally uses port 23). A request is made to get the root document (GET /), in a particular protocol (HTTP/1.0), and accepting either text or HTML. The data (i.e. HTML codes) are returned, and the connection is closed. Note: the ending empty line is required. Conversely, consider:

```
HTTP/1.0 200 OK
Server: Netscape-Enterprise/3.0K
Date: Sun, 03 May 1998 22:25:37 GMT
      Content-type: text/html
      Connection: close

<HTML>
<HEAD>
...
```

These are the data returned from the previous request. First, the server responds with the protocol (HTTP/1.0 in this example), gives the corresponding code (200 OK), provides details of the server (Netscape-Enterprise), date and time, and the format of the following data (text/html). Finally, an empty line separates the header from the actually HTML code.

This type of processing is called "stateless". This makes HTTP only slightly, yet importantly, different from FTP. FTP has "state"; an FTP session has a series of settings that may be altered during the course of a dialog between client and server. For example, the "current directory" and "download data type" settings maybe be changed during an FTP dialog. HTTP, on the other hand, has no such interaction—the conversation is limited to a simple request and response. This has been the most limiting aspect of HTTP. Much current Web development has centered around dealing with this particular limitation of the protocol (i.e. cookies).

Although HTTP is very limited, it has shown its flexibility through what must be one of the most explosive and rapidly changing technological landscapes ever. This flexibility is made possible via the protocol's format negotiations. The negotiation begins with the client identifying the types of formats it can understand. The server responds with data in any of those formats that it can supply (text/html in the above example). In this manner, the client and server can agree on file types yet to be invented, or which depend on proprietary formats. If the client and server cannot agree on a format, the data is simply ignored.

6. Dynamic Web Technologies

Web technologies evolved beyond the original concept in several important respects. We examine HTML forms, the Common Gateway Interface, plug-ins, executable content, and push technologies.

6.1 Common Gateway Interface

The support of the Common Gateway Interface (CGI) within HTTP in 1993 added interactive computing capability to the Web. Here is a one-line C program that formats the standard greeting in basic HTML. (Note: make sure the binary is marked executable. Also, often the binary will need to have a. cgi extension to tell the HTTPD server that it should be executed rather than simply displayed). Any program capable of reading from "standard input" and writing to "standard output" can be used as a CGI program, although the interpreted language Perl has, by far, been the most used. The following code fragment illustrates this point:

```
main() {
   printf("Content-type: text/html\n\n<html><body>
          <h1>Hello World\!</body></html>\n");
}
```

Many are surprised to find the amount of data a CGI program has access to from the apparent anonymous browser (more on this later). For example, a CGI program can identify what Web page referred the user to this site, the browser the user is using, the user's IP address, and a host of other information (including the host) (see below):

```
DOCUMENT_ROOT           /home/csci/public_html
```

GATEWAY_INTERFACE	CGI/1.1
HTTP_ACCEPT	image/gif, image/x-xbitmap, image/jpeg, image/pjpeg, image/png, /
HTTP_ACCEPT_CHARSET	iso-8859-1, *,utf-8
HTTP_ACCEPT_ LANGUAGE	en
HTTP_CONNECTION	Keep-Alive
HTTP_HOST	entropy.uark.edu
HTTP_REFERER	http://dangermouse.uark.edu/~dblank/samples/
HTTP_USER_AGENT	Mozilla/4.04 [en] (X11; I; Linux 2.0.33 i686)
PATH	/sbin:/usr/sbin:/bin:/usr/bin
QUERY_STRING	
REMOTE_ADDR	130.184.201.233
REMOTE_HOST	dangermouse.uark.edu
REQUEST_METHOD	GET
SCRIPT_FILENAME	/home/dblank/public_html/scm.cgi
SCRIPT_NAME	/~dblank/scm.cgi
SERVER_ADMIN	root@localhost
SERVER_NAME	entropy.uark.edu
SERVER_PORT	80
SERVER_PROTOCOL	HTTP/1.0
SERVER_SOFTWARE	Apache/1.2.5

In general, a CGI program has access to environment information regarding the network transaction. This browser data is relayed to the CGI program via environment variables.

A CGI program may create a specialized Web page that is based on any of the above variable values. For example, if a user did not come from a specific Web page, then the user could be rejected. In the example below, one could test HTTP_REFERER to see if it equals "http://dangermouse.uark.edu/~dblank/samples/". If it does, more data would be shown; otherwise a message indicating inappropriate access could be displayed.

```
include <stdlib.h>
main() {
  if (strcmp(getenv("HTTP_REFERER"),
        "http://dangermouse.uark.edu/~dblank/samples/")
        == 0 ) printf("Content-type: text/html\n\n<html><body><h1>Welcome\!");
  else
     printf("Content-type: text/html\n\n<html><body><h1>Access Denied<p>"); printf("</body></html>\n");
}
```

In this case, "more data" is a dynamic Web page. This CGI C program tests to make sure that the user is coming from a particular HTTP referrer.

Perhaps the most important use of CGI to this point has been the dynamic processing of CGI forms which enable input from the Web user-client to be passed to the server for processing (discussed below). While, in theory, CGI programs can provide server-side programming for virtually any Web need, network bandwidth constraints and transmission delays may make some heavily interactive and volumetric applications infeasible.

6.2 Forms

Forms were added to HTML version 2 around 1994. Forms allow users to give feedback to servers through standard GUI objects: text boxes, check boxes, buttons, etc. (see Fig. 4).

The HTML code below produced the screen in Fig. 4. Sections of HTML code are marked between the <FORM> and </FORM> tags. In this example, the CGI program (discussed below) is executed when the "View" button is clicked. Three additional pieces of data are sent to the executing program via environment variables: passwd, file, and html. Passwd and file are both textual, and html is a boolean check box. Notice that passwd is of type "password" which makes text typed into the area appear as asterisks.

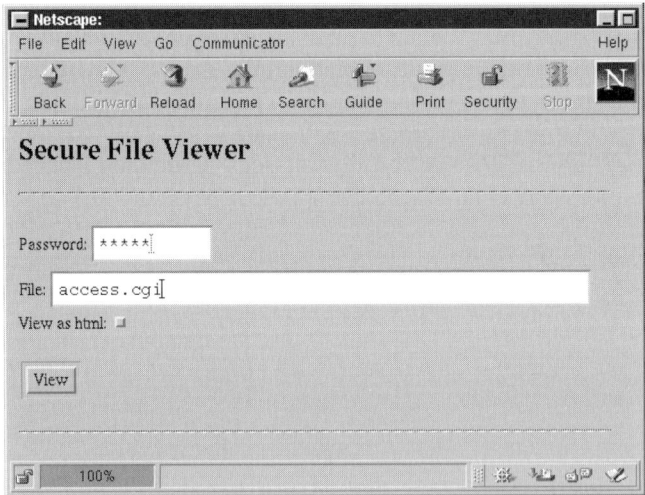

FIG. 4. Screen dump of Secure File Viewer form.

The word "checked" appearing at the end of the checkbox tag indicates that is initially true (i.e. checked).

```
<HTML>
<BODY>
<h1>Secure File Viewer</h1>
<HR>
<FORM METHOD="POST" ACTION="access.cgi">
Password:
<input type=password name=passwd value="" size=10></input>
File: <input type=text name=file value="" size=50></input><br>
View as html: <input type=checkbox name=html checked>
<br>
<br>
<input type="submit" name="submit" value=" View ">
</FORM>
<HR>
</BODY>
</HTML>
```

The final piece of this form is the actual program that is run when "View" is pressed. This program, `access.cgi`, is shown below:

```
#!/usr/bin/perl
require "cgi-lib.pl";
&ReadParse(*input);
if ($input{'passwd'} eq 'himom') {
  if ($input{'html'}) {
     exec "echo Content-TYPE: text/html; echo; cat
     ".$input{'file'} || die;
  } else {
      exec "echo Content-TYPE: text/plain; echo; cat
     ".$input{'file'} || die;
  }
} else {
  print "Content-type: text/html\n\n"; print
"<HTML><BODY><HR>"; print "Error not the correct
password!\n";
}
print "<HR></BODY></HTML>\n";
1;
```

We observe that this is a simple Perl script that checks a password before viewing a source file.

This program should be marked as executable, and requires the standard Perl library `cgi-lib.pl`.

`Access.cgi` is a CGI program (described below) written in Perl that checks for a password ("himom" in this case), and displays a file either as HTML or as plain text depending on the checkbox. This method of password protecting files is not secure: anyone with access to the file system can read `access.cgi` and therefore view the password (read access is required in order to execute a CGI script on most Web servers). Currently, there is not a foolproof method for allowing password-bearing Web surfers to have access to files while preventing general file system users. Many sites have a dedicated server with no general-purpose users for just this purpose, thereby making this form secure.

Forms were a welcome addition to early HTML standards. However, the amount of dynamic interaction allowed is quite limited.

6.3 Helper apps

So-called "Helper apps" are extensions of the network browser metaphor which diminished the browser-centricity by supporting multimedia through separate, special-purpose "players." In this way, a wider range of multimedia could be rendered than could be economically and practicably built into the browser itself.

This trend toward helper apps began in 1994. By the year's end most Web browsers included generic launchpads which could spawn pre-specified multimedia players based on the filetype/file extent (`.WAV` designated MS Window's audio file, `.QT` designated Quicktime, etc.). In practice, one simply downloaded the autonomous helper apps which could cover the range of multimedia desired.

The generic launchpad was a significant technological advance for two reasons. First, it de-coupled the evolutionary paths, and hence the development paces, of browsers and multimedia. The first multimedia Web browsers relied entirely on internal media perusers, thereby creating a bottleneck as the pace of development of new multimedia formats exceeded that of the internal perusers. By de-coupling, both browser and multimedia developers could advance independently without fear of incompatibility.

Second, generic launchpads spawn external processes which execute independently of the Web browser and hence render the multimedia in an external window. This process-independence discourages the development of helper apps that are proprietary to a particular browser, which led to the rapid growth of freeware, shareware and commercial helper apps that are now available for popular client platforms. That the helper apps could be used in isolation of the browser became a collateral advantage for easy perusal of local multimedia files as well.

This generic, browser-independent approach toward rendering multimedia would be challenged twice in 1996, first by "plug-ins" and then by "executable content."

6.4 Plug-ins

"Plug-in" (alt. "Add-on") technology increased the media-rendering capability of browsers while avoiding the time-consuming spawning of so-called "helper apps" through the browser's launchpad. The speed advantage of the plug-ins, together with the tight coupling that exists between the plug-ins and the media formats which they render, made them a highly useful extension.

Plug-ins, as the name implies, are external applications which extend the browser's built-in capability for rendering multimedia files. However, unlike helper apps plug-ins render the media "inline"—that is, within the browser's window in the case of video, or with simultaneous presentation in the case of audio. In this way the functionality of the plug-in is seamlessly integrated with the operation of the browser. Plug-ins are often proprietary and browser-specific because of this tight integration. Some of the more popular current plug-in technologies are Web telephony, virtual reality and 3-D players, and real-time (or, "streaming") audio and video. (The word "streaming" has come to mean the ability of a multimedia file to begin to be experienced by the user before the entire file has completely downloaded. For example, an hour-long audio file may begin playing after a few seconds of downloading and continue playing while the rest of the file is downloaded. This works by having the plug-in download a buffer of data prior to execution, thereby keeping just ahead of the player.)

Plug-ins proved to be a useful notion for creating extendable browsers. However, there was a rub: plug-in developers must write and compile code for each target platform. Although most modern platforms support C and C++ compilers, porting plug-in applications is still non-trivial. This requirement was eliminated through the notion of executable content.

6.5 Executable Content

Executable content continues the theme of tight integration between multimedia peruser and browser, but with a slight twist. In the case of executable content, the multimedia and the peruser are one. That is, an enabled browser will download the executable files which render the multimedia and execute them as well, all within the browser's own workspace on the client.

The advent of executable content added a high level of animated media rendering and interactive content on the client side. There are many methods with which to implement data in an executable content paradigm. One example is to simply use the plug-in technology described above. However, this method requires that the user previously download the necessary plug-in. In addition, developers would be required to write and maintain their code on all platforms that they want to support, as mentioned.

A better solution was to provide a standard environment for programming so that programs could be treated as ubiquitously as HTML. While there are several competing paradigms for Web-oriented executable content, including JavaScript, Telescript, and Active-X, the cross-platform language, Java [21, 26], was the clear environment of choice by early 1997. Sun Microsystems created Java so that developers could produce platform-independent modules that are executable on enabled Web browsers. A Java program run on the Web is called an applet.

```
public class HelloWorld extends java.applet.Applet {
    public void paint(java.awt.Graphics g) {
        g.drawString("Hello World!");
    }
}
```

This applet is a sample program written in Java and stored with the filename `HelloWorld.java`. It displays the standard greeting.

The development and use of a Java Applet runs as follows:

(1) A programmer writes an object-oriented program (ending with `java`; see above).
(2) A compiler (Sun's version is written in Java) translates the source code into Java byte-code (also called a class file as they end with `.class`).
(3) A Java virtual machine (JVM), usually located in a browser, interprets the byte-code into machine-specific commands.

Java has probably sparked more activity in computer science than the Web itself. In one important sense, Java is a computer. The Java language has commands for performing normal operations, but also includes methods for rendering graphical objects. The concept of "Java" actually has three, very different parts. These are: the JVM, the Java syntax, and the Java byte code compiler. Currently, all of these are tightly integrated, but are slowly becoming three distinct parts. For example, any language could (theoretically) be compiled for the JVM. Programmers could continue to write in (a subset) of C++ or COBOL, and their code would live on running in modern browsers. Also, browsers are utilizing the concept of "just-in-time" (JIT) compilation. This allows the server computer to compile the Java byte-code to native code right after downloading. The Java syntax is also being compiled directly to native code so that it may act as a "regular" general-purpose language as well.

These issues are further complicated by a huge amount of research in related areas. For example, Sun has recently developed a chip that actually implements the JVM in hardware.

Not surprisingly, this latest extension of the Web, which involves executing foreign programs downloaded across the networks, is not without security risk. However, Java has been designed from the ground up with security issues in mind.

Currently, Java runs in one of two modes: application or applet. In application mode, Java has full access to one's system (printers, drives, monitor, etc.)—there are no security limitations. This allows programmers to write general-purpose applications. Corel has written versions of their popular office suite is such a manner, which allows it to run on any machine with a JVM.

However, most of the interest in Java has been in its applet mode. The designers of Java were sensitive to security issues, and therefore general access to the client's system could not be permitted. Although this greatly restricts what Java applets can do, it is a relatively secure system [13]. For the first time, such applets offer the ability for safe executable content. (Note that Java 1.1 permits a user to allow Java applets to have full or partial control of the client's machine, disks, etc. This greatly enhances the power of applets, but creates a more complex security control system for the user.)

Java has been the most successful executable content language, but there are many others. Tcl [17, 24] (pronounced "tickle") has also become a popular scripting language for executable content, but does require a plug-in in order to operate as it is not built into the current browsers. Tcl was "retrofitted" for Web use with security features (the so-called "Safe Tcl" version). Tcl, like Java, supports basic programming functions as well as a graphical user interface (GUI).

Probably the second most successful technology for executable content is Microsoft's Active-X. Active-X is not a language, but rather a method for dynamically downloading and using shared libraries. Active-X is generally a Windows-only solution that requires programmers to build the executable content under that OS. However, a third party developer, Ncompass (www.ncompass.co.uk) has developed a method for Unix systems running Netscape's Navigator to execute Active-X executables. This technique shows Active-X's similarity to plug-ins, as NCompass has been implemented as such.

However, unlike Java, Active-X has no security model. An Active-X program in execution has the full range of OS functions available to it as would any typical application [13]. This illustrates the tradeoff between providing applets with greater power and flexibility on the one hand and providing the host with greater security on the other. Java and Active-X take different approaches to this trade-off.

To minimize the potentially disastrous security problem with Active-X, Microsoft attempts to deal with the security issue with "certification." Certification is the formal procedure of listing your company and programs with an official registrar (Verisign is one such company). Internet Explorer (the only current browser supporting Active-X) will only allow Active-X applets that have been certified and accepted by the user to be downloaded and executed (Java 1.1 applets may also be certified). Of course, there is nothing to prevent a programmer from doing devious things after their Active-X control has been installed on a machine once it has been certified. Certification does not prevent evil-doers, but at least one knows where the harm came from afterwards. Because of these properties, Active-X is really only a choice for Windows-only intranets where clients can faithfully trust their servers.

As can be seen, browsers are a complex environment supporting many kinds of interacting scripts, plug-ins, etc. As of early 1998, many security problems were still being reported in the media.

6.6 Programming

Java can also be used as a server scripting language (such a server side program is sometimes called a "servlet"). Usually, one wants server code to be as small and fast as possible, and Java doesn't currently meet these criteria. However, it makes a good prototyping language as it has many built-in functions that make it extremely useful for Web-based server applications (see source code, below). When there are native compilers (i.e. compilers that produce machine code rather than byte code) for server machines, Java will not only be the best prototyping language for these applications, but will be the best Rapid Application Development (RAD) tool as well.

The following is a very small (insecure) Web server written in Java (after Niemeyer and Peck [15]). This program runs on a server and retrieves HTML files to standard browsers. Warning: this little server can serve up any file on your computer, so don't use it on a machine containing sensitive data.

```
*********************** File Httpdaemon.java
import java.net.*;
import java.io.*;
import java.util.*;
public class Httpdaemon {
   public static void main (String argv[] ) throws IOException {
```

```
    ServerSocket ss = new
            ServerSocket(Integer.parseInt(argv[0]));
    while (true) {
      new HttpdConnection( ss.accept() );
    }
  }
}
class HttpdConnection extends Thread {
  Socket sock;
  HttpdConnection(Socket s) { //constructor
    sock = s; setPriority(NORM_PRIORITY - 1); start();
  }

  public void run() {
    try {
      OutputStream out = sock.getOutputStream();
      String req = new
DataInputStream(sock.getInputStream()).readLine();
      System.out.println("Request: " + req);
      StringTokenizer st = new StringTokenizer( req );
      if ( (st.countTokens() >= 2) &&
st.nextToken().equals("GET")) {
        if ( (req = st.nextToken()).startsWith("/") )
            req = req.substring(1); if ( req.endsWith("/")
|| req.equals("") )
            req = req + "index.html";
        try {
            FileInputStream fis = new FileInputStream
( req ); byte [] data = new byte [fis.available() ];
fis.read( data ); out.write( data);
        } catch (FileNotFoundException e) {
            new PrintStream(out).println("404 Not Found");
        }
      } else new PrintStream(out).println("400 Bad
Request");
      sock.close();
    } catch (IOException e) {
    System.out.println("I/O error " + e);
    }
  }
}
```

6.7 DHTML

The idea of Dynamic HTML is to expose the set of events that allows a Webmaster to program a page to respond to many common interactions between the user and the document. The proposed Dynamic HTML event model is based on two powerful features for controlling the document's behavior: event bubbling and default actions. Whenever the user interacts with the page an event is fired. The user generates events in the standard ways: moving the mouse, clicking a mouse button, or typing on the keyboard within a document. Changes in document state can also fire events include the loading of the document, images, or objects.

DHTML is similar to JavaScript, except DHTML is even less stable, neither Microsoft nor Netscape support it, and neither Microsoft nor Netscape have determined exactly how it should work. Future browser support for DHTML is unknown [12].

6.8 Server-Side Includes

Server-Side Includes (SSI) are another method of dynamically creating webpage content. SSIs are commands which are parsed and processed by the web server. SSIs may be the easiest method for the Web master to create dynamic Web pages. Consider this simple HTML code:

```
<HTML>
<BODY>
<!--#echo var="LAST_MODIFIED" -->
</BODY>
</HTML>
```

To automatically add a "last modified" date to a page requires a simple `#echo` SSI command as shown above. This Web page would display text in the form of "`Monday, 15-Jun-98 03:09:31 CDT`." Notice that the SSI command is sandwiched between `<!--` and `-->`. These HTML tags signal a comment, and therefore, are ignored by browsers if the server does not support SSI.

SSIs are useful for several reasons:

- they create easy to maintain code; all commands stay in the HTML files;
- they help create structured, uniform sites;
- they are easy for non-programmers to use.

An SSI is composed of four main commands, `#config`, `#echo`, `#include`, and `#exec`, which allow a Web master to config settings, display information, include source files, and execute programs respectively. For example, one could include a standard footer with the SSI `<!--#include virtual="footer.txt" -->`.

TABLE III
SUMMARY OF SCRIPTING LANGUAGES (AFTER LAIRD AND SORAIZ [12])

Scripting language	Advantages	Disadvantages	Source
JavaScript	Standard in browsers	Only works in browsers	http://developer.netscape.com/one/javascript
MetaCard	Easy for nonprogrammers to learn	Very small customer base	http://www.metacard.com
Perl	Widely used and dominant in CGI; specialized extensions are available	GUI, Windows, Mac OS maintenance given less attention	http://www.perl.org
Python	A clean, portable, maintainable language	Base of Python expertise still small	http://www.python.org
Rexx	Available for well integrated with all IBM OSes, including mainframes	Impoverished library of facilities compared to Perl, Python, and Tcl	http://www.rexxla.org
Tcl	Simple syntax, easily learned, extensible	Clumsy for arithmetic and some other operations	http://tclconsortium.org
VBScript	Resembles Visual Basic	Single source; useful only with Microsoft Web products	http://www.microsoft.com/scripting/vbscript/default.htm

However, the SSI directives have recently been further enhanced. SSI now includes: `#set`, `#if`, `#else`, and `#endif`. This creates a powerful programming environment for creating dynamic HTML pages as the program below illustrates. This is a sample HTML page which uses the environment variable `HTTP_USER_AGENT` to dynamically determine what text to display.

```
<HTML>
<!-- #if expr="$HTTP_USER_AGENT = /^Mozilla/" -->
You are using a Netscape Browser
<!-- #else -->
You are using another browser
<!-- #endif -->
</HTML>
```

6.9 Push Technologies

An interesting technology "about face" occurred in the mid-1990s. The Web witnessed the deployment of information acquisition tools which went beyond the original "information-pull" concept behind the Web. "Push technology" or "push-phase technology" [4] found wide use in 1996–97—to the regret of many MIS managers who watched their corporate bandwidth wither away under the strain! In its most basic form, push technology is an automated delivery environment which produces timely downloads of information without end-user involvement. In this capacity, it is seen as the most recent offshoot of an evolutionary path which begins with telegraphy.

Early wire services (e.g. Associated Press, Reuters) were also "pushy" in the same sense as modern push clients. Both distribute information automatically without requiring end-user requests. Email is pushy in this regard as well—one : one in the interpersonal case, and one : many when done with distribution lists and alias files. Television and radio are also pushy. Like email, Web push is inherently digital and network-based, and like television and radio and the wire services, it supports a wide range of broadcasting and applications. The most recent incarnation of push technology is a close descendent of the "server push" concept developed by Netscape in 1995. The principle behind this Web extension was "dynamic updating". It was thought that there were likely to be many situations in which it would be desirable to continuously update Web browser windows with volatile information. Over the past few years, server-push has been used to produce multi-cell animations, slide shows, "ticker tapes", automatic pass-through of Web splash pages, and so forth. Dynamic updating was a way of overcoming the "stateless" protocol of the Web, which disconnects the client-server connection immediately after each transaction cycle, as previously described.

Actually, server-push was just one-half of Netscape's dynamic updating duo. The other half was client-pull. Server-push refreshed information displayed on the client through pre-determined, timed, server-initiated transmissions of HTML documents. However, this approach is server-invasive, requiring special server-side executables to create and deliver the refresh stream, and accordingly server push has fallen into disuse (a "deprecated feature", in Web terminology).

Client-pull, on the other hand, remains in use within the Netscape community for the display of constantly-updated HTML pages. Unlike server-push, client-pull requires no special programs to operate. The Web browser client initiates an HTTP connection and request for information from a server when it sees a particular token of the <META> tag in an HTML document. To illustrate, the tag

<META http-equiv="refresh" content="5;url=
http://www.widget.com">

would cause a pull-compliant browser to refresh the current browser window with the document at http://www.widget.com five seconds after loading the current page. Without a URL specified, the browser will refresh itself with a reload of the current page. The "pull" is shut off as soon as a document is reached which does not have a refresh <META> tag.

For both server-push and client-pull, the idea is a simple one: provide data downloads without requiring user intervention. However, early server-push and client-pull technologies were deficient in one major respect: they were both context- and content-insensitive. That is, all accesses to a URL—whether pushed or pulled—produced the same results for all users at any given moment in time. This context/content insensitivity became the bête noir of Netscape's dynamic updating technology because it produced an information access and delivery system that wasn't scalable—the delivery of numerous, complex, timely, and personalized documents require as many URLs as there are documents. In order to minimize information overload, some mechanism needed to be created to build the content and context sensitivity into the push technology, itself.

Current push client-server environments (see Table, IV) have many characteristics in common. For one, they are set up to distribute both internal (to the vendor) and third party information. Second, most push environments require proprietary clients which operate independently of any Web browser. Third, they mainly rely on a "client-polling" (or "smart pulling") model of triggering downloads (counterintuitive as it seems, most "push" environments are not technically push at all, but are called push because the client-polling is user-transparent).

TABLE IV

SELECTED PUSH TECHNOLOGY VENDORS (PROGRAMS)—CLIENT-SIDE ONLY

BackWeb	www.backweb.com
Global Village (NewsCatcher)	www.globalvillag.com
inCommon (Downtown)	www.incommon.com
Intelliserv	www.verity.com
Intermind (Communicator)	www.intermind.com
Lanacom (Headliner)	www.lanacom.com (now part of BackWeb)
NewsEDGE	www.newsedge.com
Pointcast	www.pointcast.com
Marimba (Castanet)	www.marimba.com
Wayfarer (Incisa)	www.wayfarer.com

However, push clients also differ in some respects. For one thing, some produce revenue by subscription while others (e.g. Pointcast) achieve revenue through advertising. Though most of the clients are built around Java and HTML, some rely on Microsoft's Channel Definition Format and XML. Some support SQL database interface, where others support some mix of Common Gateway Interface (CGI), SQL, Open Database Connectivity, and so forth. All environments vary with respect to the type and variety of end-user filtering tools.

Though no silver bullet, modern push technology holds out promise of several advantages:

(1) automatic downloads—in some cases "differential downloading" which only downloads the files that have changed;
(2) automated announcements of updated content;
(3) coherent information streaming via content channels;
(4) delivery and rendering independence from browser;
(5) automated but interactive Web document management;
(6) managed delivery;
(7) server-side information filtering and screening.

Currently, hundreds, if not thousands, of media-rich (if not content-rich) channels are available for push technology use. That these channels provide useful information to some end-user communities is beyond dispute. What remains to be seen is whether future push development will develop end-user controls and filters adequate to the challenge of accommodating each information consumer's personal bandwidth.

6.10 State Parameters

A method of keeping track of state in the client-server communication is by passing messages via additional arguments. For example, one can pass additional parameters to a CGI program via the URL by placing a question mark followed by a list of messages (strings) which are separated by plus signs:

dangermouse.uark.edu/samples/params.cgi
?hithere+whatsup?+buddy

The Perl code below would give the following results:

```
hithere
whatsup\?
buddy
```

which are stored in the normal command line variables (@ARGV in Perl's case). Notice that the second question mark is treated as data. The program below, params.cgi, is a Perl [22, 23] script, which illustrates how one could keep track of state via additions to the URL and environment variables.

```
#! /usr/bin/perl
print "Content-type: text/html\n\n";
print "<html>\n";
print "<head>\n";

print "$ARGV[0]<br>\n";
print "$ARGV[1]<br>\n";
print "$ARGV[2]<br>\n";
print "<body></html>\n"
```

Another method allowing client and server to communicate information such as state is the use of hidden fields. This method uses fields in a Web form. As stated, a form is Web page that accepts user input. Input can be given in text boxes, check boxes, or button selects. There can be many forms per Web page. Here is a section of a Web page that defines a form and two input fields: id and password:

```
<form method=post>
Enter ID: <input name="id"> <br>
Enter password: <input type=password name="password"> <br>
<input type=hidden name="date" value="01/06/1999"> <br>
<input type="submit" name="continue">
</form>
```

There are actually four types of fields on this form: a text box (id), a password-type text box such that text typed appears as asterisks (password), a hidden field (date), and a button (continue). All field values are stored in operating system environment variables which can then be accessed by CGI programs. For example, the program displayed above would create three environment variables named id, password, and date.

As with most new technology, we trade a little privacy for ease of use. This will probably always be the case on the Internet.

7. Security and Privacy

To the average user, the Internet and its protocols seem very safe. However, this is far from the case. The Internet was set up in a cooperative environment, and still remains so to this day. For example, IP relies on servers all over the world acting as a giant bucket-brigade to pass message packets around from place to place. There is barely anything except ethics keeping advanced users from "peeking" at messages as they go by one's server on their way to other destinations.

Two technologies that have emerged to fix this major security hole are the Secure Socket Layer (SSL) and S-HTTP.

7.1 Secure Socket Layer

The Secure Socket Layer is a security protocol that sits on top of TCP/IP to prevent eavesdropping, tampering, or message forgery over the Internet. The latest version of the SSL protocol (Version 3.0) has been submitted to the IETF and is available as an Internet Draft.

7.2 Secure HTTP (S-HTTP)

Secure HTTP was developed by Enterprise Integration Technologies (www.eit.com) to keep commercial transactions protected. S-HTTP is a secure protocol over HTTP for identification when entering into a server. Both the server and the client identify each other using a public key system. S-HTTP encrypts certain pages that flow between the Web server and the client. This encryption is usually only done to pages that contain sensitive information, such as a credit card number. That means that if anyone attempts packet sniffing or eavesdropping in any way, the intruder will see only the encoded message.

For the Web to become a medium for commonplace commerce, security and privacy must become seemlessly integrated into it. Currently, it takes extra effort for Web users and servers to insure they are communicating over a secure line. When secure communication is the default, we expect on-line electronic transactions to be the most common method of paying bills, buying products, and performing most other types of commercial interactions.

7.3 Cookies

A cookie is another technique for allowing clients and servers to keep track of state. Cookies were created by Netscape corporation. The program below is a Perl script that attempts to set a cookie on any client that reads the Web page (given that the client's browser is cookie-capable, and that the user accepts it). The cookie will automatically be retrieved from the client's machine and stored in the HTTP_COOKIE environment variable whenever a page is accessed from the DOMAIN specified in the META tag.

```
#! /usr/bin/perl
print "Content-type: text/html\n\n";
print "<html>\n";
print "<head>\n";
print "<META HTTP-EQUIV=\"Set-Cookie\" ";
print " CONTENT=\"CODENAME=Smith";
print " EXPIRES=Mon, 01-06-99 12:00:00 GMT;";
print " PATH=/;DOMAIN=.uark.edu\">\n";
print "<body><h1>";

print $ENV{'HTTP_COOKIE'};
print "<br>\n";
print $ENV{'SERVER_NAME'};
print "<br>\n";

print "</body></html>\n"
```

Cookies are composed of two parts: the field name, and the field data. In this example, the field name is CODENAME and the data is "Smith." Whenever a page is accessed at the .uark.edu domain, the HTTP_COOKIE environment variable will contain "CODENAME=Smith" and possibly other cookie field/data pairs, separated by semicolons. This particular cookie will expire on 1 June 1999 as specified in the EXPIRES clause. Until then, the cookie's information will be stored on the user's disk. Netscape's Navigator stores cookie information in a file called "cookies"—e.g. \Programs\Netscape\Navigator\cookies.txt in the case of Netscape running under Windows. After accessing the above Web page, there would be an entry in the cookie file similar to:

```
.uark.edu TRUE / FALSE 915624000 NAME Smith
```

If the EXPIRES clause is not given, the cookie will expire when the browser is exited and will never be stored on disk.

There is an additional keyword that may appear in the META clause for use with Netscape browsers: SECURE. If the SECURE keyword appears, then the Netscape client will only send the field/data pair back if the client and server are communicating over a secure protocol, such as the Secure Socket Layer (SSL). Of course, the field/data pair could be encoded on the server, thereby protecting sensitive information even without SSL.

Because of privacy issues, the use of cookies continues to be hotly debated. According to the most recent Web survey [18] only 22% of the Web users surveyed accept cookies from any source, while 23% receive a warning before cookies are set, allowing them to make a decision on a case-by-case, and approximately 6% refuse all cookies. Surprisingly, the remaining survey participants either didn't know what a cookie was or didn't care about having a policy.

Cookies can help make the Web experience more useful by recording information on individual network transactions, which can streamline subsequent interactions. Despite this advantage, many remain concerned about the potential loss of privacy by allowing Web servers to "track" them.

Factors which mitigate against privacy concerns include:

(1) Only the domain that sets a cookie can read that cookie.
(2) Sites can only set cookies for their domain.
(3) All of the information that is stored in the cookie on the client's machine could easily be stored on the server.
(4) There is a hard limit to how many cookie field/data pairs a client can store (Netscape's Navigator can hold 300 total) and a limit per domain (20 for Navigator). This guards against "denial of services" attacks so that wayward servers can't gobble up a client's diskspace by giving it too many cookies to eat.
(5) Cookie data is typically encoded or is composed of a random site-based database key.

Given these points, one realizes that cookies might be the lesser of two evils: having the client store tracking data or having the server store tracking data. If the server keeps tabs on the browsers, the end-user might never know. Of course, the volume of data collected by highly-active servers would discourage unrefined cookie collection. Since servers do keep tabs of network transactions (e.g. in the form of values of environment variables) perhaps not much privacy is breached.

Here is a typical entry that was generated when the above Web page was accessed (from the Apache Web server's default settings for logging):

```
dangermouse.uark.edu - - [31/May/1998:22:01:19 -0500] "GET /samples/hw.cgi HTTP/1.0" 200 194
```

If the client stores the data, one could change it, delete it, and generally be aware of what sites are openly keeping track of state. Anonymous browsing is impossible, although there are some steps one can take to be less obvious:

(1) Use an "anonymizer". An anonymizer is a "go-between" web site. A user asks the anonymizer to retrieve a Web page, the anonymizer does so, and returns the HTML data back to the user. Unfortunately, one must trust the anonymizer, for it knows who is accessing what pages.
(2) Physically move to a different computer. This prevents Web sites from having accurate data. Of course, this is not always a possibility.
(3) Use dynamically assigned IP numbers.

Although cookies cannot get to data on your hard drive, they can be used to track you. For example, DoubleClick Corporation (http://www.doubleclick.com/) uses cookies to keep track of your browsing from many thousands of Web sites. This data can then be sold to marketing companies. Whenever a DoubleClick ad appears, a request is made from their site for the advertising graphic. Doing so not only retrieves the image, but allows them to check your cookies, and assign you an ID if you haven't been to a DoubleClick-sponsored site before. Afterward, whenever you go to a site with a DoubleClick ad, they can keep statistics on your visits.

The latest versions of Netscape Navigator provide a method of refusing cookies that are issued from sites other than the one that you currently are viewing. This will foil most global tracking schemes (such as DoubleClick's) without interfering with the more useful cookies that keep track of local state (i.e. for shopping carts). Of course, one could also simply delete the cookie file thus throwing a monkey wrench into the usefulness of the cookie technology. (On systems supporting symbolic links, one can simply `ln -s /dev/null` cookies and cookies are automatically sent to the void.)

In addition to server logs, security issues also include the client machine. One should consider that typical modern browsers leave a trail of exactly what has been viewed over the Internet. Such evidence can be found in a browser's cache, a directory of temporary files documenting every graphic and HTML page viewed.

The interactions between all of the types of scripting and dynamic Web technologies is still not well defined. For example, the code below is a JavaScript program that discovers a visitor's IP address. Although this information can also be found in a CGI's environment variables, as well as a server's access log files, if JavaScript could access more personal data (such as the user's email address) and give that to the server, then privacy is further lost.

```
<html>
<head>
<title>Get IP Address</title>
</head>
<HR>Getting IP Address...</HR>
<SCRIPT LANGUAGE="JavaScript">
<!--
function getIP() {
   if (navigator.javaEnabled()) {
       baseAddress = java.net.InetAddress.getLocalHost()
userDomain = baseAddress.getHostName() return
(userDomain.toString())
   } else {
        return null
   }
}
domainName = getIP()
alert('You are ' + domainName + ' and I now know it!')
//-->
</SCRIPT>
</body>
</html>
```

8. The Web as a Social Phenomenon

The social effect of the Web is not well understood. Not surprisingly, the zeal to harness and exploit the richness of Web resources and technology, combined with the desire to capitalize on commercial Web services, have taken precedence over efforts to understand the social dimensions of Web use.

Much of what little we know of Web behavior seems to be derived from two disparate sources. Descriptive statistics produced by the Web surveys are most useful to measure isolated events and independent activities—e.g. how many Windows users use Netscape.

The second source is the study of the use of email. Email's status as a de facto paradigm of "interpersonal though not-in-person communication" makes it a useful testbench for testing hypotheses about network behavior, generally. Since email and the Web share several characteristics, e.g. they both minimize the effects of geographical distance between users, they are both based on user-centric models of communication, both rely on self-imposed interrupts, both are paperless and archivable by default, both create potential security and privacy problems, and neither requires continuous endpoint-to-endpoint network connectivity, email can teach us something about Web behavior.

However, both sources provide incomplete views of Web behavior. Descriptive statistics tell us little about either the causes of emerging trends or the connections and associations between various aspects of Web use (e.g. to what extent, if any, do anonymous Web engagements promote discussion of controversial topics?).

There are differences between email and the Web as well. Email deals with network, peer-to-peer communication partnerships, where the present Web remains primarily an information-delivery system. Email, in its most basic form at least, exemplifies push-phase technology, while the current Web is mostly pull-phase in orientation. Of course, the onset of new technologies such as Web teleconferencing and virtual communities, will change the nature of such comparisons.

While definitive conclusions about the social aspects of Web use remain elusive, some central issues have been identified for future study (see Table V). We are slowly coming to understand the capabilities of the Web for selected applications and venues. To illustrate, early use convincingly demonstrated that the Web was a popular and worthwhile medium for presenting distributed multimedia, even though we cannot as yet quantify the social benefits and institutional costs which result from this use. As CGI was added to the Web, it became clear that the Web would be an important location-independent, multi-modal form of interactivity—although we know little about the motivations behind such interactivity, and even less about how one would measure the long-term utility for the participants and their institutions.

8.1 Virtual Communities

As mentioned above, the Web's primary utility at the moment is as an information delivery device—what some authors have called the "document

TABLE V

SOCIAL ISSUES AND WEB BEHAVIOR

- How central is location transparency to Web use? To what extent will Web "communities" be used to replace or enhance veridical counterparts?
- How will future Web technologies deal with information overload?
- To what extent will interactive and participatory Web engagement become enticing and immersive?
- What are the benefits and weaknesses of anonymous engagement and relative identity environments. Will relative identity havens create new problems for law enforcement?
- To what extent will Web engagement enhance or supplement alternative modes of information exchange?
- What technologies will emerge to reduce Web transaction friction?
- etc.

TABLE VI

POTENTIAL ADVANTAGES AND DISADVANTAGES OF ELECTRONIC COMMUNITIES

Advantages	Disadvantages
• potential for dynamic involvement where membership may be transitory and the infrastructure of the community informally defined	• quality of experience may not justify the participation, or may degrade over time
	• potential loss of privacy by invasive Web technologies such as global tracking via cookies, CGI environment variable recording, and the like
• location transparency for members, as all electronic communities are potentially global	
• capability of self-administration and self-organization by a membership in continuous flux	• some forms of electronic communication lack intensity, and some may lack content (e.g. more information exchange doesn't imply better information exchange)
• creation of "thought swarms" through the continuous, interactive stimulation of participants	• not all experiences translate well into the electronic realm, as documented by the easy
• increased attention on content	• misinterpretation of email and the "flaming" that can ensue

phase" of the Web. However, more powerful and robust Web applications will soon begin to take hold. Perhaps the most significant future application will involve the construction of virtual communities.

Virtual, or electronic, communities, are examples of interactive and participatory forums conducted over digital networks for the mutual benefit of the participants and sponsors. They may take on any number of forms. The first attempts to establish virtual communities dates back to the mid-1980s with the community, "freenet" movement. While early freenets offered few services beyond email and Telnet, many quickly expanded to offer access to documents in local libraries and government offices, Internet relay chats, community bulletin boards, and so forth, thereby giving participants an enhanced sense of community through another form of connectivity.

Virtual communities of the future are likely to have both advantages and disadvantages when compared to their veridical counterparts (Table VI).

9. Conclusion

The World Wide Web represents the closest technology to the ideal of a completely distributed network environment for multiform communication. As such, it may be thought of as a paradigm shift away from earlier network protocols.

Many feel that the most significant impact of the Web will not be felt until the 21st century, when technologies are added and converged to make the Web a fully interactive, participatory, and immersive medium by default.

Security and privacy will undoubtedly continue to be important issues as new methods are integrated into current Web technologies. The complexity of interacting components is nearly out of hand at this point; future Web protocols may help create the appropriate structure necessary for continued robust Web development.

The world will continue to become a smaller place as cultures continue to be only a click away. The Web promises to have one of the largest impacts on general society of any technology thus far created. For a more thorough-going analysis of the Web's future by its founder, see references [6] and [7].

ACKNOWLEDGMENTS

We wish to thank Marvin Zelkowitz and anonymous reviewers for their comments on earlier drafts of this chapter.

REFERENCES

[1] ACM Electronic Communities Project, `http://www.acm.org/~ccp/` (information on the use of the Web for Electronic Communities).
[2] Berghel, H. (1998). The client side of the World Wide Web. *Encyclopedia of Computer Science* 4th edn (ed. by Anthony Ralston, Edwin Reilly, and David Hemmendinger). Petrocelli.
[3] Berghel, H. (1998). Who won the mosaic war? *Communications of the ACM*, October.
[4] Berghel, H. (1998). Push technology. *Networker*, 2(3), 28–36, ACM Press.
[5] Berghel, H. (1997). Email: the good, the bad and the ugly. *Communications of the ACM*, **40**(4), 11–15.
[6] Berners-Lee, T. (1996). WWW: Past, present and future. *Computer*, **29**(10), 69–77.
[7] Berners-Lee, T., Cailliau, R., Luotonen, A., Nielsen, H., and Secret, A. (1994). The World Wide Web. *Communications of the ACM*, **37**(8), 76–82.
[8] Bush, Vannevar (1945). As we may think. *Atlantic Monthly*, July. Online at `www.isg.sfu.ca/~duchier/misc/vbush/`).
[9] Comer, D. (1997). *The Internet Book: Everything You Need to Know About Computer Networking and How the Internet Works*. Prentice-Hall, Inc., Upper Saddle River, NJ.
[10] Englebart, D. (1986). The augmented knowledge workshop. *The History of Personal Workstations: Proceedings of the ACM Conference*, (ed. K. Anderson). ACM Press, New York, pp. 73–83.
[11] Flanagan, D. (1996). *Java in a Nutshell*. O'Reilly & Associates, Inc. Sebastopol, CA.
[12] Laird C., and Soraiz, K. (1998). Get a grip on scripts. *BYTE*, June. The McGraw-Hill Companies, Inc. New York, NY.
[13] McGraw, G., and Felten, E. W. (1997). *Java Security: Hostile Applets, Holes, and Antidotes*. John Wiley and Sons, Inc.
[14] Nelson, T. (1995). The heart of connection: hypermedia unified by transclusion, *Communications of the ACM*, **38**(8), 31–33.

[15] Niemeyer, P., and Peck, J. (1966). Exploring Java. O'Reilly & Associates, Inc. Sebastopol, CA.
[16] NSFNET Backbone Traffic Distribution Statistics, April, 1995. http://www.cc.gatech.edu/gvu/stats/NSF/merit.html.
[17] Ousterhout, J. (1994). Tcl and the Tk Toolkit. Addison-Wesley Publishing Company. Reading, MA.
[18] Pitkow, J., *et al.*, GVU's WWW User Surveys, http://www.cc.gatech.edu/gvu/user_surveys/.
[19] Quercia, V. (1997). Internet in a Nutshell. O'Reilly & Associates, Inc. Sebastopol, CA.
[20] Roberts, D. (1996). Internet Protocols. Coriolis Books, Scottsdale, AZ.
[21] Sun Microsystems (1995). *The Java Language: a White Paper.* Web document. URL http://java.sun.com.
[22] *The Perl Journal.* (http://tpj.com) Readable Publications, Inc. Somerville, MA.
[23] Wall, L., and Schwatz, R. (1991). *Programming Perl.* O'Reilly & Associates, Inc. Sebastopol, CA.
[24] Welch, B. (1997). Practical Programming in Tcl and Tk. Prentice Hall, Inc. Upper Saddle River, NJ.
[25] WWW Security FAQ http://cip.physik.uni-wuerzburg.de/www-security/wwwsf6.html
[26] Java for 1998. *PC Magazine*, 7 April 1998.

Progress in Internet Security

RANDALL J. ATKINSON AND J. ERIC KLINKER

@Home Network
PO Box 5712
Santa Clara, CA 95056-5712
USA

Abstract

This chapter surveys the state of security within the Internet protocol suite, including standard protocols and also widely used non-standard protocols. Key security technologies such as DNS Security, Secure Sockets Layer, and Internet key management are reviewed. Selected application and infrastructure technologies are reviewed, with both threats and security approaches being discussed. Some non-technical challenges to deploying a more secure Internet are also discussed. Progress made towards a more secure Internet during the past decade is highlighted throughout the chapter.

```
1. Introduction .................................................. 220
   1.1  Protocol Layering ....................................... 221
2. The Internet Protocol ......................................... 222
   2.1  IP Addressing ........................................... 222
   2.2  Threats and Issues ...................................... 222
3. Security for the Internet Protocol ............................ 224
   3.1  IP Authentication Header ................................ 225
   3.2  Encapsulating Security Payload .......................... 226
   3.3  Future Directions ....................................... 227
4. Routing Protocols and Technology .............................. 227
   4.1  Threats and Issues ...................................... 228
   4.2  Intra-domain Unicast Routing ............................ 229
   4.3  Inter-domain Unicast Routing ............................ 231
   4.4  Multicast Routing ....................................... 232
5. Domain Name System ............................................ 234
   5.1  Threats and Issues ...................................... 234
   5.2  Current Technology ...................................... 235
   5.3  Secure Dynamic DNS Update ............................... 235
6. Dynamic Host Configuration Protocol (DHCP) .................... 236
   6.1  Threats and Issues ...................................... 236
   6.2  Technology Directions ................................... 237
7. Key Management ................................................ 237
   7.1  Unicast Key Management with ISAKMP ...................... 238
   7.2  Multicast Key Management ................................ 239
```

8.	Public Key Infrastructure	239
9.	Network Management	241
	9.1 Threats and Issues	242
	9.2 Current Status	242
	9.3 Future Directions	242
10.	Interactive Applications	243
	10.1 Threats and Issues	243
	10.2 Status and Future Directions	244
11.	Electronic Commerce	244
	11.1 Transport Layer Security (TLS)	245
	11.2 Threats and Issues	245
	11.3 Current Technology	246
	11.4 Future Directions	248
12.	Electronic Mail	248
	12.1 Threats and Issues	248
	12.2 Current Technology	249
	12.3 Future Directions	250
13.	Other Considerations	250
14.	Conclusions	251
References		251

1. Introduction

As the Internet has become widely used over the past several years, there has been increasing concern about security of the Internet. This concern has not only been focused on electronic commerce applications, but also on security of the Internet infrastructure and of private networks interconnected with the global Internet. It is worthwhile to highlight the distinction between the World Wide Web (WWW) and the global Internet. The Web is a particular application that uses the Internet protocol suite for communication between the systems that make up the Web. In particular, the Web uses the Hyper-Text Transfer Protocol (HTTP) as its application-layer protocol. In turn, HTTP uses the Transmission Control Protocol (TCP) to provide reliability for the actual data which is sent via the Internet Protocol (IP). Security that is specific to the Web is discussed in section 11 of this chapter.

During the past few years, the Internet Engineering Task Force (IETF), which is the standards body for the Internet, has made significant progress in adding cryptographic security to various components of the Internet architecture, not only within electronic commerce applications, but also within the infrastructure technology that keeps the Internet operating reliably. The Internet community, including the IETF, has an electronic document series which contain not only standards and specifications, but also general information and humour relating to the Internet. Each document in this series is known as a "Request for Comments (RFC)". The phrase "request for comments" might seem quaint today, but reflects the Internet's origins more than 20 years ago in the research and development community. It is important to note that while all IETF standards are specified in RFC documents, not all RFC documents specify IETF standards. Internet standards are developed by the IETF using a completely open process, wherein each participant represents himself, rather than his employer. Most of the standards development is done using mailing lists which are set up by working groups. However, three times each year, there are meetings of many different IETF working groups at an IETF meeting. Anyone may participate in the development of Internet standards.

This chapter describes the current state of Internet security technology, including both infrastructure and also applications. Each technology area within the Internet protocol suite is discussed in its own section. Each technology area's section describes the perceived risks, the current security capabilities, and likely future directions in that portion of the Internet protocol suite.

Often, non-technical barriers impede the deployment of more comprehensive and trustworthy approaches to Internet security. For example, the vendor and user communities generally prefer to avoid patented technologies (e.g. RSA) due to the perceived higher costs. Also, commercial concerns about the timing of standards and community distrust of some technologies (e.g. key escrow) can delay the adoption of new technologies. Meanwhile, the number and sophistication of attacks on the Internet continue to increase. Whereas most attacks a decade ago were targeting specific hosts, many current attacks are upon the Internet infrastructure itself. Despite this, significant progress has been and is being made to create and deploy a more secure global Internet.

1.1 Protocol Layering

The Internet community has for many years used a five layer protocol model to describe networking protocols. At the top is the Application Layer, which includes not only the application itself but also some of the functions that the OSI community would categorize as part of the Presentation Layer and Session Layer. The Web's Hyper-Text Transfer Protocol (HTTP) is an example of an application layer protocol. Next, the Internet protocol model has the Transport Layer, which has capabilities nearly the same as the OSI community's Transport Layer. The Transmission Control Protocol (TCP) is an example of a Transport Layer protocol. Next comes the Internet Layer, which consists of the Internet Protocol (IP) itself. Below the Internet Layer, comes the Link Layer and finally the Physical Layer. Within the Link Layer, the IEEE has defined the Logical Link Control (LLC) sublayer, which provides data framing, and the Media Access Control (MAC) sub-layer which controls access to the physical media. Ethernet is an example of a Link-Layer protocol, while RJ-45 wiring is an example of a Physical Layer implementation.

2. The Internet Protocol

The Internet Protocol (IP) is the basis for the global Internet. IP provides transportation for upper-layer protocol information from one computer system to one or more destination computer systems. This transportation is not reliable, rather IP provides an unreliable datagram service. If reliability is required, it needs to be provided by upper-layer protocols, such as TCP.

2.1 IP Addressing

Each IP datagram contains a Source Address and a Destination Address. The Destination Address in a given IP datagram is used to route that datagram to its destination(s). IP supports both unicast (i.e. point-to-point) and multicast (i.e. one-to-many) transmissions. Because people find it inconvenient to remember IP addresses, the Internet developed a naming system, the Domain Name System, which can be used by applications to automatically map from easily remembered names (e.g. `ftp.ietf.org`) to the IP address(es) corresponding with that name. The Domain Name System (DNS) is discussed in a separate section later in this chapter.

The current Internet relies on IP version 4 (IPv4), which has 32-bit addresses [76]. The IETF is developing IPv6, which has 128-bit addresses, as a proposed replacement for IPv4 [26]. The Internet layer includes not only the Internet Protocol itself, but also the Internet Control Message Protocol (ICMP), which provides network control messages essential for proper operation of the global Internet [70].

Unicast applications that require end-to-end reliability use the Transmission Control Protocol (TCP) at the transport-layer [71]. Other applications, including multicast applications, typically use the User Datagram Protocol (UDP) at the transport layer [68]. UDP does not provide reliability, but is capable of working well with IP multicasting.

2.2 Threats and Issues

There are a number of risks at the Internet layer or just below the Internet layer. This section describes some of these threats. Subsequently possible protection mechanisms for those threats will be described. Threats involve not only unicast traffic [10] but also multicast traffic [9].

For example, on LANs the Address Resolution Protocol (ARP) is used to resolve an Internet-layer address into a MAC-layer address (e.g. Ethernet address) [74]. ARP operates using a simple unauthenticated request/response protocol. A node desiring to know the MAC address for a given IP address sends out an ARP request packet. Any device on that LAN segment may send an ARP response providing the answer. Although one typically wishes for the destination host to be the only responder, there is no protection against an adversary on that LAN from providing a false response that would redirect a victim's traffic to the adversary. Similar attacks are feasible using extensions to ARP such as Inverse ARP, where a host knowing its MAC address seeks to discover its IP address, and Proxy ARP, where a gateway responds on behalf of a node not on that IP subnet [13].

In normal operation, ICMP messages are used to redirect traffic from one host or gateway towards another host or gateway. Similarly, an ICMP Unreachable message is normally used to indicate that a particular destination is currently not reachable. However, a forged ICMP Unreachable or ICMP Redirect message can also be used to implement a denial of service attack on a victim. Because ICMP messages are at the Internet layer, an Internet-layer security mechanism can be used to protect ICMP from use as an attack vector. While IPv6 uses a slightly different set of ICMP messages than IPv4, the basic design remains the same [22].

Finally, the ICMP Router Discovery system has issues similar to those with ARP [25]. In ICMP Router Discovery, a host seeking its gateway sends out an ICMP Router Solicit message. Normally, each gateway on that IP subnet will then send an ICMP Router Advertisement message. The initial host then configures a gateway based on the Router Advertisements that it receives. If an adversary were to forge an ICMP Router Advertisement message, the initial host could be fooled into sending its outbound traffic to the adversary instead of to its legitimate gateway. This could be used to eavesdrop on victim traffic or to implement a denial-of-service attack. A crucial difference between the ARP attack and this attack is that ICMP could be protected if cryptographic authentication were available at the Internet layer, whereas ARP cannot be protected via Internet-layer security mechanisms.

As the IETF worked to design IP version 6 (IPv6), consideration was given to designing a protocol that would be easier to secure from these kinds of attacks. For example, ARP was dropped completely for IPv6. Instead, IPv6 uses a system known as Neighbor Discovery (ND) when hosts need to discover each other's MAC addresses [65]. ND includes an IPv6 version of Router Discovery, thus eliminating any need for ARP or its relatives. Because ND is based on ICMP messages, ND can be fully protected via Internet-layer authentication mechanisms. However, most of the issues that affect IPv4 also affect IPv6.

Many organizations operating IP-based networks use packet filters at their administrative boundaries to reduce risk of breakins from outside their network. These packet filters are sometimes referred to as *firewalls*, even if a full-blown firewall might not be in use. Alternately, many hosts now employ address-centric access control lists to reduce risk of intrusions [86]. Such packet filters commonly use the Source IP Address, Destination IP Address, upper-layer protocol (e.g. TCP, UDP, or ICMP), Source Port, and Destination Port information to make policy decisions. All of these items are present in either the IP header or in the upper-layer protocol (e.g. UDP or TCP) header. However, it is not difficult to forge an IP packet. In the absence of per-packet cryptographic authentication, an adversary can often get past a packet filtering firewall using forged IP packets. If per-packet cryptographic authentication were used, this kind of attack would not be possible. Moreover, cryptographic security mechanisms at the IP layer could be used to protect upper-layer protocols and applications without changing the upper-layer technology.

In addition, there are a variety of attacks on upper-layer protocols (e.g. TCP) that can be precluded by the use of cryptographic authentication at the IP layer. These include TCP SYN flooding [20], TCP Sequence Number prediction [62], and others [10]. UDP Port Flooding attacks and forged ICMP Redirect attacks can also be protected using cryptographic authentication at the IP layer [19, 58]. A non-cryptographic approach to precluding TCP Sequence Number prediction has been identified [11].

3. Security for the Internet Protocol

As part of the IPv6 design effort, Atkinson proposed a set of Internet-layer security mechanisms. These mechanisms were designed to be widely deployable (i.e. deployable even in locations where use of encryption or other confidentiality mechanisms is regulated), to be independent of any particular cryptographic algorithm (i.e. permitting any cryptographic algorithm to be used with the mechanism without major design changes), to be decoupled from any particular key management technology (i.e. permitting a wide variety of key management techniques to be used), and to provide protection to the IP layer and also to any protocol above the IP layer [1]. Additionally, since multicasting is a requirement for all IPv6 implementations, these IP security mechanisms are designed to support both multicast and unicast IP datagrams. After being initially developed for IPv6, these mechanisms were then retrofitted to also work well with IPv4.

IP-layer security can be very useful in protecting not only the Internet Protocol, but also other upper-layer protocols and applications. It is not a panacea, however. Because encrypted data generally cannot be compressed, one adverse side effect of encrypted IP traffic is that link-layer compression will generally not work. This can be a significant issue on low speed dialup modem connections. Use of these cryptographic mechanisms with the Internet Protocol reduces the security risks, but decreases both the effective bandwidth available to users and possibly the end-to-end throughput.

The concept of a *security association* is crucial to understanding IP security. A security association is the entire set of security configuration information related to a given IP session. A security association typically includes the Source IP Address, Destination IP Address, Security Parameters Index, cryptographic key(s) in use, the cryptographic algorithms and modes in use, the lifetime of the security association, and all other information relating to that IP security session. The Security Parameters Index (SPI) is an opaque 32-bit integer carried in each IP packet protected via IP security. The combination of the Destination IP Address and the Security Parameters Index uniquely identifies a particular security association. Because IP security needs to support not only unicast traffic but also multicast traffic, the SPI needs to be interpreted in the context of the Destination IP Address. The use of the SPI field provides decoupling between the IP security mechanism in use and the key management system in use. Later in this chapter, several key management systems will be described. Any key management scheme that permits secure distribution of keys and other elements of an IP security association can be used. The IP security standards specify the ISAKMP approach as the preferred, mandatory-to-implement, approach to unicast key management.

3.1 IP Authentication Header

The first IP security mechanism is known as the IP Authentication Header (AH)[2]. This provides authentication without confidentiality to the portion of the IP header (including IP options) that does not change during transit and also to the upper-layer data (e.g. TCP, UDP, ICMP, or IGMP) carried in the IP datagram. Because this mechanism does not provide confidentiality, restrictions on use of encryption in some countries (e.g. France) or export of encryption from some countries (e.g. most NATO countries) are not an impediment to widespread deployment of this mechanism. By providing cryptographic authentication (including packet origin authentication and data integrity), AH can be used to preclude the forgery attacks on IP and ICMP that were described above.

The Authentication Header consists of a single optional header inserted immediately after the IP header itself. AH contains several data fields. First there is a Next Header field, which indicates which protocol follows the AH header and a header length field. Next there is an SPI field. AH also includes a sequence number, which is used to reduce the risk of replay attacks, where an adversary replays a legitimate packet later in order to disrupt an IP session. Finally, there is cryptographic authentication data. This authentication data is the output of a cryptographic hash function computed over the invariant fields of the IP datagram. The authentication data field is variable length in order to support all possible cryptographic authentication algorithms.

In order to have widespread interoperability among the various implementations of AH, a common cryptographic algorithm is needed. The IETF selected the Message Digest 5 (MD5) algorithm [83]. MD5 is used in many IETF protocols when a cryptographic hash function is needed. In part this is because MD5 is openly specified and is not patented. Another reason is that MD5 has been subjected to open peer review in the cryptographic community for several years. Although some issues with MD5 were recently discovered, none of those issues apply to MD5 as it is used in the IP Authentication Header. As insurance, the SHA-1 cryptographic hash function has also been specified for optional use with AH [66].

3.2 Encapsulating Security Payload

For situations where authentication alone is not sufficient, the Encapsulating Security Payload (ESP) was created [3]. ESP was designed to provide confidentiality and optional integrity for upper-layer protocol data. Later, the IETF decided to create a variant of ESP that provides authentication without confidentiality [53]. This was done because some vendors believed they could optimize performance by having a different packet syntax than that used by AH. However, because ESP does not provide any protection for IP options or for many of the fields in the basic IP header, there are situations where the IP Authentication Header is preferred over the authentication-only mode of ESP. For many of the issues with TCP/IP security (for example: TCP sequence number prediction, TCP SYN flooding attacks), use of either AH or ESP is sufficient to remove the vulnerability of attack.

ESP can be used in two different modes. Although these modes are described separately, a clever implementation can use a single code path to support both modes. The first mode is known as transport mode. In transport mode, the outbound IP packet is split into two parts immediately after the IP header. The upper-layer protocol information is then processed through ESP, an ESP header is prepended, and the result is then concatenated to the original IP header. In tunnel mode, the entire original IP packet is processed through ESP, an ESP header is prepended, and finally a new clear-text IP header is prepended to that. In either mode, the ESP header contains a 32-bit Security Parameters Index field and, if necessary, a variable-length cryptographic Initialization Vector (IV). An IV is only needed when certain kinds of cryptographic algorithms are in use for the ESP-protected IP session; the IV field is zero-length when it isn't needed.

ESP also needs to have standardized default cryptographic algorithms to ensure interoperability of different implementations. For ESP, the IETF chose to use the Data Encryption Standard (DES) in Cipher-Block-Chaining (CBC) mode for confidentiality and MD5 for authentication and integrity [67].

3.3 Future Directions

Firewall vendors are already incorporating the Encapsulating Security Payload into their products, usually as components of a Virtual Private Network solution. In the future, most firewalls are likely to include this VPN capability. Further, firewalls are likely to provide security services, including key management and also encryption, on behalf of their interior intranet hosts. Hardware-based encryption is likely to appear in firewalls because software-based encryption tends to be quite slow. The use of AH with firewalls could permit the firewall to begin making IP-layer access control decisions based on authenticated information, replacing the current practice of making those decisions based on unauthenticatable information. However, the advent of AH and ESP is unlikely to induce organizations to remove their firewalls.

IP-layer security will likely become widely deployed during the next several years. As time progresses, the current use of DES for encryption is likely to be replaced by the Advanced Encryption Standard (AES) that is currently being studied by the US National Institute of Standards and Technology (NIST) [69]. The algorithm-independence of the IP security protocols makes such algorithm changes straight forward.

4. Routing Protocols and Technology

IP datagrams are routed from their source to their destination using the Destination Address field in the IP header. Unlike circuit-switched technologies such as ISDN or the telephone system, the Internet routes each packet separately, potentially along a different path than other packets of the same IP session. With IPv4, these addresses are 32 bits in size, while with IPv6 these addresses are 128 bits in size. Routing is the process of determining the best next hop to take along the path from the source to the destination. Each hop along the path will forward the packet to the next hop independently. That is, the Internet does not normally predetermine the path from source to destination at the time the packet is created and originally sent out towards the destination.

For very small networks, static routing, where routes are configured manually might be used. However, static routing cannot scale to a large corporate network or the global Internet. Also, static routing does not permit the routers to dynamically learn of topology changes, thus making the network less resilient to change.

By contrast, dynamic routing scales well to global networks and increases the reliability of the network. With dynamic routing, routing protocols are used to inform the routers of topology changes. This ensures that each router knows how best to route each packet at the moment the router actually forwards the IP datagram. Thus, routing protocols are needed to convey the topology information about the network to each of the routers in the network.

Routing protocols are often differentiated by their scope. An intra-domain routing protocol distributes internal routing information within a single administrative domain (e.g. a corporation). An inter-domain routing protocol is used to convey routing information (both topologic data and policy data) between different administrative domains (e.g. between a corporation and its Internet Service Provider (ISP) or among several ISPs). Alternately, routing protocols can be distinguished by whether they convey information for unicast (i.e. one-to-one) traffic or they convey information for multicast (i.e. one-to-many or many-to-many) traffic.

4.1 Threats and Issues

During this decade, attacks on the Internet infrastructure have become increasingly common. Among these have been attacks on the routing protocols themselves. This is a clever attack strategy because attacking the routing infrastructure can have greater impact than attacking individual hosts in the network. If one can subvert routing, then eavesdropping on traffic becomes much easier. Also, if routing protocol traffic is lost or false routing protocol traffic is injected, then a widespread denial of service attack is possible.

Historically, most routing protocols have used clear-text reusable passwords to authenticate the routing information in the packet. Unfortunately, this is not sufficient, since passive eavesdropping has been commonplace for several years [17]. When clear-text reusable passwords are in use, the adversary merely eavesdrops on the routing protocol traffic, extracts the clear-text password, and then forges a packet that contains false routing information and the extracted clear-text password.

There are at least three approaches that could be taken to reduce this risk. The first would be to change to using one-time passwords rather than reusable passwords. The second would be to go to the more comprehensive approach of applying cryptography to authenticate the origin of the routing protocol packet and ensure the integrity of the received packet. The third would entail applying cryptography to authenticate not only the packet but also the origin of each individual routing information element (e.g. Link-state advertisements) in the routing protocol packet. The second approach is being widely deployed, while the third approach has been experimentally specified for OSPF (see below).

4.2 Intra-domain Unicast Routing

There are several different unicast routing protocols used for intra-domain traffic. The most widely used is probably the Routing Information Protocol (RIP) because it is easy to implement, configure, and operate. RIP does not scale well to larger networks, so the Open Shortest Path First (OSPF) protocol was created and standardized to support larger networks. Finally, a number of backbone network operators have chosen to use the Integrated ISIS as the interior routing protocol within their backbones. Bellovin published one of the first papers on security issues in Internet routing protocols [10].

4.2.1 Routing Information Protocol (RIP)

The Routing Information Protocol, version 2 (RIPv2) is an enhanced version of RIP that includes support for important routing features such as class-less addressing and variable-length subnet masks [37]. RIPv2 is a distance-vector protocol that has been in use for many years. Because RIPv2 uses a distance-vector algorithm, it is easier to implement in a router having limited resources (e.g. memory or CPU).

RIPv2 historically has used clear-text reusable passwords, with all the security issues previously described. However, recent work by Baker and Atkinson has specified a keyed cryptographic hash function for use in authenticating the origin and data integrity of RIPv2 packets [5]. While this technique is on the IETF standards-track and is becoming widespread in many brands of commercial router, it is not perfect. For example, this technique cannot prevent a replay attack, where an adversary would replay an out-of-date RIPv2 packet sent in the past by a legitimate sender.

This technique is currently used with manual key distribution, where the router operator configures the cryptographic key on each router by hand. However, the standard specifies the hooks necessary to use a dynamic key management protocol if desired. At present, no standard exists for dynamic key management with RIPv2, though one is likely to be created in the next several years.

4.2.2 Open Shortest Path First (OSPF)

Because RIPv2 uses a simple distance-vector routing algorithm, it does not scale well to larger networks. This drove the creation and standardisation of the link-state interior routing protocol known as Open Shortest Path First (OSPF) [63]. OSPF is currently at version 2. OSPFv2 can support both unicast and multicast IP routing, though most sites are only using it for unicast routing.

Initially, OSPFv2 only supported clear-text reusable passwords. However, at about the same time as RIPv2 was enhanced with standardization of a keyed cryptographic hash function, OSPFv2 was also enhanced. Nearly the same technique was used in the standard approach for OSPFv2 and RIPv2 cryptographic authentication. The OSPFv2 cryptographic hash technique has the same limitations (e.g. replay attack) that the RIPv2 cryptographic hash technique has. Hence, OSPFv2 also currently uses manual key distribution, but could use dynamic key management without major changes if a standard were created. The same dynamic key management technology would probably be used for both RIPv2 and OSPFv2 when such a standard is created in the future. Murphy has specified a fine-grained authentication scheme that authenticates the origin of each OSPF Link State Advertisement (LSA) [64]. However, this scheme is not implemented in commercial products because it is perceived to have excessive computational costs for current commercial routers.

4.2.3 Integrated-ISIS

In the late 1980s and early 1990s, there was much controversy surrounding the selection of a standard interior link-state routing protocol. While the IETF eventually selected OSPFv2, the International Standards Organisation (ISO) continued to specify the Intermediate System to Intermediate System (ISIS) routing protocol for ISO Connection-Less Network Protocol (CLNP) traffic. Digital Equipment Corporation invented an enhancement to ISIS that supported not only ISO CLNP traffic, but also Internet Protocol (IP) traffic. This variant is known as Integrated-ISIS (I-ISIS). Many Internet backbones uses I-ISIS rather than OSPFv2 as their interior routing protocol, largely because one large router vendor has a higher quality I-ISIS implementation than OSPFv2 implementation.

Because I-ISIS was originally specified for use only with ISO CLNP traffic, I-ISIS uses the ISO Connection-Less Network Protocol (CLNP) as its underlying network protocol. In theory, CLNP has similar security properties to IP. However, because CLNP has not been commercially successful, there is no significant global CLNP infrastructure. Most backbone operators use CLNP only among their backbone routers, with no other user community able to send CLNP traffic into the backbone. This makes it a bit harder in practice to subvert I-ISIS routing. However, there is at least one known instance of I-ISIS routing being subverted after a successful telnet session-stealing attack on a backbone operator's router [18]. In response to this, Li has recently proposed using the same cryptographic hash technique specified for OSPFv2 with I-ISIS [55]. At present, there is only one known implementation of this cryptographic technique for I-ISIS. Consequently, there is negligible deployment of cryptographically protected I-ISIS.

4.3. Inter-domain Unicast Routing

Originally, the Internet used the Exterior Gateway Protocol (EGP) for exterior routing. EGP uses a link-state algorithm, requiring each backbone router to know the entire backbone topology. This had scaling issues and constrained the Internet to having a single backbone. As the US Government funding for the Internet backbone faded out in the late 1980s and early 1990s, a new approach was needed that would scale better and would also permit multiple, separately operated but interconnected, backbones to exist concurrently.

Thus, the Border Gateway Protocol (BGP) which uses a Path-Vector routing algorithm, replaced EGP as the standard exterior routing protocol for the Internet [82]. At present, BGPv4 is widely deployed for exterior routing within the global Internet. BGP uses TCP for its transport, unlike RIPv2, which uses UDP, and OSPF, which uses IP directly. This use of TCP transport makes BGP vulnerable to any attack possible on TCP sessions. In the mid-1990s, *TCP session stealing* attacks became commonplace [18]. Subversion of BGP routing was first noticed in the early 1990s, but has never been tremendously widespread.

To counter the problems with BGP security, Heffernan specified a new MD5 authentication option within the TCP protocol. This used the same kind of cryptographic hash function used successfully with other routing protocols and has since been openly documented and implemented by other vendors.

However, other, more sophisticated attacks on BGP are possible, such as when a valid participant in a BGP session intentionally or deliberately injects false routing information to its peers. This kind of attack cannot be prevented by the simplistic cryptography used with BGP at present. In order to prevent this sort of attack, authorization information on which IP routing prefixes may be advertised, and by which administrative domains, needs to be both available and able to be cryptographically authenticated. Further, each prefix advertisement would need to be authenticated using a cryptographic method binding an authorized administrative domain to each IP routing advertisement sent via BGP. Such techniques would probably require use of asymmetric cryptography. The adverse performance impacts of asymmetric cryptography in a router could be significant. At present, there is little vendor interest in this issue, though the problem is being studied in the research community.

4.4 Multicast Routing

The previous discussion of routing focused primarily on routing for unicast (i.e. point-to-point) traffic. Unicast traffic represents the vast majority of the traffic on today's Internet. However, multicast (i.e. many-to-many or one-to-many) traffic has grown significantly during the past several years due to the creation of the Multicast Backbone (MBONE). The MBONE is a virtual backbone interconnecting a large segment of the global Internet. Multicast traffic uses the same Internet Protocol that is used for unicast traffic. The primary difference between unicast and multicast IP traffic is that all multicast packets have a destination IP address that is in the Class D portion of the IP address space. Another difference is that multicast routing does not have an inter-domain/intra-domain technology split at present. Some might argue that the lack of a distinct inter-domain multicast routing algorithm is itself a security problem because there is no mechanism for expressing multicast routing policy with one's adjacent administrative domains. There are a range of security issues in multicast routing that are discussed in this section.

4.4.1 *Internet Group Membership Protocol (IGMP)*

As with unicast traffic, several protocols are used to route multicast traffic. At the lowest level, the Internet Group Membership Protocol is used to control the reception of multicast traffic on a given IP subnet or LAN segment [36]. IGMP is a derivative of ICMP, which was discussed above. Consequently, IGMP and ICMP have similar security properties. A host that wishes to join a multicast group sends an IGMP Join message to the multicast group address. The first-hop multicast router then grafts that subnet onto the multicast routing tree and begins transmitting packets destined for that multicast group to that subnet. The multicast routing will periodically verify that at least one host on that subnet wishes to listen to that multicast group. Also, a host that leaves a multicast group will normally send an IGMP Leave message to indicate that it is no longer listening to that multicast group. These mechanisms help ensure that IP multicast traffic is only sent where listeners exist, thus using bandwidth more efficiently than IP broadcast.

An adversary could forge an IGMP Join message on a subnet in order to decrease available bandwidth on that subnet. Alternately, an adversary could forge an IGMP Leave message to cause the multicast traffic to no longer be sent to that subnet. Neither of these represents a large operational risk because the problems will be automatically corrected by the hosts participating in that multicast group. In order to prevent multicast routing loops, each multicast router subjects incoming multicast traffic to a Reverse Path Forwarding (RPF) check that verifies that acceptability of each multicast packet's source IP address. If that RPF check fails, the multicast router will drop the packet rather than forward it. This RPF check, which is unique to IP multicasting, will tend to detect and drop forged IP multicast traffic. It has been proposed to add an IGMP Source Quench type message to eliminate traffic from a specific source. If that were adopted, unauthenticated messages of that type could be used to deny multicast service to a legitimate sender.

4.4.2 Distance-Vector (DVMRP) and Protocol-Independent Multicast (PIM) Routing Protocols

The Distance-Vector Multicast Routing Protocol (DVMRP) is probably the most commonly used multicast routing protocol [81]. This is an updated version of the original multicast routing protocol invented by Deering in 1988 [89]. The second most commonly used multicast routing protocol is probably Protocol Independent Multicast (PIM) [35]. DVMRP and PIM each use their own special types of IGMP messages to transfer information about the multicast routing topology among multicast routers. Consequently, each has approximately the same set of security issues and potential solutions that IGMP has. The one additional potential security is the injection of incorrect multicast routing information via a forged PIM or DVMRP message. This could be prevented by using IP security or another cryptographic authentication technique. The PIM specification indicates that they intend to rely on IP security mechanisms to protect PIM routing messages. Unfortunately, the lack of scalable multicast key management at present, makes it impractical to use IP security to protect PIM traffic.

4.4.3 Core-Based Trees Multicast Routing Protocol (CBT)

An alternative multicast routing protocol that is gaining popularity is Core-Based Trees (CBT), developed by Crowcroft, Ballardie, and Tsuchiya [7, 8]. CBT is primarily intended as an inter-domain multicast routing protocol. CBT is somewhat simpler than other multicast routing algorithms, making it more likely to be correctly implemented. CBT routing messages are carried using IP. CBT messages could also be protected using IP security provided that appropriate key management facilities existed. As noted elsewhere in this chapter, the designers of CBT also have designed a key management system that works well with CBT-based multicasting. So, unlike PIM, CBT appears to have a practical approach to using IP security to protect multicast routing messages.

5. Domain Name System

The Domain Name System (DNS) is used to map between IP addresses and domain names, identify mail exchangers and key exchangers for domains, and other information central to the operation of the global Internet [60, 61]. The DNS has been crucial to making the Internet usable by large numbers of people because most people find it much easier to remember textual names than to remember abstract IP address numbers or application port numbers. The DNS is organized hierarchically based on structured names, known as domain names. There is a relatively small set of top-level domains (TLDs), most of which are assigned on a one-TLD per country basis. This hierarchical approach permits the DNS to scale reasonably well, though there have been some scaling issues with especially popular international TLDs, such as *.COM*. The DNS replaced an earlier, non-scalable system using text files updated manually. The DNS hierarchy relies on a system of delegation that includes replicated servers and caching of DNS information. This helps ensure that the failure of any single DNS server cannot eliminate the entire DNS service for a given domain.

5.1 Threats and Issues

Because the DNS is important and central to operation of the global Internet, it has been a popular target for attacks during the mid and late 1990s [40]. Adversaries have falsified DNS information for various purposes, including attacking specific hosts, impersonating servers (e.g. for Web sites), and impersonating hosts (e.g. for intercepting email) [10]. More recently, many sites use firewalls. Those firewalls rely in part upon the accuracy of the DNS information and upon unauthenticated information in the header of each IP datagram transiting the firewall in making their policy decisions. So subverting the DNS can lead to breach of the security policy that the firewall is intended to enforce. Regrettably, the DNS has not historically incorporated any cryptographic protections against false information being injected into the system.

5.2 Current Technology

More recently, Donald Eastlake and Charles Kaufman have devised cryptographic security extensions to the Domain Name System [33]. These DNS security extensions are backwards compatible with the existing DNS, making gradual deployment easier. The extensions are designed to permit authentication of information contained within the DNS and also to permit the DNS to store public key information associated with IP addresses or domain names stored in the DNS.

The first extension is the Signature (SIG) record, which is used to provide a cryptographic binding between a data element and the domain name associated with that data element. The SIG record contains the type of DNS record being signed, the identity of the signer, the time of the signature, the expiration time for the signature, the cryptographic algorithm in use, and the digital signature itself. The inclusion of the additional data elements beyond the signature itself is essential to providing a trustworthy response and to handling the time-varying nature of DNS data effectively.

The second extension is the Public Key (KEY) record, which is used to indicate the public key for some fully qualified domain name, such as a host computer or router. The KEY record must be used in conjunction with a valid SIG record to ensure that a false public key is not associated with the entity using that domain name.

Atkinson has recently proposed another DNS extension that builds upon the DNS security extensions. This is the Key eXchanger (KX) record [4]. A KX record is associated with a domain-name. When a node wishes to initiate a key management transaction with another node, the first node looks for a KX record for the second node in the Secure DNS. If present, the KX record indicates which nodes provide key management services for the second node. This can be useful in locating security gateways and in easing the deployment of secure services which use dynamic key management.

5.3 Secure Dynamic DNS Update

With the advent of dynamic assignment of IP addresses to hosts using DHCP (described below), there is a requirement to be able to dynamically update the information stored within the DNS. Dynamic DNS Update would be a simple way to subvert the DNS and lead to the previously described attacks if it were not secured. Thus, Eastlake devised the Secure Dynamic DNS Update protocol to prevent attacks via the DNS dynamic update procedures [32]. Secure Dynamic DNS Update uses digital signatures from DNS security specification to protect update requests and update responses. This ensures that updates are only accepted from an authorized party. The authorization is controlled by possession of the correct cryptographic keys. However, the authors of this specification observe that any DNS zone permitting dynamic updates is inherently less secure than a DNS zone configured statically using off-line signing.

6. Dynamic Host Configuration Protocol (DHCP)

With the success of TCP/IP in the corporate community during the past several years, there has been a need for automated configuration of networking for desktop PCs and laptop computers. Most users neither know how to configure the TCP/IP parameters on their desktop computer nor desire to know how to do this. The need for automated network configuration of desktop computers has been met by the Dynamic Host Configuration Protocol (DHCP) [29]. With DHCP, the computer sends out a DHCP Request when it boots up, this is relayed to the DHCP server responsible for that LAN, and then the DHCP server sends a DHCP reply back to the requesting computer. This reply contains the IP address and other networking configuration needed by the requesting computer. The requesting computer then configures itself using the information contained in the DHCP reply message, sparing the user the effort of manual configuration.

6.1 Threats and Issues

While DHCP meets the need for automated configuration of computers, it also creates some risks. For example, a false DHCP reply could be forged by an adversary located somewhere along the path from the requesting computer to the DHCP server. This might cause the requesting computer to have an invalid non-functional configuration—creating a denial-of-service attack. Perhaps more dangerous, such a forged DHCP reply message might place the requesting computer into a configuration that appeared to work fine, but was inconsistent with the security policy of the network administrator. Gudmundsson and Droms have also documented specific security requirements for the DHCP protocol [41]. The crux of their analysis is that mutual authentication of the client and server and authentication of DHCP protocol messages is essential to have a secure and trustworthy DHCP.

6.2 Technology Directions

At present, DHCP lacks cryptographic authentication mechanisms that would be needed to prevent a forged DHCP reply from being successful. Very recently, Ralph Droms has proposed a technique for DHCP authentication to address these issues [30]. His approach provides for the use of HMAC-MD5 [54] to provide authentication for DHCP message origin and to provide message integrity during transit. This technique is very similar to that used with SNMPv2 and for routing protocol authentication.

Droms also describes a method whereby the DHCP server chooses a master key. Each DHCP client has its own unique key with the DHCP server that is the result of a cryptographic hash of the server's master key and the CLIENT-ID of that DHCP client. This would simplify key management on the DHCP server since it would only need to know a single master key and could compute the per-client key as necessary. However, this approach would require that each DHCP client be preconfigured with the correct client key. Since most DHCP user communities rely on DHCP for all of the requesting computer's network configuration, it is unclear whether they would be willing to configure a public key into each computer using DHCP because of the administrative overhead.

It is possible that once a Public Key Infrastructure (PKI) were established, each DHCP client could be configured with its own public and private key pair plus the public authentication key for its PKI directory server. With this information preconfigured into each client, it should be possible to derive a scalable session key distribution scheme applicable not only to DHCP but also for other protocols (e.g. ISAKMP, routing protocols).

7. Key Management

Key management is used to create, update, and remove cryptographic keys and related security associations among the parties involved in a secure session or security system. In most security systems, the single most important component is key management. If the adversary knows the key(s) in use, then the innate strength of the cryptographic algorithm(s) protecting the data just does not matter. Key management is often the most arcane and abstruse component of a security system. There are a number of approaches to key management that are used within the Internet. This section highlights the technologies used now and likely to be used in the near future for

Internet key management. Other technologies used in some portions of the Internet for key management include Kerberos, which was developed originally for MIT's Project Athena but could be extended for use with routing protocol authentication, IP security, or other security protocols. Kerberos uses the Needham-Schroeder technology to implement a scheme built around key distribution centers [70, 71].

7.1 Unicast Key Management with ISAKMP

With the advent of IP security (i.e. Authentication Header and Encapsulating Security Payload), the need for a standardized key management scheme became acute. Circa 1993, Karn proposed a monolithic key management protocol based upon Diffie-Hellman technology [50, 28]. Ultimately, a very similar scheme having a more modular design was selected by the IETF. The selected approach uses the Internet Security Association and Key Management Protocol (ISAKMP) framework [57]. This protocol framework can support multiple key exchange algorithms and multiple security protocols.

The IETF has selected the Internet Key Exchange (IKE) for standardization with IP security [44]. IKE is directly derived from Orman's Oakley proposal [66]. In turn, Oakley is a kind of Diffie-Hellman key exchange [28] that includes authentication of the identities of the parties and provides the essential property of *Perfect Forward Secrecy*. A Diffie-Hellman exchange permits the secure establishment of a shared session key between two parties. Perfect Forward Secrecy ensures that compromise of any single session key (e.g. via a brute force attack) does not lead to compromise of any other session key. In short, with Perfect Forward Secrecy there is no master key, whose compromise would lead to the compromise of dependent session keys.

Unless the identities of the parties are mutually authenticated, there is a potential risk from a man-in-the-middle attack [84]. In the Internet, any of the Public Key Infrastructure techniques discussed above can be used to support the mutual authentication of the parties to the session key exchange. Because of its scalability and already ubiquitous use, the DNS is likely to be widely used as a PKI to support IP Security.

A Domain of Interpretation (DOI) document specifies how ISAKMP and IKE are used to support a particular security protocol. In large part, the DoI specifies the set of security protocol parameters (e.g. session key lifetime, sensitivity label) that can be negotiated for a given Security Association that is being created using ISAKMP. ESP and AH are currently supported by the IP Security Domain of Interpretation [73]. In the near future, other standardized DoIs might support RIPv2 Cryptographic Authentication, OSPFv2 Cryptographic Authentication or the Secure Shell (SSH).

7.2 Multicast Key Management

Unlike unicast key management, which is relatively well understood technology, scalable multicast key management remains a research area. This section describes several approaches that have been proposed within the Internet community and are being considered for possible future use and standardization.

Ballardie, who is a designer of the CBT multicast routing protocol, has proposed extending the CBT routing protocol to provide scalable key distribution as well [6]. This approach would constrain the key distribution scheme to using trusted routers to distribute keys to nodes below them in the multicast routing topology. Not all routers need be trusted. The scalability of the approach is proportional to the number of trusted routers, however. This proposal has very good scaling properties and should be straightforward to implement. Because it uses the multicast routers for key distribution, key distribution is always performed from a reasonable location in the multicast routing topology. However, this approach does place constraints on the user's trust model that might not be acceptable to all potential users.

Harney and Muckenhirn have proposed using a heirarchy of Key Distribution Centres (KDCs) to support multicast key distribution [45, 46]. Their Group Key Management Protocol (GKMP) does not require that any router be trusted. The scalability of the approach is proportional to the number of trusted KDCs and to the effective distribution of KDCs within the multicast routing topology. When the KDCs are co-located with multicast routers, this approach is very similar to Ballardie's approach.

Atkinson has proposed using very simplistic public-key cryptography to solve the quite narrow problem of multicast key distribution to support OSPFv2 or RIPv2 routing protocol authentication. This approach requires each router to have its own public key/private key pair. Each router is then configured with the public key and IP address of each adjacent router. Each router then creates a symmetric session authentication key and transmits that key, encrypted in the sending routers private key, to each of its neighbours. The neighbour decrypts this session key using the sender's public key and associates that session key with its sender. Thereafter, the router receiving the OSPFv2 or RIPv2 packet uses the source IP address to locate the correct session key to use in authenticating the routing update packet.

8. Public Key Infrastructure

Virtually all of the techniques outlined in this chapter have relied on public key cryptography for one purpose or another. However, there needs to be an automated, yet secure, method of verifying and distributing public key information. Users can't be expected to remember long strings of numbers for public key use any more than they can be expected to remember the IP address for a particular host. A public key infrastructure (PKI) is used to fulfil these needs. Public key certificates are usually used to authentically bind an entity's identity with its public key(s). A public key certificate is usually issued by a certification authority (CA). A PKI needs to have one or more certification authorities.

A public key certificate is a data structure which contains the name of the user and his public key but also contains other information (like an expiration data). This structure is digitally signed with the private key of the CA and placed in an easily retrievable location, often referred to as the repository. To use a certificate (say for secure e-mail) a sender would acquire the certificate of the intended recipient and validate it by checking the digital signature using the public component of the CA which issued the certificate. If successful, the user can be assured that the public key contained in the certificate belongs to the intended recipient and it is safe to encrypt a symmetric key with this public key. The message data can be encrypted with the symmetric key and the encrypted symmetric key can be placed in the secure e-mail header.

For the above approach to work, it is necessary to have an assured copy of the public key of the CA. It might be necessary to acquire another certificate signed by a more authoritative CA for this purpose. This process may be repeated, creating a chain of certificates referred to as the certification path. There are several different approaches to PKI being undertaken within the Internet community. As described above, the DNS is being extended to add security and to add the ability to distribute public keys for domain-names. Also, there are efforts to enhance the ITU's X.509 version 3 certificate technology for use within the global Internet.

Certificate based key management and early attempts at forming a public key infrastructure were proposed as part of the PEM RFCs in 1993 [46]. Those documents specified the use of X.509 certificates, first introduced in 1988 as part of the X.500 Directory Service [48]. Early attempts to implement a PKI with the original version of X.509 certificates led to the adoption of additional fields in the certificates resulting in the X.509v3 certificate. This reduced some of the restrictive nature of early PKI implementations allowing for more flexible certification hierarchies and naming conventions. The IETF's PKIX working group is developing standards for X.509v3 based key management [4]. Though X.509 was originally proposed as a part of an overall X.500-based directory service, the current specifications realize that X.500 directory servers might not be widely deployed in the global Internet. Therefore, other means of certificate and CRL retrieval are possible including the use of FTP, HTTP, or LDAPv3 [88].

The goal of PKI is to make certificate use as seamless and automated as possible, both for the end user and the CA administrator. If this goal is not achieved, the security of the Internet will suffer. A misconfigured or compromised CA can do tremendous damage.

The structure of the certification path represents the most significant difference between X.509v1 and X.509v3 PKI. Version 1 required a strict top down hierarchy with *a priori* knowledge of specific CAs built into the certification path. Version 3 relaxes many of these restrictions. For instance, certification paths may start with a CA in the user's own domain.

As mentioned above there is a certain lifetime associated with a certificate. However, there may be times when a certificate must be revoked before the lifetime has expired. This is done by adding the certificate to a certificate revocation list or CRL. CRLs are generated and signed by CAs and stored in the repository along with the certificates. In addition to the certificate verification process mentioned above, the user must also retrieve the latest CRL and verify that the certificate is not contained in the CRL. CRLs are periodically (hourly, daily, or weekly) reissued by the CA. The advantage of this approach is that CRLs can be distributed and stored in the same manner that certificates are. The obvious disadvantage of this approach is that the time granularity of revocation is limited to the CRL issue period. On-line, real-time verification is possible but imposes additional security requirements which are not necessary in the CRL-based approach.

9. Network Management

In any large network, scalable network management requires the use of a network management protocol. Within the global Internet, the Simple Network Management Protocol (SNMP) is used [14]. SNMP version 1, which is most widely deployed at present, supports basic operations such as GET, GET-NEXT, and SET on the data elements contained within each Management Information Base (MIB). The Management Information Base is the set of configuration parameters and system statistics that a person managing a system might need. SNMP is used to automate and protect access to that information by the person(s) managing the system. SNMPv1 also supports the asynchronous transmission of a TRAP from a managed device to its management station to inform the management station of an interesting or anomalous event occurring. Later, SNMPv2 enhanced these basic operators with important new operators such as GET-BULK [15, 38]. Nearly all active devices in the Internet support SNMP, though it is currently used more for network monitoring than for network management.

9.1 Threats and Issues

SNMPv1 recognized the need for security of the network management system. Because of technology limitations at the time, SNMPv1 only specified clear-text reusable passwords, which are known as *community strings*. A given managed device will typically support several concurrent community strings, each having its own permissions. In SNMPv1, a given community string can have either read-only permission or read-write permission. SNMPv1 does not support multiple views or stronger authentication. If an adversary were able to discover the community string of some network device, the adversary could then change the configuration of that network device and cause significant damage. For example, if the device were a packet filtering router, the adversary might be able to remove or alter packet filters critical to the security policy of the network operator. As passive attacks became more widespread on the Internet, the limitations of the community string approach became more widely understood. This caused many operators to configure their SNMP agents to only provide read-only access, which limited the operator's ability to use SNMP to actually manage the device remotely.

9.2 Current Status

With the development of SNMPv2, security was an important design goal. SNMPv2 was the first of many protocols to use a keyed cryptographic hash function to provide authentication without confidentiality. SNMPv2 also included optional encryption provided through the use of DES in Cipher-Block-Chaining mode. Unfortunately, the Internet community had significant issues with the view-based access control model required by SNMPv2 and it never achieved widespread deployment. While many implementations added support for non-security features such as 64-bit counters and the GET-BULK operator, users were stuck with the disclosing passwords of SNMPv1.

9.3 Future Directions

Recently, SNMP version 3 was approved. This includes many of the cryptographic features originally developed for SNMPv2. SNMPv3 supports both authentication without confidentiality, using a keyed cryptographic hash function, and confidentiality, using DES in CBC mode. SNMPv3 supports several security models [12, 90]. The *User Security Model* provides access control mechanisms for SNMPv3 that are oriented around the notion of a user, without incorporating a per-user view mechanism that would have permitted different users to have different views into the MIBs. This model appears to be garnering significant support from SNMPv3 implementers, primarily because it appears to be easier to implement than the view-based access control model. Perhaps just as important, SNMPv3 appears likely to achieve widespread deployment and use before the end of this decade. As SNMPv3 is deployed, the goal of scalable distributed network management will become reality in the operational Internet.

10. Interactive Applications

The Internet has long used protocols such as telnet, rlogin, and rsh to provide users with access over the network to remote systems [79, 49]. These protocols remain widely used and help many organisations use expensive computing resources (e.g. supercomputers) more efficiently. The remote shell application (rsh) has also been widely used to facilitate remote system administration via various scripting languages. Applications implementing these protocols generally rely on the Domain Name System, described previously, to provide mapping between the domain name of the communicating systems and the IP addresses used by those systems. These protocols generally use the Transmission Control Protocol (TCP) at the transport layer and always use the Internet Protocol at the Internet layer.

10.1 Threats and Issues

Unfortunately, neither rlogin, rsh, nor telnet provides confidentiality to data sent over the network or authentication of the session endpoints [17]. When passive attacks first became widespread, many users changed from using reusable disclosing passwords to using one-time passwords to reduce risk [42, 43]. Even before then, many users were concerned about rlogin and rsh because they use the concept of unauthenticated *trusted hosts* as part of their authorization and authentication scheme. In short, rsh and rlogin simply trusted that packets received with a source IP address that was in the list of trusted IP addresses were valid. No further checks were performed. Unfortunately, it is easy to forge an IP packet. In this era of inexpensive PCs, IP packet forgery is quite commonplace, making the concept of trusted hosts entirely unworkable. Other issues with the rlogin command have been discovered over the years [21].

Other users worked to enhance the existing remote terminal applications or worked to develop new applications to provide greater security through cryptographic techniques. Several efforts were undertaken to provide an encryption option to telnet. Unfortunately, telnet option negotiation itself was not protected by most of these projects, so the adversary could defeat the encryption by forging a telnet control packet disabling that option. Since most telnet client implementations do not permit users to see the option negotiation, users were not aware that their telnet encryption had been disabled. One such project had the misfortune of an implementation error in key management that caused security to be compromised.

10.2 Status and Future Directions

One effort that has been rather more successful than the others is the development of the Secure Shell (SSH) application [91]. SSH provides an interface similar to the older rsh or rlogin applications of Berkeley UNIX. However, SSH does not rely on the older concept of trusted hosts. Instead, SSH employs cryptography both for authentication of users to hosts and also to protect user data transiting the network. User authentication is supported via public-key authentication, while data confidentiality is supported by stream ciphers (e.g. DES-CBC, IDEA). SSH implementations commonly support several different stream ciphers and permit users and administrators to configure which ciphers are acceptable on a given system.

One major security issue with SSH is that its integrated key management scheme is a pure Diffie-Hellman approach, making it vulnerable to the well known man-in-the-middle attack. SSH does not support the use of any form of PKI to authenticate the endpoints in the key exchange. SSH also does not support the use of any form of PKI to authenticate users or hosts to each other. In order to safely use SSH, one must configure it to disallow new hosts from establishing sessions and configure the SSH public key of each authorized host manually on each other authorized host. Finally, users need to exercise thought in configuring SSH so that it isn't used with a stream cipher that is too weak for the data requiring protection.

11. Electronic Commerce

Many users view the Internet primarily as a platform for conducting electronic commerce. For the past several years, this has primarily been in the form of World Wide Web sites with advertising and product information accessible to potential customers. However, in the past two years, there has been a significant increase in actual commerce conducted over the Web, including the transmission of sensitive information (e.g. credit card numbers) from customers to the firms selling the products. Concern about eavesdropping attacks has led to the development of upper-layer security mechanisms designed to provide confidentiality and integrity to data being transmitted over the network. The placement of security just above the transport-layer permits it to be implemented solely inside an application. This can be convenient because it does not require any modifications to the operating system underneath the application, as use of IP Security would require. The leading approach is now known as Transport Layer Security (TLS) [27]. TLS is directly derived from the Secure Sockets Layer (SSL) technology originated at and promoted by Netscape Communications.

11.1 Transport Layer Security (TLS)

The transport layer of the network model is responsible for providing reliability when conducting sessions or transactions on top of the Internet Protocol and IP based networks. Common "sessions" include Web browsing, file transfer, and remote access. Transport Layer Security (TLS) is commonly used to secure these kinds of applications.

The strong push for TLS originates from electronic commerce. Electronic commerce has been around for years, not in form of Web based commerce, which is mainly customer-to-business oriented, but in electronic data interchange or EDI. EDI is primarily a business-to-business model and is predominantly conducted over private value-added networks (VANs) which exist apart from the global Internet. There has been a recent push to leverage Internet connectivity to order to implement VANs using Virtual Private Networks and security mechanisms available at the network layer. Another recent trend is to encapsulate EDI information into MIME format and conduct EDI over email [23]. Security in this instance reduces to general email security covered in the next section.

However, the EDI model does not work well for customer-to-business transactions, and the popularity of these transactions is literally exploding with the wide acceptance of Web-based commerce. The general process behind customer-based electronic commerce is the sharing of information, followed by ordering and payment and may also include a support relationship. The sharing of information is analogous to the storefront where a seller advertises products and services that are available. This is easily done though Web sites or electronic catalogues and is generally conducted using the Hyper-Text Transfer Protocol (HTTP). TLS in the initial phase of interaction is not a major concern, but TLS is very important when a customer orders and pays for products electronically. If ongoing support is necessary, this support may be conducted at the transport layer as well, but is probably more suited to applications such as electronic mail, which is discussed below in more detail.

11.2 Threats and Issues

Significant user interaction with other parties on the Internet is maintained via a transport mechanism (e.g. HTTP, FTP). Securing these transactions is of paramount concern especially when commerce is involved and financial assets are changing hands between the communicating parities. Potential customers in this new medium need to be assured that information such as credit card numbers, account balances, and stock transactions are secure and authentic. Without such reassurances the new paradigm of Web-based commerce would fall apart.

While the privacy of personal communication is often important, there is nothing which heightens anxiety about security more than placing personal finances at risk. As such, the entire gamut of security threats is often considered when conducting these types of transactions. In an environment where transport layer security did not exist, eavesdropping attacks conducted just outside the electronic commerce site could silently gather credit card or other important information as it flowed into or out of the site. However, protecting the information sent in the transaction is not enough given the threat of replay attacks where certain transactions (say an electronic transfer of funds) are captured and re-sent over and over again by some malicious third party. Message tampering is another concern. Changing the amount of a transaction, or adding additional information to a valid transaction are classic examples of the threats posed by message tampering.

Masquerading attacks can be serious as well. To gather a large number of credit cards someone might masquerade as a seller of books on the Internet. Or on the other hand, someone may be in possession of stolen credit card information and masquerade himself as a valid card holder to potential sellers. Without authenticating the parties involved in the transactions, masquerading attacks are trivial to conduct and can have considerable impact.

To guard against these additional threats, the technology must deliver message integrity as well as authentication of the parties involved. Consider the credit card transaction over the Internet. Protecting the credit card number is important, but protecting the integrity of the transaction, authenticating buyers as valid holders of the credit card number, and authenticating sellers as valid recipients of this information are important as well.

11.3 Current Technology

Basic Transport Layer Security is widely deployed today in the form of the Secure Sockets Layer (SSL) developed by Netscape Communications. SSL is intended to provide channel-oriented security and as such is a protocol layer that sits just above TCP/IP and beneath the application layers (Fig. 1). It seeks to secure all traffic between two connected parties as well

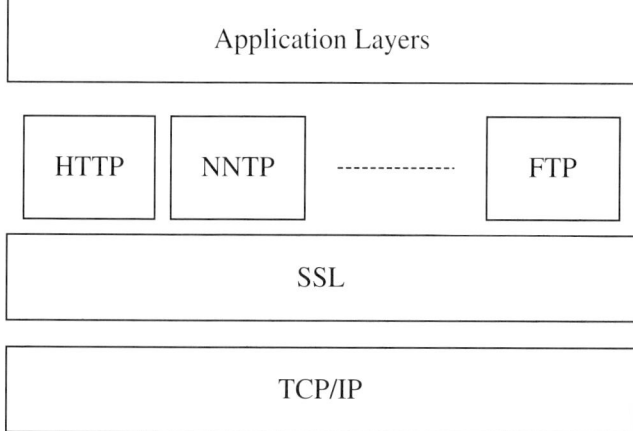

FIG. 1. Protocol diagram with Secure Socket Layer.

as provide some authentication of the parties involved. When used to its fullest extent, the protocol can effectively prevent eavesdropping, tampering and forgery attacks. However, because SSL and TLS do not protect the TCP header itself, they cannot protect against the TCP Sequence Number Prediction, TCP SYN Flooding, or other attacks upon TCP itself. In this way, the difference between the protections offered by IP Security and SSL/TLS is highlighted.

SSL uses public key cryptography to negotiate a common symmetric key and algorithm. Public key cryptography also plays a role in authentication using digitally signed certificates. SSL typically uses X.509v3 certificates. Each of these actions takes place before the transfer of data and together form the handshake phase of the protocol. Regrettably, the SSL protocol makes the authentication of end parties optional and in doing so opens up the possibility for man-in-the-middle attacks when anonymous transactions occur.

SSL supports a wide variety of algorithms and ciphers. For asymmetric algorithms, the protocol allows for the use of popular techniques such as RSA and Diffie-Hellman. When hash functions are required, SSL generally uses both the MD5 and the SHA-1 cryptographic hash functions in tandem. Performing Message Authentication Code (MAC) computations in this manner can reduce the risk from the potential discovery of a catastrophic flaw in either algorithm. Finally, a wide variety of bulk ciphers and key lengths can be negotiated, including RC2, RC4, DES, 3DES and with key lengths ranging from 40 bits (exportable) to 168 bits. Since SSL provides channel-oriented security it is common practice to layer HTTP over SSL and simply distinguish traffic intended to be secure from other traffic by using a different port number. This use of HTTP over SSL is by far the most common use of SSL today.

11.4 Future Directions

SSLv3, with some slight modification, is being standardized by the IETF as Transport Layer Security (TLS) v1. There is also a move underfoot to allow secure and insecure HTTP traffic to use the same port number. However, even in TLSv1, authentication of the server and client remains optional. Technology to help authenticate credit card holders and merchants is being pursued in the form of the Secure Electronic Transaction protocol or SET [87]. SET is being driven by the credit card industry, though its adoption has been slow. This is partially because SSL has been so successful in bootstrapping Web-based commerce. Although another impediment is the large amount of infrastructure necessary to conduct a SET. Though it should be noted that SET is slightly more versatile in that it secures credit card transactions independently from the applications performing the transactions.

12. Electronic Mail

Electronic mail has long since been the most popular application on the Internet. It is one of the most efficient means of communication possible between two parties. It supports the user without high bandwidth, real time connectivity, or continuous connectivity. E-mail, in essence, provides text (and lately multimedia) based communication between two end users. It relies on the DNS to route the messages across a series of mail relays until the final destination is reached, while IP routing is used for the actual packets that carry the message between each pair of mail relays. At each mail relay, the message is brought back up to the application layer as it is delivered on to the next hop or to the final recipient.

12.1 Threats and Issues

E-mail is very susceptible to eavesdropping attacks, either in transit on the wire or at the mail relays as the mail is being forwarded. Nothing is done to protect the data in transit and the e-mail may wait on an intermediate mail relay for some time before being passed along. During that period any party with administrative access to the relay machine has access to the data in the e-mail. Authentication of e-mail is another serious concern. It is trivial to spoof e-mail by source routing fraudulent messages through authentic mail relays (which stamp their identity on the message) and the end result appears to originate from an authentic domain name. Nor is message integrity assured as the message can be changed by unauthorized parties at any time during transit. And there is no mechanism in place to determine if the message was actually received by the intended party.

Also, using a secure electronic mail program could provide a false sense of security if the encryption algorithm negotiated between two implementations is weak. It is estimated that 40-bit RC2 can be broken by brute force in a matter of hours. To worsen matters, this algorithm is often the lowest common denominator negotiated between two secure e-mail implementations.

As the user base of the Internet continues to grow, unsolicited bulk e-mail is becoming another serious problem. Often referred to as *spam*, such mailings constitute denial-of-service attacks on legitimate mail servers that are being subverted to distribute the spam.

12.2 Current Technology

Electronic mail security is not a newly recognized problem. Privacy Enhanced Mail (PEM) [56, 52] was one of the first solutions available. PEM laid the groundwork for both secure e-mail and a public key infrastructure (PKI) for certificate-based key management. However, PEM has recently been moved to historical status by the IETF. Technologies in use today include S/MIME v2 [31], a secure e-mail technology which provides for the Multipurpose Internet Mail Extensions (MIME) encapsulation of digitally signed and encrypted objects. Another secure e-mail approach is Pretty Good Privacy (PGP) developed by Philip Zimmerman [92] and the extension of PGP called PGP/MIME to handle multimedia data [34].

There are many similarities between the two protocols but they differ in one important area, key management. S/MIME relies on the X.509v3 certification hierarchy being developed as part of the IETF's PKIX Working Group, while PGP utilizes a peer-based approach know as the web-of-trust. In PGP, the decision to trust a key is made by the end user. Furthermore, users can sign the keys of other users to generate the "web" portion of the trust relationship. This trust model is the most significant drawback to PGP as this type of key management makes scaling difficult, especially as the Internet community continues to grow. Also, little scientific work has been done on the web-of-trust security model. Both techniques provide confidentiality and authentication, using a symmetric algorithm to encrypt the message and asymmetric algorithms to protect the symmetric key and a keyed hash algorithm to provide a digital signature.

Other notable encryption schemes for e-mail include MIME Object Security Services (MOSS) [39, 24] and the US Government's X.400 based Message Security Protocol (MSP) [68], which closely resembles S/MIME in structure and process. In addition, MSP provides for the non-repudiation of messages through a signed receipt capability. Non-repudiation is a guarantee that the identical message was received by the intended recipient. The MSP effort is unlikely ever to be widely used outside the US Government because of its cost, complexity, and lack of support for Internet electronic mail standards.

12.3 Future Directions

The future of e-mail security lies in the wide availability of implementations. Some, such as PGP are add-on packages to current e-mail applications. Others will be tightly integrated into the mail application itself. Protocols which rely on the certification hierarchy will live or die by the availability of X.509v3 and a certification authority hierarchy on the Internet. Other secondary issues such as the availability of the directory service for certificate and CRL retrieval will also help determine the degree to which e-mail security is seamlessly available throughout the Internet.

13. Other Considerations

There are a number of other considerations that will affect the progress of Internet security. For example, although the Internet is global, many countries regulate the use of technologies that can provide confidentiality (e.g. encryption). Other countries, notably the USA, only regulate export of such technology. These regulations are one reason that Internet-based networking protocols commonly specify the use of cryptographic hash functions to provide strong authentication. Lack of widely deployable encryption has already impacted the growth of electronic commerce and is likely to continue to be a hindrance in the future.

Another issue is the widespread availability of a public key infrastructure (PKI). Deployment of one or more PKI systems in the Internet community will greatly facilitate not only electronic commerce but also infrastructure security techniques that require key management systems. For example, lack of a PKI to use with ISAKMP/IKE is already impeding deployment of the IP Authentication Header and IP Encapsulating Security Payload.

Regardless of how sound a given security technology might be, that technology cannot be fully successful unless it is implemented by vendors and deployed by users. Vendor choices for security technology have had and will continue to have significant impact on the security properties of the deployed Internet. For example, without Netscape's support, Secure Sockets Layer would never have developed into the IETF's transport-layer security standard. Similarly, without cisco's support, BGP security would be a much more serious problem today.

A curious issue has emerged recently within the Internet community. As so-called firewalls have been widely deployed over the past four or five years, there has been increasing demand that all protocols be "firewall friendly". For some, this means that all information should be provided as clear-text to the firewall. Unfortunately, for a security protocol to be firewall-friendly, it might not be able to provide the kind of end-to-end security that is ultimately desired by most users and network operators. The issue will affect whether key technologies such as IP security become widely deployed to provide end-to-end protections or are only narrowly deployed to fill niche requirements such as virtual private networks.

14. Conclusions

A decade ago, it was not clear that the Internet would evolve into anything more than a large-scale research prototype. At that time, the protocols and technologies used in the Internet did not generally provide significant security to users, administrators, or network operators. The advent of the World Wide Web application has changed the Internet permanently, with exponential growth in users and with the commercial pressures for security to support electronic commerce. As the Internet has grown, the number of skilled and motivated adversaries has also increased. By the late 1980s, some governments were believed to be behind some of the attacks occurring on the Internet [85]. By the late 1990s, the threat environment is much more challenging.

In the past decade, significant progress has been made towards a more secure Internet. This progress has not only been in applications such as electronic commerce, but also within the Internet infrastructure itself. However, significant technical and social challenges remain to be solved if the Internet is to become widely useful for commercial purposes.

REFERENCES

[1] Atkinson, R. (1995). *Security Architecture for the Internet Protocol*, RFC-1825, August.
[2] Atkinson, R. (1995). *IP Authentication Header*. RFC-1826, August.
[3] Atkinson, R. (1995). *IP Encapsulating Security Payload (ESP)*. RFC-1827, August.
[4] Atkinson, R. (1997). *Key Exchange Delegation Record for the DNS*. RFC-2230, October.

[5] Baker, F., and Atkinson, R. (1997). *RIP-2 MD5 Authentication*. RFC-2082, January.
[6] Ballardie, A. (1996). *Scalable Multicast Key Distribution*. RFC-1949, May.
[7] Ballardie, A. (1997). *Core Based Trees (CBT version 2) Multicast Routing*. RFC-2189, September.
[8] Ballardie, A. (1997). *Core Based Trees (CBT) Multicast Routing Architecture*, RFC-2201, September.
[9] Ballardie, A., and Crowcroft, J. (1995). Multicast-specific security threats and counter-measures. *Proceedings of the 1995 Internet Society Symposium on Network and Distributed System Security*, San Diego, CA, February.
[10] Bellovin, S. M. (1989). Security problems in the TCP/IP protocol suite. *ACM Computer Communications Review*, **19**(2), 32–48, April.
[11] Bellovin, S. (1996). *Defending Against Sequence Number Attacks*. RFC-1948, May.
[12] Blumenthal, U., and Wijnen, B. (1998). *User-based Security Model (USM) for version 3 of the Simple Network Management Protocol (SNMPv3)*. RFC-2264, January.
[13] Bradley, T., and Brown, C. (1992). *Inverse Address Resolution Protocol*. RFC-1293, January.
[14] Case, J. D., Fedor, M., Schoffstall, M. L., and Davin, C. (1990). *Simple Network Management Protocol (SNMP)*. RFC-1157, 1 May.
[15] Case, J., McCloghrie, K., Rose, M., and Waldbusser, S. (1993). *Introduction to version 2 of the Internet standard Network Management Framework*, RFC-1441, April.
[16] J. Case, *et al*. Message Processing and Dispatching for the Simple Network Management Protocol (SNMP), RFC-2262, January 1998.
[17] Computer Emergency Response Team, ongoing network monitoring attacks. *CERT Advisory 94:01*, 3 February 1994. http://www.cert.org/advisories/CA-94.01.ongoing.network.monitoring.attacks.html
[18] Computer Emergency Response Team, IP spoofing attacks and hijacked terminal connections. CERT Advisory 95:01, 23 January 1995, http://www.cert.org/advisories/CA-95.01.IP.spoofing.attacks.and.hijacked.terminal.connections.html
[19] Computer Emergency Response Team, UDP port denial-of-service attack. CERT Advisory 96:01, 8 February 1996. http://www.cert.org/advisories/CA-96.01.UDP_service_denial.html
[20] Computer Emergency Response Team, TCP SYN flooding and IP spoofing attacks, CERT Advisory 96:21, 19 September 1996. http://www.cert.org/advisories/CA-96.21.tcp_syn_flooding.html
[21] Computer Emergency Response Team, Vulnerability in rlogin/term. CERT Advisory 97:06, 6 February 1997. http://www.cert.org/advisories/CA-97.06.rlogin-term.html
[22] Conta, A., and Deering, S. (1995). *Internet Control Message Protocol (ICMPv6) for the Internet Protocol Version 6 (IPv6)*. RFC-1885, December.
[23] Crocker, D. (1995). *MIME Encapsulation of EDI Objects*. RFC-1767, March.
[24] Crocker, S., Freed, N., Galvin, J., and Murphy, S. (1995). *MIME Object Security Services*. RFC-1848, October.
[25] Deering, S. (1991). ICMP Router Discovery Messages, RFC-1256, September.
[26] Deering, S., and Hinden, R. (1995). *Internet Protocol, Version 6 (IPv6) Specification*. RFC-1883, December.
[27] Dierks, T., and Allen, C. (1997). *The TLS Protocol version 1.0*. RFC-2246, January.
[28] Diffie, W., and Hellman, M. E. (1976). New directions in cryptography. *IEEE Transactions on Information Theory*, IT-11, 644–654, November.
[29] Droms, R. (1997). Dynamic Host Configuration Protocol, RFC-2131, March.

[30] Droms, R. (ed.) (1998). *Authentication for DHCP Messages*. Work in progress, June.
[31] Dusse, S., Hoffman, P., Ramsdell, B., Lundblade, L., and Repka, L. (1998). *S/MIME Version 2 Message Specification*. RFC-2311, March.
[32] Eastlake, D. (1997). Secure DNS Dynamic Update, RFC-2137, April.
[33] Eastlake, D., and Kaufman, C. (1997). Domain Name System (DNS) Security Extensions, RFC-2065, January.
[34] Elkins, M. (1996). MIME Security with PGP, RFC-2015, October.
[35] Estrin, D., Farinacci, D., Helmy, A., Thaler, D., Deering, S., Handley, M., Jacobson. V., Liu. C., Sharma. P., and Wei. L. (1997). *Protocol Independent Multicast-Sparse Mode (PIM-SM): Protocol Specification*. RFC-2117, June.
[36] Fenner, W. (1997). *Internet Group Management Protocol, Version 2*, RFC-2236, November.
[37] Fuller, V., Li, T., Yu, J., and Varadhan. K. (1993). *Classless Inter-Domain Routing (CIDR): an Address Assignment and Aggregation Strategy*, RFC-1519, September.
[38] Galvin, J., and McCloghrie, K. (1993). *Security Protocols for version 2 of the Simple Network Management Protocol (SNMPv2)*. RFC-1446, April.
[39] Galvin, J., Murphy, S., Crocker, S., and Freed, N. (1995). *Security Multiparts for MIME: Multipart/Signed and Multipart/Encrypted*, RFC-1847, October.
[40] Gavron, E. (1993). *A Security Problem and Proposed Correction With Widely Deployed DNS Software*. RFC-1535, October.
[41] Gudmundsson, O., and Droms R. (1998). *Security Requirements for the DHCP Protocol*. Work in progress, March.
[42] Haller, N., and Atkinson, R. (1994). *On Internet Authentication*. RFC-1704, October.
[43] Haller, N., and Metz, C. (1996). *A One-Time Password System*, RFC-1938, May.
[44] Harkins, D., and Carrel, D. (1998). *The Internet Key Exchange (IKE)*. RFC-2409, November.
[45] Harney, H., and Muckenhirn, C. (1997). *Group Key Management Protocol (GKMP) Specification*. RFC-2093, July.
[46] Harney, H., and Muckenhirn, C. (1997). *Group Key Management Protocol (GKMP) Architecture*. RFC-2094, July.
[47] Housley, R., Ford, W., Polk, W., and Solo, D. (1999). *Internet X.509 Public Key Infrastructure: Certificate and CRL Profile*.
[48] International Telecommunications Union (1997). *ITU-T Recommendation X.509 (1997E): Information Technology—Open Systems Interconnection—The Directory: Authentication Framework*, June.
[49] Kantor, B. (1991). *BSD Rlogin*. RFC-1258, 1 September.
[50] Karn, P. (1993). Presentation to IP Security Working Group at IETF meeting.
[51] Karn, P., Metzger, P., and Simpson, W. (1995). *The ESP DES-CBC Transform*, RFC-1829, August.
[52] Kent, S. (1993). *Privacy Enhancement for Internet Electronic Mail: Part II Certificate-Based Key Management*. RFC-1422, February.
[53] Kent, S. T., and Atkinson, R. J. (1998). *IP Encapsulating Security Payload*. RFC-2406, November.
[54] Krawczyk, H., Bellare, M., and Canetti, R. (1997). *HMAC: Keyed-Hashing for Message Authentication*. RFC-2104, February.
[55] Lee, A. J. (1998). Private communication, June.
[56] Linn, J. (1993). *Privacy Enhancement for Internet Electronic Mail: Part I: Message Encryption and Authentication Procedures*. RFC-1421, February.
[57] Maughan, D., Schertler, M., Schneider, M., and Turner, J. (1998). *Internet Security Association and Key Management Protocol (ISAKMP)*. Work in progress, July.

[58] Medin, M. (1991). NASA/Ames Research Centre, private communication, December.
[59] Metzger, P., and Simpson, W. (1995). *IP Authentication using Keyed MD5*, RFC-1828, August.
[60] Mockapetris, P. V. (1987). *Domain names—concepts and facilities*. RFC-1034, 1 November.
[61] Mockapetris, P. V. (1987). *Domain names—implementation and specification*, RFC-1035, 1 November.
[62] Morris, R. T. (1985). A weakness in the 4.2 BSD TCP/IP software, *Computing Science Technical Report 117*, AT&T Bell Laboratories, Murray Hill, NJ, February.
[63] Moy, J. (1998). *OSPF Version 2*, RFC-2328, April.
[64] Murphy, S., Badger, M., and Wellington, B. (1997). *OSPF with Digital Signatures*. RFC-2154, June.
[65] Narten, T., Nordmark, E., and Simpson, W. (1996). *Neighbor Discovery for IP Version 6 (IPv6)*. RFC-1970, August.
[66] National Institute of Standards and Technology (1993). *Secure Hash Standard*. Federal Information Processing Standard, Publication 180, US Department of Commerce, May.
[67] National Institute of Standards and Technology (1993). *Data Encryption Standard*. Federal Information Processing Standard, Publication 46–2, US Department of Commerce, December.
[68] National Institute of Standards and Technology (1997). *Message Security Protocol 4.0, Revision A*. SDN.701, 6 February.
[69] National Institute of Standards and Technology (1997). Announcing request for candidate algorithm nominations for the Advanced Encryption Standard (AES). *Federal Register*, **16**(177) 48051–48058, 12 September.
[70] Needham, R. M., and Schroeder, M. D. (1978). Using encryption for authentication in large networks of computers. *Communications of the ACM*, **21**(12), December.
[71] Neuman, B. C., and T'so, T. Y. (1994). Kerberos: An authentication service for computer networks. *IEEE Communications*, **32**(9), September.
[72] Orman, H. (1998). *The Oakley Key Exchange*. Determination Protocol. RFC-2412, November.
[73] Piper, D. (1998). Internet IPsec Domain of Interpretation for ISAKMP, RFC-2407, November.
[74] Plummer, D. C. (1982). *Ethernet Address Resolution Protocol: Or converting network protocol addresses to 48.bit Ethernet address for transmission on Ethernet hardware*. RFC-0826, 1 November.
[75] Postel, T. (1980). *User Datagram Protocol*. RFC-0768, 28 August.
[76] Postel, J. (1981). *Internet Protocol*. RFC-0791, 1 September.
[77] Postel, J. (1981). *Internet Control Message Protocol*. RFC-0792, 1 September.
[78] Postel, J. (1981). *Transmission Control Protocol*. RFC-0793, 1 September.
[79] Postel, J., and Reynolds, J.K. (1983). Telnet Protcol Specification, RFC-854, May.
[80] Postel, J., and Reynolds, J. K. (1983). *Telnet Option Specifications*. RFC-0855, May.
[81] Pusateri, T. (1998). *Distance Vector Multicast Routing Protocol version 3 (DVMRPv3)*. Work in progress, March.
[82] Rekhter, T., and Li, T. (1995). *A Border Gateway Protocol 4 (BGP-4)*. RFC-1771, March.
[83] Rivest, R. (1992). *The MD5 Message-Digest Algorithm*. RFC-1321, April.
[84] Schneier, B. (1996). *Applied Cryptography*, John Wiley & Sons, New York, pp. 48–49.
[85] Stoll, C. (1989). *The Cuckoo's Egg: Tracking a Spy Through the Maze of Computer Espionage*.
[86] Venema, W. (1992). TCP Wrapper: Network monitoring, access control, and booby traps, *Proceedings of the 3rd USENIX UNIX Security Symposium*, USENIX Association, pp. 85–92, Baltimore, MD, September.

[87] Visa, *SET Secure Electronic Transaction Specification*, Book 3: Formal Protocol Definition, 31 May 1997.
[88] Wahl, M., Howes, T., and Kille, S. (1997). Lightweight Directory Access Protocol (LDAPv3), RFC-2251, December.
[89] Waitzman, D., Partridge, C., and Deering, S. E. (1988). *Distance Vector Multicast Routing Protocol*. RFC-1075, 1 November.
[90] Wijnen, B., Presuhn, R., and McCloghrie, K. (1998). *View-based Access Control Model (VACM) for the Simple Network Management Protocol (SNMP)*. RFC-2265, January.
[91] Ylonen, T. (1996). SSH—Secure Login Connections over the Internet, *Proceedings of the 6th USENIX Security Symposium*, USENIX Association, San Jose, CA, July.
[92] Zimmerman, P. R. (1995). *PGP Source Code and Internals*, MIT Press, Boston, MA.

Digital Libraries: Social Issues and Technological Advances

HSINCHUN CHEN

Artificial Intelligence Lab
Management Information Systems Department
University of Arizona
Tucson, Arizona 85721
USA
hchen@bpa.arizona.edu
http://ai.bpa.arizona.edu

ANDREA L. HOUSTON

ISDS Department
3194B4 CEBA
E. J. Ourso College of Business Administration
Louisiana State University
Baton Rouge, LA 70803
USA
ahoust2@lsu.edu

Abstract

The location and provision of information services has dramatically changed over the last ten years. There is no need to leave the home or office to locate and access information now readily available on-line via digital gateways furnished by a wide variety of information providers, (e.g. libraries, electronic publishers, businesses, organizations, individuals). Information access is no longer restricted to what is physically available in the nearest library. It is electronically accessible from a wide variety of globally distributed information repositories—"digital libraries".

In this chapter we will focus on digital libraries, starting with a discussion of the historical visionaries, definitions, driving forces and enabling technologies and some key research issues. We will discuss some of the US and international digital library projects and research initiatives. We will then describe some of the emerging techniques for building large-scale digital libraries, including a discussion of semantic interoperability, the "Grand Challenge" of digital library research. Finally, we offer our conclusions and a discussion of some future directions for digital libraries.

1. Introduction 258
2. Digital Libraries: Historical Overview 259
3. What Is a Digital Library? 261
   3.1 Creating Digital Library Content 262
   3.2 Indexing and Filtering Information 263
   3.3 Supporting Universal Access 264
   3.4 Preservation 264
4. Drives towards Digital Libraries 265
   4.1 Economics 265
   4.2 Improved Level of Service 266
   4.3 New Technologies 266
   4.4 Standards 267
5. Digital Library Research Issues in the Social Context 268
   5.1 Economic Issues 268
   5.2 Legal Issues 270
   5.3 Quality and Security Issues 273
   5.4 Social Issues 274
6. Digital Library Research Activities: An Overview 276
   6.1 Digital Library Research Activities in US 277
   6.2 Digital Library Activities in Other Countries 293
7. Digital Library Research Issues in Semantic Interoperability 299
   7.1 Digital Library Grand Challenge: Semantic Interoperability .. 299
   7.2 Research Towards Semantic Interoperability in Digital Libraries 300
8. Conclusions and the Future 306
Acknowledgments 308
References 309

1. Introduction

Over the last ten years, the way one finds or acquires information has dramatically changed. It is no longer necessary to leave the home or office to locate and access the vast amounts of information now readily available online via digital gateways, furnished by a wide variety of information providers (e.g. libraries, electronic publishers, businesses, organizations, individuals) [99]. Information access is no longer restricted to what is physically available in the nearest library but is electronically accessible from a wide variety of globally distributed information repositories.

Information is no longer simply text and pictures. It is electronically available in a wide variety of formats many of which are large, complex (i.e. video and audio) and often integrated (i.e. multimedia). This increased variety of information allows one to take virtual tours of museums, historical sites and natural wonders, attend virtual concerts and theater performances, watch a variety of movies, and read, view or listen to books, articles, lectures and music, all through digital libraries.

In this chapter we will focus on digital libraries, starting with a discussion of the historical visionaries, definitions, driving forces and enabling technologies and some key research issues. We will discuss some US and international digital library projects and research initiatives. We will then describe some of the emerging techniques for building large-scale digital libraries, including a discussion of semantic interoperability, the "Grand Challenge" of digital library research. Finally, we offer our conclusions and a discussion of some future directions for digital libraries.

2. Digital Libraries: Historical Overview

The ideas of several visionaries and their dreams for the future helped initiate the digital library concept. Three, whose ideas predate the computer, had visions based on entirely different technologies (microfilm and analog machines), so it is their ideas not their designs that predicted digital libraries.

Watson Davis founded the American Documentation Institute (ADI) in 1937 (renamed the American Society for Information Science (ASIS) in 1968). Davis was a pioneer in the field of subject indexing and was interested in documentation and in document classification and distribution. He interacted with the other visionaries of the time: Vannevar Bush (who discussed methods for indexing microfilm documents) and H. G. Wells.

In 1937 Davis published an article in *Science News Letter* (now *Science News*) predicting "a new way of duplicating records, manuscripts, books and illustrations" which would significantly change scholarly communication. The article also predicted greater information accessibility and inexpensive publication of manuscripts [72]. Davis foresaw the proliferation of journals and the difficulty of locating and integrating relevant information from several different journals. Other Davis ideas related to digital libraries include [23]: (1) *one big library*—from which users can order information from the nearest library with guaranteed prompt delivery and reasonable prices; (2) *auxiliary publications*—a repository of document copies available on-demand, replacing paper-oriented publications; (3) *one big journal*—one central location listing *all* publications in one index; and (4) *a world brain*—an idea presented in 1937 by H. G. Wells.

Herbert George Wells was an English novelist best known for science fiction (e.g. *The Time Machine*, *The Invisible Man*, and *The War of the Worlds*). Inspired by discussions with Watson Davis, Wells proposed a *World Encyclopedia* (presented at the 1937 World Congress of Documentation in Paris and described in his book, *World Brain*). He believed that the assembling and distribution of world knowledge was extremely ineffective, handicapping anyone relying on organized information for decision making. His solution, *Permanent World Encyclopedia*, was a *distributed* microfilm-based repository of all world knowledge divided into different topics, subtopics and levels consisting of "selections, extracts, quotations, very carefully assembled with the approval of outstanding authorities in each subject, carefully collated and edited and critically presented ... alive and growing and changing continually under revision, extension and replacement from the original thinkers" [72, 98].

His quote: "The time is close at hand when any student, in any part of the world, will be able to sit with his projector in his own study at his or her convenience to examine *any* book, *any* document, in an exact replica" [98] is now almost true, especially in the network form that he envisioned. The idea of a repository or encyclopedic intelligence is still being pursued (e.g. the CYC project initiated by Douglas Lenat in 1985).

Vannevar Bush was an American electrical engineer who oversaw US government support of scientific research during World War II. In 1945, Bush published an essay "As We May Think" in *Atlantic Monthly* describing a hypothetical information retrieval and annotation system called "Memex", a personal desksize machine that would store and retrieve abstracts of scientific articles [8]. Some interesting "Memex" features from a digital library perspective are: (1) using technology to organize and retrieve information, (2) creating "trails" (chains of associations) of information, (3) electronically annotating existing documents, (4) the idea that a desksized machine could store and use the contents of an entire university library, and (5) the idea of a community of scholars sharing and exchanging information. The descriptions of "Memex" trails sound remarkably like hypertext links. Although his technical implementation designs for "Memex" were not achievable, the description is similar to the gateway access digital libraries provide.

Prior to the Second World War, Bush described the "information overload" problem. In his words: "scientific literature is expanding faster than man's ability to understand, let alone control it ... publication has been extended far beyond our present ability to make real use of the record" [9]. The problem as he saw it was that "before knowledge can be used it has to be selected out of an undifferentiated mass ... knowledge that can not be selected is lost" [65]. Bush recognized that associative indexing could mimic human associative memory. He was concerned about the problems humans encounter when searching information indexed by an unfamiliar vocabulary or ontology—a phenomenon called the "vocabulary problem" or "semantic barrier" [63]. He blamed the problem on the "artificiality of systems of indexing" [9] rather than on the ambiguity of language.

There are many others who were influential in setting the stage for digital libraries. Some of them include:

- *Warren Weaver*—an MIT professor who in 1945 wrote an essay proposing machine translation [97], which initiated a stream of

research on machine translation and on statistical approaches to language and text analysis (the latter made famous by Gerald Salton [81], generally considered the father of modern information retrieval).
- *J. C. R. Licklider*—a former Director of the Information Processing Techniques Office (IPTO) division of the Pentagon's Advanced Research Projects Agency (ARPA) who established the funding priorities leading to the development of the Internet, and the invention of the "mouse," "windows," and "hypertext". He is best known for three publications: (1) *Man-Computer Symbiosis* (1960) which describes his vision of computing which led to IPTO funding priorities mentioned above; (2) *The Computer as a Communications Device* (1968, co-authored with Robert Taylor), which discusses the future predicting that by the year 2000 millions of people would be on-line, connected by a global network; and (3) *Libraries of the Future* [51].
- *Ted Nelson*—influential in the development of hypertext, he coined the term "hypertext" in his paper "A file structure for the complex, the changing and the indeterminate" presented at the 1965 ACM national conference and is known for the Xanadu project.
- *William Wulf*—who wrote a white paper on national collaboratories in 1988 while working for NSF and has been influential in collaboratory research [18, 103].

3. What is a Digital Library?

What exactly is a digital library? A good general definition is that it is an entity concerned with "the creation of information sources and the movement of [that] information across global networks" [1] specifically identifying and delivering *relevant* information to interested parties. A digital library could be characterized as "a collection of distributed autonomous sites (servers) that work together to give the consumer the appearance of a single cohesive collection" [1]. In practice, each site will most likely store a large amount of information in a wide variety of formats on a wide variety of storage media [53]. Individuals accessing the information will have a wide range of expertise in key access-related areas such as computer literacy, collection navigation abilities, and domain knowledge [4].

Digital libraries are characterized by "collaborative support, digital document preservation, distributed database management, hypertext, information filtering, information retrieval, instructional modules, intellectual property rights, multimedia information services, question answering and reference services, resource discovery and selective dissemination of information" [30]. They allow information to be accessed globally, copied error-free, stored compactly, and searched rapidly. "A true digital library also provides the principles governing what is included and how the collection is organized" [49]. Advances in information technology have enabled digital libraries, and contributed to a blurring of traditional information-related roles. Anyone with access to the right equipment (a computer and access to storage on a server) can become an information provider and consumer.

Creating and maintaining a digital library typically involves the following phases:

- creating digital library content
- indexing and filtering information
- supporting universal access, and
- preservation.

3.1 Creating Digital Library Content

The first decision to be faced when creating a digital library is to determine what information to provide and what information to discard, either permanently (disposal) or through archiving. Unfortunately most of the information digital libraries wish to provide is not digitized, calling for additional decisions (i.e. determining digitization priorities and cost-effective conversion processes). Conversion challenges include both a technological component (e.g. advances in OCR technology and storage media) and an evaluation component (e.g. selection, prioritization, and choosing the appropriate level(s) of digitized quality).

Another major problem is the dynamic nature of digitized information [40]. The content can change over time, requiring the storage of either multiple copies or versions or some mechanism that allows version differentiation [50]. Other related challenges include identifying methods to capture and index continuous media in real time and techniques for processing, storing and managing vast volumes of extremely complex electronic information [1, 96].

Finally, since hypertext links allow digital libraries to provide pointers or links to information (as opposed to a digital copy), digital libraries must decide what form of access they will provide. Concerns about information ownership and archiving are becoming extremely important as a result. For example, if a digital library decides to provide a pointer or link to a certain piece of information, what happens when the owner(s) of the electronic copy decide it is no longer cost-effective to keep it? What are the responsibilities of the owner(s) to notify pointer or link owners of changes to or deletions of the original (a classic problem on the World Wide Web)?

3.2 Indexing and Filtering Information

After the acquisition and storage issues are resolved, the next set of challenges involve finding ways to make the *right* information available to the *right* individuals at the *right* time [41, 53]. Customers must be able to identify or locate potentially relevant information, filter it so that only the most relevant information is returned, and organize it (via ranking or categorization) into manageable units. Intelligent artificial agents will probably be heavily involved in future information location and filtering efforts [5, 44].

There are at least two different kinds of information location processes. The first kind is useful in a broad-based search where the information need has not yet been specifically defined. Relevant information will probably be widely dispersed among several distributed heterogeneous information sources. The key challenge is to present a seamless integration of information to the customer. Individuals interested in this kind of search will probably want the information to be summarized for quick perusal [90]. An alternative is to provide effective organization and categorization techniques that chunk information into manageable units which do not overwhelm human cognitive abilities.

The second kind of information identification process involves a very narrow, well-defined and focused search. This kind of search requires very detailed information. Because precision will be most important, effective filtering techniques will be required to return a small amount of the *most* relevant information.

In either case, the user interface will be critical. Even the most relevant information is worthless if the customer cannot understand the presentation [84]. The best digital libraries will have uniform but customizable, dynamic user interfaces that can smoothly integrate existing common data types (text, numeric, audio, video and image) from structured and unstructured sources with specialized types of data (maps, three-dimensional data, and continuous graphical data) and, potentially, new data types [1]. These systems will incorporate algorithms and techniques that enable semantic interoperability, so that humans can search in unfamiliar domains of knowledge (each with its own specialized vocabulary and ontology) using familiar vocabularies and ontologies [4, 53].

Another important aspect of information location, is finding key *relationships*, especially in distributed, heterogeneous information sources. Data mining, the extraction of patterns, associations and anomalies from large data sources [2], is a very promising research area that may produce significant payoffs for large-scale, complex multimedia digital library applications.

3.3 Supporting Universal Access

The ultimate goal of a digital library is universal access, which is consistent with the traditional library goal of providing public access to information. To accomplish universal access, digital libraries need to solve the problems of integrating distributed heterogeneous information and information sources by designing and implementing effective user interfaces that solve the "vocabulary problem" (via semantic interoperability, to be discussed in detail) [88].

One of the challenges to providing universal access is devising techniques that will support a wide variety of information display devices in handling voluminous, diverse and complex information. Not only is there a variety of operating systems in the computer domain, but there are a wide variety of display devices (e.g. palm tops, televisions, fax machines, video monitors, modems, and other information "appliances") to cope with. Accommodating legacy display devices and receivers is probably a more difficult problem than accommodating and integrating legacy information and information sources [93].

Another major challenge is the limited amount of bandwidth available for the transmission of electronic information to accommodate an increasing number of users and increasingly complex (and large) data sets. For equitable universal access to be achieved, intelligent use of the bandwidth, including the ability to guarantee bandwidth for a given period of time (in particular for law enforcement and emergency situations) must be identified and policies to support such uses enacted. These challenges, combined with the economic pressures faced by digital libraries, have led to a perception that information providers behave as "gate-keepers" of a service (or set of services), providing a "gateway" to knowledge [25, 26, 68, 78]. The current government and industry funded Internet-II project was designed to help alleviate some future problems in supporting universal access to digital libraries.

3.4 Preservation

Electronic media do not disintegrate as readily as other types. Paper is particularly vulnerable because it is susceptible to the problems of acid paper and binding disintegration as well as to destruction through innocent physical handling and vandalism. Other media (including tape, images, negatives, vinyl records, etc.) are susceptible to disintegration due to pollution, catastrophic events (floods, and other natural disasters), humidity, light, insect and other kinds of pests, mold and mildew, vandalism and human handling. However, constant changes and various enhancements in electronic document format (e.g. MARC, SGML, HTML, XML, etc.) and associated incompatibility problems will need to be addressed carefully in this digital age.

4. Drives Towards Digital Libraries

Over the past decade, several trends have steadily encouraged the transition to and expansion of digital libraries. The four major drivers are: economics, accessibility, new technologies, and standards.

4.1 Economics

It is cheaper to produce, store, distribute, and reproduce electronic information. Furthermore, digital libraries can cooperate with each other by providing a gateway (links) to information managed or provided by others, allowing specialization as well as conservation of acquisition and production budgets while still providing access to a wide range of information [49]. Other economic pressures driving libraries towards digitization include:

- *Inflation*: the rapid rise in library operating costs (especially in acquisition or collection expansion of scholarly journals). In the past 20 years, journal prices have soared by 400 percent while book and monograph prices have increased by 40% [31].
- *Volume*: the explosion in the amount, variety and complexity of information.
- *Maintenance*: the preservation crisis in existing collections, especially with regard to acidic paper (nationally the replacement cost of disintegrating print materials extrapolates to approximately $35–$45 billion [31]).
- *Multimedia*: the increasing amount of multimedia information that requires special viewing or listening facilities and different cataloging and storage requirements.
- *Collaboration*: the advantages from resource sharing among libraries and other information providers (both economically and in improved level of service).
- *Timeliness*: electronic information is easy to produce, distribute, and duplicate with few of the problems of multiple handling and redistribution, allowing a dramatic savings in costs [33].
- *Scholarly communication*: the severe cost problem associated with scholarly communication [26], in particular the excessive cost of

providing access to an *appropriate* number of scholarly journals [6, 31, 49] to maintain an *adequate* level of service. For example, according to Andrew Odlyzko of Bell Lab, "a good mathematics library spends $100,000 per year on journal subscriptions, plus twice more on staff and equipment. [The] US spends as much money buying mathematics journals as NSF [the National Science Foundation] spends on mathematical research" [66].

4.2 Improved Level of Service

Digital libraries have the ability to provide a previously unattainable level of service, i.e. "individual words and sentence search and delivery of information to the user's desk—information that does not decay with time, whether it is words, sounds or images" [49]. Information that was either previously unavailable or difficult to acquire is now readily available electronically (i.e. large government collections). Access to information can be improved in several different ways: access time (retrieval speed and/or timeliness), availability (recall), content (relevance), improved visualization (user interface) or some combination [6]. Historically, research has been focused on generic improvements to information access. The current trend is to *individually* customize or tailor user information access methods and interfaces.

Since the production and distribution of electronic information eliminates multiple handling and redistribution, there is a dramatic savings in time from production to use. Electronic information need only be created and stored *once* to be immediately available over a network *simultaneously* to multiple users as opposed to multiple copies being generated over time and provided via traditional (postal and/or manual) distribution channels [41, 49, 77]. Many Internet news Web sites offer information in real-time, for example, with no time delay in printing or delivery.

4.3 New Technologies

To effectively meet the information needs of their clients, digital libraries need to use a combination of technological advances and have the ability to design, construct, manage, and use global electronic networks [57]. They must be able to adapt rapidly to dynamic changes in technology and to cope with the size, scale, and complexity of both the networks themselves and the information available through them [4].

Many technological advances in information production, management and distribution are responsible for *enabling* digital libraries. They are too numerous to describe in detail but include such things as advances in:

(1) storage media;

(2) digitization or information capturing techniques (i.e. OCR technology);
(3) automatic indexing and organizing of large volumes of information [88];
(4) computing speed;
(5) network technology (including data compression);
(6) content-based search and retrieval [90];
(7) feature-based or texture-based search and retrieval [91];
(8) full-text indexing;
(9) resource or knowledge discovery;
(10) multimedia and hypertext;
(11) standards (i.e. Standardized General Mark-up Language (SGML) and Hypertext Mark-up Language (HTML), and Z39.50);
(12) object-oriented techniques; and
(13) improvements in user-interface design and data visualization [26, 42, 53, 76].

In the next section, we will review some of the recent technical advances in several large-scale, high-impact digital library projects. In particular, we will review new technologies that aim to improve semantic interoperability in digital libraries.

4.4 Standards

In order for digital libraries to be truly global gateways, it is important to have internationally accepted technical standards for electronic information representation, formatting, transmission, and protocols. This is the only way to ensure compatibility and therefore interoperability between equipment, data, practices and procedures necessary to achieve universal access [41, 42, 70, 93] and global electronic information exchange. Unfortunately, there are many social, cultural and political barriers to developing international standards, even when the benefit is clear to all.

Several international organizations are involved in standard development, including the International Organization for Standardization (ISO)—which was responsible for the SGML (Standardized General Mark-up Language). Another organization, IETF (Internet Engineering Task Force—see www.ietf.org) is specifically interested in Internet architecture and smooth Internet interaction and operation [42]. One of the most important standards from a digital library perspective is Z39.50 (the distributed information retrieval standard, see lcweb.loc.gov/z3950/agency/) which was adopted by ISO as the ISO 23950 standard [30, 61].

At a national level, while information and document standards such as SGML, HTML, TEI (Text Encoding Initiative), VRML (Virtual Reality

Modeling Language), and MARC (Machine-Readable Cataloging) exist, in practice most electronic information exchange occurs via e-mail, anonymous ftp, Gopher, and Web browser platforms with TeX, LaTeX, PostScript, PDF, ASCII text, and Word and WordPerfect formatted documents. Most of these formats do not have mechanisms to distinguish the contributions of multiple authors or versions, nor do they have the ability to include active links to other information. Many of the formats used in practice are commercial, proprietary, and therefore not platform independent which means they are not universally accessible. Will common practice dictate what standards become accepted or will some governing body take responsibility for thoughtful and independent (unbiased) standards development? If a set of standards is accepted and adopted, what kind of translation capability from these "legacy" formats will be provided? Careful research and policy related to standards will be needed to achieve a truly universal digital library community.

5. Digital Library Research Issues in the Social Context

Digital libraries allow people to interact with each other and information in novel ways. As is often the case with new technology, these abilities have become available ahead of the societal norms, conventions, and policies that help monitor, guide and evaluate their use. As a result, some economic, social, and legal issues have arisen in response to digital libraries and the technologies that have enabled them.

5.1   Economic Issues

While electronic information may be cheap to produce, store, modify and distribute, it is much harder to determine a fair or market price and cost for it than for a physical object. To date, there is no commonly accepted economic model that can accurately and fairly determine either costs or prices for digital library services.

Historically, information-related services were typically not broken down into individual transactions or unit priced [78]. As a result, most digital libraries and their clients have little idea what an information transaction is worth [49]. This is such a difficult challenge that Saracevic and Kantor [85] developed a derived taxonomy to address the problem of determining and measuring the *value* of a library's information and services. Customers know that electronic information has an almost zero incremental reproduction and viewing cost and therefore expect that access should be free or extremely cheap.

Digital library services are not free, however. Some method of compensation is necessary. Currently, there are at least two basic compensation models: (1) allowing free access but charging for content (i.e. freely accessing the index and table of contents, but charging for anything more) and (2) charging for access but allowing free perusal and consumption of the content [49]. These two models are not mutually exclusive and both co-exist on the Internet.

Several different digital library funding models have been proposed, but the basic models are either time-based (unlimited access for a given unit of time, e.g. a month), request-based (per request), or some combination of both [1, 26]. Some proposed models include [49]:

- institutional (public and private) subsidies—the current model for most digital libraries;
- "free" general services and charging by transaction for unusual services, especially those requiring human intervention;
- charging for everything—assuming that information services can be transactionalized and costed. Common suggestions include charging by: connect time, CPU usage, fee-per-search, fee-per-hit or retrieval, and download fees. A problem with all of these suggestions is that people generally do not understand how they work, creating a situation where charges appear to be unpredictable and resulting in unreasonable or unpredictable behavior;
- subsidizing services through advertising (typical of magazines, television, and the Web);
- other subsidizing mechanisms (for example, pledge breaks—public appeals for donations similar to public television and radio);
- taxes or other sources of public funds;
- subscriptions (pay for a given period, i.e. a year) or licenses (viable concept in the software market);
- memberships similar to "buying clubs" where individual consumers pool their resources to allow access to information (pricing issues could be resolved via price discrimination, non-linear pricing and service bundling [43]);
- charge authors a per-unit fee for the "privilege" of having their information and services accessible, then charge users for the nominal incremental cost of accessing the information (similar to a per-page author charge under consideration by some journals);
- opportunity cost—measuring the opportunity cost of providing information or a service as opposed to measuring the cost of expended resources. "Opportunity cost is determined by the relationship between

supply and demand for a given resource, so that the opportunity cost of an idle resource is close to zero but that of an over-utilized resource is so high that it is basically unaffordable" [1]; and
- using a detailed byte-by-byte charging algorithm—an interesting idea from Ted Nelson (CNRI) and CMU's NetBill project [49].

Current cost models and financial instruments used in traditional information production and consumption do not adequately address the needs of digital libraries. Fixed cost models are insensitive to changes in content and costs. Electronic information comes in a variety of formats with different associated production and distribution costs. Flexible and adaptable cost models are required to handle this diversity and complexity [1, 20]. Economic models for digital libraries require a series of specialized costing and pricing algorithms that can dynamically determine the cost and price of information or services and modify the model with a variety of environmental factors [20, 49, 70].

5.2 Legal Issues

Digital libraries exchange electronic information on a global level. Therefore, national governments will have to negotiate an international-level policy framework that can accommodate the exchange of information across international boundaries and differences in cultural values and laws (especially with respect to copyright, intellectual property, privacy, information ownership, fraud and other business crimes, taxation and currency exchange) [57, 74].

Now that almost anyone can be an electronic information provider, it is easier to perpetuate ethically questionable acts. For example, it is harder to prevent plagiarism in the digital age. The shear volume of electronic information makes it very difficult to enforce copyright laws or even to detect illegal copies. False representation and false information can easily be provided electronically, leading to concerns about information quality. These ethical considerations are challenging enough within a given nation or culture, but digital libraries are global, and different nations and cultures have very different perspectives, definitions, and social guidelines with respect to concepts such as plagiarism, copyright laws, "fair use" and "truth in advertising" [79]. How can internationally accepted ethical codes be developed and enforced in light of these issues?

In the United States, more localized legal issues surrounding digital libraries include [49]:
- *Ownership issues.* When a library owns a physical copy, decisions about acquisition and archiving are relatively straightforward. If a

digital library only owns a link or gateway connection to the information, certain kinds of ownership problems arise [28]. For example, if a digital library decides to cancel its subscription to regularly published information (such as a journal), how will access be controlled? Obviously access to future issues should not be permitted but the right to access past issues has already been negotiated and paid for. Dynamically having to keep this kind of information results in complicated record-keeping and access control policies, procedures and processes for digital libraries. What should be done about an information provider that goes out of business or an information item that goes "out of print." In both cases the information provider can no longer afford (or wish) to support physical storage. How can the rights of owners of *links* to that information be protected?

- *Unauthorized access.* Electronic information appears to be more vulnerable to unauthorized access, theft and fraud than physical copies as such incursions are harder to detect. A variety of techniques are being investigated to help protect electronic information, including "firewalls," electronic signatures, encryption, special "rendering" or viewing software or hardware, and electronic watermarks.
- *Liability.* Traditionally US law distinguishes between authors and publishers who *are* held responsible (liable) for information that they have produced and distributors (the post office, libraries and bookstores) who *are not.* Digital libraries can distribute as well as produce information, raising difficult legal questions regarding their responsibility for information published, displayed or distributed from their sites. In situations where electronic information has multiple authors and multiple versions, how can expertise be determined and liability assigned?
- *Trademark infringement.* Trade-marked images (for example a state or university seal or a commercial caricature) can be copied or scanned and used as wall-paper or images in electronic information. Many organizations require notification and/or payment for using trademarks (trademark use is often interpreted as an organizational endorsement). How will these rights be protected?
- *Copyright and intellectual property rights.* Copyright issues, in particular copyright violation and the related intellectual property rights issues, are major digital library legal issues [49]. Pamela Samuelson [82, 83] from Berkeley is a well-known authority on the topic.

Virtually anything that can be copyrighted can also be digitized. Once digitized, anyone with a computer can copy it, modify it and distribute it to anyone else who has access to a network. Electronic information is easy to copy and redistribute, but it is difficult to distinguish a valid copy from an illegal one. The regulations that exist today (e.g. no downloading at all; no electronic storage—view only; no copies or distribution, even internally; no copies or distribution to third parties; and specific limitations on various types of use) are largely ignored [41]. Information providers (i.e. publishers) implicitly endorse this behavior by "looking the other way" in many instances. What are the responsibilities of digital libraries in enforcing copyright laws applying to the information and services they provide?

New copyright laws and practices, at least with respect to electronic information, are going to have to be created because the speed of technological advancements have left legal systems far behind [41, 95]. In the US, several proposals are being considered [49, 52]. Since new laws and practices must be enforceable, they must rely on new technology to help protect copyrighted material from unauthorized access [19, 32], reproduction, manipulation, distribution, and performance or display. New technology will probably also assist in the detection of copyright violations through new methods of authentication, management of copyright protected material (such as the clearing house model used predominantly by the music industry), and licensing techniques [41].

Several methods to protect intellectual property rights and copyright of electronic information are currently under investigation. They include [49]:

(1) *Fractional access*: this only applies to very large information sources (e.g. LEXIS/NEXIS) whose value lies in the *volume* of information and the knowledge that can be gleaned from analyzing the *entire* collection. There is no economic advantage to copying small portions of the data, and illegally copying the entire data source should be relatively easy to detect.
(2) *Interface control*: this requires a proprietary interface to access information, implying that universal access is no longer possible.
(3) *Hardware locks or "dongles"*: these are the hardware equivalent of interface control (a software solution). Access to information is restricted by proprietary access hardware (video games such as Sega or Nintendo are good examples).
(4) *Information repositories*: legitimate copies are *only* available from one large repository or source; any other copy is *not* legitimate. Some organizations exploring this approach include: in the US InterTrust (previously EPR—Electronic Publishing Resources) and CNRI (Corporation for National Research Initiatives, currently working with the US Copyright Office) and in Europe, Imprimatur

(Intellectual Multimedia Property Rights Model and Terminology for Universal Reference).
(5) *Steganography*: the embedding of hidden messages in information. Each legal copy is labeled with a different identification number allowing illegal copies to be tracked back to the original purchaser (i.e. "digital water-marks"—see [34] for a good example). The major problems are that the "hidden" codes or messages are easy to remove, hard to insert and while the method appears to work with complex images it does not work with simple text and may not even apply to audio data.
(6) *Encryption*: information is encrypted (sometimes in cryptolopes or secret envelopes), and cannot be interpreted without an encryption key (software or hardware dependent).
(7) *Economic approaches*: identifying ways to make it uneconomical to pirate or illegally copy electronic information. Ideas include: provider page charges to reduce the per-copy price, site licenses to reduce on-site cheating, and advertiser supported publications.
(8) *Flickering or "Wobbling"*: information technology that allows a customer to view but not capture information [48].

5.3 Quality and Security Issues

Publication (especially by reputable publishers and editors) lends credibility to information *content*. There is less concern about fraud, plagiarism, and unreliable or invalid information with non-electronic formats. Most non-electronic information (especially scholarly information) is subject to some kind of peer review or validation process, further augmenting perceptions of quality. Unfortunately, quality is harder to determine in on-line information. None of the existing searching engines has a way of evaluating electronic information quality (traditional information quality cues are typically missing) and therefore no way of sorting or filtering information by quality.

Lack of information about quality tends to limit searching to known experts (authors, Web sites, organizations, publishers or journals, etc.) or information recommended by known experts. Some search engines do use either an individual expert's profile or a group profile to request information (i.e. "give me information identical to what Joe Einstein requests"). Information integrity is still a problem, however, because electronic information is so easily modified. Electronic information is rarely guaranteed to be truly generated or endorsed by the expert. Currently, electronic scholarly publishing is a hotly debated topic. Much of the concern centers around questions of information and intellectual quality [26, 33, 71].

Issues of security and control are related to quality issues. Digital libraries need to address security in at least four areas [1, 41]:

(1) *Confidentiality*: protecting access to the information content (especially sensitive information, such as personal, financial or health information, and strategic business or national information) from unauthorized access and distribution.
(2) *Authenticity*: attributing information to the correct author(s) and validating it as original, accurate, and correctly attributed. This can be especially difficult in a multi-authored and multi-versioned environment [99].
(3) *Integrity*: protecting information content from unauthorized modification. This type of security involves a balance between easily enabling authorized updates and preventing unauthorized ones. The authenticity of modifications must be verifiable (challenging in a multi-author, multi-versioned environment).
(4) *Privacy*: protecting information access and usage patterns from unauthorized access and resale.

An important challenge for the implementation of any security technique is to balance the need for security with the need for performance (access and timeliness). Authorized access and modification must not be so difficult that it is never attempted, or abandoned before completion. Likewise, while validation techniques must be as accurate as technically feasible, they cannot be so time and resource intensive that the accessibility and timeliness of the information is compromised. Information is not valuable if it is not accessible, timely or useful.

5.4 Social Issues

There are several kinds of social issues faced by digital libraries. The major ones include:

- *Literacy*: in order to use a digital library a certain basic level of education or training is required, (i.e. a basic competence in the operation of a computer). Who will be responsible for providing basic computer skills and training? Should training be freely available through public education systems or should it be part of the services provided by digital libraries? Will access to training as well as access to the appropriate equipment (computer) and facilities (an account and storage space on a server) separate society into information "haves" and "have-nots"? If so, what are the implications of this division?

- *Cultural biases*: filtering and organizing electronic information to assist in coping with information overload is a useful service. Unfortunately, the result, deliberate or unintentional, is that the cultural biases and social values of the service provider are imposed [6]. The simplest example of this is language bias. Should information be accessed in the language in which it was generated, or should part of a digital library's information service be the ability to translate information into the customer's language of preference? One interesting approach in Japan is the MHTML project which provides multilingual browsing capability to a collection of Japanese fairy tales. The server can handle Japanese, Korean, Chinese, Thai, and several European languages including French and English [55].

    Translation of words (written or spoken) is relatively straightforward, but what about translation of non-language information (i.e. images or music)? Furthermore, information considered publicly appropriate for one group of people may be offensive or even illegal for another [42]. One solution may be to develop highly sensitive and individually customizable user-interfaces that could accommodate a given individual or group's cultural and linguistic preferences [29].

- *Ethical considerations*: the traditional librarian's perspective is that libraries have a responsibility to ensure socially and economically equitable public access to information [6]. However, not all governments, organizations or social groups support universal access and may, indeed, actively attempt to restrict access to certain kinds of information deemed inappropriate.

    Universal access also involves ethical issues related to censorship and cultural bias. Not all information is appropriate for all groups. Different individuals and cultures have different opinions about the accessibility and even the definition of material that could be considered inappropriate due to background (racial, religious, cultural), sex (including sexual preference), age and health. Included here is such information as: pornography, material generated by hate groups and other racial or religious persecutors, sexual predators (particularly child predators), drug dealers, terrorists and other criminals [49]. Should there be a limit on what information a digital library can provide access to? How could such a limitation be imposed and by whom? Or should there be limits on what kinds of information an individual can receive (who has the authority to determine and impose such limitations, and how might it be accomplished)?

- *Equality*: this issue addresses questions such as, is there equal access to information and do individuals have an equally likely chance of providing it. Experiences from some forms of electronic scholarly publication (i.e. e-print archive for high-energy physics) is very positive. Access is more equal in the electronic version than the printed version as the information is posted, and anyone can access it [33]. There are other instances, in the vast biomedical collections for example, where the volume of information is so huge that information is typically requested by a very small set of well-known and respected authors, journals, research centers, or some combination of those, making it extremely difficult for newcomers to get recognized and accepted. Fears about the lack of quality control in electronic information drive this tendency even more dramatically. There may be no difficulty in equitably providing electronic information, but how can consumers be encouraged to access it equitably?

6. Digital Library Research Activities: An Overview

In the last five years, there has been an explosion of digital library research, digital library initiatives and digital library programs both in the United States and around the world. In briefly describing some of these efforts, we have tried to suggest their breadth and variety. As these programs are constantly growing, expanding and changing, the most current source of information about them can be found through their Web pages, from which we have heavily drawn in the following sections. We apologize if the sites that we list have changed or are no longer active. There are many more digital library efforts than can possibly be included in this chapter. We have tried to offer descriptions of programs with which we are most familiar or consider interesting. Obviously, there are many interesting efforts that we may have missed.

The focus of digital library initiatives can either be *research* or technically oriented, primarily coming out of major research-oriented computer science departments, and emphasizing new methodologies, new technologies, new tools and new methods of storing and accessing information, or it can be *library* or socially oriented, examining collections and social issues and concerns related to digital libraries. In the United States, the federally funded digital library initiative projects are at the research end of the spectrum, while most of the digital library projects in other countries, like Japan, are more library and collection oriented [49]. However, many large-scale digital library projects incorporate both components, but in different proportions.

From an international perspective, the first US federally funded Digital Library Initiative (DLI), described in more detail below, has made at least two fundamental contributions. First, the research effort is substantial and is beyond the scope and definition of other digital library projects. All DLI projects are heavily research oriented and focus on exploring and identifying new scalable technologies for large-scale digital library content and users. Second, each project has been given a great deal of autonomy in defining the scope and focus of its research. While any large digital library effort requires resources commonly found only at the national level, and indeed most of the international digital library efforts are national government level efforts, this US effort essentially provides research "seed money," with minimal governmental intervention [42]. The response and support of this four-year research effort from the digital library community, both in the US and internationally, have been overwhelming.

6.1 Digital Library Research Activities in US

Many digital library research activities and programs are in progress in the United States and the number is rapidly increasing every month. Most of the research and work has occurred in the public sector and in institutions of higher learning, although the private sector has often generously contributed funding and technology exchange. As electronic commerce increases in its influence and its impact on the US economy, we believe that the private sector will become more involved in digital library research programs.

Because the US federal government has been responsible for the majority of the funding for US digital library efforts, this section is divided into two parts: US digital library initiatives that are federally funded and others. It is clear that the US government intends to continue funding this important research. Two new federally funded US digital library initiatives are the DLI-2 (Digital Library Initiative—Phase 2) announced in the spring of 1998, and the International Digital Library Initiative (announced in the fall of 1998). The international initiative will be jointly funded by the US and other nations' governments and organizations and will stress international cooperation and internationally distributed and accessible collections.

6.1.1 The NSF/NASA/DARPA Funded Digital Library Initiative (DLI)

In September 1993, the National Science Foundation (NSF) announced a jointly funded digital library initiative in conjunction with the National Aeronautics and Space Administration (NASA) and the Defense Advanced Research Projects Agency (DARPA). A total of $24.4 million was awarded to six research consortiums composed of major research universities, industry and other interested organizations. This initiative has been the flagship research effort for the National Information Infrastructure (NII) program.

The projects' focus was to be on dramatically advancing the *technology* involved in collecting, storing, and organizing digital information, and making that technology available for searching, retrieval and processing via communication networks. Particular emphasis was to be placed on user-friendliness and leveraging prior research in high performance computing and communications technology. The four-year projects (1994–1998) are centered at Carnegie Mellon University, the University of California, Berkeley, the University of California, Santa Barbara, the University of Illinois at Urbana-Champaign, the University of Michigan, and Stanford University.

The digital library effort was identified as a "National Challenge" (a fundamental application that has broad and direct impact on US competitiveness and the wellbeing of its citizens) in the Information Infrastructure Technology Applications component of the US High Performance Computing and Communications Program (HPCC). The key technological issue has been how to index, locate and display information of interest from very large, distributed (potentially internationally distributed) digital information repositories (or collections). In essence this involves developing infrastructures or architectures and tools for multimedia information retrieval on the Internet [88]. The six projects are briefly described in alphabetical order in the next six subsections.

6.1.1.1 Carnegie Mellon University: Informedia (www.informedia.cs.cmu.edu/)
The title of this $4.8 million project is: "Full Content Search and Retrieval of Video." It is also called the Informedia project. The principal investigator is Howard Wactlar of the School of Computer Science. Industrial partners and collaborators include:

- *corporations*—BBC (British Broadcast Communications), Bell Atlantic Network Services, The Boeing Company, Digital Equipment Corporation, the Vira I. Heinz Endowment, Intel Corporation, Microsoft Inc., Motorola, QED Communications (WQED in Pittsburgh, Pennsylvania, a public television station); and
- *educational institutions*—the Fairfax Virginia County Public Schools, the Open University in the United Kingdom, and the Winchester Thurston School in Pittsburgh, Pennsylvania.

The testbed database consists of 1000 hours of digital video from the archives of public television station WQED/Pittsburgh, Electronic Field Trips on video from the Fairfax County Virginia public school system and video course material produced by the BBC for the Open University. The research is primarily concerned with creating and searching this interactive on-line digital video library by capitalizing on a number of techniques for which Carnegie Mellon University is famous [49]:

- *image analysis*—partitioned video, image feature, frame classification from the Machine Vision project,
- *speech recognition*—the Sphinx, HEARSAY projects,
- *face recognition*—matching faces to names in voice transcript, and
- *natural language understanding*—using content-based video retrieval, video paragraphs, and segmentation and experience from the Tipster, Ferret and Scout projects.

The project is also investigating various methods of protecting the collection's intellectual property data rights and techniques to provide security and privacy through network billing, variable pricing and access control (NetBill project).

The Informedia project digital video library system was created by Carnegie Mellon University and WQED/Pittsburgh and allows users to access, explore and retrieve video science and mathematics materials. Informedia integrates speech, image and natural language understanding technologies. The digital library is populated by automatically encoding, segmenting and indexing video data that is partitioned into scenes using image analysis (image and frame features), speech recognition (including both closed captioned transcripts and automatically generated transcripts using the CMU speech recognition abilities from Sphinx and HEARSAY projects), face recognition (matching faces with names in the transcripts), and natural language understanding. The collection is chunked or segmented into video clips or video "paragraphs" (using visual scenes or conversations as boundaries). Video data contains temporal and spatial information and is typically massive and unstructured, making it extremely difficult to segment. The ultimate goal is full-content and knowledge-based search and retrieval of the video collection. Usability studies are conducted using K-12-age children from the Winchester Thurston School in Pittsburgh, Pennsylvania and investigate questions related to human factors such as learning, interaction and motivation [96].

Video user-interface requirements are more challenging than those of other multimedia collections, so various new techniques and approaches are under investigation. Especially challenging is the need for data representation for video clips which will allow "video skimming" by users to determine the relevance of a particular video segment. Problems encountered in the resolution of video error and variability caused by music and noise mixed with speech, segmentation of long fragments of video, inappropriate language models, error-prone closed-captioned data and scripts, acoustic modeling, identification of speaker change, and speech recognition for keyword retrieval [96] are also being studied. Issues involving human-computer interaction, pricing and charging for digital video use, and privacy and security are being addressed as part of the research program. More detail is available from the project's homepage listed above, including links to a series of publications on the project [96].

6.1.1.2 University of California at Berkeley (elib.cs.berkeley. edu/)
The title of this $4 million project is "Work-centered Digital Information Services." The principal investigator is Robert Wilensky of the Computer Science Department. Partners and collaborators in the project include:

- *University of California partners*—Office of the President, University of California at Berkeley Division of Computer Science, Office of Information Systems and Technology, Research Program in Environmental Planning and Geographic Information Systems, and School of Information Management and Systems;
- *State and federal agencies and organizations*—California Department of Fish and Game, California Department of Water Resources, California Environment Resources Evaluation System, California Land Use Planning Network, California Resources Agency, California State Library, San Diego Association of Governments, Shasta County Office of Education, Sonoma County Library, and USDA Forest Service;
- *Industrial partners*—Hewlett Packard (HP), Informix, IBM Almaden, Phillips Research, The Plumas Corporation, Ricoh California Research, The State of California Resources Agency, Sun Microsystems, and Xerox Corporation (Xerox PARC); and

The primary testbed database contains environmental information. Primary research topics for the project include [49]:

- *image content queries*—under investigation primarily at Xerox PARC using the Cypress engine and metadata or derived data generated at data acquisition time;
- *techniques for database extraction from documents*—including a variety of data formats from tables to spreadsheets or databases;
- *multivalent documents (MVD)*—a new digital document model which involves the creation of multiple potentially distributed layers of the same document, each containing different "behaviors;"

- *natural language processing (NLP)*—lexical disambiguation, and statistically based NLP; and
- *automatic categorization*—TileBars based on TexTile analysis which represent document content.

Other research areas include: automated indexing; intelligent retrieval and search processes; database technology to support digital library applications; new approaches to document analysis; and data compression and communication tools for remote browsing. A prototype digital library was created and contains environmental information to be used for the preparation and evaluation of environmental data, impact reports and related materials. The research prototype will eventually be deployed in the State of California as a full-scale CERES production system.

The project's main goal is to develop technologies for intelligent access to massive, distributed collections of photographs, satellite images, maps, full text documents, and "multivalent" documents. To accomplish this the project has focused on user needs assessments and a "simple" architecture consisting of information repositories, interoperable clients, indexing and searching techniques, interoperability mechanisms and protocols (e.g. ZQL—a Berkeley designed protocol that combines the SQL and Z39.50 protocol standards). The UC Berkeley project has created an interesting approach to image representation, "Blobworld," which locates objects by grouping low-level image properties (color, texture, symmetry) together into coherent units in a hierarchical manner. Users can query the image database by indicating on a given photograph regions central to their query. Blobworld returns images that contain regions that match user input. More detail can be obtained from the project's homepage mentioned above (including some very interesting demonstrations of their work and a list of publications) [100].

6.1.1.3 University of California at Santa Barbara: Alexandria (alexandria.sdc.ucsb.edu/)

The focus of this $4 million project is on "Spatially-referenced Map Information." It is also called ADL (Alexandria Digital Library). The principal investigator is Terrence R. Smith of the Departments of Computer Science and Geology. Partners include:

- *academic groups from the University of California at Santa Barbara*—Center for Remote Sensing and Environmental Optics, Departments of Computer Science and Electrical and Computer Engineering, Graduate College of Education, Map and Imagery Laboratory, and National Center for Geographic Information and Analysis (NCGIA);

- *academic researchers from NCGIA at other institutions*—University of Maine at Orono and State University of New York at Buffalo (SUNY-Buffalo);
- *libraries*—Library of Congress, St Louis Public Library, SUNY-Buffalo Library, UC Center for Library Automation and US Geological Survey Library; and
- *industrial partners*—AT&T, Conquest, Digital Equipment Corporation (DEC), Environmental Systems Research Institute (ESRI), and Xerox.

The project testbed database consists of maps, aerial photographs, atlases, gazetteers, and other spatially indexed information. The research focus is on [49]:

- *spatial indexing and retrieval*;
- *rapid response to image data queries*—including multi-resolution image storage and display;
- *image processing using features*—(i.e. texture, color, shape, location); and
- a variety of problems related to a distributed (i.e. across the Internet) digital library for geographically referenced information (i.e. all the objects in the library will be associated with one or more regions, or "footprints," on the surface of the Earth).

The primary project goal is to provide a comprehensive set of library services for spatially indexed and geographic information. The user interface supports both textually based and visually based queries focusing particularly on content-based searching. The collection is indexed using both top-down techniques (metadata based on a combination of USMARC, US Machine-Readable Cataloging, and FGDC, Federal Geographic Data Committee standards) and bottom-up automatic techniques.

The project is centered at the University of California, Santa Barbara (UCSB) because of its major map and image collections and its strong research focus in the area of spatially indexed information. The project is expected to expand to include other UCSB components, and other interested libraries such as the SUNY-Buffalo Library, the Library of Congress, the United States Geological Survey Library and the St. Louis Public Library. Facilities for geographical information interfaces, electronic catalogues, and information storage and acquisition will be included at each prototype test site. More detail is available from the project's homepage mentioned above (including a demonstration and a list of publications), and from [91] and [92].

6.1.1.4 University of Illinois at Urbana-Champaign: Interspace (dli.grainger.uiuc.edu/)
The focus of this $4 million project is on "Federating Repositories of Scientific Literature." It is also called the Interspace Project. The principal investigator is Bruce Schatz of the Graduate School of Library and Information Sciences and the National Center for Supercomputing Applications at Illinois. Other principal researchers include: Ann Bishop, Hsinchun Chen (University of Arizona), and Bill Mischo. The principal partners include:

- *publishing partners and professional societies* (providers of digitized material)—Academic Press, Inc., American Association for the Advancement of Science (AAAS), American Astronomical Society (AAS), American Chemical Society (ACS), American Institute of Aeronautics and Astronautics (AIAA), American Institute of Physics (AIP), American Physical Society (APS), American Society of Agricultural Engineers (ASAE), American Society of Civil Engineers (ASCE), American Society of Mechanical Engineers (ASME), Institution of Electrical Engineers (IEE), Institute of Electrical and Electronics Engineers (IEEE), IEEE Computer Society, Institute of Physics, Tribune Company, US News and World Report, and John Wiley & Sons;
- *software and hardware providers*—BRS/Dataware, Hewlett Packard, Microsoft, Inc., NETBILL, OpenText, SoftQuad, Spyglass, and United Technologies; and
- *others*—The University of Arizona, Carnegie-Mellon University, CIC Consortium (members of the Big Ten Universities), Corporation of National Research Initiatives (CNRI), and National Center for Supercomputing Applications (NCSA).

The testbed database consists of a collection of engineering and science journals and magazines. The technology focus of the project includes investigating:

- conversion of SGML to HTML documents and the conversion of digital non-SGML documents to SGML;
- semantic retrieval using noun phrases—concept spaces;
- automatic semantic categorization using neural networks—category maps;
- supercomputing simulation of large-scale semantic analysis;
- information representation or visualization; and
- semantic interoperability or vocabulary switching across knowledge domains.

The project is based in the Grainger Engineering Library Information Center at the University of Illinois at Urbana-Champaign and is centered around engineering and science journals and magazines. The testbed prototype (called DeLIver) is a production facility at the university library. It contains hundreds of thousands of full-text documents and is accessible to thousands of users at the University of Illinois. The testbed software supports comprehensive indexing, searching, and display of the complete contents of the collection including text, figures, equations, and tables. The primary focus is on seamless *textual* information retrieval across distributed, heterogeneous digital information repositories. However, a joint project with the University California at Santa Barbara, The University of Arizona and the University of Illinois at Urbana-Champaign is also investigating information retrieval using *texture* for images (in particular, satellite images and aerial photographs) [17].

Indexing the collection combines humanly determined and assigned meta-data (a top-down approach) and automatically generated, statistical co-occurrence analysis based indexing terms (a bottom-up approach). Research includes sociological evaluation of the testbed (including a user evaluation study), technological development of *scalable* deep semantic retrieval and data visualization techniques, and a prototype design of a future scalable information system (the Interspace). The ultimate goals of the project are to bring professional quality index, search and display capability to a large digital collection that is accessible via the Internet and to develop and implement an Interspace prototype (a vision of future evolution of the Internet). More detail is available from the project's homepage listed above, which includes a list of publications and presentations on the project and from [86] and [90].

6.1.1.5 University of Michigan: UMDL (www.si.umich.edu/ UMDL/)

The focus of this $4 million project is on "Intelligent Agents for Information Location." It is also known as UMDL (University of Michigan Digital Library). The principal investigator is Daniel Atkins of the School of Information. Partners include:

- *library partners*—Ann Arbor Public Library and New York Public Library;
- *school partners*—in Ann Arbor, Michigan: Huron High School, Community High School, Roberto Clemente Student Development Center, and Ann Arbor Public School Administrative Staff and in New York: Hunter College High School, and Stuyvesant High School;
- *publishing partners*—American Mathematical Society, Association of Research Libraries (ARL), Cambridge University Press, Elsevier

Science, Encyclopedia Britannica Educational Corporation, Groliers, McGraw-Hill and University Microfilm (UMI); and

- *corporate and organizational partners*—Apple Computer, Bellcore, Eastman-Kodak, Hewlett-Packard, IBM, Sybase and UMI International.

The testbed database contains earth and space science multi-media information. The major focus of the research includes:

- *scalability*—using agents to help unify diverse collections and locate information; and
- *education*—investigating "inquiry-based education," a new teaching style that heavily utilizes the Internet and digital libraries.

Specific research topics include investigating: the use of agents to unify collections and services (scalability); conspectus search (i.e. finding appropriate collection); new educational methods (i.e. "inquiry-based education"); and several different approaches to copyright and intellectual property protection on the Internet. A critical component of the project is the testing and evaluation of the prototype system by a wide variety of users, including those from on-campus, local high schools and public libraries. Michigan has several other ongoing digital library projects (JSTOR, TULIP, and "The Making of America") that it is integrating with this effort [49].

The Michigan project is investigating the coordination of three levels or types of agents for intelligent information identification and retrieval: *user interface agents* which interact with the user to define and determine the scope of the inquiry, *mediation agents* which coordinate the requests of many user interface agents and their interactions with the collections (using a conspectus approach to searching) and *collection agents* which handle the specific details of searching various media types within a given collection. Another focus of the project is investigating the pricing of electronic access to knowledge using agents that negotiate access fees based on supply and demand or market information (see the Internet AuctionBot information on the project's web site). More detail can be obtained from the project's homepage (which also contains a list of publications, a demonstration, and links to other related sites) and [5] and [22].

6.1.1.6 Stanford University: InfoBus (walrus.stanford.edu/diglib/)
The focus of this $3.6 million project is on "Interoperation Mechanisms among Heterogeneous Services." It is also called the InfoBus project. The principal investigator is Hector Garcia-Molina of the Computer Science Department.

Participating organizations include: Association for Computing Machinery (ACM), Bell Communications Research (Bellcore), Enterprise Integration

Technologies (EIT), Hewlett-Packard Labs (HP), Hitachi Corp., Hughes Research Laboratory, Interconnect Technologies Corporation (ITC), Interval Research Corporation, Knight-Ridder Information (Dialog Information Services—DIS), MIT Press, NASA/Ames Research Center (NASA/ARC) including the Advanced Interaction Media Group and the library, Naval Command, Control and Ocean Surveillance Center (NCCOSC), O'Reilly and Associates, WAIS Inc. and Xerox PARC.

The primary focus of this project is *interoperability*. It has a small testbed database consisting of computer science literature. Primary research topics include:

- investigating different database infrastructures for digital library support primarily focusing on CORBA (the distributed-object standard developed by the Object Management Group);
- investigating different network infrastructures for digital library support; and
- investigating a World Wide Web annotation service which allows "permanent" annotation of Web pages without modification to the original.

The problems involved in the integration of a variety of heterogeneous information sources (ranging from personal sources to public library or repository sources to private or proprietary domain specific sources) at a higher level than the current transport-oriented protocols is one of the primary research thrusts of the project. The goal is to develop enabling technologies for a single, integrated "virtual" library available over the Internet that provides uniform access to a large number of networked information sources and collections, thus requiring new forms of information sharing and communication models, client information interfaces and information finding services. Another research focus is on the legal and economic issues of a networked environment. Inter-Pay, for example, is an architecture designed to provide interoperability for fee-based services, while the Stanford SCAM and COPS (Copywrite Protection Service) projects are involved with the protection of intellectual property in electronic or digital forms [70].

The heart of the Stanford project is the "InfoBus" protocol, which provides a uniform way to access a variety of services and information sources through "proxies" acting as interpreters between it and each collection's native protocol and thereby allowing access to multiple, distributed information sources. The InfoBus protocol is supported by a variety of user-level applications, which provide powerful ways to find information by using cutting-edge user interfaces for direct manipulation or through agent technology. Examples of Stanford projects involved in information location include GlOSS (Glossary-of-Servers Server) which helps identify the most relevant information sources for a particular query and SIFT (Stanford Information Filtering Tool). More detail is available from the project's homepage mentioned above, which contains some excellent links to other digital library information [35, 70].

6.1.2 Other Major US Digital Library Research Activities

There are several other major US digital library research activities. Most of them involve large-scale content creation and user testbeds.

6.1.2.1 Library of Congress (lcweb.loc.gov/) The most ambitious national level project in the United States is the Library of Congress National Digital Library Program under the direction of James Billington. This project's goal is to digitize over 5 million multimedia items from the extensive Library of Congress collection with particular focus on historical information. There are currently 32 historical collections available for keyword searching and browsing (by titles, topics, and library division by collection type—i.e. photos and prints, documents, motion pictures, maps and sound recordings). This project includes: the *American Memory project* which will become one of the testbeds for the DLI-2 initiative; *THOMAS*, which provides full text access to bills under consideration in the US House of Representatives and Senate; and *Library of Congress exhibitions* which are now indefinitely available on the Internet. Many other databases and information resources are available on-line through the Library of Congress Internet gateway. Some of these resources include: Library of Congress catalogs (which contain over 110 million items); access to catalogs at over 200 other libraries both within and outside the US (through the Z39.50 Gateway); Library of Congress Thesauri; the Vietnam Era Prisoner of War/Missing in Action and Task Force Russia Databases; Science Tracer Bullets (SCTB) Online (bibliographic guides); GLIN—Global Legal Information Network; and US Copyright Office Records.

Other digital library projects at the Library of Congress include:

- *Standards*: The Library of Congress is the maintenance agency for several key standards used in the information community, including US Machine-Readable Cataloging (MARC) formats, the Z39.50 information retrieval protocol, the Encoded Archival Description (EAD) Document Type Definition (DTD) for Standard Generalized Markup Language (SGML), and the International Standard Serial Number (ISSN).

- *The Library of Congress/Ameritech National Digital Library Competition*: With a gift of $2 million from the Ameritech Foundation, the Library of Congress is sponsoring a competition to enable public, research, and academic libraries, museums, historical societies and archival institutions (except federal institutions) to create digital collections of primary resource material. These digital collections will complement and become part of the collections of the National Digital Library Program at the Library of Congress. The Library of Congress/Ameritech National Digital Library Competition will run for three consecutive years beginning in 1996, with the expectation that eight to ten awards of up to $75,000 each will be made annually.
- *The Digital Library Federation*: Fifteen of the nation's largest research libraries and archives agreed in 1995 to cooperate on defining what must be done to bring together digitized materials that document the building and dynamics of United States heritage and cultures and will be made accessible to people everywhere. Members include: Columbia University, the Commission on Preservation and Access, Cornell University, Emory University, Harvard University, The Library of Congress, National Archives and Records Administration, The New York Public Library, Pennsylvania State University, Princeton University, Stanford University, University of California at Berkeley, University of Michigan, University of Southern California, University of Tennessee, and Yale University.

    Some of the projects include: Computer Sciences Technical Reports (CSTR) Project at Berkeley, Emory University Virtual Library, Information Infrastructure Project (Harvard University), Making of America Project (Cornell University and the University of Michigan), Networked Computer Science Technical Reports Library (NCSTRL at Cornell University), New York State Museum Bulletins Project (Columbia University), Open Book Project (Yale University) and Stanford University Computer Science Electronic and Technical Reports Library.
- *The Global Information Society*: The Library of Congress is a member of the Global Information Society and participates in the G-7 "Electronic Libraries" Project (a part of the Group 7 Bibliotheca Universalis project) with France, Japan, Germany, Canada, Italy, and the United Kingdom. The Library officially represents the United States on issues of international importance to the future of libraries.

6.1.2.2 National Aeronautics and Space Administration— NASA (www.nasa.gov/)

In addition to supporting the Digital Library

Initiatives, NASA provides the ability to search on-line its extensive collections, with particular emphasis on its earth science scientific data collection (predominantly satellite data and images). Some of the available NASA information includes: AVHRR 1 km Data Browser (Italy) Live Access to Climate Data (NOAA), Crustal Dynamics Data Information System (NASA), The Earth Science Data and Information System Project, EOS Data Information System Distributed Active Archive Centers, The Global Change Data Center, Global Hydrology Resource Center (GHRC), Guide to NASA Online Resources, National Climate Data Center (NOAA), NASA Documents on-line, NASA News Archives, NASA's Earth Observing System Earth Images and Data, NASA Facts on-line, NASA News Archives, Pathfinder Datasets, SeaWiFS Project—Ocean Color Data, The Total Ozone Mapping Spectrometer (TOMS) Project and Data, and many other NASA publications.

NASA's Digital Library Technology (DLT) project supports the development of new technologies to facilitate public access to NASA data via computer networks, placing greatest emphasis on scalable technologies that develop tools, applications, and software and hardware systems. The DLT project and the Public Use of Remote Sensing Data (RSD) project, are two related elements of the Information Infrastructure Technology and Applications (IITA) component of NASA's High Performance Computing and Communications Program (HPCC).

6.1.2.3 FedStats (www.FedStats.gov) The collection available in this multiple agency project includes statistical information (reports, charts, tables, etc.) from more than 70 different US governmental agencies. This information has two major data types (textual and numerical) and is Web accessible in a variety of formats from spreadsheets to relational databases. The major challenges include designing flexible presentation and intelligent user interfaces that can assist users in transforming raw statistics into useful information or knowledge.

6.1.2.4 IBM (www.software.ibm.com/is/dig-lib/) The IBM digital library is one of the first commercial digital library efforts in the United States. It consists of an array of products and services aimed at helping customers transform information into digital multimedia forms that can be shared with others via networks and includes tools to manage, present and protect that information. The primary focus of the IBM digital library is on *image retrieval* (e.g. Scriptorium) with particular emphasis on high quality image presentation, searching capabilities for multimedia information, and copyright and intellectual property management capabilities [34]. The IBM digital library integrates a wide array of scalable information storage, management, search, retrieval, and distribution technologies, many of which were already available, into a single architecture. Excellent examples of the IBM digital library are the El Archive General de Indies, the works of Andrew Wyeth, and the Vatican Library project, all of which can be found in [34].

6.1.2.5 The California Digital Library Project (www.lpai.ucop. edu)
The California Digital Library or CDL is the tenth system-level University of California library and is administered from the Office of the President. The University of California system (nine campuses with nine-system level libraries) owns a collection of over 29 million volumes in its 100-plus individual libraries. With the exception of the Library of Congress, this collection is the largest on the American continent. Each of the nine University of California campuses has its own library system, but the CDL (formerly known as the Division of Library Automation) is the first system-wide library with a primary emphasis on accessibility and digitization. The CDL is responsible for leading several automation and digitization projects for the University of California, and for expanding both the accessible collections (to include more public and private libraries and museums and libraries and museums from California, around the United States, and eventually the world) and extending accessibility (to include the general public). Resource sharing is obviously one important focus of CDL, but another major research area includes efforts to reduce staggering increases in costs over the last five years by exploring electronic alternatives to scholarly publishing. The first target shared collection for digitization in the CDL is a Science, Technology and Industry Collection which will include access to approximately 1000 science and technology journals when it is complete. Plans are already underway to begin processing a Humanities and Social Sciences shared digitized collection.

CDL's responsibilities include the maintenance and continuing development and expansion of MELVYL, which can search on-line the entire system's catalog, the California Academic Libraries list of Serials and approximately 120 other databases, 25 of which are commercial products such as MEDLINE. The system can be accessed either by telnet or through the Internet. The original objective of the MELVYL system was to unite and provide on-line access to the library collections of the entire University of California system. The objective has since shifted to providing state-wide and wider access to a broad range of information sources for research and education. Several other public and private libraries in California (including museums and museum collections) like the Stanford University Library are now accessible, and the goal is to continue to expand accessibility. Richard E. Lucier was named to head the CDL in October of 1997. Funding for CDL was budgeted for $1.5 million in the fiscal year 1997–98 and approximately $4 million in the fiscal year 1998–99 [64].

6.1.2.6 The DARPA D-Lib Program (www.dlib.org) D-Lib is an excellent on-line digital library reference source coordinated by CNRI and sponsored by the Defense Advanced Research Projects Agency (DARPA). The Web site provides access to the D-Lib Magazine (an on-line monthly compilation of contributed stories, commentary, and briefings); Ready Reference (an exceptional clearinghouse of pointers to other sites on the Web of interest to researchers and users of digital libraries); Technology Spotlight (a collection of demos and interesting reports and papers related to digital library research); and other information.

6.1.2.7 JSTOR (www.jstor.org/) JSTOR is a not-for-profit organization initially established with funding from The Andrew W. Mellon Foundation. It is dedicated to helping the scholarly community take advantage of advances in information technologies, in particular electronic publishing capabilities, in an effort to ease the costs of scholarly journal storage and access. The project goals are to convert back issues of paper journals into electronic formats to save space (and the capital costs associated with that space) while simultaneously improving access to journal contents and offering a solution to preservation problems associated with storing paper-based information.

A pilot project at five library test sites provided electronic access to the back files of ten journals in two core fields, economics and history. Every issue of the ten participating journals published prior to 1990—approximately 750,000 total pages—has now been converted from paper into an electronic database that resides at the University of Michigan and is mirrored at Princeton University. Using technology developed at Michigan, high-resolution (600 dpi) bit-mapped images of each page are linked to a text file generated with optical character recognition (OCR) software which, along with newly constructed Table-of-Contents indexes, permits complete search and retrieval of the journal material.

Currently the collection contains the "back files" of over 50 journals and it permits access from more than 300 universities and colleges around the world [94]. Future plans include extending the collection to more than 100 journals (by the end of 1999).

6.1.2.8 Making of America—Cornell University and the University of Michigan (moa.cit.cornell.edu/ and www.umdl.umich.edu/moa/) The goal of the Making of America (MOA) Project is to create and make accessible (over the Internet) a distributed digital library of materials on the history of the United States. The Cornell University and University of Michigan libraries have cooperated in the initial phase of MOA, which has been funded by the Andrew W. Mellon Foundation and the Charles E. Culpeper Foundation. The MOA project is designed to select complementary journals and monographs on 19th-century US history from the two universities, create digital images of the material in a manner that ensures full capture of all significant information, and provide equitable access to the combined digital collection from both campuses.

6.1.2.9 Project Open Book—Yale University (www.library. yale.edu/preservation/pobweb.htm) Yale University Library's Project Open Book is a research and development program that is exploring the feasibility and costs of large-scale conversion of preserved material from microfilm to digital imagery. The project has three overall goals:

(1) *Conversion*—create a 10,000 volume digital image library from converted microfilm and evaluate issues of workflow, quality, and cost;
(2) *Intellectual access*—enhance intellectual access through the creation of document structure and page number indexes enabling scholars to go directly to a particular page or document structure element, such as a table of contents; and
(3) *Distributed physical access*—enhance physical access to the digital library by providing distributed access over the Yale campus network and eventually over the Internet.

6.1.2.10 The Red Sage Project (www.ckm.ucsf.edu/projects/ RedSage/) The Red Sage project was a four-year (1992–96) experimental cooperative effort between the University of California at San Francisco, AT&T Bell Laboratories (Right-Pages), and Springer-Verlag to provide on-line access to 70 Springer-Verlag, American Medical Association (AMA) and other health-science related journals on molecular biology and radiology. The goal of the project was to allow researchers, clinicians, and students to search, read and print the full-page text, including graphics and photographs. Red Sage investigated technical, legal, business, and human factors issues related to network delivery of scientific journal literature.

6.1.2.11 The TULIP Project—Elsevier (www1.elsevier.nl/ homepage/about/resproj/tulip.shtml) TULIP [7] was an Elsevier Science Publishers initiative (1991–95) created to explore the issues involved in electronic scholarly journal electronic distribution. Ten universities (Carnegie Mellon University—CMU, Cornell University, Georgia

Institute of Technology, Massachusetts Institute of Technology—MIT, Princeton University, University of California (all campuses), University of Michigan, University of Tennessee, University of Washington, and Virginia Polytechnic Institute and State University) were involved in the project, which also included several official *observing* institutions (California State University, Harvard University, Pennsylvania State University, Stanford University and the University of Southern California). Approximately 60 Materials Science journal titles comprised the testbed collection. The project was especially interested in exploring economic models for electronic access, investigating the technical feasibility of networked distribution of journals, and investigating usage patterns for electronic access. One of the most significant contributions made by this project is its extensive user evaluation effort [37]. It is now a commercial product.

6.2 Digital Library Activities in Other Countries

Most digital library activities in other countries focus on collections, particularly on improving access to collections of historical, cultural or artistic significance. Many of the social issues surrounding digital libraries, especially legal issues related to copyright laws and protection of intellectual property, are also of primary importance in these activities. As most of these efforts are at a national level, the primary lead organization is the national library of the country or government agencies.

6.2.1 Canada

There are several Canadian digital library initiatives. The most recent, the Canadian Initiative on Digital Libraries (CIDL) was initiated in 1998 and comprises an alliance of Canadian libraries. CIDL's goal is to promote, coordinate, and facilitate the development of Canadian digital collections and services, emphasizing interoperability and long-term access to Canadian digital library resources. (see www.nlc-bnc.ca/cidl/).

The University of Waterloo developed text-searching software based on the Patricia tree data structure that is now being commercially sold by OpenText [49]. Waterloo is also the site of a major community network prototype and study called Canada's Technology Triangle (CTT) Community Network. This project is community-based and provides local maps, information about local businesses and local historical information available on the Internet, focusing on communication and community-building infrastructures [21] (see CTTnet.uwaterloo.ca).

The National Library of Canada, much like the US Library of Congress, provides on-line access to some of its collection through its Web homepage.

It is also involved in an extensive historical information digitization project and in the Canadian Electronic Publications Pilot Project (see www.nlc-bnc.ca/ehome.htm).

6.2.2 United Kingdom

The Follett report begun in 1993 initiated digital library activities in the United Kingdom, resulting in the E-Lib project (UK Electronic Libraries Program), which funded approximately 60 programs for a total of £20 million starting in 1995. Some of the E-Lib projects include cataloging archives, providing UK-wide e-mail services, and providing access to Web multimedia information (a distinct challenge due to the congestion on the Internet between the US and the UK). The E-Lib project focuses more on providing electronic resources and services for UK higher education than on purely scientific research. One of the most significant E-Lib achievements has been persuading publishers to treat the *entire* UK academic community as a single site for the purposes of licensing information [59]. (see www.ukoln.ac.uk/services/elib/).

The British Library began a digital library program in 1993. Similarly to other national library programs, its emphasis is on collections, preservation and improved public access. The British Library is also heavily involved in the establishment of standards and legal guidelines for copyright law and intellectual property protection with respect to digital libraries [49]. Several fascinating key projects include: the Patent Express Jukebox (CD-ROM jukebox of over one million patent records), the Electronic Beowulf Project (a huge database of digital images of the Beowulf manuscript, related manuscripts and printed texts), the Electronic Photo Viewing System (10,000 images of historical significance that are hyperlinked to descriptive text), the Network OPAC (providing ability to search on-line the British Library's 6 million bibliographic records, which is connected to all other UK university and research institutes via the UK Joint Academic Network—JANET), and conversion of microfilm to digital form [75]. Several literary and artistic treasures are available on-line through the British Library Web site, including: the Lindisfarne Gospels, the Diamond Sutra, the Magna Carta, the Sforza Hours, a Leonardo da Vinci Notebook, and the Tyndale New Testament (see www.bl.uk).

6.2.3 France

The Bibliothèque Nationale de France, the national library of France, has led the digitization effort in France. It plans to make available through its Web site 110,000 digitized books (mostly in image format), 300,000 pictures and 3,000 recordings. The most interesting component of this digitized collection is a group of 1000 14th-century manuscripts [42, 49] (see www.bnf.fr/ or the English version at www.bnf.fr/bnfgb.htm).

Frantext/ARTFL (American and French Research on the Treasury of the French Language) allows full-text access to a digitized database of classic French literature (approximately 3500 items) [42, 49]. Frantext is managed by the Institut National de la Langue Française in Paris (see ciril.fr/mastina/FRANTEXT). ARTFL is managed through the University of Chicago (see humanities.uchicago.edu/ARTFL.html).

France is a co-leader with Japan on the Group 7 project (the Bibliotheca Universalis project) whose goal is to provide global access to digitized cultural, historical and scientific multi-media information from all over the world (see www.culture.fr/culture/bibliuni/engbu1.htm).

6.2.4 Germany

Multimedia Electronic Documents (MeDoc) is a digital library project sponsored by the German Informatics Society that involves several publishers, universities and research institutions. The goal of this project is to "stimulate the use of electronic media in academic education and in scientific research" [27]. The collection currently focuses on computer science literature. The system contains a mechanism that allows the retrieval of individual book chapters or journal paper components (Fulltext Storage System—FSS). (see medoc.informatik.tu-muenchen.de).

6.2.5 Gabriel

Gabriel is a gateway server that provides access to Europe's National Libraries. Information about the server is available in three languages (German, English and French). The objective is to try to bring the European community belonging to the Conference of European National Libraries (CENL) closer together by providing a single entry point through the Internet to all of their libraries, including their collections and services. Thirty-eight national European libraries (including the Vatican City library) are connected through Gabriel (see linnea.helsinki.fi/gabriel/index.html).

6.2.6 Japan

National Diet Library is sponsoring five Electronic Library Projects. They include: Pilot Electronic Library Projects, Electronic Library of Children's Books, Asian Information Supply System, G7 (Group 7) Electronic Library Project or Bibliotheca Universalis, and Full Text Database of the Minutes of the Diet. As with most national libraries, the focus is on the collections themselves, from an acquisition and preservation perspective with the goal of improving public access to national cultural and historical information. This project is extremely ambitious in that it is attempting to digitize a wide variety of multimedia information, and information in very diverse formats (e.g. scrolls, woodblock prints, microfilms) (see www.ndl.go.jp/index-e.html).

As one of the three main projects under the Center for Information Infrastructure (CII), the Electronic Library Pilot Project offers experimental electronic access to a vast collection of diverse books and other resources existing in libraries all over Japan. One of the main goals of this project is to test the latest advances in data-processing and network technologies in preparation for future digital libraries. This is a joint project of the Information-technology Promotion Agency and the National Diet Library (see www.cii.ipa.go.jp/el/index_e.html).

The MHTML (Multilingual HTML) project is a fascinating multilingual project that allows multilingual browsing of a digital library of Japanese folk tales on the Internet. This collection can be accessed via a gateway, and can process Japanese, Korean, Chinese, Thai, and several European languages, including French and English [55] (see mhtml.ulis.ac.jp/).

The Science Information Network (SINET) is one of several projects sponsored by the Japanese National Center for Science Information Systems. This system connects universities and research institutions all over Japan and in addition is interconnected with research networks in the United States, the United Kingdom, and Thailand. NACSIS-IR is an information retrieval service that provides access to 57 different databases, allowing a user to simultaneously browse, search and retrieve information from multiple databases. NACSIS also has an electronic library service (NACSIS-ELS) which provides access to an integrated bibliographic database from several distributed sources and an electronic document delivery service of Japanese scientific journals over the Internet (see www.nacsis.ac.jp/nacsis.f-index.html).

6.2.7 Korea

Korea has a digital library pilot program developed under the supervision and guidance of the Ministry of Information and Communication. The project testbed is accessible via the Internet and provides full-text, catalogue and abstract searching and browsing. Five major libraries are involved: (1) The National Library of Korea (includes a database of old rare books available on-line), (2) The National Assembly Library (provides legislative documents similar to the Library of Congress's THOMAS project), (3) The

Science Library in KAIST, (4) The Korea Research and Development Information Center in KAIST and (5) the Korean Research Foundation). The project uses SGML and Z39.50 standards to provide interoperability between the sites and users. All information is accessible in Korean and some of it is accessible in English. Much of the challenge involved in the Korean Digital Library project has to do with the problems associated with Korean text. The language is character-based and has many stylistic differences even within a given document collection, which can negatively impact information retrieval and exchange [62] (see www.dlibrary.or.kr).

6.2.8 Singapore

Singapore is aspiring to be the "Intelligent Island" with leading edge information management as one of its top national priorities. To this end, it has electronically linked all of the libraries in the country. As its primary focus is on linking to information via the Internet, most of the electronically linked libraries function essentially as gateways [49]. The emphasis in this country is on using digital information for business and for educational purposes. One of the other major projects in Singapore is the CLiB project. This project uses the Z39.50 protocol and provides multilingual (primarily Chinese and English) searching of several heterogeneous bibliographic databases. It focuses primarily on language support issues, especially those related to representation of Chinese characters [47] (see www.lib.gov.sg/nlb.html).

6.2.9 China, Hong Kong, and Taiwan

Most of the digital library projects in this region are centered around Chinese information retrieval and digitization of local and cultural content.

Digital library research efforts in China have focused on collections, and in particular on the preservation of national literary treasures. Other Chinese digital library projects involve tackling the challenge of electronically recognizing Chinese characters, Chinese cross-lingual retrieval and developing standards for digital libraries such as the Chinese MARC record standard [49] and the Net Compass Project of Tsinghua university.

In Hong Kong, special-purpose digital libraries have been created. One of these is the Financial Digital Library project at the university of Hong Kong that serves the unique need of the Hong Kong stock market and users. Similar to the research effort in China, the Chinese University of Hong Kong has continued to research NLP-based intelligent Chinese information retrieval for digital libraries.

The Academia Sinica in Taiwan probably has the best research teams in the area of Chinese information retrieval and voice recognition. Funded by the Taiwan government for about two decades, these teams have significantly advanced Chinese input, segmentation, indexing, and analysis. Many of their techniques have been adopted in digital libraries or Internet servers of Chinese content. In addition, several projects in Taiwan have focused on cultural content digitization, including the Digital Museum project of the National Taiwan University and the art collection digitization of Palace Museum in Taipei by IBM.

The First Asia Digital Library Workshop was held in Hong Kong in August 1998. With its focus on Asia digital library research projects, the workshop attracted more than 120 participants from nine Asia/Pan-Pacific countries and has served as the catalyst for Asia digital library collaborations. Several countries have expressed strong interest in sponsoring a Second Asian Digital Library Workshop. An Asia Digital Library Consortium is also under development to help foster long-term collaboration and projects in digital library related topics in Asia (see www.ssrc.hku.hk/sym/98/adl.html).

6.2.10 Australia

Australia has several major digitization efforts that are centered at the National Gallery of Australia and the National Library of Australia and focus on historical and cultural material. One effort is digitizing aboriginal language recordings and other multimedia material relating to Australian Aborigines. Another effort, the MetaWeb Project, is focusing on developing tools for metadata creation and maintenance [49]. The National Library of Australia is involved in a project called PADI (Preserving Access to Digital Information) that is investigating issues and solutions to problems of preservation and access to digital information in the future (see www.nla.gov.au/).

6.2.11 New Zealand

The New Zealand digital library system is a federally funded research project at the University of Waikato which contains several demonstration collections (primarily in computer science, e.g. computer science technical reports, literary works, Internet FAQs, the Computists' Communique magazine) and makes them available over the Web through full-text interfaces. The digital library has expanded beyond its original computer science-oriented collection to include literary, music, and image collections and an Arabic collection accessible in Arabic. There are interfaces to access the collections in five different natural languages (English, French, German, Arabic, and Maori) [101]. The goal of this research program is to explore the potential of Internet-based digital libraries by developing systems that automatically impose structure on anarchic, uncatalogued, distributed repositories of information, thereby providing information consumers with effective tools to locate what they need and to peruse it conveniently and comfortably [102]. The project includes a collaborative effort with the German MeDoc project [27] and the *Journal of Biological Chemistry* to explore novel browsing techniques. Access is based on full-text retrieval as opposed to metadata. The most interesting part of the collection is a musical collection of 9400 international folk tunes stored in musical notation. The melody index can be used to retrieve songs using sung, hummed or played musical input [60] (see www.nzdl.org/).

7. Digital Library Research Issues in Semantic Interoperability

7.1 Digital Library Grand Challenge: Semantic Interoperability

The Information Infrastructure Technology and Applications (IITA) Working Group, the highest level of the US National Information Infrastructure (NII) technical committee, held an invited workshop in May 1995 to define a research agenda for digital libraries.

The shared vision is an entire net of distributed repositories, where objects of any type can be searched within and across different indexed collections [88]. In the short term, technologies must be developed to transparently search across these repositories, handling any variations in protocols and formats (i.e. addressing structural interoperability [70]). In the long term, technologies must be developed to handle the variations in content and meanings (knowledge) transparently as well. These requirements are steps along the way toward matching the concepts requested by users with objects indexed in collections [87].

The ultimate goal, as described in the IITA report [53], is the Grand Challenge of digital libraries:

> deep semantic interoperability—the ability of a user to access, consistently and coherently, similar (though autonomously defined and managed) classes of digital objects and services, distributed across heterogeneous repositories, with federating or mediating software compensating for site-by-site variations ... Achieving this will require breakthroughs in description as well as retrieval, object interchange and object retrieval protocols. Issues here include the definition and use of metadata and its capture or computation from objects (both textual and multimedia), the use of computed descriptions of objects, federation and integration of heterogeneous repositories with

disparate semantics, clustering and automatic hierarchical organization of information, and algorithms for automatic rating, ranking, and evaluation of information quality, genre, and other properties.

Attention to semantic interoperability has prompted several of the NSF/DARPA/NASA funded large-scale digital library initiative (DLI) projects to explore various statistical, and pattern recognition techniques, e.g. concept spaces and category maps in the Illinois project [90, 15], textile and word sense disambiguation in the Berkeley project [100], voice recognition in the CMU project [96], and image segmentation and clustering in the UCSB project [56]. "Definition and use of metadata" and "clustering and automatic hierarchical organization of information," which require significant future research, are the key components needed to build classification systems for digital libraries automatically.

7.2 Research Towards Semantic Interoperability in Digital Libraries

Library classification systems and subject-specific thesauri such as the Library of Congress classification, Dewey classification, or the NLM's Unified Medical Language Systems (UMLS) are significant human efforts to have trained librarians, who are versed in classification scheme and domain knowledge, label knowledge consistently [39, 11]. Library classification systems and thesauri often capture nouns or noun phrases and represent only limited relationships (e.g. broader terms, narrower term, etc.). The representations are often coarse, but precise. The goal of supporting indexing and searching is practical. Significant human efforts are needed to create and maintain large-scale classification systems.

Artificial intelligence representations such as semantic networks, expert systems, or ontologies represent another approach to capturing knowledge, e.g. Lenat's CYC common sense knowledge base [45, 46, 36]. Such representations are often richer and more fine-grained and the goal of capturing human intelligence is ambitious and difficult. Due to the granularity required, knowledge creation is slow and painstaking. Only experimental prototypes in small, limited domains have been created. Their usefulness in large-scale digital library applications remains suspect.

The traditional approach to creating classification systems and knowledge sources in library science and classical AI is often considered top-down since knowledge representations and formats are pre-defined by human experts or trained librarians and the process of generating knowledge is structured and well-defined. A complementary bottom-up approach to knowledge creation has been suggested by researchers in machine learning, statistical analysis, and neural networks.

Based on actual databases or collections, researchers develop programs which systematically segment and index documents in various databases (text, image, and video) and identify patterns within such databases. Analyzing databases which contain structured and numeric data (e.g. credit card usage, frequent flyer program) is often referred to as data mining or knowledge discovery [73, 54]. Generating knowledge algorithmically from multimedia databases (especially text, e.g. customer complaint e-mail, machinery repair reports, brainstorming outputs) is considered the core of knowledge management [67].

Among the semantic indexing and analysis techniques that are considered scalable and domain independent, the following classes of algorithms and methods have been examined and subjected to experimentation in various digital library applications. We also provide examples from our own research for illustration purposes.

7.2.1 Object Recognition, Segmentation, and Indexing

The most fundamental techniques in information retrieval involve identifying key features in objects. For example, automatic indexing and natural language processing (e.g. noun phrase extraction or object type tagging) are frequently used to automatically extract meaningful keywords or phrases from texts [80]. Texture, color, or shape-based indexing and segmentation techniques are often used to identify images [56]. For audio and video applications, voice recognition, speech recognition, and scene segmentation techniques can be used to identify meaningful descriptors in audio or video streams [96].

As part of the Illinois DLI project, we have developed a noun phrasing technique for textual document indexing [38]. Noun phrase indexing aims to identify concepts (grammatically correct noun phrases) from a collection for term indexing. It begins with a text tokenization process to separate punctuation and symbols. It follows by part-of-speech-tagging (POST) using variations of the Brill tagger and 30-plus grammatic noun phrasing rules. Figure 1 shows an example of tagged noun phrases for a simple sentence. (The system is referred to as AZ Noun Phraser.) For example, "interactive navigation" is a noun phrase that consists of an adjective (A) and a noun (N). In [38], we have shown that the noun phrasing technique produces more accurate indices for digital libraries (than inverted word indexing or N-gram indexing) and helps in concept-based retrieval. By using such a scalable natural language processing technique, digital libraries will be able to efficiently (automatically) and precisely index its own collections.

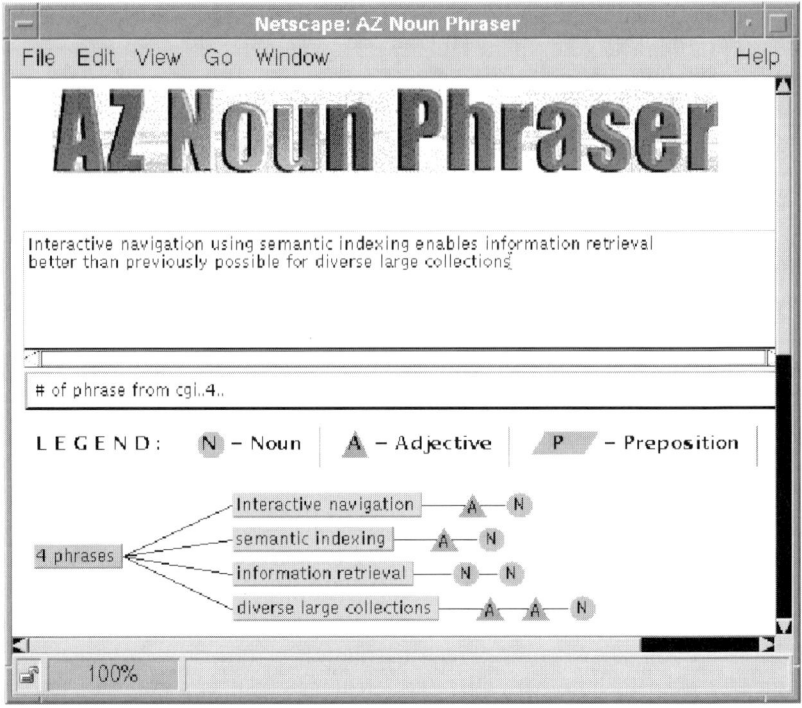

FIG. 1. Tagged noun phrases.

7.2.2 Semantic Analysis

Several classes of techniques have been used for semantic analysis of texts or multimedia objects. Symbolic machine learning (e.g. ID3, version space), graph-based clustering and classification (e.g. Ward's hierarchical clustering), statistics-based multivariate analyses (e.g. latent semantic indexing, multi-dimensional scaling, regressions), artificial neural network-based computing (e.g. backpropagation networks, Kohonen self-organizing maps), and evolution-based programming (e.g. genetic algorithms) are among the popular techniques [10]. In this information age, we believe these techniques will serve as good alternatives for processing, analyzing, and summarizing large amounts of diverse and rapidly changing multimedia information.

The *concept space* technique, developed at the Illinois DLI project is an example of semantic, statistical analysis of large-scale digital library collections [15, 12]. Concept space, like an automatic thesaurus, attempts to generate weighted, contextual concept (term) association in a collection to assist in concept-based associative retrieval. It adopts several heuristic term

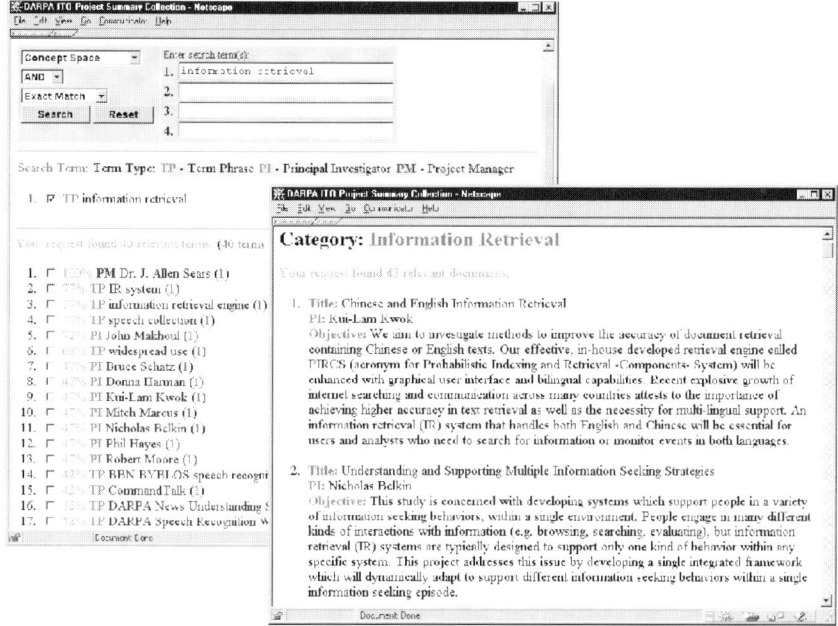

FIG. 2. Associated terms for "information retrieval".

weighting rules and a weighted co-occurrence analysis algorithm. Figure 2 shows the associated terms for "information retrieval" in a sample collection of project reports of the DARPA/ITO Program—TP (Term Phrase) such as "IR system," "information retrieval engine," "speech collection," etc. Such concept spaces have been computed for collections of the scale of 100,000 web pages [12], one million abstracts across engineering [15], and 10 million abstracts across medicine [3].

7.2.3 Knowledge Representations

The results from a semantic analysis process could be presented in one of many knowledge representations, including classification systems, semantic networks, decision rules, or predicate logic. Many researchers have attempted to integrate such results with existing human-created knowledge structures such as ontologies, subject headings, or thesauri [58]. Spreading activation based inferencing methods are often used to traverse various large-scale knowledge structures [14].

In [12] and [16], we reported a neural network-based textual categorization technique for digital library content classification. A category map is the result of performing neural network-based clustering (self-organizing) of similar documents and automatic category labeling. Documents that are similar to each other (in noun phrase terms) are grouped together in a neighborhood on a two-dimensional display. As shown in the colored jigsaw-puzzle display in Fig. 3, each colored region represents a unique topic that contains similar documents. Topics that are more important often occupy larger regions. By clicking on each region, a searcher can browse documents grouped in that region. An alphabetical list that is a summary of the 2D result is also displayed on the left-hand side of Fig. 3, e.g. Adaptive Computing System (13 documents), Architectural Design (nine documents), etc. Our current research has demonstrated the computational scalability and clustering accuracy and novelty of this technique [69, 12].

7.2.4 Human–Computer Interactions (HCI) and Information Visualization

One of the major trends in almost all digital library applications is the focus on user-friendly, graphical, and seamless HCI. The Web-based browsers for texts, images, and videos have raised user expectations of the rendering and

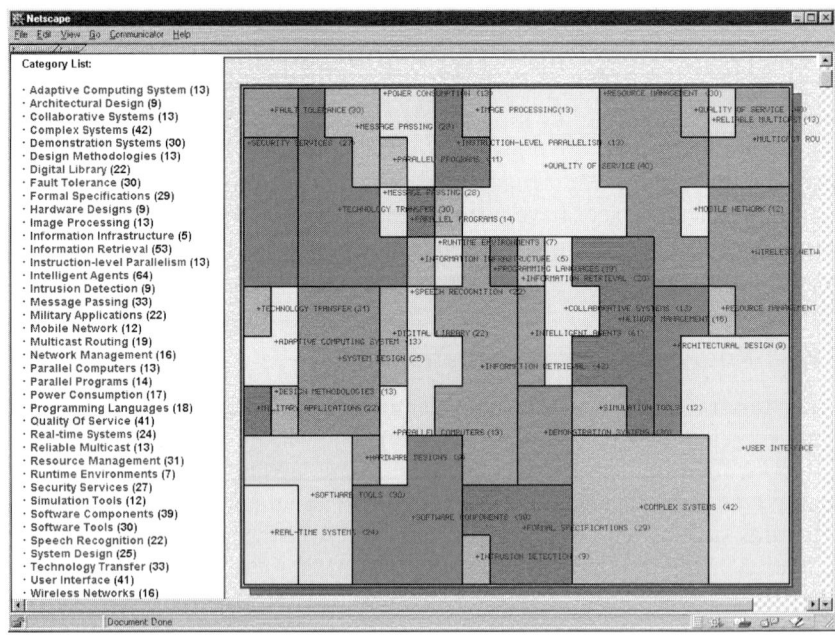

FIG. 3. Category map.

manipulation of information. Recent advances in development languages and platforms such as Java, OpenGL, and VRML and the availability of advanced graphical workstations at affordable prices have also made information visualization a promising area for research [24]. Several of the digital library research teams including Arizona/Illinois, Xerox PARC, Berkeley, and Stanford, are pushing the boundary of visualization techniques for dynamic displays of large-scale information collections.

In addition to the graphical, colored 2D display shown in Fig. 3, the same clustering results from the category map can also be displayed in a 3D helicopter fly-through landscape as shown in Fig. 4, where cylinder height represents the number of documents in each region. Similar documents are grouped in a same-colored region. Using a VRML plug-in (COSMO player), a searcher is then able to "fly" through the information landscape and explore interesting topics and documents. Clicking on a cylinder will display the underlying clustered documents.

Our initial lab experiments have confirmed the novelty and graphical appeal of such a 3D visualization metaphor, especially for the younger web generation. In particular, we found most users of digital libraries may exhibit different cognitive styles and tend to prefer one visualization

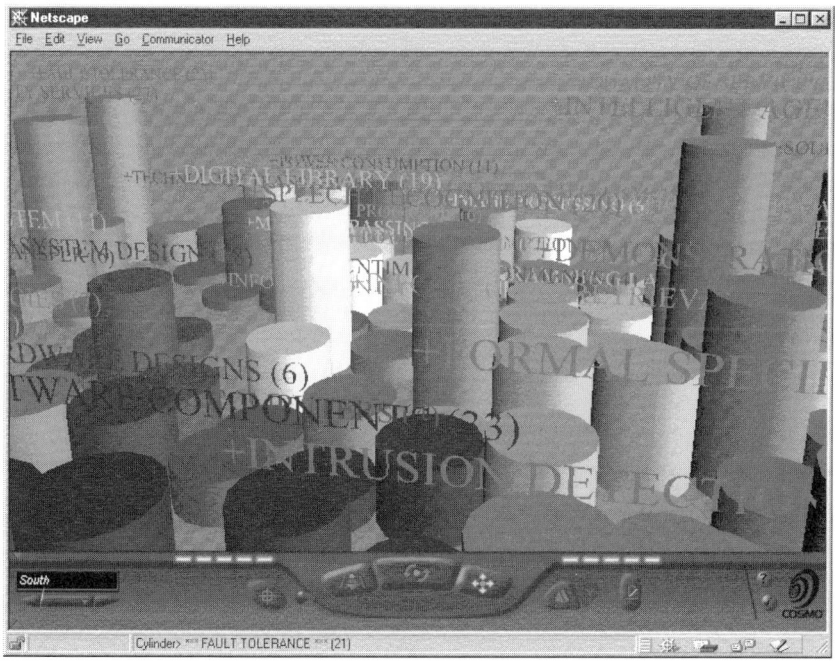

FIG. 4. VRML interface for category map.

metaphor over another (e.g. comparing 1D hierarchy, 2D jigsaw puzzle display, and 3D fly-through display). A more personalized interface may be needed for transmitting digital library content to different users. More HCI research in the context of digital libraries is critically needed in light of the richness of digital library content and media format and the diversity in user styles and needs.

8. Conclusions and the Future

The World Wide Web has made access to the Internet part of the structure of everyday life. At the same time, over the past few years, the primary interface to the Web has evolved from browsing to searching. Millions of people all over the world do Web searching every day, but the commercial technology of searching large collections has remained largely unchanged from its roots in US government-sponsored research projects of the 1960s. This public awareness of the Net as a critical infrastructure in the 1990s has caused a new revolution in the technologies for information retrieval in digital libraries, driven by the hardware revolution in network-based personal computers.

Digital libraries are a form of information technology in which social impact matters as much as technological advancement. It is hard to evaluate new technology in the absence of real users and large collections. The best way to develop effective new technology is in multi-year large-scale research projects which develop real-world electronic testbeds for actual users and which aim at developing new, comprehensive, and user-friendly technologies for digital libraries. Typically, these testbed projects also examine the broad social, economic, legal, ethical, and cross-cultural contexts and impacts of digital library research.

The May 1996 issue of the *IEEE Computer* magazine, edited by Bruce Schatz and Hsinchun Chen, was a special issue on digital libraries. The issue focused specially on the NSF/DARPA/NASA Digital Libraries Initiative (DLI). The six major projects supported by the DLI each was represented by a survey paper at the then halfway point in the initiative [88]. The February 1999 *IEEE Computer* issue, edited by the same guest editors, focuses on practical outcomes from research projects—major research testbeds and fundamental technology research that shows what the large-scale future infrastructure might become [89]. Digital libraries have become far more important nationally and internationally in 1999 than in 1996. Partially, this is due to the exponential growth of information in the Web, which the Web searchers are rapidly failing to handle successfully. This is a special case of the increasing dependence of modern society on information technology and the increasing failures of fundamental infrastructure stemming from lack of fundamental new technology.

The recently released PITAC report (President's Information Technology Advisory Committee Interim Report, August 1998) makes this point clearly. This was a report, in direct response to the President of the United States, by the leaders of information technology from industry and university. They concluded:

> Vigorous information technology (IT) research and development is essential for achieving America's 21st century aspirations. The technical advances that led to today's information tools, such as electronic computers and the Internet, began with Federal government support of research in partnership with industry and universities. All of these innovations depended on patient investment in fundamental and applied research.
>
> We have had a spectacular return on that Federal government research investment. Businesses that produce computers, semiconductors, software, and communications equipment have accounted for one-third the total growth in US production since 1992, creating millions of high paying new jobs. As we approach the 21st century, the opportunities for innovation in IT are larger than they have ever been—and more important. We have an essential national interest in ensuring a continued flow of good new ideas in IT.
>
> After careful review of the Federal programs, however, this Committee has concluded that Federal support for research in information technology is dangerously inadequate. Research programs intended to maintain the flow of new ideas in IT are turning away large numbers of excellent proposals. In addition, current support is taking a short-term focus, looking for immediate returns, rather than investigating high-risk long-term technologies. Significant new research on computers and communication systems serve our needs while protecting us from catastrophic failures of the complex systems that now underpin our transportation, defense, business, finance and healthcare infrastructure.
>
> The current Federal program is inadequate to start necessary new centers and research programs. Computers on university campuses and other civilian research facilities are falling rapidly behind the state of the art. The end result is that critical problems are going unsolved and we are endangering the flow of ideas that have fueled the information economy.
>
> To address these problems, the Federal budget for the year 2000 should include a commitment to sustained growth in IT research, along with a new management system designed to foster innovative research. The Federal IT research program must include vigorous support for fundamental and applied research and must ensure that the US research community is equipped with state-of-the art facilities.

The follow-on to the DLI is another NSF-led initiative, which builds on the successes of DLI and presages the even bigger efforts that will follow on the PITAC report. The NSF/DARPA/NLM/LC/NASA/NEH Digital Libraries Initiative Phase 2 (DLI-2) has recently made the initial awards for multi-year projects. DLI-2 will support a broader range of activities than the first DLI, including small projects and humanities topics. There will be an even stronger emphasis on working testbeds with real users and real collections.

The DLI and DLI-2 Program Director, Dr Stephen Griffin explains in [89]:

> The Digital Libraries Initiative-Phase 2 (DLI-2) supported by NSF, DARPA, NLM, LoC, NEH, NASA and other agency partners will address a refined technology research agenda and look to support new areas and dimensions in the digital libraries information lifecycle including content creation, access, use and usability, preservation and archiving. DLI-2 will look to create domain applications and operational infrastructure, and understand their use and usability in various organizational, economic, social, international contexts—in short, digital libraries as human-centered systems. DLI-2 involvement will extend far beyond computing and communications specialty communities and engage scholars, practitioners and learners in not only science and engineering but also arts and humanities. DLI-2 recognizes that knowledge access is inherently international and will actively promote activities and processes that bridge political and language boundaries, including funding through a new program in International Digital Libraries Collaborative. [see DLI-2 at www.dli2.nsf.gov]

The technologies of digital libraries will dominate the Net of the 21st century [87]. There will be a billion repositories distributed over the world, where each small community maintains a collection of their own knowledge. Semantic indexes will be available for each repository, using scalable semantics to generate search and navigation aids for the specialized terminology of each community. Concept switching across semantic indexes will enable members of one community to easily search the specialized terminology of another [13].

The Internet will have transformed into the *Interspace*, where users navigate abstract spaces to perform correlation across sources. Information analysis will become a routine operation in the Net, performed on a daily basis worldwide. Such functionality will first be used by specialty professionals then by ordinary people, just as occurred with text search on Internet. The information infrastructure will become the essential part of the structure of everyday life and digital libraries will become the essential part of information infrastructure in the 21st century.

ACKNOWLEDGMENTS

This project was funded primarily by:

- NSF/CISE "Concept-based Categorization and Search on Internet: A Machine Learning, Parallel Computing Approach," NSF IRI9525790, 1995–98.

- NSF/ARPA/NASA Illinois Digital Library Initiative project, "Building the Interspace: Digital Library Infrastructure for a University Engineering Community," NSF IRI9411318, 1994–98.
- National Center for Supercomputing Applications (NCSA), "Parallel Semantic Analysis for Spatially-oriented Multimedia GIS Data," High-performance Computing Resources Grants (Peer Review Board), on Convex Exemplar and SGI Origin2000, June 1996–June 1998 (IRI960001N).
- Department of Defense, Advanced Research Projects Agency (DARPA), "The Interspace Prototype: An Analysis Environment Based on Scalable Semantics," June 1997–May 2000 (N66001–97-C-8535).

We would also like to thank Dr Stephen Griffin of NSF, Dr Ron Larsen of DARPA, Dr Alexa McCray of NLM, Dr Larry Smarr of NCSA, and Dr Bruce Schatz of CANIS at UIUC.

REFERENCES

[1] Adam, N., and Yesha, Y. (1996). Strategic directions in electronic commerce and digital libraries: Towards a digital agora. *ACM Computing Surveys*, **28**(4), 818–835.

[2] Agrawal, R., Imielinski, T., and Swami, A. (1993). Database mining: A performance perspective. *IEEE Transactions on Knowledge and Data Engineering*, **5**(6), 914–925.

[3] Alper, J. (1998). Taming MEDLINE with concept spaces. *Science*, 281, 1785, 18 September.

[4] Atkins, D. E. (1997). Report of the Santa Fe planning workshop on distributed knowledge work environments: Digital libraries. Supported by a Grant from the National Science Foundation (NSF-IRI-9712586) to the University of Michigan School of Information, March 9–11.

[5] Atkins, D. E., Birmingham, W. P., Durfee, E. H., Glover, E. J., Mullen, T., Rundensteiner, E. A., Soloway, E., Vidal, J. M., Wallace, R., and Wellman, M. P., (1996). Toward inquiry-based education through interacting software agents. *IEEE Computer*, **29**(5), 69–75.

[6] Atkinson, R. (1996). Library functions, scholarly communication, and the foundation of the digital library: Laying claim to the control zone. *Library Quarterly*, **66**(3), July.

[7] Borghuis, M., Brinckman, H., Fischer, A., Hunter, K., Loo, E., Mors, R., Mostert, P., and Zijlstra, J. (1996). *TULIP final report*. Technical report, Elsevier Science Publishers.

[8] Burke, C. (1992). The other memex: The tangled career of Vannevar Bush's information machine, the Rapid Selector. *Journal of the American Society for Information Science*, **43**(10), 648–657.

[9] Bush, V. (1945). As we may think. *Atlantic Monthly*, July, 101–108.

[10] Chen, H. (1995). Machine learning for information retrieval: neural networks, symbolic learning, and genetic algorithms. *Journal of the American Society for Information Science*, **46**(3), 194–216.

[11] Chen, H., and Dhar, V. (1990). User misconceptions of online information retrieval systems. *International Journal of Man-Machine Studies*, **32**(6), 673–692.

[12] Chen, H., Houston, A. L., Sewell, R. R., and Schatz, B. R. (1998). Internet browsing and searching: User evaluations of category map and concept space techniques. *Journal of the American Society for Information Science*, **49**(7), 582–603.

[13] Chen, H., Martinez, J., Ng, D. T., and Schatz, B. R. (1997). A concept space approach to addressing the vocabulary problem in scientific information retrieval: an experiment on the Worm Community System. *Journal of the American Society for Information Science*, **48**(1), 17–31.

[14] Chen, H., and Ng, D. T. (1995). An algorithmic approach to concept exploration in a large knowledge network (automatic thesaurus consultation): symbolic branch-and-bound vs. connectionist Hopfield net activation. *Journal of the American Society for Information Science*, **46**(5), 348–369.

[15] Chen, H., Schatz, B. R., Ng, T. D., Martinez, J. P., Kirchhoff, A. J., and Lin, C. (1996). A parallel computing approach to creating engineering concept spaces for semantic retrieval: The Illinois Digital Library Initiative Project. *IEEE Transactions on Pattern Analysis and Machine Intelligence*, **18**(8), 771–782.

[16] Chen, H., Schuffels, C., and Orwig, R. (1996). Internet categorization and search: a machine learning approach. *Journal of Visual Communications and Image Representation*, **7**(1), 88–102.

[17] Chen, H., Smith, T. R., Larsgaard, M. L., Hill, L. L., and Ramsey, M. (1997). A geographic knowledge representation system (GKRS) for multimedia geospatial retrieval and analysis. *International Journal of Digital Library*, **1**(2), 132–152.

[18] Chen, S., Chien, Y., and Griffin, S. (1996). Agency perspectives on the digital library initiative. *IEEE Computer*, **29**(5), 23–24.

[19] Ching, N., Jones, V., and Winslett, M. (1996). Authorization in the digital library: Secure access to services across enterprise boundaries. *Proceedings of the Third Forum on Research and Technology Advances in Digital Libraries—ADL '96 Forum*, IEEE, pp. 110–119. 13–15 May, Washington, DC.

[20] Choy, D. M., Dwork, C., Lotspiech, J. B., Anderson, L. C., Boyer, S. K, Dievendorff, R., Griffin, T. D., Hoenig, B. A., Jackson, M. K., Kaka, W., McCrossin, J. M., Miller, A. M., Morris, R. J. T., and Pass, N. J. (1996). A digital library system for periodicals distribution. *Proceedings of the Third Forum on Research and Technology Advances in Digital Libraries—ADL '96 Forum*, IEEE, pp. 95–103. 13–15 May Washington, DC.

[21] Cowan, D. D., Mayfield, C. I., Tompa, F. W., and Gasparini, W. (1998). New role for community networks. *Communications of the ACM*, **41**(4), 61–63.

[22] Crum, L. (1995). University of Michigan digital library project. *Communications of the ACM*, **38**(4), 63–64.

[23] Davis, W. (1988). Documentation unfinished. *Bulletin of the American Society for Information Science*, **14**(5), 50–53.

[24] DeFanti, T., and Brown, M. (1990). Visualization: expanding scientific and engineering research opportunities. (1990). In *Visualization in Scientific Computing*, (eds G. M. Nielson, B. D. Shriver, and L. J. Rosenblum), IEEE Computer Society Press, NY.

[25] Dowler, L. (1997). Gateways to knowledge: A new direction for the Harvard College Library. In L. Dowler, editor, *Gateways to Knowledge: The role of academic libraries in teaching, learning and research*. MIT Press, Cambridge, MA.

[26] Drabenstott, K. M. (1993). Analytical review of the library of the future. Council on Library Resources, 1400 16th Street, N.W., Suite 510, Washington, DC 20036-2217. Research assistance by Celeste M. Burman.

[27] Endres, A., and Fuhr, N. (1998). Students access books and journals through MeDoc. *Communications of the ACM*, **41**(4), 76–77.

[28] Feldman, S. (1997). Advances in digital libraries '97. *Information Today*, **14**(7), 12–13.

[29] Ferguson, C. D., and Bunge, C. A. (1997). The shape of services to come: Values-based reference service for the largely digital library. *College and Research Libraries*, **58**(3), 252–265.
[30] Fox, E. A., and Marchionini, G. (1998). Toward a worldwide digital library. *Communications of the ACM*, **41**(4), 28–32.
[31] Frye, B. E. (1997). Universities in transition: Implications for libraries. In *Gateways to Knowledge: The Role of Academic Libraries in Teaching, Learning and Research* (ed. Lawrence Dowler). MIT Press, Cambridge, MA.
[32] Garrett, J. R., and Lyons, P. A. (1993). Toward an electronic copyright management system. *Journal of the American Society for Information Science*, **44**(8), 468–473.
[33] Ginsparg, P. (1997). First steps toward electronic research communication. In *Gateways to Knowledge: The Role of Academic Libraries in Teaching, Learning and Research* (ed. Lawrence Dowler). MIT Press, Cambridge, MA.
[34] Gladney, H. M., Mintzer, F., Schiattarella, F., Bescós, J., and Treu, M. (1998). Digital access to antiquities. *Communications of the ACM*, **41**(4), 49–57.
[35] The Stanford Digital Libraries Group. (1995). The Stanford digital library project. *Communications of the ACM*, **38**(4), 59–60.
[36] Guarino, N. (1995). The role of formal ontology in the information technology. *International Journal of Human-Computer Studies*, **43**(5/6), 623–624.
[37] Hitchcock, S., Carr, L., Harris, S., Hey, J. M. N., and Hall, W. (1997). Citation linking: Improving access to online journals. *Proceedings of the 2nd ACM International Conference on Digital Libraries* (Robert B. Allen and Edie Rasmussen eds.), pp. 115–122, ACM, New York, NY.
[38] Houston, A. L., Chen, H., Schatz, B. R., Sewell, R. R., Tolle, K. M., Doszkocs, T. E., Hubbard, S. M., and Ng, D. T. (1999). Exploring the use of concept space, category map techniques, and natural language parsers to improve medical information retrieval. *Decision Support Systems*, (forthcoming).
[39] Humphreys, B. L., and Lindberg, D. A. (1989). Building the unified medical language system. *Proceedings of the Thirteenth Annual Symposium on Computer Applications in Medical Care*, pages 475–480, Washington, DC: IEEE Computer Society Press, 5–8 November.
[40] Huser, C., Reichenberger, K., Rostek, L., and Streitz, N. (1995). Knowledge-based editing and visualization for hypermedia encyclopedias. *Communications of the ACM*, **38**(4), 49–51.
[41] Kalakota, R., and Whinston, A. B. (1996). *Frontiers of Electronic Commerce*. Addison-Wesley Publishing Company, Reading, MA.
[42] Kessler, J. (1996). *Internet Digital Libraries: The International Dimension*. Artech House, Inc., Boston, MA.
[43] Kluiters, C. P. (1997). Delivering "building blocks" for digital libraries: First experiences with Elsevier electronic subscriptions and digital libraries in Europe. *Library Acquisitions: Practice and Theory*, **21**(3), 273–279.
[44] Knoblock, C., Koller, D., Shoham, Y., Wellman, M. P., Durfee, E. H., Birmingham, W. P., and Carbonell, J. (1996). The role of AI in digital libraries. *IEEE Expert*, **11**(3), 8–13.
[45] Lenat, D. B., Borning, A., McDonald, D., Taylor, C., and Weyer, S. (1983). Knoesphere: Building expert systems with encyclopedic knowledge. *Proceedings of the International Joint Conference of Artificial Intelligence*.
[46] Lenat, D. B., Guha, R., Pittman, K., Pratt, D., and Shepherd, M. (1990). CYC: Toward programs with common sense. *Communications of the ACM*, **33**(8), 30–49.

[47] Leong, M. K., Cao, L., and Lu, Y. (1998). Distributed Chinese bibliographic searching. *Communications of the ACM*, **41**(4), 66–67.
[48] Lesk, M. (1996). Digital libraries meet electronic commerce: On-screen intellectual property. *Proceedings of the Third Forum on Research and Technology Advances in Digital Libraries—ADL '96 Forum*, pages 58–64. IEEE. Washington, DC, 13–15 May.
[49] Lesk, M. (1997). *Practical Digital Libraries*. Morgan Kauffmann, Los Altos, CA.
[50] Levy, D. M., and Marshall, C. C. (1995). Going digital: A look at assumptions underlying digital libraries. *Communications of the ACM*, **38**(5), 77–84.
[51] Licklider, J. (1965). *Libraries of the Future*. The MIT Press, Cambridge, MA.
[52] Lyman, P. (1996). What is a digital library? Technology, intellectual property and the public interest. *Daedalus*, **125**(4), 1–34.
[53] Lynch, C., and Garcia-Molina, H. (1995). Interoperability, scaling and the digital libraries research agenda. (1995). *A Report on the May 18–19, 1995 Information Infrastructure Technology and Applications (IITA) Digital Libraries Workshop*, 22 August.
[54] Lynch, K. J., and Chen, H. (1992). Knowledge discovery from historical data: an algorithmic approach. *Proceedings of the 25th Annual Hawaii International Conference on System Sciences (HICSS-25), Decision Support and Knowledge Based Systems Track*, pp. 70–79, Kaui, HI, 7–10 January.
[55] Maeda, A., Dartois, M., Fujita, T., Sakaguichi, T., Sugimoto, S., and Tabata, K. (1998). Viewing multilingual documents on your local web browser. *Communications of the ACM*, **41**(4), 64–65.
[56] Manjunath, B. S., and Ma, W. Y. (1996). Texture features for browsing and retrieval of image data. *IEEE Transactions on Pattern Analysis and Machine Intelligence*, **18**(8), 837–841.
[57] Mansell, R. (1996). Designing electronic commerce. In R. Mansell and R. Silverstone, editors, *Communication by Design: The Politics of Information and Communication Technologies*. Oxford University Press, New York, NY.
[58] McCray, A. T., and Hole, W. T. (1990). The scope and structure of the first version of the UMLS semantic network. *Proceedings of the Fourteenth Annual Symposium on Computer Applications in Medical Care*, pp. 126–130, Los Alamitos, CA: Institute of Electrical and Electronics Engineers, 4–7 November.
[59] McKnight, C. (1998). Many projects that depend on collaboration. *Communications of the ACM*, **41**(4), 86–87.
[60] McNab, R. J., Smith, L. A., Whitten, I. H., Henderson, C. L., and Cunningham, S. J. (1996). Toward the digital music library: Tune retrieval from acoustic input. *Proceedings of ACM Digital Libraries*, pages 11–18.
[61] Moen, W. E. (1998). Accessing distributed cultural heritage information. *Communications of the ACM*, **41**(4), 45–48.
[62] Myaeng, S. (1998). R&D for a nationwide general-purpose system. *Communications of the ACM*, **41**(4), 83–85.
[63] Nadis, S. (1996). Computation cracks semantic barrier between databases. *Science*, **272**, 1419, 7 June.
[64] Notice. (1997). University of California, November 1997. A publication of the Academic Senate, University of California, Volume 22, No. 2.
[65] Nyce, J. M. and Kahn, P. (1989). Innovation, pragmatism, and technological continuity: Vannevar Bush's Memex. *Journal of the American Society for Information Science*, **40**(3), 214–220.
[66] Odlyzko, A. M. (1996). Tragic loss or good riddance? The impending demise of traditional scholarly journals. In R. P. Peek and G. B. Newby, (eds.), *Scholarly Publishing: The Electronic Frontier*. The MIT Press, Cambridge, MA.

[67] O'Leary, D. E. (1998). Enterprise knowledge management. *IEEE Computer*, **31**(3), 54–61.
[68] Olsen, J. (1997). The gateway: Point of entry to the electronic library. In L. Dowler (ed.), *Gateways to Knowledge: The Role of Academic Libraries in Teaching, Learning and Research*. MIT Press, Cambridge, MA.
[69] Orwig, R., Chen, H., and Nunamaker, J. F. (1997). A graphical, self-organizing approach to classifying electronic meeting output. *Journal of the American Society for Information Science*, **48**(2), 157–170.
[70] Paepcke, A., Cousins, S. B., Garcia-Molina, H., Hasson, S. W., Ketcxhpel, S. P., Roscheisen, M., and Winograd, T. (1996). Using distributed objects for digital library interoperability. *IEEE COMPUTER*, **29**(5), 61–69.
[71] Peek, R. P., and Newby, G. B. (1996). *Scholarly Publishing: The Electronic Frontier*. The MIT Press, Cambridge, MA.
[72] Peterson, I. (1996). Fashioning a world brain. *Bulletin of the American Society for Information Science*, **22**(5), 10–11.
[73] Piatetsky-Shapiro, G. (1989). Workshop on knowledge discovery in real databases. *Proceedings of the International Joint Conference of Artificial Intelligence*.
[74] Prentice, A. E. (1997). Copyright, WIPO and user interests: Achieving balance among the shareholders. *The Journal of Academic Librarianship*, **23**(4), 309–312.
[75] Purday, J. (1995). The British Library's initiatives for access projects. *Communications of the ACM*, **38**(4), 65–66.
[76] Rao, R., Pedersen, J. O., Hearst, M. A., Mackinlay, J. D., Card, S. K., Masinter, L., Halvorsen, P., and Robertson, G. G. (1995). Richer interaction in the digital library. *Communications of the ACM*, **38**(5), 29–39.
[77] Reddy, R. (1996). The universal library: Intelligent agents and information on demand. In N. R. Adam, B. K. Bhargava, M. Halem, and Y. Yesha (eds.), *Digital Libraries Research and Technology Advances*, Springer-Verlag.
[78] Rockwell, R. C. (1997). The concept of the gateway library: A view from the periphery. In L. Dowler, editor, *Gateways to Knowledge: The role of academic libraries in teaching, learning and research*. MIT Press, Cambridge, MA.
[79] Rush, J. E. (1996). Foreword. In R. P. Peek and G. B. Newby, (eds.), *Scholarly Publishing: The Electronic Frontier*. The MIT Press, Cambridge, MA.
[80] Salton, G. (1989). *Automatic Text Processing*. Addison-Wesley Publishing Company, Inc., Reading, MA.
[81] Salton, G., and McGill, M. (1983). *Introduction to Modern Information Retrieval*. McGraw-Hill, New York, NY.
[82] Samuelson, P. (1995). Copyright and digital libraries. *Communications of the ACM*, **38**(5), 15–21 and 110.
[83] Samuelson, P. (1998). Encoding the law into digital libraries. *Communications of the ACM*, **41**(4), 13–18.
[84] Saracevic, T., and Kantor, P. B. (1997). Studying the value of library and information services. Part I. Establishing a theoretical framework. *Journal of the American Society for Information Science*, **48**(6), 527–542.
[85] Saracevic, T., and Kantor, P. B. (1997). Studying the value of library and information services. Part II. Methodology and taxonomy. *Journal of the American Society for Information Science*, **48**(6), 543–563.
[86] Schatz, B. R. (1995). Building the interspace: The Illinois digital library project. *Communications of the ACM*, **38**(4), 62–63.
[87] Schatz, B. R. (1997). Information retrieval in digital libraries: Bringing search to the net. *Science*, **275**, 327–334.

[88] Schatz, B. R., and Chen, H. (1996). Building large-scale digital libraries. *IEEE Computer*, **29**(5), 22–27.
[89] Schatz, B. R., and Chen, H. (1999). Digital libraries: technological advancements and social impacts. *IEEE Computer*, **31**(2), 45–50.
[90] Schatz., B. R., Mischo, B., Cole, T., Hardin, J., Bishop, A., and Chen, H. (1996). Federating repositories of scientific literature. *IEEE Computer*, **29**(5), 28–36.
[91] Smith, T. R. (1996). A digital library for geographically referenced materials. *IEEE Computer*, **29**(5), 54–60.
[92] Smith, T. R., and Frew, J. (1995). Alexandria digital library. *Communications of the ACM*, **38**(4), 61–62.
[93] Tennant, R. (1997). The grand challenges. *Library Journal*, **122**(20), 31–33.
[94] Thomas, S. W., Alexander, K., and Guthrie, K. (1999). Technology choices for the JSTOR online archive. *IEEE Computer*, **31**(2), 60–65, February.
[95] Unsworth, J. (1997). Some effects of advanced technology on research in the humanities. In *Gateways to Knowledge: The role of academic libraries in teaching, learning and research* (ed. Lawrence Dowler). MIT Press, Cambridge, MA.
[96] Wactlar, H. D., Kanade, T., Smith, M. A., and Stevens, S. M. (1996). Intelligent access to digital video: Informedia project. *IEEE Computer*, **29**(5), 46–53.
[97] Weaver, W. (1955). Machine translation of languages. In *Translation* (W. N. Locke and A. D. Booth eds.). John Wiley, New York, NY, pp. 15–27. (Reprint of 1949 memo.)
[98] Wells, H. G. (1971). *World Brain*. Books for Libraries Press, Freeport, NY.
[99] Wiederhold, G. (1995). Digital libraries, value and productivity. *Communications of the ACM*, **38**(5), 85–96.
[100] Wilensky, R. (1996). Toward work-centered digital information services. *IEEE Computer*, **29**(5), 37–45.
[101] Witten, I. H., McNab, R., Apperley, M., Bainbridge, D., Cunningham, S. J., and Jones, S. (1999). Managing multiple collections, multiple languages, and multiple media in a distributed digital library. *IEEE Computer*, **31**(2), 74–80, February.
[102] Witten, I. H., Nevill-Manning, C., McNab, R., and Cunningham, S. J. (1998). A public library based on full-text retrieval. *Communications of the ACM*, **41**(4), 71–75.
[103] Wulf, W. A. (1989). The national collaboratory—a white paper. In Towards a National Collaboratory, the unpublished report of a workshop held at Rockefeller University, Joshua Lederberg and Keith Uncapher, co-chairs, March 17–18.

Architectures for Mobile Robot Control

JULIO K. ROSENBLATT

*Department of Mechanical and Mechatronic Engineering,
J07 University of Sydney,
Sydney, NSW 2026
Australia
julio@mech.eng.usyd.edu.au*

JAMES A. HENDLER

*Department of Computer Science
A.V. Williams Building.
University of Maryland,
College Park, MD 20742
USA
hendler@cs.umd.edu*

Abstract

Effective control of mobile robots and their associated sensors demands the synthesis and satisfaction of several complex constraints and objectives in real-time, particularly in unstructured, unknown, or dynamic environments such as those typically encountered by outdoor mobile robots. For example, an autonomous vehicle may be required to follow roads, drive off-road, follow designated paths, avoid obstacles, and reach goal destinations. To function effectively, an architectural framework for these sensing and reasoning processes must be imposed to provide a structure for combining information from several different sources. Some key issues considered in planning and control architectures are whether they should be centralized or distributed, whether the reasoning should be reactive or deliberative, and whether control should be top-down or bottom-up. In addition, there is a fundamental choice to be made in the method by which information from multiple sources is combined, via sensor fusion or command arbitration. We explore the inherent problems of the mobile robot domain, the nature of the trade-offs that must be considered, consider various types of action selection, and describe some of the solutions that have been proposed and implemented in existing architectures.

1. Introduction	316
1.1 Control of Autonomous Mobile Robots	317
2. Architectures for Mobile Robot Control	319
2.1 Centralized Architectures	320
2.2 Hierarchical Architectures	325

	2.3 Behavior-based Architectures	327
3.	Command Arbitration	335
	3.1 Command Selection	335
	3.2 Command Fusion	340
	3.3 Utility Fusion	345
4.	Conclusion	347
	Acknowledgments	350
	References	350

1. Introduction

There are a number of reasons why researchers are exploring the use of autonomous mobile robots. One often-cited reason is the desire to use these robots in environments where it is dangerous or difficult for a human to go. This includes applications such as space exploration, nuclear clean-up, undersea expeditions, or dealing with hazardous environments. A second rationale is the desire to use lower-cost robots for household tasks and educational uses, much as we see personal computers used in a wide variety of home and school applications. A third proposed use is for tasks in which robotic technologies could improve human performance, such as the "smart highway" systems being explored as a way to move more cars over more distances at a greater speed with less danger. One thing all these sorts of applications have in common is that they impose significantly different requirements on robots than do traditional manufacturing and warehouse robotic tasks. In particular, they demand that the robots function in environments that were designed for humans, not for robots, or in domains such as the surface of Mars where much is unknown about the environment.

In order to function in such under-constrained, dangerous, and dynamic domains, a mobile robot must be able to sense its surroundings and determine what actions to take which are appropriate for the environment and for the goals of the robotic system. To function effectively, an architectural framework for these sensing and reasoning processes must be imposed to provide a structure for combining information from several different sources. The role of the mobile robot control system is to map perceptual and state information into action so as to achieve the desired effects. When designing a software architecture for the control of complex real-time systems such as mobile robots, there are many important issues that must be addressed. The architecture must provide the means by which the system may accomplish its multiple objectives efficiently; it must be able to satisfy real-time constraints, promote fault tolerance, and provide for the safety of the vehicle and of its surroundings.

Some key issues to be considered in the design of a planning and control architecture are whether the architecture should be centralized or distributed, whether the reasoning should be reactive or deliberative, and whether control should be top-down or bottom-up. As we shall see, these do not represent dichotomies, but rather continuous spectra along which various architectures lie. In addition, there is a fundamental choice to be made in the method by which information from multiple sources is combined, via sensor fusion or command arbitration. In section 2, we explore the inherent problems of the mobile robot domain, the nature of the trade-offs that must be considered, and describe some of the solutions that have been proposed and implemented in existing architectures.

Section 3 explores the issues involved in action selection. In a distributed architecture, it is necessary to decide which behaviors should be controlling the vehicle at any given time and to select among the candidate actions proposed by the various modules. Systems that combine command inputs via arbitration to determine an appropriate course of action fall into two broad categories, command selection and command fusion. Each of these is discussed in detail, and a third alternative, utility fusion, is introduced as well.

Finally, we conclude with a summary of the types of architectures that have been used to date for autonomous mobile robot control, and compare them in terms of the trade-offs described in this chapter.

1.1 Control of Autonomous Mobile Robots

There have been many actual and proposed uses for mobile robots, especially for gaining access to areas that are unreachable by or dangerous to humans, such as cleanup of hazardous waste sites, land mine removal, inspection of nuclear power stations, military reconnaissance missions, subsea exploration, and interplanetary exploration. Other proposed and actual uses include the automation of highly routine tasks such as mail delivery or the inspection and waterproofing of heat tiles underneath the space shuttles. A new emphasis has also been placed upon the incorporation of robotic technology in passenger vehicles in order to improve both the safety and efficiency of highway driving. Finally, a growing perception is that robots can be used either for routine tasks in the home (vacuuming, loading the dishwasher, etc.) or for educational or children's entertainment applications (several recent projects focus on the design of low-cost, robot "animals" to be programmable pets for school-aged children).

One of the key characteristics of most mobile robot domains is that uncertainty plays a large role. Prior knowledge of the environment may be incomplete or may not exist at all. The environment is typically dynamic, so that reasoning must occur rapidly enough to be able to respond to unexpected events. Posterior knowledge gained via sensing is incomplete, inaccurate, and uncertain, as is knowledge of the effects of those actions decided upon and taken by the system. Thus, the effective control of mobile robots and their associated sensors demands the synthesis and satisfaction of a number of complex constraints and objectives in real-time. An architecture must connect the perception, planning, and control modules and provide a structure with which the system may be developed, tested, debugged, integrated, and understood.

Another important aspect of mobile robot systems is the need to combine information from several different sources such as video cameras, laser range finders, sonars, and inertial navigation systems; they must also be capable of combining objectives for a system that is to perform diverse tasks such as following roads, driving off-road, following designated paths, avoiding obstacles, and reaching goal destinations, as well as allowing for teleoperation in many cases. Because of the disparate nature of the raw sensor data and the internal representations used by such subsystems, combining them into one coherent system which integrates all their capabilities has historically been difficult.

Thus, the role of an architecture for mobile robot control is to provide a means that allows the mapping of perceptual and state information into action so as to achieve the desired effects, as shown schematically in Fig. 1. When designing such a software architecture for the control of complex real-time systems such as mobile robots, there are many issues that must be addressed. First and foremost, the architecture must provide the means by which the system may accomplish its objectives efficiently; it must be able to satisfy real-time constraints, promote fault tolerance, and provide for the safety of the vehicle and of its surroundings. It must allow for purposeful goal-oriented behavior yet retain the ability to respond to potentially dangerous situations in real-time while maintaining enough speed to be useful.

A second crucial consideration in the design of a mobile robot architecture is the ease with which a system may be developed. It should not be overly restrictive so that a wide variety of independently developed modules

FIG. 1. Processing world input and state information to generate commands.

may be integrated within its structure. It must provide a framework for sensing and reasoning processes to be conducted in a timely fashion within the context of purposeful, goal-oriented behavior. While many general purpose architectures are computationally equivalent or nearly so, the ease with which various classes of systems may be instantiated within them varies greatly. A crucial yet often neglected consideration in the design of a mobile robot architecture is the ease with which a system may be developed, tested, debugged, and understood, as well as adapted to novel domains and applications. Additionally, in a rapidly developing field such as mobile robot navigation, it is highly desirable to be able to add new subsystems without disrupting established functionality, thus requiring that an architecture allow evolutionary development, with new subsystems added to an existing platform without the need for extensive reworking.

To achieve all this, there are some key issues that must be considered in the design of a mobile robot control architecture. These are:

- whether the architecture should be centralized or distributed,
- whether the reasoning should be reactive or deliberative,
- whether input combination should occur via sensor fusion or command arbitration, and
- whether control should be top-down or bottom-up.

These issues, which are interrelated and must be considered together, should not be treated as dichotomies, but rather as continuous spectra. While some architectures take extreme positions on these issues and have been demonstrated in very narrowly defined niches, pragmatism dictates that there is a vast middle ground to be explored; reasonable trade-offs can and should be considered in the design of a system order to achieve its desired capabilities. The question then becomes not "which one?" but rather "how much of each?" for a particular class of domains. In the sections that follow, classes of architectures will be described in terms of these trade-offs.

2. Architectures for Mobile Robot Control

A number of different approaches have been suggested for designing architectures for autonomous mobile robots functioning in complex domains. In this section, we overview a number of the key issues that have been explored and some of the different types of architectures that have been used in robotics projects. We focus on architectures that have been demonstrated in the control of physical, as opposed to simulated, robots, and primarily on those that have been shown to work in complex natural, rather than artificial, domains.

2.1 Centralized Architectures

The earliest mobile robot systems, such as Shakey the Robot [36] and the Stanford Cart [34], operated by gathering all available sensory data, creating a complete model of its static environment, planning an optimal series of actions within the context of that model, and then executing that plan. The robot would then stop to gather more information and the process would repeat, as illustrated in Fig. 2. Robotic systems of this sort were capable primarily of moving about artificial environments consisting of a room with simple static obstacles. Due to inherent bottlenecks, problems arose with the use of highly centralized architectures when applied to more challenging environments. In particular, this approach requires the fusion of a number of different sensory inputs into a single world model and then the performance of "deliberative" planning with respect to this world model.

2.1.1 Sensor Fusion

Architectures that perform *sensor fusion* construct a single unified *world model* based on all available sensory data [14], such as an *occupancy grid* which represents objects within a map [15], or a symbolic model containing assertions about world states [36]. This world model is then used for planning actions, as illustrated in Fig. 3. This approach has the advantage of being able to combine evidence to overcome ambiguities and noise inherent in the sensing process, but has the disadvantage of creating a computationally expensive sensory bottleneck. In such architectures, all sensor data must be collected and fused into a single monolithic world model, and a complete path considering all relevant information must be planned within this model before any single action can be taken, no matter how simple or urgent that action may be.

Another difficulty with sensor fusion is that information from disparate sources such as maps, sonar, and video are generally not amenable to combination within a single representational framework that is suitable for planning such dissimilar tasks as following roads and avoiding obstacles. For

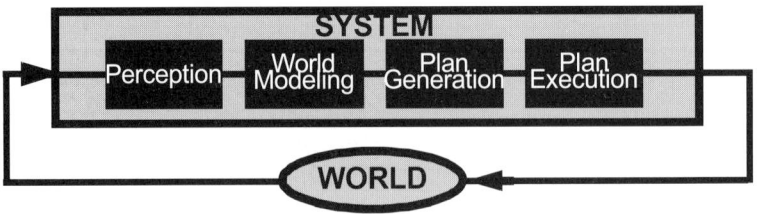

FIG. 2. Traditional functional decomposition of centralized systems.

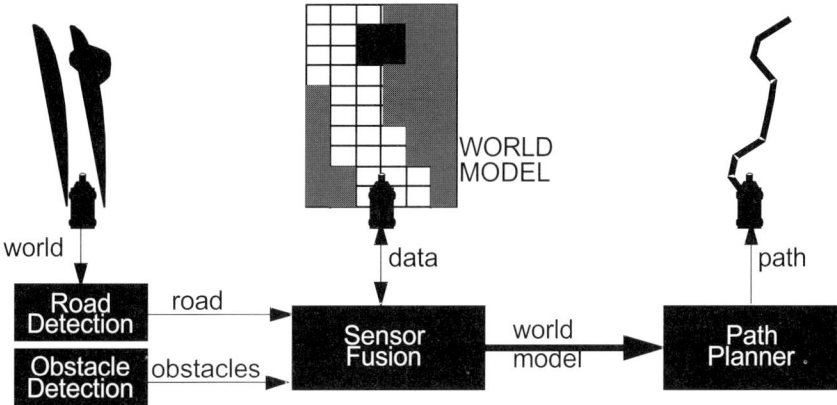

FIG. 3. Sensor fusion creates a centralized world model for planning.

example, although the ALVINN system [40] uses an artificial neural network to associate video images of roads with appropriate steering directions, and has been one of the most successful road-following systems to date, it has been less successful than other systems which use range data for the purpose of obstacle avoidance, such as that described in [28]. Thus, by requiring a single representation for all sensor and map data, a centralized architecture does not allow specialized modules to use other representations and algorithms best suited to the task at hand. A single monolithic world model is also more difficult to develop, maintain, and extend.

2.1.2 Deliberative Planning

Using the world model created in the previous step, the system would then generate plans, i.e. a predetermined series of actions designed to attain a particular goal. Deliberative planners function by searching through a state space to find a sequence of operators that result in the goal state G being reached from the start state S, as illustrated by the "Optimal Plan to Goal" in Fig. 4. Some of the earliest work in robot control architectures, such as Shakey [36], attempted to reason by manipulating abstract symbols using only first-order predicate logic; the world state was represented as a set of truth values for the objects of interest and their relevant properties. Likewise, the goal state consisted of a set of desired truth values. Actions were described by their preconditions, i.e. what had to be true before the action could be taken, and by their effects, a list of assertions to be added or deleted from the world state as result of the action taken. A theorem prover-based planner, STRIPS [35], would then "prove" the possibility of the

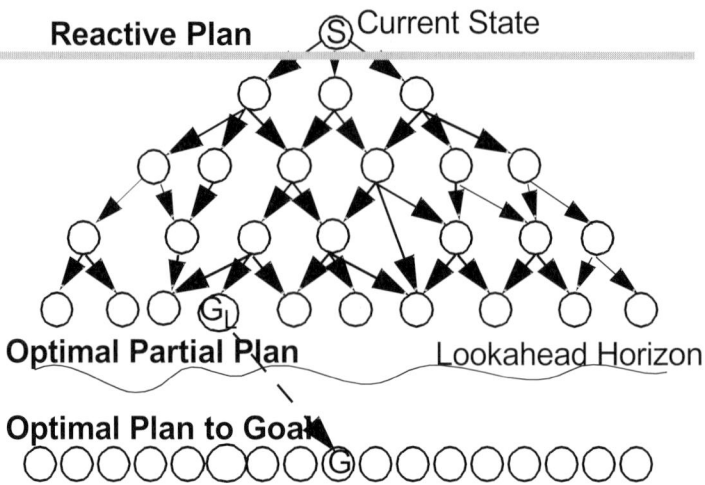

FIG. 4. Levels of planner deliberation. Optimal plan to goal, optimal partial plan to subgoal, and reactive plan without search.

achievement of the desired goal state from the initial state via a series of planned actions which it generated and then handed off to a run-time execution module.

This was an important first step in the automatic creation of plans for robotic action, but it was immediately apparent that it suffered from some severe drawbacks. The most obvious shortcoming of this system was its slowness, due to the combinatorial explosion of the search process. The robots would need to stop and deliberate for a very long period of time before they could move another step, and even on today's computers (many times more powerful than the processors of the 1960s used by SHAKEY) real-time needs would not be met. Furthermore, no sensing or planning took place during the execution of a step, and the effects of an action were assumed to have occurred without verification, thus rendering the robots unresponsive to their environment. The plan would be handed to an execution module responsible for performing each step of that plan. Such systems contain no parallelism and no pipelining; once a plan has been formulated, it is blindly followed in an open-loop fashion, regardless of whether the actual environment differs from the model, and regardless of whether or not the commanded actions actually have the desired effect. Robotic systems of this sort had the advantage of being able to produce an optimal plan in a rational, coherent fashion, but they were limited in their usefulness due to their lack of reactivity to an uncertain or dynamic environment; the robotic systems which operated in this manner were only capable of moving very slowly

(~0.004 km/hr) and only in simple static environments. In short, SHAKEY was an important existence proof that autonomous mobile robots could actually be built, and a seminal work in defining many of the basic concepts in such robotics, but a long way from a practical system for solving complex tasks.

2.1.3 Partial Plans

As a partial solution to the impracticality of a full search through all possible world states assuming perfect knowledge, a planner may instead expand the search only so far as a lookahead horizon that may be defined by either informational or processing limitations. This "Optimal Partial Plan", shown in Fig. 4, finds the optimal path to a subgoal G_L at the search horizon lookahead depth. Such a scheme limits the combinatorial explosion of the full search space and allows for an iterative solution towards the goal which may be recomputed in real-time, taking into account the latest available information as it becomes available. Thus the need to compute the entire plan off-line is obviated, and instead it becomes possible to *interleave planning and execution*, i.e. search up until the lookahead horizon, execute that plan, search again from the ensuing vehicle state, and iterate until the goal is reached. In addition, maintenance goals that have no specific end state, such as preserving the safety of the robot, may be dealt with in this manner.

Abstraction hierarchies were also introduced as a mechanism for dealing with the exponential nature of the search space, as well as the limitations of *a priori* knowledge. As shown in Fig. 5, a plan to achieve the top level goal is determined by searching in a high level abstract search space; intermediate states of that plan can then be used as subgoals at a lower level of abstraction. This process recurses until primitive actions are composed into a directly achievable plan. This refinement of high level plans into primitive actions may either occur off-line within the planner, or on-line during execution with a functional hierarchy constructed to mirror the task hierarchy.

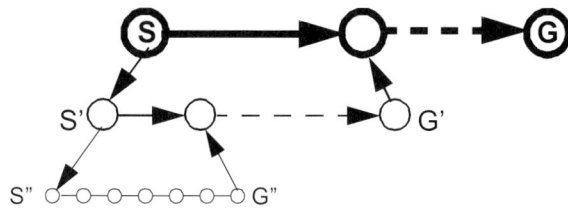

FIG. 5. Recursive abstraction hierarchy.

2.1.4 Non-symbolic Planners

Mobile robot systems were subsequently developed which were still highly centralized, but which did not use the highly symbolic logic of deliberative planners. Because they did not guarantee the optimality of their plans, these systems could process information at faster rates and therefore were capable of driving a vehicle at faster speeds. At Carnegie Mellon University (CMU), the Navlab vehicles, shown in Fig. 6, provided a testbed for more complex capabilities for outdoor mobile robots, operating at higher speeds and on rougher terrain than the indoor robots that preceded them [18, 47]. A system developed on these platforms was capable of following roads and stopping when an obstacle was detected in the vehicle's path [54]; this system was adapted to the DARPA Autonomous Land Vehicle (ALV) at Lockheed Martin to demonstrate applications of the technology [55]. While such centralized systems allowed the vehicles they controlled to move at significantly faster speeds than their forebears (~4.0 km/hr), they were not responsive enough for more complicated maneuvers such as obstacle avoidance, and because of their monolithic nature they were difficult to maintain and to augment with new capabilities. In contrast, recent CMU vehicles, using a parallel distributed processing architecture, have been able to drive on highways at speeds commensurate with the posted speed limits, for long periods of time [21]. In a 1997 experiment entitled "No Hands Across America", CMU researchers had an autonomous vehicle drive from Pittsburgh to the West Coast. The vehicle had a maximum speed of approximately 80 miles/hour and drove without human intervention approximately 98% of the time.

FIG. 6. CMU Navlab vehicles.

Centralized architectures provide the ability to coordinate, in a coherent fashion, multiple goals and constraints within a complex environment; however, a purely centralized architecture is clearly not appropriate for a real-time system where the environment is dynamic or uncertain. In addition to introducing potentially harmful delays, a centralized architecture also leads to brittleness because the system may fail entirely if any single part of it is not functioning properly; thus, any modifications or additions made to a system function could cause a catastrophic error. In order to overcome the limitations inherent in a purely centralized architecture, schemes for allowing distributed processing to occur were developed.

2.2 Hierarchical Architectures

In order to overcome the limitations inherent in a purely centralized architecture and address the need for greater responsiveness in a mobile robot system, hierarchical architectures were developed. The highest level of an hierarchical architecture performs in much the same way as the earlier systems; however, rather than a single monolithic structure mapping these high level plans directly into motor-level commands, the highest level passes down its plans to intermediate levels that translate them into lower level commands, which are in turn passed to the level below. Hierarchical architectures are a type of distributed system in which the modules are organized into multiple control levels which operate at varying granularities, levels of abstraction, and time scales.

One class of hierarchical architectures decompose the task itself in a recursive manner, following the abstraction hierarchy shown in Fig. 5. A plan to achieve the highest level task is created and subtasks are recursively spawned to achieve subgoals of that plan until primitive actions achieve the desired result, as shown in Fig. 7 for the Task Control Architecture (TCA) [48]. Other systems, such as RAPS, allow higher levels to selectively enable and disable modules at lower levels [16].

In another class of hierarchical architectures that use a homogeneous functional decomposition, each level is constructed of the same modules, albeit at different levels of reasoning, as shown in Fig. 8. Each level operates in parallel at a different rate, so that the lowest levels are free to respond to immediate stimuli without having to wait for higher level reasoning processes, thus providing varying trade-offs between long-term correctness and completeness and short-term survival and relevance. Within the NASREM architecture, developed at the National Bureau of Standards (currently NIST), each and every level had the same *SENSE-PLAN-ACT* structure, but operated at different scales of time and space, thus providing varying trade-offs between assimilation and responsiveness [2].

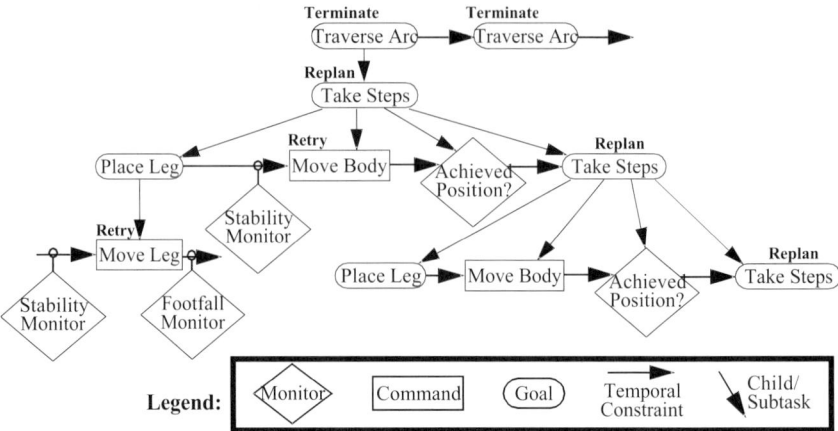

FIG. 7. Hierarchical architecture with recursive task decomposition. (Figure reproduced from [49], with permission.)

While these hierarchical frameworks effectively bypass the sequential bottlenecks of purely centralized systems, their recursive decomposition imposes a rigid structure which has been found in practice to be overly constraining because whatever structure is chosen is usually not appropriate at all levels. In addition, the design and operation of strictly hierarchical architectures is expected to proceed in a top-down manner where each level controls the level beneath it, often imposing overly rigid constraints, and assumes that its commands will execute as anticipated. Since expectations are not always met, there is a need to monitor the progress of desired actions

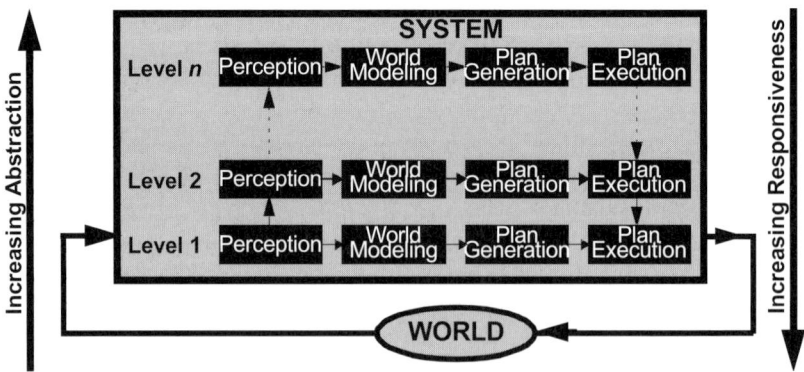

FIG. 8. Hierarchical architecture with recursive functional decomposition. Lower levels are more reactive and higher levels are increasingly deliberative.

and to report failures as they occur. To deal with this, monitoring processes are attached to the actions, as can be seen in Fig. 7 for TCA [49]. In an unstructured, unknown, or dynamic environment, this approach introduces complexities and inefficiencies which can sometimes be avoided if higher level modules participated in the decision-making process without assuming that their commands will be strictly followed [39].

2.3 Behavior-based Architectures

As a response to the complexities and inefficiencies of centralized and hierarchical systems in controlling autonomous robots, a new generation of behavior-based architectures emerged which were designed in a bottom-up fashion to provide greater reactivity to the robot's surroundings. The seminal work in this area was developed by Rodney Brooks of MIT and called the Subsumption Architecture [10]. Such behavior- or schema-based architectures constitute a radically different class of robot control systems. Rather than constructing the system of functional modules such as perception and planning, the system is composed of specialized task-achieving modules, or behaviors, that operate independently. Each behavior only receives as input that information specifically needed for its task, thus avoiding the need for sensor fusion and its inherent bottlenecks. A behavior encapsulates the perception, planning and task execution capabilities necessary to achieve one specific aspect of robot control. Thus, in such an architecture, not only the processing, but the actual control of the robot itself is distributed across multiple independent modules. The overall functioning of the system is defined not by a complex internal structure that seeks an optimal sequence of actions, but rather by the interaction between simple behaviors and a complex world as the system seeks to satisfice, i.e. achieve reasonable performance among a set of basic constraints necessary for the survival of the robot [Simon, 1967].

In principle, a behavior-based system may be developed in a bottom-up, evolutionary manner because behaviors are essentially self-contained and capable of achieving their specific purpose whether or not other particular modules have been developed and are present in the system. Because an individual component in a behavior-based architecture is capable of producing meaningful action, behaviors can be composed to form levels of competence, each of which endows the robotic system with a particular externally manifested capability, as shown in Fig. 9. In theory, successive levels can be incrementally added in order to enhance the functionality of the robot without disrupting previously established capabilities.

In contrast to hierarchical architectures, all behaviors in the Subsumption Architecture are active at all times, in the sense that they always process

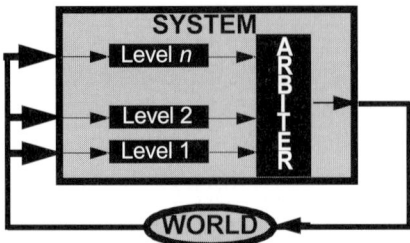

FIG. 9. Levels of competence in a behavior-based architecture.

data as it is available. The control structure is bottom-up because each behavior determines for itself whether or not it is relevant to the current situation, based on the data that it receives. For example, a behavior designed to detect and avoid obstacles based upon sonar data would continually check this data to determine if there were obstacles in the robot's path; when obstacles were detected, the behavior would issue avoidance commands, otherwise it would remain quiescent.

Behavior-based architectures are more responsive to their environment and are less susceptible to catastrophic failure than other types of architectures. They are also more robust because if any one part of the system fails, the rest of the system continues to function independently. As described above, behavior-based architecture also facilitates the evolutionary creation of robust systems. However, a completely distributed system also has its disadvantages; in general, the behavior produced does not reflect the multiple objectives and constraints that the system is subject to at any given moment, thus leading to significantly suboptimal performance. The sequence of actions produced may result in an incomplete plan that does not find a solution even when one does exists. Additionally, the interactions, both between modules and between the system and its environment, are less predictable and more difficult to understand and modify than in a purely centralized system.

Hierarchical and behavior-based approaches can also be combined. An approach called supervenient hierarchies allowed a simulated robot to show both planned and reactive behaviors by using a partial order among its operations such that a higher level action could only receive input from, and issue commands to, a lower level action [51]. This approach was unified with a subsumption-based robotics approach to create behavior hierarchies, in which behaviors were used to replace the more symbolic actions of the earlier supervenience system. Behavior hierarchies were developed for a number of robotic tasks, and the approach was used to allow a combination of telerobotic and autonomous behaviors to be combined in the control of the Secondary Camera And Maneuverability Platform (SCAMP), shown in

FIG. 10. The SCAMP robot controlled by behavior hierarchies.

Fig. 10, a robot being developed by NASA-funded researchers for use in space applications [46].

2.3.1 Command Arbitration

As described above, a behavior is a self-contained module which maps input data into actions. However, each individual behavior is only concerned with one specific aspect of controlling the robot to achieve a specific sub-task, and the particular data sensed and the particular actions decided upon by that behavior are only relevant to that one sub-task. Therefore, in a behavior-based system, it is necessary to select among or combine the actions suggested by the various behaviors to produce an action that meets the needs of the overall system; this is the role of the Command Arbitration

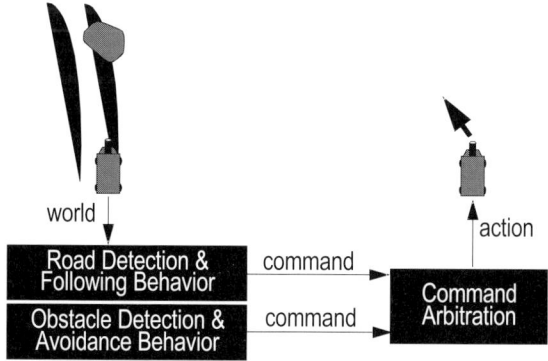

FIG. 11. Command arbitration combines behavior outputs to produce action.

module shown in Fig. 11. By appropriately combining behavior commands through arbitration, a robot control system can respond to its environment without suffering the problems inherent in sensor fusion such as bottlenecks; however, command arbitration runs the risk of losing information valuable to the decision-making process. Therefore a careful balance must be struck between completeness and optimality on the one hand versus modularity and efficiency on the other.

In the Subsumption Architecture, GAPPS [22], and the Hughes architecture [38], among others, command selection is achieved by having priorities assigned to each behavior; all of the behaviors issue commands, and the one with the highest priority is given control while the rest are ignored. Other architectures perform command fusion, i.e. they combine the commands from individual behaviors so that decisions may be made based on multiple considerations while preserving the modularity and reactivity of distributed systems.

Command fusion can be accomplished through the use of potential fields [26], in which each behavior, or schema, outputs a force vector, and the resultant vector obtained through their addition is used to decide the motion of the robot. The Hughes architecture was reworked to allow behaviors to vote for and against a range of possible actions that could be combined [39]; this eventually led to the development of the Distributed Architecture for Mobile Navigation, or DAMN [41]. A similar type of command fusion has also been achieved in rule-based systems using fuzzy logic [58]. Another type of arbiter performs action selection via utility fusion. Within the utility fusion framework, behaviors indicate the utility of various possible world states and the arbiter determines the next action within a probabilistic framework based on the maximization of expected utility [42]. The issues involved in command arbitration will be discussed in greater detail in section 3.

Another type of bottom-up control structure is the emergent architecture, in which behaviors receive activation and inhibition from other behaviors, all of whom are competing for control of the robot [30, 52]. Both hierarchical structures and pre-defined prioritizations are avoided to allow the greatest possible reactivity to the current situation. In the emergent architecture, a behavior receives activation based on the current situation as with any other bottom-up mechanism but, via motivations, a behavior also receives activation from those current goals to which it contributes, as well as inhibitions from achieved goals with which the behavior would interfere. Spread of activation occurs forward from achieved effects and backward from desired effects through successor and predecessor links, respectively. The competition among behaviors arises by way of conflicter links between behaviors that would interfere with each other. Such an architecture is more flexible and reactive than a preprogrammed structure, but has the disadvantage of being less predictable [32].

2.3.2 Reactive Architectures

Behavior-based architectures also serve as a counterpoint to deliberative planners in that these architectures typically seek to minimize the use of internal representations, arguing that "the world is its own best model" [11]. Rather than constructing an explicit model, planning a course of action within that model, and mapping that plan into concrete actions, reactive architectures are designed to respond directly to sensory stimuli, using compiled procedural knowledge to map perceptions instantaneously to actions. As indicated by the "Reactive Plan" shown earlier in Fig. 4, reactive execution performs no lookahead and explicit evaluation of possible future states. Problems with uncertainty in perception are avoided by sensing at a rate rapid enough so that false readings have a limited impact; problems with uncertainty in action are avoided by acting at all moments on the currently perceived world. No assumptions are made about the persistence of previously observed states.

There are several drawbacks to a purely reactive approach, however. First, there is an often unrealistic assumption that the robot's sensors and the algorithms which process them are essentially free of harmful noise and that they cannot benefit from evidence combination between consecutive percepts. Secondly, disallowing the use of internal representations requires that all environmental features of immediate interest be visible to the robot's sensors at all times, thus adding unnecessary constraints and reducing the flexibility of the overall system. Without internal representations and plans, there is also no means to direct the robot towards a goal unless the cues are directly observable; to compensate, reactive systems must wander around a great deal, essentially performing a random walk, until they happen to reach a point where the means of achieving a goal becomes apparent. Further contributing to their inefficiency, they have no explicit means of avoiding or detecting local minima along the way.

The capabilities of a system that prohibits any internal state whatsoever, as well as any intermodule communication, was investigated in the MIT AI Lab using Herbert [12]. The system was carefully constructed for the specific task of collecting Coke cans in an office environment; however, its generality and robustness to changes in its environment were severely limited. Few reactive architectures are actually taken to such an extreme and maintain some degree of internal state, each finding various trade-offs in the reactive/deliberative spectrum. Behaviors in the Subsumption Architecture contain finite state machines to remember which mode it is operating in along with some minimal state information, and a network of behaviors was defined that was capable of learning a topological map [33].

2.3.3 Non-Reactive Architectures

Although behavior-based architectures have come to be associated with reactive planning, there are several examples of systems that do maintain complex internal representations. For example, "motor schemas" [6] map perception directly into action but also maintain local state as needed to perform their task. In DAMN, each behavior module uses those representations and planning paradigms deemed most suitable for the task for which it is responsible [44]. While an attempt is made to keep the perception and planning components of a behavior as simple as possible without sacrificing dependability, they can and often do maintain arbitrarily complex internal representations of the world. Similarly, since DAMN behaviors are not constrained as to what processing takes place within them, a behavior may do as little or as much deliberation as is appropriate for its role in the system. Thus, behaviors range from simple proprioceptive responses to sophisticated map-based reasoning. While the arbiters in DAMN use information from behaviors that are at any degree of reactivity or deliberation, the arbiters themselves may perform lookahead to produce action that responds to immediate circumstances and possibilities and yet considers the consequences of its actions in terms of predicted future states. In this way DAMN is similar to the approaches that interleave planning and execution, but rather than performing the lookahead up to the limits of available information, DAMN performs just enough lookahead to determine the next immediate action.

The situated-action approach has been proposed as another means of representing the world and deciding responses directed towards achievement of goals. Where deliberative architectures use compiled symbolic knowledge of how to *act* according to a given plan and reactive architectures use compiled procedural knowledge of how to *react* to a given stimulus, situated architectures such as GAPPS use compiled knowledge of how to *interact* with a given environment [22]. This approach avoids the limitations of reactive agents because internal representations may be arbitrarily complex [31]. In the Pengi system, internal representations are constrained to have a direct deictic referent in the immediate world [1]. Because no abstract symbols are used, the problem of unique object identification is reduced to the relatively easier task of object recognition. Situated agents have been somewhat successful when applied to limited tasks in simulated domains, but their usefulness in physical robotic applications has been more limited. Both reactive planners and situated agents also suffer from their limited ability to represent and reason about possible future states of the world; in addition to possible inefficiencies, this lack of forethought can also lead to states from which it is impossible to recover and successfully complete a given task.

2.3.4 Inter-Module Communication

An issue which must also be addressed in distributed systems is the nature of the communications between modules. Direct communications between modules provide the system designer with a high degree of control over the operation of the system, which may be desirable when modules are engineered to interact in a very narrowly defined manner (e.g. [10, 47]). However, this makes extensions and modifications to the system difficult, and greatly limits the extent to which the system may be reused in different domains. Indirect communications via media such as a blackboard or a broadcast mechanism provides a layer of abstraction in the inter-module interface, thus simplifying the task of interchanging modules or adding new ones to a system; this flexibility comes at the cost of increased overhead, resulting in reduced efficiency and throughput (e.g. [18, 19, 38]). Another form of indirect communication is those cases where no information at all is transmitted within the system from one behavior to another [12]. In *command fusion* architectures such as motor schemas [6], fuzzy control [23], and DAMN [41], each behavior communicates its intentions with a central arbiter or coordinator rather than with each other, thus allowing development and execution of each module to proceed completely independently; however, the central module may represent a bottleneck, and there may be benefits derived from mutually shared information that cannot be realized without inter-module communication.

2.3.5 Hybrid Architectures

Generally speaking, the exclusive use of symbols has been found to be inappropriate for the "lower levels" of control (high speed decision-making based on immediate sensor readings). However, symbolic representations appear to be useful for planning that involves prior knowledge of the domain and task. As with higher level programming knowledge, the expectation is that a compiler or translator will efficiently reduce these abstract plans into directly executable low level actions. Likewise, numerical computations are invaluable for low level control, but are less appropriate when attempting to reason about processes and goals which are best described and understood at a higher level of abstraction, in much the same way that writing code in an assembly language is inappropriate for all but the lowest level of programming.

Hybrid architectures are based on the view that deliberative planning and reactive control are equally important for mobile robot navigation; when used appropriately, each complements the other and compensates for the other's deficiencies, allowing for purposeful goal-oriented behavior while

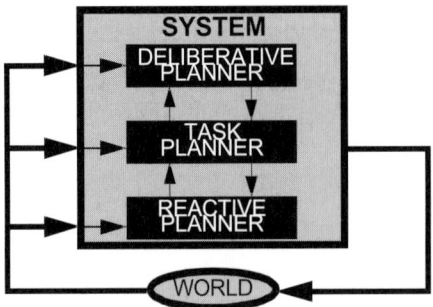

FIG. 12. Hybrid control architecture.

retaining the ability to respond to potentially dangerous situations in real-time. As shown schematically in Fig. 12, hybrid architectures consist of layers, each composed of different reasoning elements operating within various paradigms. At the top level is a deliberative planner which assimilates all available information and creates long-term global plans to be used by the lower levels. The lowest level consists of a behavior-based reactive planner which responds in real-time to sensory stimuli, but when possible also takes into account the higher level considerations or constraints passed down to it from above. In many hybrid architectures, an intermediate level also appears between the high level symbolic reasoning of the deliberative planner and the low level numerical computations of the reactive planner operating at the actuator control level [17], resulting in the three-layer architecture shown. Because of its ability to synthesize centralized and distributed approaches, the hybrid architectures have been gaining increasing popularity among the robotics community as a means of utilizing the complementary strengths and weaknesses of deliberative and reactive architectures [20].

In order to achieve a symbiosis of deliberative and reactive elements, a hybrid architecture was first proposed which incorporated a behavior-based system as the lower level of an layered architecture, thereby providing the reactivity of the former and the control structure of the latter [38]. This Hughes architecture was successfully used to implement a system which was the first autonomous cross-country map and sensor-based system for a mobile robot [13, 37]. The Hughes architecture consists of a behavior-based subsystem which is exclusively responsible for control of the vehicle, and an event-driven higher level module that selectively enables and disables groups of behaviors in a *behavior pool*, as shown in Fig. 13, according to the currently appropriate mode of operation, thus allowing several behaviors to operate at once rather than predetermining a single active subtask module as in hierarchical architectures. The highest planning level of this architecture

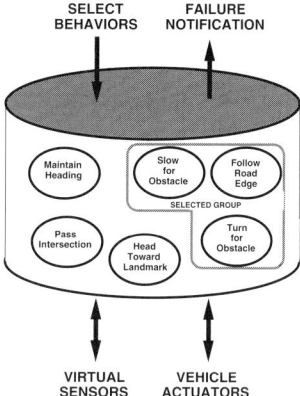

FIG. 13. Behaviors in the Hughes architecture are selectively activated from a pool. (Figure reproduced from [38], with permission.)

does not issue commands to lower levels in a strictly top-down manner, but instead participates in the shared control of the robot, providing *plans as advice* to the system rather than a plan as a sequence of actions to be executed [39]. This structure, referred to as a *free flow hierarchy* has been shown to perform action selection in a robust manner and to be suitable for complex tasks [56].

3. Command Arbitration

As discussed above, in a distributed architecture it is necessary to decide which behaviors should be controlling the robot at any given time and to select among the candidate actions proposed by the behaviors. By appropriately combining behavior commands through arbitration, a robot control system can respond to its environment without suffering the problems inherent in sensor fusion. Instead of performing sensor fusion, the system must combine command inputs to determine an appropriate course of action. Systems that combine command inputs to determine an appropriate course of action fall into two broad categories, command selection and command fusion. In addition, a more recent type of action selection mechanism, called utility fusion, is described.

3.1 Command Selection

In a distributed architecture, it is necessary to decide which behaviors should be controlling the vehicle at any given time. In some architectures this is achieved by having priorities assigned to each behavior; having all the

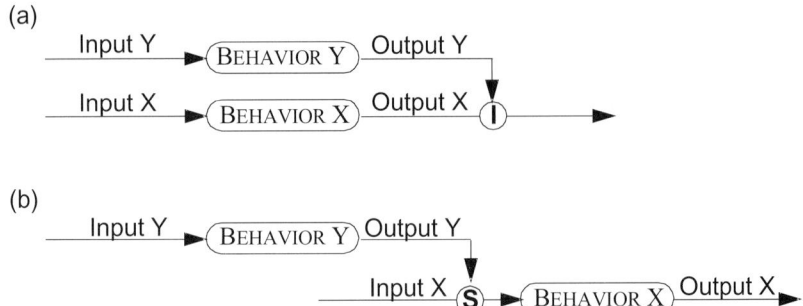

FIG. 14. Combining behaviors in the subsumption architecture. Behaviors interact via (a) inhibition, or (b) suppression.

behaviors issue commands, and assigning control to the one with the highest priority. This allows for quick responses to new situations and stimuli, although the prioritization only allows one module to affect control at any given time.

3.1.1 Command Selection Architectures

3.1.1.1 Subsumption Architecture The Subsumption Architecture [10] is perhaps the most well-known example of an architecture that employs priority-based command selection. In this architecture, the prioritization is implicit in the wiring of behavior modules; a higher level behavior can override the output of a lower level behavior via an *inhibition* link, as shown in Fig. 14a. While Behavior Y is dormant, the output of Behavior X is used to control the vehicle. When Y is active, its output inhibits the output of X and is used to control the vehicle instead. In a similar fashion, a higher level behavior can overwrite the input of a lower level behavior via a *suppression* link, as shown in Fig. 14b. Behavior X operates as before, unaware of the source of its input; under normal circumstances the input source is the same as always, but when Y is active then its output is used as input to X instead. The Subsumption Architecture is designed to grow in an evolutionary manner; the higher level capability of Behavior Y is added to the system without disturbing the lower level capabilities already offered by X. These behaviors can thus be composed to form *levels of competence*, each of which endows the robotic system with a particular externally manifested capability.

3.1.1.2 GAPPS In the GAPPS architecture [22], priorities are compiled into a *mediator*, which combines inputs from the behaviors through a combinatorial logic circuit which yields the system output, as shown in

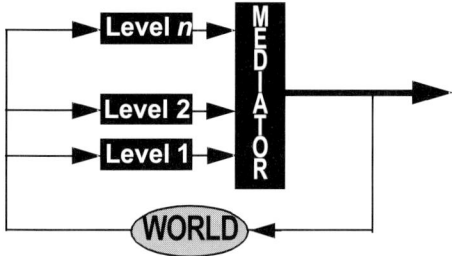

FIG. 15. Combinatorial circuits for action selection in the GAPPS architecture.

Fig. 15. This decomposition is recursive and hierarchical; each level may be composed of sub-levels sending their output to a mediator, whose output is in turn used as input to a higher level mediator. Thus, more complex arbitration is possible without loss of real-time performance. As in the Subsumption Architecture, behaviors within GAPPS are implemented as finite state automata whose operation and intermodule communication are highly constrained.

3.1.1.3 Hughes architecture

The lowest level of the hybrid Hughes architecture [38] also consists of a similar distributed control mechanism. However, a centralized blackboard [19] is used for arbitration and communication between behaviors whose priorities are explicit and can be changed dynamically, as shown in Fig. 16. Unlike the Subsumption Architecture and

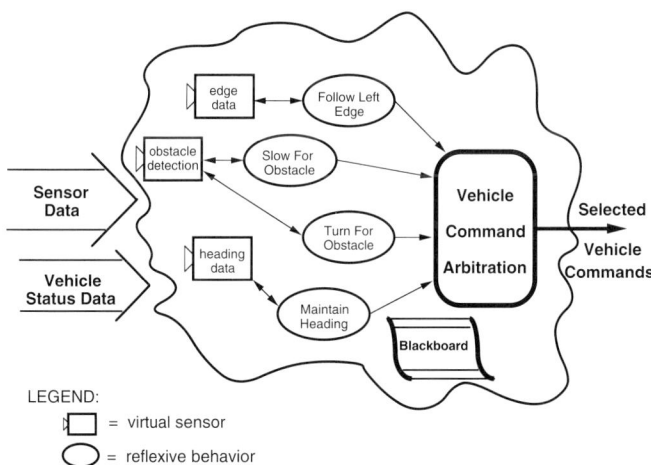

FIG. 16. Communication and arbitration among behaviors via a central blackboard. (Figure reproduced from [38], with permission.)

GAPPS, the implementation of behaviors in the Hughes architecture is not limited to a particular paradigm, and arbitrary communication between modules may occur via the blackboard. However, as with the CMU Codger system [47], it was found in practice that modules have very narrow communication needs with other specific modules, and a general framework such as a blackboard introduces unnecessary latencies and bottlenecks, as well as increasing system complexity.

3.1.2 Limitations of Command Selection

As discussed in section 2, behavior-based architectures successfully avoided the sensing and planning bottlenecks of centralized systems, thus gaining the important advantage of reactivity. Additionally, these architectures introduced the important notion of decomposing the system according to the tasks to be achieved, rather than the traditional functional decomposition, along with the associated idea of incremental, evolutionary system development. However, the objectives of independent behavior development and the accumulative addition of new capabilities were not realized in practice. One of the requirements for a robot control system is that it be capable of satisfying multiple, possibly conflicting goals [50]. As the name "subsumption" implies, this is achieved in command selection architectures by having one behavior's commands completely override another's. While this is an effective scheme for choosing among incompatible commands, it does not provide an adequate means for dealing with multiple goals that can and should be satisfied simultaneously.

This inability to compromise stems from the fact that priority-based selection of commands masks all of the knowledge within each individual behavior that was used to reach its decision. In the process of selecting a command, a behavior may weigh several alternatives before making its ultimate choice. In other behaviors, it may be more natural to merely rule out certain inappropriate actions rather than selecting a desirable one, yet their only means of expression is to completely suppress or inhibit the outputs of other behaviors. A compromise between behaviors cannot be achieved in such an all-or-nothing scenario; whenever one behavior's output is inhibited by another, the information and knowledge represented by that behavior is completely lost to the system.

Consider, for example, the evolutionary development of a system that is capable of avoiding obstacles while following a road in scenarios like that suggested by Fig. 17a. Adopting the symbology of the Subsumption Architecture, the initial system would consist of a Follow-Road behavior as shown in Fig. 17b. A second behavior, Avoid-Obstacles, is then developed

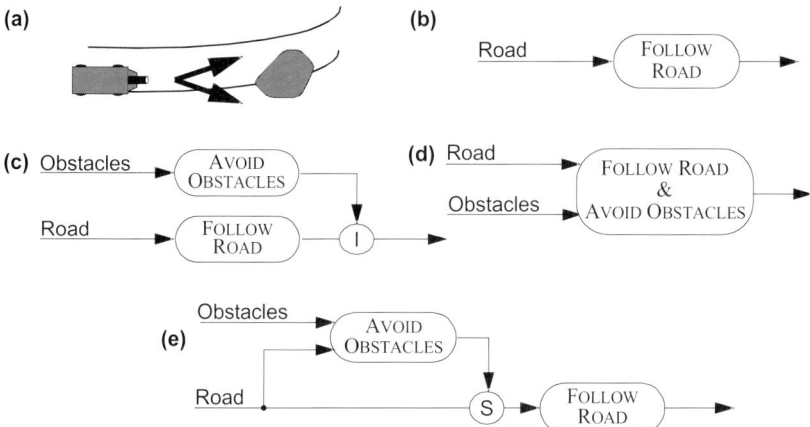

FIG. 17. Prioritized selection of behavior commands. (a) vehicle on road that with obstacle; (b) road-following behavior; (c) addition of obstacle avoidance behavior via inhibition; (d) integration of behaviors into one large behavior; (e) integration of behaviors via suppression.

to provide the ability to detect and avoid obstacles. The obvious way to add it to the system is to effectively give it a higher priority via an inhibition link, as shown in Fig. 17c.

Since, in general, there are no obstacles to be avoided, Avoid-Obstacles is usually quiescent, so that most of the time Follow-Road controls the vehicle as it always has. Then, as the vehicle approaches an obstacle, the Avoid-Obstacles behavior perceives it and begins to send obstacle avoidance commands which inhibit the output of the Follow-Road behavior, thus taking over control of the vehicle until it has passed the obstacle, at which point Follow-Road resumes control. The difficulty with this approach arises when the Avoid-Obstacles behavior is active; during that time, the output of the Follow-Road behavior is ignored, and thus the road-following capability of the system is temporarily disabled. As illustrated by the arrows in Fig. 17a, when an obstacle is in front of the vehicle, Avoid-Obstacles may issue commands for the vehicle to turn either left or right to avoid the obstacle, but has no knowledge that it is preferable to go left so as to stay on the road.

These types of problems were encountered by a robot control system that was developed using the prioritized behavior-based paradigm [24]. In this system, the limitations of priority-based arbitration were overcome by creating one larger behavior which received both road and obstacle data and internally combined the procedural knowledge of both the road-following and obstacle avoidance behaviors, as shown in Fig. 17d. Another possibility, shown in Fig. 17e, would be to have the newly added obstacle avoidance behavior also receive road data, combine the two representations, and suppress the input to the road-following behavior with a new input that would effectively deceive the road-following behavior into taking the correct action. Although these techniques provide a means of controlling the vehicle so that it would stay on the road even when avoiding obstacles, such practices fundamentally violate the desired architectural features of modularity, independent development, distributed perception, and distributed control [43].

Another problem with one behavior completely inhibiting the output of another is that it undermines one of the purported advantages of behavior-based architectures: that a given level of competence, once established, can always be relied upon to imbue the system with certain capabilities, regardless of subsequent additions to the system. If the output from a lower level is inhibited, or if its input data is suppressed so that it is acting upon data for which it was not developed, then any assurance of performance and capability which that level previously provided can no longer be relied upon.

3.2 Command Fusion

A different means of action selection is to combine commands from various behaviors. Prioritization only allows one module to affect control at any given time—the output of other modules, and thus the knowledge contained within them, is lost. To overcome this limitation, some architectures perform *command fusion*, i.e. they combine the commands from individual behaviors so that decisions may be made based on multiple considerations while preserving the modularity and reactivity of distributed systems.

Schemas are independent modules which represent perceptual information and contain processes for deciding how to act on that information [3]. They constitute a distributed system for reasoning and for acting, either externally to change the state of the physical world or internally to change the state of the system. Unlike the priority-based arbitration above, which selects the command output by a single behavior, the outputs of all the schemas are combined in order to produce an action that reflects multiple considerations. This combination of schemas can also be prioritized, in that each schema may have a weight associated with its output command that reflects the importance of the command or the certainty of the information on which it is based. Two different schema models were developed to explain behaviors that were observed in frogs. The Orientation Selection model chooses among orientations based on a summation of excitatory and inhibitory influences from each schema, and the Vector Field model of path planning associates motor actions with schema objects and combines them through vector addition [4].

3.2.1 Command Fusion Architectures

3.2.1.1 Potential Fields
Potential Fields is a method of planning robot trajectories, originally developed for manipulators, based on combining vector fields [7, 26, 27]. It provides a means of performing command fusion based on attractive and repulsive forces exerted by mapped or detected objects. For example, an attractive field of vectors is associated with the goal location, and a repulsive field is associated with obstacles, as shown in Fig. 18. The magnitude of the vector indicates the strength of the choice for moving in that particular direction, i.e. a small vector at a point means that heading in a different direction would have a relatively small effect, while a large vector indicates that the choice of orientation at that position is an important one. The strength of the vectors diminishes with distance from the object creating the field. The schemas are then combined by summing their associated vector fields.

In the Vector Field model [4], the entire field is created at once, and then a path is planned through it and followed to the goal, as shown in Fig. 18a. This would be advantageous if the obstacle and goal locations were known with certainty *a priori*; however, to be responsive to a changing and incompletely known environment, it has been found in practice that it is necessary for a robot to reevaluate its path often. In the Motor Schema framework for mobile robot control [6], as in most practical applications of potential fields, only the force vector for the current robot position is calculated for each schema, as shown in Fig. 18b. The process is then repeated from the next

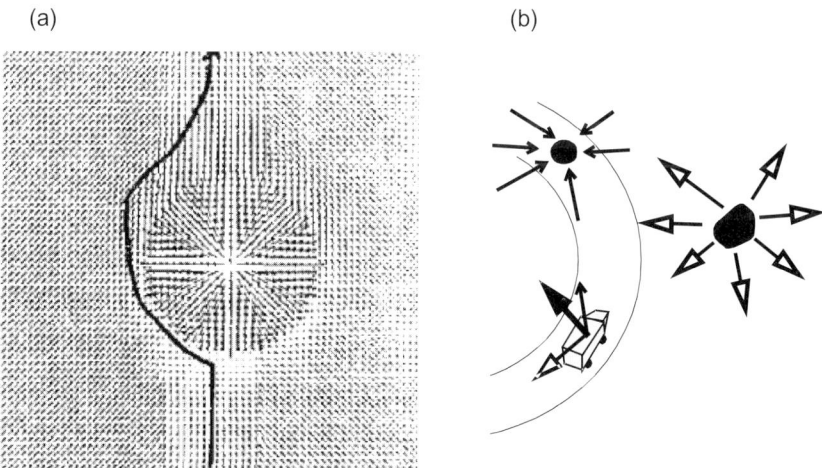

FIG. 18. (a) Combined potential fields for obstacle and goal schemas, and resulting path (reproduced from [5], with permission); (b) vector addition from potential field motor schemas.

robot position to be evaluated, taking into consideration any new perceptual information that may have become available. This type of command fusion allows multiple behaviors to be instantiated and their outputs combined for a variety of different tasks and environments.

One problem with these approaches is that arbitration via vector arithmetic can result in an averaged command which is not satisfactory to any of the contributing behaviors; for example, a robot cannot pass through closely spaced obstacles. This is problematic for robots that wish to explore areas that may only be accessible by passing through narrow entrances such as doorways. There also exist conditions under which potential fields suffer from oscillations and instability [9]. The root of these limitations is that, like priority-based architectures, each behavior simply outputs a single command, which is insufficient for effective command fusion.

3.2.1.2 Fuzzy Logic   Many control systems have been constructed using fuzzy logic [29], including many developed for mobile robot navigation [23, 45]. Fuzzy logic defines a mathematics in which set membership is not binary; an object has a degree of membership in a set which lies in the real numbered interval between 0 and 1, inclusive. For example, Fig. 19a shows the fuzzy membership sets for left, straight, and right; a point at some orientation θ on the x-axis belongs to each of the three sets to the extent indicated by their functions. The black circle indicates the presence of an obstacle at that orientation, so it belongs to the set left with value 0.8, and the sets straight and right with value 0.0.

If-then rules take these fuzzy variables as antecedents and produce inferences as a result [58]. For example, there may be a rule of the form "If there is an obstacle on the left, then turn right" with an associated fuzzy multiplier of 0.75, which produces the fuzzy output shown in Fig. 19b. Figure 19c shows the output of several such rules, which are then summed to produce the result in Fig. 19d. Various *defuzzification* strategies such as selecting the maximum value or the center of mass to select a single crisp output to be sent to the controller; however, many of these are not appropriate for mobile robot control because they effectively average commands, which can produce results which are poor at satisfying any of the goals of the system, as in the case shown in Fig 19e.

3.2.1.3 DAMN   The DAMN system was designed to permit the exploitation of a number of different arbitration schemes. In one particular scheme, each behavior votes for or against various alternatives in an actuator command space. Each behavior generates a vote between −1 and +1 for every possible command, with negative votes being against and positive votes for a particular command option. Each behavior also has an associated

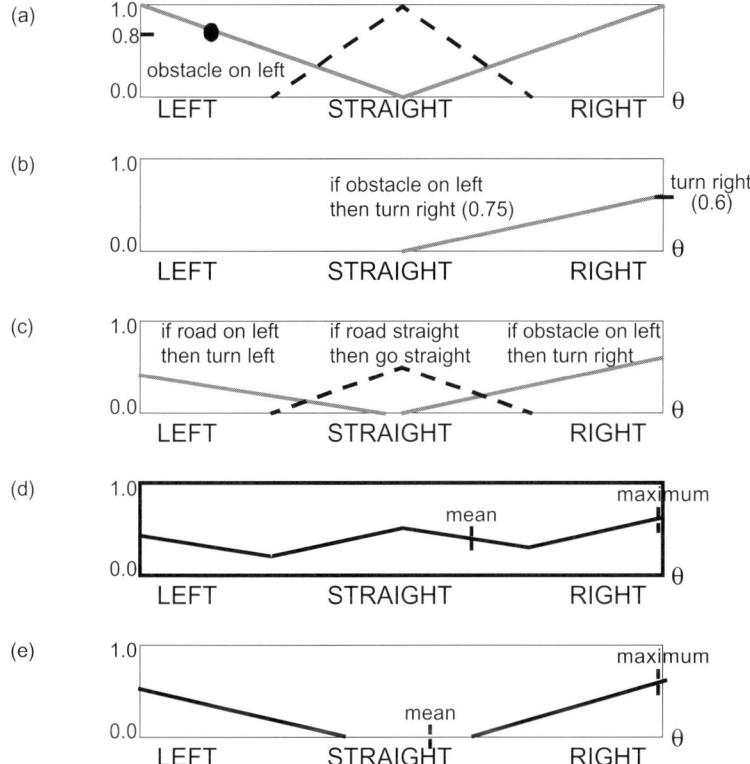

FIG. 19. Command fusion via fuzzy logic. (a) fuzzy membership sets; (b) output of rule to turn right when an obstacle is on the left; (c) output of several fuzzy rules; (d) sum of all rule outputs and defuzzification strategies; (e) center of mass defuzzification yields averaged commands.

weight which reflects its priority relative to other behaviors. The arbiter then computes a weighted sum of the votes received for each candidate command, and selects that action which has the highest total score.

For example, a turn arbiter receives votes for a fixed set of vehicle curvatures. Each behavior votes for or against each of a set of possible orientations. Fig. 20 (a and b) shows the votes from two behaviors, one for obstacle avoidance and one for road following, plotted with vote value v as a function of curvature κ. The obstacle avoidance behavior is voting most in favor of soft left turns, less so for far right, and against soft right or hard left. The road-following behavior votes most strongly for a soft right that would keep the vehicle centered on the road, and the strength of the vote falls off as the curvature deviates from the desired turn. Because avoiding obstacles was deemed more important than staying on the road, behavior weights of 0.8 and

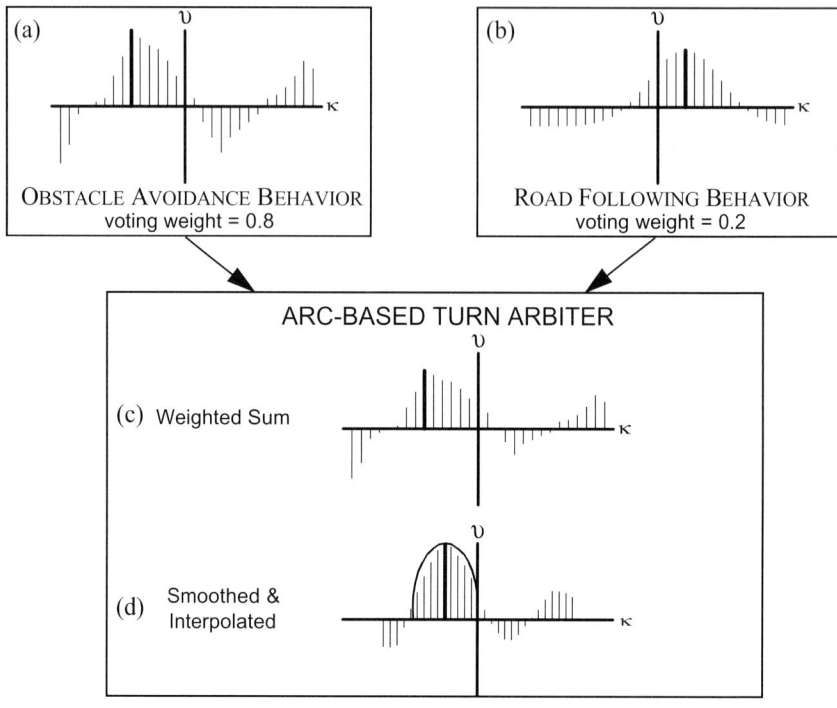

FIG. 20. DAMN turn arbitration process. (a and b) votes from two behaviors are sent to the arbiter; (c) the arbiter combines the votes as a weighted sum; (d) the votes are smoothed and an interpolated maximum value is selected.

0.2 were assigned, respectively. The arbiter then combines these votes as a weighted sum, shown in Fig. 20c. The resulting histogram is then smoothed, the orientation with the highest value is selected as the direction to move in, and finally sub-pixel interpolation is performed to overcome the effects of discretization, as shown in Fig. 20d. The resulting turn command steers clear of the obstacles while staying as centered on the road as possible.

This type of DAMN arbitration is very similar to fuzzy logic systems, and in fact has been recast into this framework [57]. However, the behaviors are not rule-based and do not necessarily use fuzzy membership, but instead are free to independently evaluate each possible action and thus produce a distribution which may take on any shape. After the arbiter smoothes the combined inputs, it performs the equivalent of defuzzification using the "maximum" criterion. Other defuzzification strategies such as center of mass assume a unimodal function, and in the general case an averaging of inputs would select inappropriate commands. For example, the weighted sum in Fig. 20c has two areas of positive votes, one for soft left turns and another for hard right; selecting the center of mass would result in a soft right turn, which has negative vote sums and would have bad effects such as driving the vehicle directly into an obstacle.

This method of command fusion is very general and many different types of behaviors for various tasks have been readily integrated within it, including off-road navigation, road following, and map-based planners, yielding combined systems with greater capabilities (e.g. [28, 53]).

3.2.2 Limitations of Command Fusion

Whether summing vectors in potential fields, combining rules by fuzzy logic, or combining votes in the DAMN actuation-space approach, the arbiter may be fusing commands proposed by the behaviors which are not physically realizable; for example, a vehicle turn command may require a change in the commanded curvature which exceeds the steering wheel actuator's torque capabilities. Command fusion methods do not in general account for vehicle dynamics and kinematic constraints; thus they may produce commands which are not executable by the system being controlled. Another important difference between the commanded and actual vehicle trajectories is due to the system delays arising from latencies in data acquisition, data processing, intermodule communications, and actuator response. Given the continuous motion of the vehicle, these delays imply that by the time the command is being executed the vehicle is no longer in the state at which the behavior commands were generated. Stable control requires that the system anticipate these latencies and allow the behaviors to consider actions that are kinematically achievable and which originate from the point where the vehicle will actually be when the command is executed [25].

Domains such as mobile robot navigation necessarily contain a great deal of uncertainty. There exists uncertainty in the sensing of internal state such as vehicle position, uncertainty in perception such as the location or shape of an object, and uncertainty in the effects of actions, e.g. due to slippage. These uncertainties are accounted for in an ad hoc manner in behavior-based systems, for example by "growing" the size of observed obstacles by some fixed amount or by "fuzzifying" the inputs to a system and using fuzzy reasoning to determine an approximately appropriate output [23].

3.3 Utility Fusion

Utility fusion is a means of action selection introduced as an alternative to both the command selection and command fusion approaches. Evidence concerning the desirability of possible world states is obtained from multiple independent sources and combined via *utility fusion*. The determination of what the next action taken should be is then based on this combined evidence. In this paradigm, behaviors do not select or express preferences for actions but instead determine the utility of possible world states. It is then the responsibility of the arbiter to determine which states are actually attainable and how to go about achieving them.

Unlike command arbitration or command fusion systems, the utility fusion arbiter does not simply select among or combine actions proposed by behaviors. Instead, the arbiter is provided with much richer evaluation information from behaviors, thus allowing for more intelligent decision-making. The arbiter accumulates utility and probability evaluations from the behaviors and bases its decision-making on the combined evidence, so that the limitations of command fusion systems may be overcome.

In contrast to sensor fusion systems, utility fusion does not create a world model. The information combined and stored by the utility fusion arbiter does not represent a sensed feature of the world, but rather the desirability of being in a particular state according to some criterion defined by the behavior. The processing of sensory data is still distributed among behaviors, so the presence of bottlenecks and other difficulties associated with sensor fusion is avoided.

For example, a utility map-based path arbiter for steering control has been developed. Behaviors communicating with the path arbiter vote on the desirability of various possible vehicle locations, and the arbiter maintains a local map of these votes. Fig. 21 shows polygons of positive utility that a road-following behavior has sent based on detected road location, with the greatest value being the polygon closest to the center of the detected road, and polygons of negative utility that an obstacle avoidance behavior has sent,

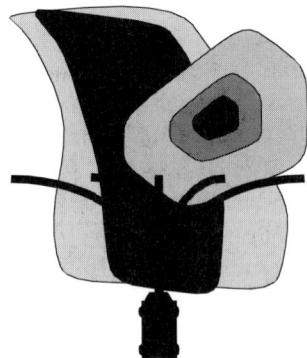

FIG. 21. Map-based path arbiter voting. Darker polygons reflect higher vote utility values; striped polygons indicate negative utilities. Arcs indicate trajectories evaluated by the arbiter.

with the greatest value being the polygon closest to the center of the detected obstacle. Based on the vehicle's current state, the path arbiter evaluates the possible trajectories which may be followed, shown in the figure as arcs emanating from the vehicle. The utilities are summed along each arc, and the arbiter selects that one for which the total is the greatest.

Utility theory gives a unified conceptual framework for defining votes and weights and dealing with uncertainty. Because we are attempting to decide which among a set of possible actions to take, it is natural to make judgments on the usefulness of each action based on its consequences. If we assign a utility measure $U(c)$ for each possible consequence of an action, then the *expected utility* for an action a is:

$$U(a) = \sum_c U(c) \cdot P(c|a,e)$$

By casting the voting scheme for this class of arbiter within the framework of utility theory, uncertainty within the system is explicitly represented and reasoned about within the decision-making processes. Utility theory teases apart the value of the consequence of an action from the probability that the consequence will occur and provides a Bayesian framework for reasoning about uncertainty [8]. Each behavior votes for the subjective utility of the vehicle being in the various particular locations of concern to that behavior, e.g. obstacle locations or road locations. The behavior also expresses any uncertainty associated with the perception process as covariances in a multi-dimensional normal distribution. The arbiter can then use utility theory to reason explicitly about the uncertainty in position and control of the vehicle and apply the Maximum Expected Utility criterion to select the optimal action based on current information. Utility fusion represents a compromise between sensor fusion and command fusion, in order to retain some of the properties of coherence and rationality of the former while achieving the responsiveness and robustness of the latter.

4. Conclusion

Effective control of mobile robots and their associated sensors demands the synthesis and satisfaction of several complex constraints and objectives in real-time, particularly in unstructured, unknown, or dynamic environments such as those typically encountered by outdoor mobile robots. Another important aspect of mobile robot systems is the need to combine information from several different sources such as video cameras, laser range finders, sonars, and inertial navigation systems. They must also be capable of combining objectives for a system that is to perform diverse tasks—for example, an autonomous vehicle may be required follow roads, drive off-road, follow designated paths, avoid obstacles, and reach goal destinations. To function effectively, an architectural framework for these sensing and reasoning processes must be imposed to provide a structure for combining information from several different sources. The architecture should allow for purposeful goal-oriented behavior yet retain the ability to respond to potentially dangerous situations in real-time while maintaining enough speed to be useful. An architecture must connect the perception, planning, and control modules and provide a structure with which the system may be developed, tested, debugged, integrated and understood.

When designing a software architecture for the control of complex real-time systems such as mobile robots, there are many important issues that must be addressed. The architecture must provide the means by which the system may accomplish its multiple objectives efficiently. It must be able to satisfy real-time constraints, promote fault tolerance, and provide for the safety of the robot and of its surroundings. Some key issues to be considered in the design of a mobile robot control architecture are whether the architecture should be centralized or distributed, whether the reasoning should be reactive or deliberative, whether input combination should occur via sensor fusion or command arbitration, and whether control should be top-down or bottom-up.

Deliberative planning and reactive control both play an important role in mobile robot navigation; when used appropriately, each complements the other and compensates for the other's deficiencies. Reactive components provide the basic capabilities which enable the robot to achieve low-level tasks without injury to itself or its environment, while deliberative components provide the ability to achieve higher-level goals and to avoid mistakes which could lead to inefficiencies or mission failure. Because reactivity is essential for any real-time system, robots must avoid the sensing and planning bottlenecks of purely centralized systems. However, in a distributed system, it is necessary to specify how information is to be combined and used to generate action in an intelligent, coherent manner. While sensor fusion creates a bottleneck, command arbitration runs the risk of losing information valuable to the decision-making process. Therefore, a careful balance must be struck between completeness and optimality on the one hand versus modularity and efficiency on the other. Systems that combine command inputs to determine an appropriate course of action fall into two broad categories, command selection and command fusion.

In architectures which employ priority-based command selection such as the Subsumption Architecture, action selection is achieved by assigning priorities to each behavior. All of the behaviors issue commands and the one with the highest priority is given control while the rest are ignored. This allows for quick responses to new situations and stimuli, although, by definition, prioritization only allows one module to affect control at any given time. While this is an effective scheme for choosing among incompatible commands, it does not provide an adequate means for dealing with multiple goals that can and should be satisfied simultaneously. A compromise between behaviors cannot be achieved in such an all-or-nothing scenario; whenever one behavior's output is overridden by another, the information and knowledge represented by that behavior is completely lost to the system.

Architectures that perform command fusion combine the commands from individual behaviors so that decisions may be made based on multiple considerations while preserving the modularity and reactivity of distributed systems. Command fusion provides a mechanism for the concurrent satisfaction of multiple goals, and allows modules to be completely independent, thus allowing incremental, evolutionary system development. In systems that perform command fusion, the decision-making process is based on combining command inputs from multiple behaviors, and is therefore able to simultaneously satisfy multiple goals. Such systems are largely distributed, but they must also contain a central module that receives commands from the various behaviors and combines them in some manner. Motor schemas provide a general framework for command fusion, but because they are implemented as potential fields they are subject to the problems of command averaging and local minima, among others.

In addition, a new means of action selection, via utility fusion, was introduced as a solution to some observed shortcomings of behavior-based systems. Instead of voting for actions, behaviors indicate the utility of various possible world states, and it is the responsibility of the arbiter to determine which states are actually attainable and how to go about achieving them. The utility fusion arbiter determines the next action based on the maximization of expected utility, thus providing a unified conceptual framework for defining the semantics of votes and for dealing with uncertainty. This new approach strikes a balance between action selection and sensor fusion and has been found to yield many benefits.

The essential trade-offs in the design of a mobile robot control architecture considered in this chapter were centralized vs distributed processing, reactive vs deliberative reasoning, sensor fusion vs command arbitration, and top-down vs bottom-up control. The properties of some representative architectures along these four dimensions are summarized in Table I. While these four issues are interrelated and must be considered together, it can be seen in this table that they are at least partially separable.

TABLE I
CHARACTERIZATIONS OF DESIGN TRADE-OFFS MADE IN REPRESENTATIVE ARCHITECTURES

Architecture	Centralized/ distributed	Fusion/ arbitration method	Deliberative/ reactive	Top-down/ bottom-up
Shakey	Centralized	Sensor fusion	Deliberative	Top-down
Navlab	Centralized	Sensor fusion	Hybrid	Bottom-up
GAPPS	Centralized	Command selection	Hybrid	Bottom-up
NASREM	Hierarchical	Sensor fusion	Hybrid	Top-down
TCA	Hierarchical	Sensor fusion	Hybrid	Top-down
DAMN utility	Hybrid	Utility fusion	Hybrid	Hybrid
DAMN actuation	Hybrid	Command fusion	Hybrid	Hybrid
Motor schemas	Distributed	Command fusion	Hybrid	Hybrid
Hughes	Distributed	Command selection	Hybrid	Hybrid
Behavior hierarchies	Distributed	Command selection	Reactive	Hybrid
Subsumption	Distributed	Command selection	Reactive	Bottom-Up

On one extreme is the architecture developed for control of Shakey the Robot [36]; it is deliberative, centralized, uses sensor fusion, and control is top-down. This is collectively known as a "centralized" architecture, but as can be seen, there are several variables that can be independently manipulated. At the opposite extreme is the prototypically "reactive" Subsumption Architecture [10]. In between are hybrid architectures which contain both deliberative and reactive elements and vary along the other three dimensions.

ACKNOWLEDGMENTS

This paper necessarily had to omit many interesting aspects of modern work in robotics. We focused primarily on control aspects of architectures, slighting other issues such as the coordination of multiple robots, the use of vision as a sensor, and implementation details of the various approaches we outlined. A collection of recent papers including more on these aspects can be found in a special issue of the *Journal of Experimental and Theoretical Artificial Intelligence*, 9(2/3) (1997), which contains a number of papers on implemented architectures for mobile robots. This research was supported in part by grants from ONR (N00014-J-91-1451), ARPA (N00014-94-1090, DABT-95-C0037, F30602-93-C-0039), and ARL (DAAH049610297). Dr Rosenblatt's work at Carnegie Mellon University under the UGV project was supported by ARPA under contracts DACA76-89-C-0014 and DAAE07-90-C-R059, and by the National Science Foundation under NSF Contract BCS-9120655. Julio Rosenblatt was supported in part by a Hughes Research Fellowship.

REFERENCES

[1] Agre, P., and Chapman, D. (1987). Pengi: An implementation of a theory of activity. *Proceedings of the AAAI Sixth National Conference on Artificial Intelligence*, pp. 268–272, Seattle, WA, July.

[2] Albus, J., McCain, H., and Lumia, R. (1987). *NASA/NBS Standard Reference Model for Telerobot Control System Architecture* (NASREM), NBS Tech. Note 1235, Gaithersburg, MD.
[3] Arbib, M. A. (1992). Schema theory. In *The Encyclopedia of Artificial Intelligence*, 2nd edn (S. Shapiro ed.), Wiley-Interscience, pp. 1427–1443.
[4] Arbib, M. A., and House, D. H. (1987). Depth and detours: An essay on visually-guided behavior. In *Vision, Brain, and Cooperative Computation* (M. A. Arbib and A. R. Hanson eds.), Bradford Book/MIT Press, Cambridge, MA, pp. 129–163.
[5] Arkin, R. (1987). Motor schema-based navigation for a mobile robot: An approach to programming by behavior. *Proceedings of IEEE International Conference on Robotics and Automation*, Raleigh, North Carolina, 31 March–3 April.
[6] Arkin, R. (1989). Motor schema-based mobile robot navigation. *International Journal of Robotics Research*, **8**(4), August pp. 92–112.
[7] Barraquand, J., and Latombe, J. C. (1993). Nonholonomic multibody mobile robots: Controllability and motion planning in the presence of obstacles. *Algorithmica* **10**(2–4), 121–155.
[8] Berger, J. (1985). *Statistical Decision Theory and Bayesian Analysis*, 2nd edn. New York: Springer.
[9] Borenstein, J., and Koren, Y. (1991). Potential field methods and their inherent limitations for mobile robot navigation. *Proceedings of the International Conference on Robotics and Automation*, Sacramento, California, 9–11 April.
[10] Brooks, R. (1986). A robust layered control system for a mobile robot. *IEEE Journal of Robotics and Automation*, vol. RA-2, no. 1, pp. 14–23, April.
[11] Brooks, R. (1991). Intelligence without reason. *Proceedings of International Joint Conference on Artificial Intelligence*, Sydney, Australia, August, pp. 569–95.
[12] Connell, J. (1989). A behavior-based arm controller. *IEEE Transactions on Robotics and Automation*, **5**(6), 784–791.
[13] Daily, M., Harris, J., Keirsey, D., Olin, K., Payton, D., Reiser, K., Rosenblatt, J., Tseng, D., and Wong, V. (1988). *Autonomous Cross-Country Navigation with the ALV, IEEE Conference on Robotics and Automation*, Philadelphia, PA, April.
[14] Durrant-Whyte, H. (1986). *Integration, Coordination, and Control of Multi-Sensor Robot Systems*, PhD dissertation, University of Pennsylvania, Philadelphia, PA.
[15] Elfes, A. (1986). A sonar-based mapping and navigation system. *Proceedings of IEEE International Conference on Robotics and Automation*, San Francisco, CA, pp. 1151–1156.
[16] Firby, J. (1994). Task networks for controlling continuous processes. *Proceedings of the Second International Conference on AI Planning Systems*, Chicago IL.
[17] Gat, E. (1992). Integrating planning and reacting in a heterogeneous asynchronous architecture for controlling real-world robots. *Proceedings of AAAI Eleventh National Conference on Artificial Intelligence*, San Jose, CA, 12–16 July, pp. 823–28.
[18] Goto, Y., and Stentz, A. (1987). Mobile robot navigation: The CMU system, *IEEE Expert*, **2**(4), 32–43.
[19] Hayes-Roth, B. (1985). A blackboard architecture for control. *Artificial intelligence*, 26, 251–321. Reprinted in Bond, A., and Gasser, L. (eds.), *Readings in Distributed Artificial Intelligence*, Morgan.
[20] Hexmoor, H., and Kortenkamp, D. (eds.), (1995). *Proceedings of the 1995 AAAI Spring Symposium on Lessons Learned from Implemented Software Architectures for Physical Agents*, Stanford, CA, March 27–29: AAAI Press, Menlo Park, CA.
[21] Jochem, T., Pomerleau, D., Kumar, B. and Armstrong, J. (1995). "PANS: A portable navigation platform." *Proceedings of the IEEE Symposium on Intelligent Vehicles*, Detroit, Michigan, 25–26 September.

[22] Kaelbling, L., and Rosenschein, S. (1990). Action and planning in embedded agents. *Designing Autonomous Agents* (P. Maes ed.), MIT Press, pp 35–48.
[23] Kamada, H., Naoi, S., and Gotoh, T. (1990). A compact navigation system using image processing and fuzzy control, *IEEE Southeastcon*, New Orleans, April 1–4.
[24] Keirsey, D., Payton, D., and Rosenblatt, J. (1988). Autonomous navigation in cross-country terrain. *Proceedings of Image Understanding Workshop*, Cambridge, MA, April.
[25] Kelly, A., and Stentz, A. (1997). An analysis of requirements for rough terrain autonomous mobility. *Autonomous Robots*, **4**(4), December.
[26] Khatib, O. (1990). Real-time obstacle avoidance for manipulators and mobile robots. *Proceedings of International Conference on Robotics and Automation*, Ohio, 13–18 May.
[27] Krogh, B., and Thorpe, C. (1986). Integrated path planning and dynamic steering control for autonomous vehicles, *Proceedings of the IEEE International Conference on Robotics and Automation*, San Francisco, CA, pp. 1664–1669.
[28] Langer, D., Rosenblatt, J., and Hebert, M. (1994). A behavior-based system for off-road navigation. *IEEE Journal of Robotics and Automation*, **10**(6), 776–782, December.
[29] Lee, C. (1990). Fuzzy logic in control systems: fuzzy logic controller—Parts I & II. *IEEE Transactions on Systems, Man and Cybernetics*, **20**(2), March/April.
[30] Maes, P. (1989). How to do the right thing. *Connection Science Journal*, **1**(3), 291–323.
[31] Maes, P. (1990). Situated agents can have goals. *Robotics and Autonomous Systems*, **6**, 49–70.
[32] Maes, P. (1991). A bottom-up mechanism for action selection in an artificial creature. *Animals to Animats: Proceedings of the Adaptive Behavior Conference, '91* (S. Wilson and J. Arcady-Meyer eds.). MIT Press, February.
[33] Mataric, M. (1992). Integration of representation into goal-driven behavior-based robots. *IEEE Transactions on Robotics and Automation*, **8**(3), 304–312, June.
[34] Moravec, H. (1990). The stanford cart and the CMU rover. *Autonomous Robot Vehicles* (I. Cox, and G. Wilfong eds.), Springer-Verlag.
[35] Nilsson, N. (1980). *Principles of Artificial Intelligence*. Tioga Pub. Co., Palo Alto.
[36] Nilsson, N. (1984). *Shakey the Robot*. SRI Tech. Note 323, Menlo Park, CA.
[37] Olin, K., and Tseng, D. (1991). Autonomous cross-country navigation. *IEEE Expert*, **6**(4), August.
[38] Payton, D. (1986). An architecture for reflexive autonomous vehicle control. *IEEE International Conference on Robotics and Automation*, San Francisco, CA, April 7–10.
[39] Payton, D., Rosenblatt, J., and Keirsey, D. (1990). Plan guided reaction. *IEEE Transactions on System Man and Cybernetics*, **20**(6), 1370–1382.
[40] Pomerleau, D. (1993). *Neural Network Perception for Mobile Robot Guidance*. Kluwer Academic Publishing, Boston, MA.
[41] Rosenblatt, J. (1997). The distributed architecture for mobile navigation. *Journal of Experimental and Theoretical Artificial Intelligence*, **9**(2/3), 339–360, April-September.
[42] Rosenblatt, J. (1998). Utility fusion: map-based planning in a behavior-based system. *Field and Service Robotics*, Springer-Verlag.
[43] Rosenblatt, J., and Payton, D. (1989). A fine-grained alternative to the subsumption architecture for mobile robot control. *Proceedings of the IEEE/INNS International Joint Conference on Neural Networks*, Washington DC, **2**, 317–324, June.
[44] Rosenblatt, J., and Thorpe, C. (1995). Combining multiple goals in a behavior-based architecture. *Proceedings of International Conference on Intelligent Robots and Systems* (IROS), Pittsburgh, PA, August 7–9.
[45] Saffiotti, A. (1997). The uses of fuzzy logic in autonomous robotics: a catalogue raisonn´e, *Soft Computing*, **1**(4):180–197, Springer-Verlag.

[46] Seeliger, O., and Hendler, J. (1997). Supervenient hierarchies of behaviors in robotics. *Journal of Experimental and Theoretical AI*, **9**(2/3).
[47] Shafer, S., Stentz, A., and Thorpe, C. (1986). An architecture for sensor fusion in a mobile robot. *Proceedings of IEEE International Conference on Robotics and Automation*, pp. 2002–2011, San Francisco, CA, April.
[48] Simmons, R. (1994). Structured control for autonomous robots. *IEEE Transactions on Robotics and Automation*. **10**(1), 34–43, February.
[49] Simmons, R. (1995). Towards reliable autonomous agents. *AAAI Spring Symposium on Software Architectures*, Stanford CA, March.
[50] Simon, H. (1967). Motivational and emotional controls of cognition. *Models of Thought*, Yale University Press, 1979, pp. 29–38.
[51] Spector, L., and Hendler, J. (1994). The use of supervenience in dynamic-world planning. *Proceedings of Second International Conference on AI Planning Systems*, (K. Hammond ed.), pp. 158–163. Menlo Park, CA: AAAI Press.
[52] Luc Steels (1994). Emergent functionality in robotic agents through on-line evolution. *Proceedings of Artificial Life IV*, Cambridge, MA, pp. 8–14.
[53] Stentz, A., and Hebert, M. A. (1995). Complete navigation system for goal acquisition in unknown environments. *Proceedings of International Conference on Intelligent Robots and Systems* (*IROS, 95*), August.
[54] Thorpe, C. (ed.) (1990). *Vision and Navigation: The Carnegie Mellon Navlab*, Kluwer, New York.
[55] Turk. M., Morgenthaler, D., Gremban, K., and Marra, M. (1988). VITS—A vision system for autonomous land vehicle navigation. *IEEE Transactions on Pattern Analysis and Machine Intelligence*, **10**(3).
[56] Tyrell, T. (1993). The use of hierarchies for action selection. *Adaptive Behavior*, **1**(4), 387–420.
[57] Yen, J., and Pfluger, N. (1992). A fuzzy logic based robot navigation system. *Proceedings of the AAAI Fall Symposium*.
[58] Zadeh, L. (1973). Outline of a new approach to the analysis of complex systems and decision processes. *IEEE Transactions on Systems, Man and Cybernetics*, **3**(1), January.

Author Index

Numbers in italics indicate the pages on which complete references are given.

A

Abbott, M.B., 12, *115*
Acharya, S., *178*
Adam, N., 261, 262, 263, 269, 270, 274, *309*
Agrawal, R., 161, *175*, 263, *309*
Agre, P., 332, *350*
Albus, J., 325, *351*
Alexander, K., 291, *314*
Alonso, R., 151, 161, *175*, *178*
Alper, J., 303, *309*
Al-Shaer, E., 3, *118*
Amir, E., 122, 171, 174, *176*
Anderson, L.C., 270, *310*
Apperley, M., 298, *314*
Arbib, M.A., 340, 341, *351*
Arkin, R., 332, 333, 341, *351*
Armstrong, J., 324, *351*
Atkins, D.E., 261, 263, 266, 285, *309*
Atkinson, R., 224, 225, 226, 229, 235, 240, 243, *251*, *252*, *253*, 266, 275, *309*
Atkinson, R.J., 226, *253*

B

Bachmann, D., 122, 129, 142, 167, 170, *176*
Badger, M., 230, *254*
Badrinath, B.R., 121, 122, 124, 125, 127, 131, *175*
Bainbridge, D., 298, *314*
Baker, F., 229, *252*
Baker, M.G., 131, 142, *175*
Bakken, D.E., 18, 34, *118*
Balakrishnan, H., 142, 171, 174, *177*
Ballardie, A., 222, 234, 239, *252*
Barraquand, J., 341, *351*
Barton, S., 69, *115*
Bector, R., 8, 9, 15, 16, 17, 25, 27, 29, 52, 54, 72, 73, *118*
Bellare, M., 237, *253*
Bellovin, M., 222, 224, 225, 234, *252*

Bellovin, S., 224, *252*
Berger, J., 347, *351*
Berghel, H., 183, 189, 206, *217*
Berners-Lee, T., *217*
Bernstein, P., 151, *175*
Bershad, B.N., 167, 171, *177*
Bescós, J., 273, 289, 290, *311*
Bhargava, B., *177*
Bhargava, M., 151, *178*
Birmingham, W.P., 261, 263, 285, *309*, *311*
Bishop, A., 263, 267, 284, 300, *314*
Black, J.K., 7, 34, *115*
Blumenthal, U., 242, *252*
Borenstein, J., 342, *351*
Borghuis, M., 292, *309*
Borning, A., 300, *311*
Bostic, K., 40, *117*
Box, D., *114*
Boyer, S.K., 270, *310*
Braden, R., 16, *114*
Bradley, T., 223, *252*
Breitbart, Y., 148, 151, 156, 161, *175*
Brewer, E.A., 122, 171, 174, *176*
Bright, M., 122, 134, 136, 137, 141, 145, *176*
Bright, M.W., 122, 139, 140, 144, 145, 153, *176*
Brinckman, H., 292, *309*
Brooks, R., 327, 331, 333, 336, 350, *351*
Brown, C., 223, *252*
Brown, M., 305, *310*
Bukhres, O., 151, *178*
Bunge, C.A., 275, *311*
Burghardt, F., 122, 171, 174, *176*
Burke, C., 260, *309*
Buschmann, F., 82, 83, *115*
Bush, V., *217*, 260, *309*

C

Cailliau, R., *217*
Canetti, R., 237, *253*

Cao, L., 297, *311*
Carbonell, J., 263, *311*
Card, S.K., 267, *313*
Carey, M., 161, *175*
Carr, L., 293, *311*
Carrel, D., 238, *253*
Case, J.D., 241, *252*
Chapman, D., 332, *350*
Chehadeh, C., 145, *176*, *177*
Chen, H., 263, 264, 267, 278, 284, 299, 300, 301, 302, 303, 304, 306, 308, *309*, *310*, *311*, *312*, *313*, *314*
Chen, S., 261, *310*
Chien, Y., 261, *310*
Ching, N., 272, *310*
Choi, J.-D., 30, *115*
Choy, D.M., 270, *310*
Christopher, A., 245, *252*
Clark, D.D., 29, *115*
Cleeland, C., 9, 13, 29, 81, *118*
Cole, T., 263, 267, 284, 300, *314*
Comer, D., 180, 183, *217*
Computer Emergency Response Team, 224, 228, 231, 243, *252*
Connell, J., 331, 333, *351*
Conover, J., 140, *176*
Conta, A., 223, *252*
Cormen, T., 156, *176*
Cousins, S.B., 267, 270, 286, 287, 299, *313*
Cowan, D.D., 293, *310*
Cox, J.J.R., 10, 15, 22, 31, 34, *115*
Cranor, C., 9, 22, *115*
Crocker, D., 245, *252*
Crocker, S., 250, *252*, *253*
Crowcroft, J., 222, *252*
Crum, L., 285, *310*
Cunningham, S.J., 298, 299, *312*, *314*
Custer, H., *115*
Cytron, R., 30, *115*

D

Dadam, P., 137, 167, *177*
Daily, M., 334, *351*
Dang, X., *115*
Dartois, M., 275, 296, *312*
Dash, K., 145, *176*
Davin, C., 241, *252*
Davis, W., 259, *310*

Deering, S., 222, 223, 233, *252*, *253*
Deering, S.E., 233, *255*
DeFanti, T., 305, *310*
deLespinasse, A.F., 142, 171, *176*
Demers, A., 122, 142, 171, 173, *176*
Dhar, V., 300, *309*
Dierks, T., 245, *252*
Dievendorff, R., 270, *310*
Diffie, W., 238, *252*
Dittia, Z.D., 10, 15, 22, 31, 34, *115*
Doszkocs, T.E., 301, *311*
Dowler, L., 264, *310*
Drabenstott, K.M., 264, 265, 267, 269, 273, *310*
Droms, R., 236, 237, *252*, *253*
Druschel, P., 12, *115*
Durfee, E.H., 261, 263, 285, *309*, *311*
Durrant-Whyte, H., 320, *351*
Dusse, S., 249, *253*
Dwork, C., 270, *310*

E

Eastlake, D., 235, 236, *253*
Eide, E., 5, 8, 12, 29, *115*
Elfes, A., 320, *351*
Elkins, M., 249, *253*
Elmagarmid, A., 125, 126, *176*
Endres, A., 295, 299, *310*
Englebart, D., 188, *217*
Estrin, D., 233, *253*
Eykholt, J., 69, *115*

F

Farinacci, D., 233, *253*
Faulkner, R., 69, *115*
Fay-Wolfe, V., 7, 34, *115*
Fedor, M., 241, *252*
Feldman, S., 271, *310*
Felten, E.W., 201, *217*
Fenner, W., 232, *253*
Ferguson, C.D., 275, *311*
Ferrante, J., 30, *115*
Firby, J., 325, *351*
Fischer, A., 292, *309*
Flanagan, D., *217*
Flores-Gaitan, S., 20, 21, 30, 55, 101, *118*

Ford, B., 5, 8, 12, 29, *115*
Ford, W., *253*
Fox, A., 122, 171, 174, *176*
Fox, E.A., 262, 267, *311*
Franklin, M., *178*
Freed, N., 250, *252*, *253*
Frei, K., 5, 8, 12, 29, *115*
Frew, J., 282, *314*
Frye, B.E., 265, 266, *311*
Fuhr, N., 295, 299, *310*
Fujita, T., 275, 296, *312*
Fuller, V., 229, *253*
Furukawa, T., 125, 126, *176*

G

Galvin, J., 241, 250, *252*, *253*
Gamma, E., 23, 57, 82, 86, 87, 103, 105, *115*
Garcia-Molina, H., 135, 148, 151, 161, *175*, *176*, 261, 263, 267, 270, 286, 287, 299, *312*, *313*
Garrett, J.R., 272, *311*
Gasparini, W., 293, *310*
Gat, E., 334, *351*
Gavron, E., 234, *253*
Georgakopoulos, D., 150, 151, 161, 162, *175*, *176*
Gifford, D.K., 142, 171, *176*
Gill, C.D., 21, 25, 28, 32, 103, *116*
Gingell, R., *115*
Ginsparg, P., 265, 273, 276, *311*
Gladney, H.M., 273, 289, 290, *311*
Glover, E.J., 261, 263, 285, *309*
Gokhale, A., 8, 9, 12, 13, 18, 20, 21, 27, 29, 30, 55, 80, 82, 84, 85, 101, 103, 105, 112, 113, *115*, *116*, *118*
Goodman, N., 151, *175*
Gopalakrishnan, R., 9, 10, 22, 25, *116*
Goto, Y., 324, 333, *351*
Gotoh, T., 333, 342, 345, *352*
Gray, J., 123, 124, 137, 146, *176*
Gremban, K., 324, *353*
Gribble, S.D., 122, 171, 174, *176*
Griffin, S., 261, *310*
Griffin, T.D., 270, *310*
Guarino, N., 300, *311*
Gudmundsson, O., 236, *253*
Guha, R., 300, *311*

Guillemont, M., 74, *116*
Guthrie, K., 291, *314*

H

Hadzilacos, V., 151, *175*
Hall, W., 293, *311*
Haller, N., 243, *253*
Halvorsen, P., 267, *313*
Handley, M., 233, *253*
Harbour, M.G., 17, 20, 59, *116*
Hardin, J., 263, 267, 284, 300, *314*
Harkins, D., 238, *253*
Harney, H., 239, 240, *253*
Harris, J., 334, *351*
Harris, S., 293, *311*
Harrison, T., 8, 9, *118*
Harrison, T.H., 3, 6, 8, 10, 23, 25, 28, 31, 43, 50, 59, 67, 84, 85, 87, 93, 95, 97, 101, 104, *116*, *117*, *118*
Hasson, S.W., 267, 270, 286, 287, 299, *313*
Hayes-Roth, B., 333, 337, *351*
Hearst, M.A., 267, *313*
Hebert, M., 321, 345, *352*
Hebert, M.A., 345, *353*
Heidemann, J., 167, 170, *177*
Helal, A., 127, *177*
Hellman, M.E., 238, *252*
Helm, R., 23, 57, 82, 86, 87, 103, 105, *115*
Helmy, A., 233, *253*
Henderson, C.L., 299, *312*
Hendler, J., 328, 329, *353*
Henning, M., 6, *116*
Hexmoor, H., 334, *351*
Hey, J.M.N., 293, *311*
Hill, L.L., 284, *310*
Hills, A., 167, *176*
Hinden, R., 222, *252*
Hitchcock, S., 293, *311*
Hoenig, B.A., 270, *310*
Hoffman, P., 249, *253*
Hole, W.T., 303, *312*
Honeyman, P., 122, 129, 142, 167, 170, *176*
Hoschka, P., 12, 30, *116*
House, D.H., 340, 341, *351*
Housley, R., *253*
Houston, A.L., 301, 302, 303, 304, *310*, *311*
Howes, T., 240, *255*
Hu, J., 82, 91, 93, *116*

358 AUTHOR INDEX

Hubbard, S.M., 301, *311*
Humphreys, B.L., 300, *311*
Hunter, K., 292, *309*
Hurson, A., 122, 134, 136, 137, 139, 140, 141, 144, 145, 153, *176*
Hurson, A.R., *177*
Huser, C., 262, *311*
Huston, L., 122, 129, 142, 167, 170, *176*

I

Imielinski, T., 263, *309*
Information Technology – Portable Operating System Interface (POSIX), 17, *116*
International Telecommunications Union, 240, *253*

J

Jackson, M.K., 270, *310*
Jacobson, V., 233, *253*
Jain, P., 23, 29, 38, 83, 87, 107, *116*
Jing, J., 125, 126, *176*
Jochem, T., 324, *351*
Johnson, D.B., 167, *176*
Johnson, R., 23, 57, 82, 86, 87, 103, 105, *115*
Jones, S., 298, *314*
Jones, V., 272, *310*
Joseph, A.D., 122, 131, 132, 141, 142, 171, *176*

K

Kaashoek, M.F., 122, 131, 132, 141, 142, 171, *176*
Kaelbling, L., 332, 336, *352*
Kahn, P., 260, *312*
Kaka, W., 270, *310*
Kalakota, R., 263, 266, 267, 272, 274, *311*
Kalogeraki, V., 18, *116*
Kamada, H., 333, 342, 345, *352*
Kanade, T., 262, 279, 280, 300, 301, *314*
Kantor, B., 243, *253*
Kantor, P.B., 263, 268, *313*
Karels, M.J., 40, *117*

Karn, P., 238, *253*
Katz, R.H., 142, 171, 174, *177*
Kaufman, C., 235, *253*
Keirsey, D., 327, 330, 334, 335, 339, *351*, *352*
Kelly, A., 345, *352*
Kent, S., 249, *253*
Kent, S.T., 226, *253*
Kessler, J., 267, 275, 277, 295, *311*
Ketcxhpel, S.P., 267, 270, 286, 287, 299, *313*
Khanna, S., 7, 16, 40, 62, 73, *116*
Khatib, O., 330, 341, *352*
Khosla, P.K., 23, 38, *118*
Kille, S., 240, *255*
Kirchhoff, A.J., 300, 302, 303, *310*
Kistler, J.J., 122, 142, *177*
Kleiman, S., 69, *115*
Klein, M.H., 17, 20, 59, *116*
Kluiters, C.P., 269, *311*
Knoblock, C., 263, *311*
Koller, D., 263, *311*
Koren, Y., 342, *351*
Kortenkamp, D., 334, *351*
Korth, H., 153, *177*
Krawczyk, H., 237, *253*
Krogh, B., 341, *352*
Krupp, P., 7, 34, *115*
Kumar, B., 324, *351*
Kumar, P., 173, *177*

L

Lai, S.J., 122, *176*
Laird, C., 204, 205, *217*
Langer, D., 321, 345, *352*
Larsgaard, M.L., 284, *310*
Latombe, J.C., 341, *351*
Lavender, R.G., 23, 83, 86, 99, *116*
Layland, J., 17, 20, 59, *116*
Le, M.T., 122, 171, 174, *176*
Lee, A.J., 231, *253*
Lee, C., 342, *352*
Lee, M., *115*
Lehoczky, J.P., 7, 34, 81, *117*
Leiserson, C., 156, *176*
Lenat, D.B., 300, *311*
Leong, M.K., 297, *311*
Lepreau, J., 5, 8, 12, 29, *115*

AUTHOR INDEX

Lesk, M., 262, 265, 266, 268, 269, 270, 271, 272, 273, 275, 276, 279, 280, 282, 285, 293, 294, 295, 297, 298, *312*
Levine, D., 8, 9, 15, 16, 17, 25, 27, 29, 52, 54, 72, 73, *118*
Levine, D.L., 6, 8, 9, 10, 21, 23, 25, 28, 31, 32, 43, 50, 59, 67, 84, 85, 93, 97, 103, 104, *116*, *118*
Levy, D.M., 262, *312*
Li, T., 229, 231, *253*, *254*
Licklider, J., *312*
Lim, J.B., *177*
Lin, C., 300, 302, 303, *310*
Lindberg, D.A., 300, *311*
Lindstrom, G., 5, 8, 12, 29, *115*
Linn, J., 249, *253*
Liu, C., 17, 20, 59, *116*, 233, *253*
Livny, M., 161, *175*
Loo, E., 292, *309*
Lotspiech, J.B., 270, *310*
Lu, Y., 297, *311*
Luc Steels, 330, *353*
Lumia, R., 325, *351*
Lundblade, L., 249, *253*
Luotonen, A., *217*
Lyman, P., 272, *312*
Lynch, C., 261, 263, 267, 299, *312*
Lynch, K.J., 301, *312*
Lyons, P.A., 272, *311*

M

Ma, W.Y., 300, 301, *312*
McCabe, T.J., 110, *117*
McCain, H., 325, *351*
McCloghrie, E., 242, *255*
McCloghrie, K., 241, *252*, *253*
McCray, A.T., 303, *312*
McCrossin, J.M., 270, *310*
McDonald, D., 300, *311*
McGill, M., 261, *313*
McGraw, G., 201, *217*
Mackinlay, J.D., 267, *313*
McKnight, C., 294, *312*
McKusick, M.K., 40, *117*
McNab, R., 298, 299, *314*
McNab, R.J., 299, *312*
Maeda, A., 275, 296, *312*
Maes, P., 330, 332, *352*

Manjunath, B.S., 300, 301, *312*
Mansell, R., 266, 270, *312*
Marchionini, G., 262, 267, *311*
Marra, M., 324, *353*
Marshall, C.C., 262, *312*
Martin, G.P., 122, *176*
Martinez, J., 308, *310*
Martinez, J.P., 300, 302, 303, *310*
Masinter, L., 267, *313*
Mataric, M., 331, *352*
Maughan, D., 238, *253*
Mayer, J., 127, *177*
Mayfield, C.I., 293, *310*
Medin, M, 224, *254*
Mehrotra, S., 153, *177*
Melliar-Smith, P., 18, *116*
Metz, C., 243, *253*
Metzger, P., *253*, *254*
Meunier, R., 82, 83, *115*
Miller, A.M., 270, *310*
Mintzer, F., 273, 289, 290, *311*
Mischo, B., 263, 267, 284, 300, *314*
Mockapetris, P.V., 234, *254*
Moen, W.E., 267, *312*
Mogul, J.C., 142, 171, 174, *177*
Moon, S., *177*
Moravec, H., 320, *352*
Morgenthaler, D., 324, *353*
Morris, R.J.T., 270, *310*
Morris, R.T., 224, *254*
Mors, R., 292, *309*
Moser, L., 18, *116*
Mostert, P., 292, *309*
Motorola ReFLEX Fact Sheet, 127, 131, *177*
Moy, J., 230, *254*
Muckenhirn, C., 239, 240, *253*
Mullen, T., 261, 263, 285, *309*
Mummert, L.B., 122, 142, *177*
Mungee, S., 7, 8, 9, 10, 15, 16, 17, 20, 21, 25, 27, 29, 30, 31, 32, 52, 54, 55, 72, 73, 82, 91, 93, 101, *116*, *117*, *118*
Murphy, S., 230, 250, *252*, *253*, *254*
Myaeng, S., 297, *312*

N

Nadis, S., 260, *312*
Naoi, S., 333, 342, 345, *352*
Narten, T., 223, *254*

National Institute of Standards and Technology, 222, 226, 227, 238, 250, 254
Needham, R.M., 222, 238, *254*
Nelson, T., 188, *217*
Neuman, B.C., 222, 238, *254*
Nevill-Manning, C., 299, *314*
Newby, G.B., 273, *313*
Ng, D.T., 301, 303, 308, *310*, *311*
Ng, T.D., 300, 302, 303, *310*
Nielsen, H., *217*
Niemeyer, P., 202, *218*
Nilsson, N., 320, 321, 350, *352*
Noble, B., 173, *177*
Noble, B.B., 127, *177*
Noble, B.D., 167, *177*
Nordmark, E., 223, *254*
NSFNET Backbone Traffic Distribution Statistics, *218*
Nunamaker, J.F., 304, *313*
Nyce, J.M., 260, *312*

O

Obenza, R., 17, 20, 59, *116*
Object Management Group, 3, 6, 11, 19, 20, 80, *117*
Odlyzko, A.M., 266, *312*
O'Leary, D.E., 301, *312*
Olin, K., 334, *351*, *352*
Olsen, J., 264, *313*
Orman, H., *254*
Ortiz, R., 137, 167, *177*
Orwig, R., 303, 304, *310*, *313*
Ousterhout, J., 204, *218*

P

Padmanabhan, V.N., 142, 171, 174, *177*
Paepcke, A., 267, 270, 286, 287, 299, *313*
Pagels, M., 12, *115*
Pakzad, S., 122, 134, 136, 137, 139, 140, 141, 144, 145, 153, *176*
Partridge, C., 233, *255*
Parulkar, G., 8, 9, 15, 16, 17, 22, 25, 27, 29, 52, 54, 72, 73, *115*, *117*, *118*
Parulkar, G.M., 9, 10, 15, 22, 25, 31, 34, *115*, *116*

Pass, N.J., 270, *310*
Payton, D., 327, 330, 333, 334, 335, 337, 339, 340, *351*, *352*
Peck, J., 202, *218*
Pedersen, J.O., 267, *313*
Peek, R.P., 273, *313*
Perl Journal, The, 209, *218*
Pertersen, K., 122, 142, 171, 173, *176*
Perterson, T., 129, *177*
Peterson, I., 259, 260, *313*
Peterson, L.L., 12, *115*
Pfluger, N., 344, *353*
Phoha, S., 145, *176*
Piatetsky-Shapiro, G., 301, *313*
Pinckney, T., 122, *176*
Piper, D., 238, *254*
Pitkow, J., 181, 212, *218*
Pitoura, E., *177*
Pittman, K., 300, *311*
Plummer, D.C., 223, *254*
Polk, W., *253*
Pollak, B., 17, 20, 59, *116*
Pomerleau, D., 321, 324, *351*, *352*
Popek, G., 167, 170, *177*
Postel, J., 222, 243, *254*
Postel, T., *254*
Prakash, R., 137, 142, *177*
Pratt, D., 300, *311*
Prentice, A.E., 270, *313*
Presuhn, R., 242, *255*
Price, M., 173, *177*
Pryce, N., 31, 87, 95, 101, *118*
Purday, J., 294, *313*
Pusateri, T., 233, *254*
Pyarali, I., 6, 8, 40, 82, 91, 93, 100, 104, *116*, *117*

Q

Quarterman, J.S., 40, *117*
Quercia, V., 180, *218*

R

Rabaey, J., 122, 171, 174, *176*
Rajkumar, R., 7, 34, 81, *117*
Ralya, T., 17, 20, 59, *116*
Ramamritham, K., 35, *117*

AUTHOR INDEX 361

Ramsdell, B., 249, *253*
Ramsey, M., 284, *310*
Rao, R., 267, *313*
Ratner, D., 167, 170, *177*
Reddy, R., 266, *313*
Rees, J., 122, 129, 142, 167, 170, *176*
Reichenberger, K., 262, *311*
Reiher, P., 167, 170, *177*
Reiser, K., 334, *351*
Rekhter, T., 231, *254*
Repka, L., 249, *253*
Reuter, A., 123, 124, 137, 146, *176*
Reynolds, J.K., *254*
Riggs, R., 3, *118*
Ritchie, D., 16, *117*
Rivest, R., 156, *176*, 226, *254*
Roberts, D., 180, *218*
Robertson, G.G., 267, *313*
Rockwell, R.C., 264, 268, *313*
Rogers, A., 126, 127, 131, *177*
Rohnert, H., 82, 83, *115*
Roscheisen, M., 267, 270, 286, 287, 299, *313*
Rose, M., 241, *252*
Rosen, B.K., 30, *115*
Rosenblatt, J., 321, 327, 330, 332, 333, 334, 335, 339, 340, 345, *351*, *352*
Rosenschein, S., 332, 336, *352*
Rostek, L., 262, *311*
Rundensteiner, E.A., 261, 263, 285, *309*
Rush, J.E., 270, *313*
Rusinkiewicz, M., 150, 151, 161, 162, *175*, *176*

S

Saffiotti, A., 342, *353*
Sakaguichi, T., 275, 296, *312*
Salem, K., 151, 161, *175*
Salton, G., 261, 301, *313*
Samuelson, P., 271, *313*
Saracevic, T., 263, 268, *313*
Satyanarayanan, M., 122, 141, 142, 167, 173, *177*
Schantz, R., 18, 34, *118*
Schatz, B.R., 263, 264, 267, 278, 284, 299, 300, 301, 302, 303, 304, 306, 308, *310*, *311*, *313*, *314*
Schertler, M., 238, *253*
Schiattarella, F., 273, 289, 290, *311*

Schmidt, D.C., 3, 6, 7, 8, 9, 10, 12, 13, 15, 16, 17, 18, 20, 21, 22, 23, 25, 27, 28, 29, 30, 31, 32, 38, 40, 43, 50, 52, 54, 55, 58, 59, 67, 72, 73, 80, 81, 82, 83, 84, 85, 86, 87, 89, 91, 92, 93, 95, 97, 98, 99, 100, 101, 102, 103, 104, 105, 107, 112, 113, *115*, *116*, *117*, *118*
Schneider, M., 238, *253*
Schneier, B., 238, *254*
Schoffstaff, M.L., 241, *252*
Schroeder, M.D., 222, 238, *254*
Schuffels, C., 303, *310*
Schwatz, R., 209, *218*
Secret, A., *217*
Seeliger, O., 329, *353*
Seshan, S., 122, 142, 171, 174, *176*, *177*
Sewell, R.R., 301, 302, 303, 304, *310*, *311*
Sha, L., 7, 34, 81, *117*
Shafer, S., 324, 333, 338, *353*
Sharma, P., 233, *253*
Shepherd, M., 300, *311*
Sheth, A., 150, 162, *176*
Shivalingiah, A., 69, *115*
Shoham, Y., 263, *311*
Silberschatz, A., 148, 151, 153, 156, 161, *175*, *177*
Simmons, R., 325, 326, 327, *353*
Simon, H., 327, 338, *353*
Simpson, W., 223, *253*, *254*
Singhal, M., 137, 142, *177*
Skinner, G., 167, 170, *177*
Smith, L.A., 299, *312*
Smith, M., 69, *115*
Smith, M.A., 262, 279, 280, 300, 301, *314*
Smith, T.R., 267, 282, 284, 310, *314*
Sohn, K., *177*
Solo, D., *253*
Soloway, E., 261, 263, 285, *309*
Sommerlad, P., 82, 83, *115*
Soraiz, K., 204, 205, *217*
Spector, L., 328, *353*
Spreitzer, M., 122, 142, 171, 173, *176*
Stal, M., 82, 83, *115*
Stallings, W., 127, 131, *177*
Stanford Digital Libraries Group, 287, *311*
Stankovic, J.A., 13, 35, *117*, *118*
Stein, D., 69, *115*
Stentz, A., 324, 333, 338, 345, *351*, *352*, *353*
Stevens, S.M., 262, 279, 280, 300, 301, *314*

Stewart, D.B., 23, 38, *118*
Stoll, C., 251, *254*
Streitz, N., 262, *311*
Suda, T., 83, 107, *118*
Sugimoto, S., 275, 296, *312*
Sun Microsystems, 187, 200, *218*
Surendran, N., 7, 10, *117*
Swami, A., 263, *309*

T

Tabata, K., 275, 296, *312*
Tauber, J.A., 122, 131, 132, 141, 142, 171, *176*
Taylor, C., 300, *311*
Tennant, R., 264, 267, *314*
Tennenhouse, D.L., 27, 29, *115*, *118*
Terry, D., 122, 142, 171, 173, *176*
Thaler, D., 233, *253*
Theier, M., 122, 142, 171, 173, *176*
Thomas, S.W., 291, *314*
Thompson, H.G., 151, *175*
Thorpe, C., 324, 332, 333, 338, 341, *352*, *353*
Thuraisingham, B., 7, 34, *115*
Tolle, K.M., 301, *311*
Tompa, F.W., 293, *310*
Treu, M., 273, 289, 290, *311*
Tseng, D., 334, *351*, *352*
T"so, T.Y., 222, 238, *254*
Turk, M., 324, *353*
Turner, J., 238, *253*
Turner, J.S., 22, *117*
Tyrell, T., 335, *353*

U

Unsworth, J., 272, *314*

V

Varadhan, K., 229, *253*
Veijalainen, J., 142, 151, *178*
Venema, W., 224, *254*
Vidal, J.M., 261, 263, 285, *309*
Vinoski, S., 3, 25, 97, *118*
Visa, 248, *255*

Vlissides, J., 23, 57, 82, 86, 87, 103, 105, *115*
Voll, J., 69, *115*

W

Wactlar, H.D., 262, 279, 280, 300, 301, *314*
Wahl, M., 240, *255*
Waitzman, D., 233, *255*
Waldbusser, S., 241, *252*
Waldo, J., 3, *118*
Wall, L., 209, *218*
Wallace, R., 261, 263, 285, *309*
Watson, T., 167, 171, 172, *177*, *178*
Weaver, W., 260, *314*
Weeks, M., 69, *115*
Wegman, M.N., 30, *115*
Wei, L., 233, *253*
Welch, B., 122, 142, 171, 173, *176*, 201, *218*
Wellington, B., 230, *254*
Wellman, M.P., 261, 263, 285, *309*, *311*
Wells, H.G., 260, *314*
Weyer, S., 300, *311*
Whinston, A.B., 263, 266, 267, 272, 274, *311*
Whitten, I.H., 299, *312*
Wiederhold, G., 258, 274, *314*
Wijnen, B., 242, *252*, *255*
Wilensky, R., 281, 300, *314*
Williams, D., 69, *115*
Winograd, T., 267, 270, 286, 287, 299, *313*
Winslett, M., 272, *310*
Witten, I.H., 298, 299, *314*
Wollrath, A., 3, *118*
Wolski, A., 142, 151, *178*
Wong, V., 334, *351*
Wulf, W.A., 261, *314*
WWW Security FAQ, *218*

Y

Yegyazarian, A., 129, *177*
Yen, J., 344, *353*
Yeo, L.H., 122, *176*
Yesha, Y., 261, 262, 263, 269, 270, 274, *309*
Ylonen, T., 244, *255*
Yu, J., 229, *253*

Z

Zadeck, F.K., 30, *115*
Zadeh, L., 330, 342, *353*
Zaslavsky, A.Z., 122, *176*
Zdonik, S., *178*

Zhang, A., 151, *178*
Zhao, W., 35, *117*
Zijlstra, J., 292, *309*
Zimmerman, P.R., 249, *255*
Zinky, J.A., 18, 34, *118*

Subject Index

A

Abstract factory pattern, 87, 104–5
Acceptor-Connector pattern, 86, 93–6
Access devices, 129–31
ACE C++ wrapper facades, 89
ACID properties, 123, 124, 137, 146
Active demultiplexing, 28
Active object pattern, 86–7, 97–100
Active transaction, 159
Active-X, 201–2
Address Resolution Protocol (ARP), 223
Admission controller, 18
Advanced Encryption Standard (AES), 227
Advanced Networks and Services (ANS), 183
Alexandria Digital Library (ADL), 281–2
American Documentation Institute (ADI) (now American Society for Information Science (ASIS)), 259
Andrew File System (AFS), 167
Anonymizer, 213
Application data units (ADUs), 30
Application layer, 221
  protocol, 220, 221
Application-programming interface (API), 172
ARPANET, 182
Asynchronous transfer mode (ATM), 126
ATM Port Interconnect Controller (APIC), 10, 29, 31
Atomic commit protocol, 151
Atomicity, 123
Attacks, 224, 228–9, 231–2, 234–5, 246–9
Augment project, 188
Australia, digital libraries, 298
Authenticity, 274
Automatic indexing, 301
Autonomous Land Vehicle (ALV), 324
Autonomy, 132, 147
Average response time, 163

B

Basic Transport Layer Security, 246
Bayou project, 172–3
Blackbox benchmarks, 63–7
Blackbox site, 157
BNU project, 171
Border Gateway Protocol (BGP), 231–2
  version 4 (BGPv4), 231
British Library, 294
Browsing, 122

C

California Digital Library (CDL) Project, 290–1
Canada, digital libraries, 293–4
Canada's Technology Triangle (CTT) Community Network, 293
Canadian Initiative on Digital Libraries (CIDL), 293
Carnegie Mellon University (CMU), 278–80, 324
Cells, 127
Cellular network, 126–7
Certificate revocation list (CRL), 241
Certification authority (CA), 240–1
China, digital libraries, 297–8
Chorus ClassiX, performance results, 73–9
Cipher-Block-Chaining (CBC), 227
Clear-text reusable passwords, 228–9
Coda, 167–70
Command-line options, 102
Common data representation (CDR), 19
Common Gateway Interface (CGI), 194–6, 209, 213, 215
Common Object Request Broker Architecture. See CORBA
Communication autonomy, 135
Communication utilization, 165
Community strings, 242
Concept space technique, 302

Concurrency control, 146–58
  algorithms, 162
  global transactions, 124
  MDAS, 152–8
  MDBMS, 123, 137–8, 141, 151–2
  V-locking, 158–65
Concurrent transactions, 150
Confidentiality, 274
Conflicting data, 136
Connection-Less Network Protocol (CLNP), 231
Connection mediums, 128
Consistency, 123
Cookies, 211–14
Copyright, 270–3
CORBA, 1–118
  efficient and predictable stubs and skeletons, 29–30
  evaluation for high-performance real-time systems, 3–13
  limitations for real-time applications, 6–8
  overcoming limitations for high-performance and real-time applications, 8–13
  reference model, 3–6
  supporting real-time scheduling, 31–50
CORBA/ATM hardware platform, 61
CORBA/IDL interface, 35
CORBAplus, 62, 64
  blackbox benchmarks, 65
  concurrency architecture, 68
  connection architecture, 68
  whitebox benchmarks, 67–8
Core-Based Trees (CBT) multicast routing protocol, 234
Cornell University, 291–2
CPU utilization, 164
Cryptographic algorithms, 225
Cryptographic authentication, 224, 229, 237, 238
Cryptographic keys, 225, 237–9
Cryptographic mechanisms, 225
  see also Encryption
Cultural biases, 275

D

Daedalus/GloMop project, 173–4

DARPA Autonomous Land Vehicle (ALV), 324
DARPA D-Lib Program, 291
Data distillation, 142–3
Data Encryption Standard (DES), 227
Data heterogeneity, 122
Data integration, 122
Data mining, 263
Database management system (DBMS), 121, 124, 134, 135, 137, 140, 159
Databases, 121
DCOM, 3
Deadlocks, 156–7
  detection, 157, 159–60
Decision-making process, 132
Deferred synchronous calls, 5
Depth first search (DFS) policy, 156
Design autonomy, 135
Desktop computing devices, 129
Destination Address, 222
Diffie-Hellman approach, 244, 247
Digital libraries, 257–314
  Australia, 298
  Canada, 293–4
  characterization, 261–2
  China, 297–8
  content creation, 262
  copyright, 270, 271–3
  definition, 261
  drives towards, 265–8
  economic issues, 268–70
  economic pressures, 265–6
  enabling technologies, 266–7
  equality of access, 275–6
  ethical considerations, 275
  France, 294–5
  funding models, 269–70
  future directions, 306–9
  Germany, 295
  Grand Challenge, 299–300
  historical overview, 259–61
  Hong Kong, 297–8
  improved level of service, 266
  indexing and filtering information, 263
  information location processes, 263
  intellectual property rights, 271–3
  Japan, 295–300
  Korea, 296–7
  legal issues, 270–3

SUBJECT INDEX

liability issues, 271
new technologies, 266–7
New Zealand, 298–9
ownership issues, 270–1
preservation of media, 264–5
quality issues, 273–4
research activities
  in US, 277–93
  overview, 276–99
  semantic interoperability, 299–306
  social context, 268–76
security, 273–4
Singapore, 297
standards, 267–8
Taiwan, 297–8
trademark infringement, 271
United Kingdom, 294
universal access, 264
user interface, 263
see also Electronic information
Digital Library Federation, 288
Digital Library Initiative (DLI), 276–87
  Phase 2 (DLI-2), 277
Direct conflict, 147–50
Dirty read, 146
Disk utilization, 164
Distance-Vector Multicast Routing Protocol (DVMRP), 233
Distributed Architecture for Mobile Navigation (DAMN), 330, 332, 333, 342–5
Distributed object computing (DOC) middleware, 3
Distribution transparency, 122
Domain Name System (DNS), 222, 234–6, 240
  attacks, 234–5
  current technology, 235
  Secure Dynamic Update, 235–6
Domain of Interpretation (DOI), 238
Dongles, 272
DoubleClick Corporation, 213
Durability, 123
Dynamic Host Configuration Protocol (DHCP), 235–7
  technology directions, 237
  threats and issues, 236–7
Dynamic HTML (DHTML), 203–4
Dynamic invocation interface (DII), 5–6
Dynamic skeleton interface (DSI), 6

E

Earliest deadline first (EDF), 32
EDI, 245
Electronic commerce, 244–8
  current technology, 246–8
  future directions, 248
  threats, 245–6
Electronic information
  economic issues, 268–70
  flickering or wobbling, 273
  standards, 267–8
  unauthorized access, 271
  see also Digital libraries
Electronic information provider, 270
Electronic mail (E-mail), 248–50
  current technology, 249–50
  future directions, 250
  threats, 248–9
Electronic media, preservation, 264–5
E-Lib project, 294
Encapsulating Security Payload (ESP), 226
Encryption, 227, 273
Ethernet, 222
Ethical considerations, digital libraries, 275
European Backbone (EBONE) project, 183
Executable content, 199–202
Execution autonomy, 135
Exterior Gateway Protocol (EGP), 231

F

FedStats, 289
Ficus, 170
FIDONET, 183
File Transmission Protocol (FTP), 192
Firewalls, 224, 227, 234–5
Forced conflicts under full autonomy, 150–1
Format differences, 136
Forms, 196–8
Fractional access, 272
France, digital libraries, 294–5
Full autonomy, forced conflicts under, 150–1
Fuzzy logic, 342

G

Gabriel, 295

GAPPS, 330, 332, 336-8
General Inter-ORB Protocol (GIOP), 7, 19-23, 30, 59
Generalized Markup Language (GML), 190
Germany, digital libraries, 295
Global conflict, 149, 150
Global information access, 120
Global information sharing process, 160
Global locking algorithm, 153-6
Global locking scheme (GLS), 152
Global locking tables, 153-4
Global parameters, 160-1
Global scheduler, 141
Global serialization, 149
Global subtransactions, 160-1
Global throughput, 162
Global transaction manager (GTM), 123, 148, 154, 157
Global transactions, 147, 159
  percent completed, 163
Global transduction manager (GTM), 152
Gopher, 180
Graphical user interface (GUI), 201
Group Key Management Protocol (GKMP), 239

H

Hardware locks, 272
Helper apps, 198-9
Heterogeneity and site autonomy, 134-6
Heterogeneous data, 133-4
Heterogeneous data access, 133, 136
  in mobile environment, 119-78
Heterogeneous remote access to data (HRAD), 122
HMAC-MD5, 237
Hong Kong, digital libraries, 297-8
HTML, 180, 185, 187-92, 207, 213
  evolution, 189
HTTP, 91, 180, 185, 186, 188, 192-4, 207, 220, 245
  see also Secure HTTP (S-HTTP)
Human-computer interactions (HCI), 304-6
Hypernym, 145, 153
Hypertext Markup Language. *See* HTML
Hypertext Transfer Protocol. *See* HTTP
Hyponym, 145

I

IBM digital library, 289-90
ICMP, 222, 223, 232
  Router Advertisement, 223
  Router Solicit, 223
IDL compiler, 5, 29-30
IIOP, 5, 19-23, 30, 87, 93, 94, 97, 110, 112, 113
  concurrency architectures, 98
  event loop, 91
  hard-coded strategy usage, 107
  operating system interaction, 88
Implementation Repository, 6
Indexing
  and filtering information, 263
  automatic, 301
  term, 301
  textual document, 301
Indirect conflict, 147-8
InfoBus project, 285-7
InfoPad project, 174
Information identification process, 263
Information Infrastructure Technology and Applications (IITA) Working Group, 299
Information repositories, 272-3
Information visualization, 304-6
Informedia project, 278-80
Integrated-ISIS (I-ISIS), 230-1
  routing protocol, 229
Integrity, 274
Intellectual property rights, 271-3
Inter-domain unicast routing, 229-32
Interface control, 272
Interface Definition Language (IDL), 19
  see also Real-time IDL (RIDL)
Interface Repository, 6
Intermediate System to Intermediate System (ISIS), 230
Internet, 120, 306
  infrastructure, 182-3
  interactive applications, 243-4
  security, 219-55
    and privacy, 210
    status and future directions, 244
  threats, 222-4, 243-4
  vs. World Wide Web (WWW), 220
Internet II project, 183

Internet Control Message Protocol. *See* ICMP
Internet Engineering Task Force (IETF), 220–2, 226
Internet Explorer, 186
Internet Group Membership Protocol (IGMP), 232–3
Internet Inter-ORB Protocol. *See* IIOP
Internet Key Exchange (IKE), 238
Internet Protocol (IP), 180, 220–4
  addressing, 222
  Authentication Header (AH), 225–6
  security, 224–7, 245
  Security Domain of Interpretation, 238
  version 4 (IPv4), 222, 227
  version 6 (IPv6), 223, 224, 226
Internet Relay Chat (IRC), 184
Internet Security Association and Key Management Protocol (ISAKMP), 225, 238
Internet service provider (ISP), 126, 228
Interoperable object reference (IOR), 19
Interspace Project, 283–4
Intra-domain unicast routing, 229–31
Intranet, 186
IPC mechanism, 74
ISDN, 227
Isolation, 122, 123

J

Japan, digital libraries, 295–300
Java, 202
Java RMI, 3
Java virtual machine (JVM), 200–1
JSTOR, 291

K

Kernel-level locking overhead, 72–3
Key Distribution Centres (KDCs), 239
Key eXchanger (KX) record, 235
Key management, 237–9
  multicast, 239
  unicast, 238–9
Knowledge representations, 303–4
Korea, digital libraries, 296–7

L

Library of Congress, 287–8
  standards, 287
Library of Congress/Ameritech National Digital Library Competition, 288
Limited resources, 122
Link Layer, 221–2
Literacy, 274
Little Work project, 170–1
Local area network (LAN), 121, 125–7, 171, 182, 186, 223
Local conflict, 149, 150
Local serialization, 149
Local transactions, 147, 159, 160
Location transparency, 122
Lock contention, 100–2
Locking schemes, 72–3, 151–6
  see also V-locking
Logical Link Control (LLC) sub-layer, 221
Lost update, 146

M

MAC-layer address, 223
Making of America (MOA) Project, 291–2
Management Information Base (MIB), 241
Maximum urgency first (MUF), 32
MDAS, 157–9, 165–6
  concurrency control, 152–8
  future directions, 166–7
  global throughput varying the number of local sites, 162
MDBMS, 121–4, 134–41
  concurrency control, 123, 137–8, 141, 151 2
  global, 136
  issues, 136–8
  serializability approaches, 141–2
  serializability solutions, 150–2
  transaction processing model, 147–9
Media Access Control (MAC) sub-layer, 221–2
Message Authentication Code (MAC), 247
Message Digest 5 (MD5)
  algorithm, 226
  authentication, 231
MIME Object Security Services (MOSS), 250

miniCOOL, 62, 64
  blackbox benchmarks, 66
  concurrency architecture, 70
  connection architecture, 69
  using Chorus IPC, 75–7
  using TCP, 77–8
  whitebox benchmarks, 69–70
Minimum laxity first (MLF), 32
Missing data, 136
Mobile-aware projects, 169, 171–4
Mobile computing, 134
Mobile data access system (MDAS), 119, 123, 124, 139–46
  summary of issues and solutions, 143
  transaction processing model, 147–9
Mobile environment
  heterogeneous data access in, 119–78
  issues, 131–4
  networking, 125–34
Mobile robot control architectures, 315–53
  abstraction hierarchies, 323
  Avoid-Obstacles, 338–9
  behavior-based architectures, 327–35
  centralized architectures, 320–5
  Command Arbitration, 329–30, 335
  command fusion, 333, 340–5
    limitations, 345
  command selection, 335–40
    limitations, 338–40
  deliberative planning, 321–3
  design approaches, 318–35
  Follow-Road behavior, 338–9
  hierarchical architectures, 325–7
  Hughes architecture, 337–8
  hybrid architectures, 333–5
  inter-module communication, 333
  key issues in design, 319
  map-based path arbiter voting, 346
  non-reactive architectures, 332
  non-symbolic planners, 324–5
  overview, 317–19
  partial plans, 323
  reactive architectures, 331
  role of, 318
  sensor fusion, 320–1
  Subsumption Architecture, 331, 336
  utility fusion, 345–7
Mobile support system, 131–2
Mobile-transparent projects, 167–71
Mobility issues, 125–34

Modem connection, 126
Motor Schema, 341
MT-Orbix, 57–8, 62, 64
  blackbox benchmarks, 65
  concurrency architecture, 70
  connection architecture, 70
  whitebox benchmarks, 70
MUF, 49
Multicast Backbone (MBONE), 232
Multicast key management, 239
Multicast routing, 232–4
Multicast traffic, 232
Multidatabase management systems. *See* MDBMS
Multipurpose Internet Mail Extensions (MIME), 249

N

Naming differences, 136
NASREM architecture, 325
National Aeronautics and Space Administration (NASA), 288–9
Natural language processing, 301
Navlab vehicles, 324
Neighbor Discovery (ND), 223
Netscape Navigator, 185, 212, 213
Network computing (NC) device, 129
Network management, 241–3
New Zealand, digital libraries, 298–9
NII, 278
Noun phrase indexing, 301
NSFNET Backbone, 180–1

O

Object adapters, 6, 25–9, 93
Object recognition, 301
Object Request Brokers. *See* ORBs
Odyssey project, 173
OMG IDL stubs and skeletons, 5
Open Shortest Path First (OSPF) protocol, 229
  version 2 (OSPFv2), 230, 239
ORB Core, 5, 18–25
  active connection architecture, 51–2
  alternative concurrency architectures, 54–60

components, 24
demultiplexing events using reactor pattern, 90–3
efficient and predictable memory management, 30–1
extensibility and portability, 23–5
leader/follower connection architecture, 52–4
leader/follower thread pool architecture, 56
multiplexed connection architectures, 51–4
non-multiplexed connection architectures, 54
reactor-per-thread-priority architecture, 58–60
real-time
design, 50–82
scheduling and dispatching of client requests, 25
threading framework architecture, 57–8
worker thread pool architecture, 55
ORB endsystem, 49–50
architectural components and features for high-performance real-time, 13–31
benchmarking testbed, 60–3
client benchmarking configuration, 63
dispatcher, 41
hardware configuration, 61
non-determinism, 80–2
priority inversion, 80–2
requirements for high-performance and real-time, 10
server benchmarking configuration, 61–2
ORBs, 1–118, 3
architectural components and features for high-performance real-time endsystems, 13–31
consolidation of strategies using abstract factory pattern, 104–5
contribution of patterns to middleware, 109–13
conventional demultiplexing strategies, 26–7
design challenges and patterns that resolve them, 109
dynamically configurable middleware, 83–5
real-time middleware, 82
with service configurator pattern, 105–9
extensibility
pattern improvement overview, 85–7
to retargeting on new platforms, 84–5
via custom implementation strategies, 85
via dynamic configuration of custom strategies, 85
high-performance real-time I/O subsystem, 15–18
interface, 5
managing connections using acceptor-connector pattern, 93–6
optimized demultiplexing strategies, 27–9
simplifying concurrency using Active Object pattern, 97–100
statically configured, 83–4
strategy configurations, 104
support interchangeable behaviors with strategy pattern, 101–4
use of patterns to resolve design challenges, 87–109
OS dispatcher, 40
OS platforms, 4

P

Paging network, 127
Password, 228–9
PDA (personal digital assistant), 129–31
Perfect Forward Secrecy, 238
PGP/MIME, 249
Physical Layer, 221–2
2PL scheme, 153
Plug-ins, 199
Portable computers, 129
Portable handheld devices, 129
Portable Object Adapter (POA), 6
Preprocessor macros, 102
Presentation Layer, 221
Pretty Good Privacy (PGP), 249
Priorities assignment, 49
Priority inversions, 100–2
Privacy, 274
Internet, 210
Pretty Good Privacy (PGP), 249
Privacy Enhanced Mail (PEM), 249
Private data, 121

Project Open Book, 292
Protocol Independent Multicast (PIM)
    routing protocols, 233
Protocol layering, 221
Public data, 121
Public key cryptography, 247
Public Key Infrastructure (PKI), 237–41, 244, 249, 250
Public Key (KEY) record, 235
Push technologies, 206–8

Q

Quality of service (QoS), 3, 7–11
    guarantees, 2, 17
    information, 27, 33, 37
    mechanisms, 74
    parameters, 15
    requirements, 17–19, 31–2, 34–9, 82, 83, 97, 114
    specification, 34–5
Query languages, 137
Query processing, 137, 140
Queued remote procedure calls (QRPC), 171–2
Queuing mechanism, 142

R

Rapid Application Development (RAD), 202
Rapid cache validation, 170
RAPS, 325
Rate monotonic analysis (RMA), 20, 31
Rate monotonic scheduling (RMS), 17, 20, 31, 59
Rates groups, 20
RDOs, 171–2
Reactor pattern, 86, 90–3
Real-time dynamically configurable, ORB middleware, 82
Real-time I/O (RIO) subsystem, 17
Real-time IDL (RIDL) schemas, 35, 39
Real-time inter-ORB protocol (RIOP), 20, 22
Real-time operating systems (RTOS), 74
Real-time ORB Core
    design, 50–82
    scheduling and dispatching of client requests, 25

Real-time scheduling service, 32–4
    and run-time scheduler, 17–18
Real-time threads, 47–9
Real-time vs. high-performance tradeoffs, 13
Red Sage project, 292
Remote access devices, 130
Remote access network architecture, 125–7
Remote access system, 122
Remote access to data, 121
Remote procedure call (RPC), 171
Request for Comments (RFC), 220–1
Request priority assignments, 49–50
Resource utilization, 164
Reverse Path Forwarding (RPF), 233
RJ-45 wiring, 222
Robots. *See* Mobile robot control architectures
Routing Information Protocol (RIP), 229–30
    version 2 (RIPv2), 229–31, 239
Routing protocols
    Core-Based Trees (CBT) multicast, 234
    integrated-ISIS (I-ISIS), 229
Routing protocols and technology, 227–34
Rover project, 171–2
RT_Info, 45–50
RT_Info struct, 37–9
RT_Operation, 47, 48, 50
    interface, 35–7
    priority assignments, 44–5

S

Satellite network, 127
Schedulability, 49
Schema integration, 136–7, 140
Secondary Camera And Maneuverability Platform (SCAMP), 328–9
Secure Electronic Transaction (SET) protocol, 248
Secure HTTP (S-HTTP), 210
Secure Shell (SSH) application, 244
Secure Socket Layer (SSL), 210, 245–7
    version 3 (SSLv3), 248
Security
    digital libraries, 273–4
    Internet, 219–55
    Internet Protocol (IP), 224–7, 245
    Transport Layer Security (TLS), 245, 248
    user model, 242

Security association, 225, 238
Security Parameters Index (SPI), 225
Semantic analysis, 302–3
Server-Side Includes (SSI), 204–6
Service Configurator pattern, 29, 87, 105–9
Session Layer, 221
SGML, 188–9
SHA-1 cryptographic hash function, 226
Shared data, 121
Signature (SIG) record, 235
Simple Mail Transfer Protocol (SMTP), 193
Simple Network Management Protocol (SNMP)
  current status, 242
  future directions, 242
  version 1 (SNMPv1), 241–2
  version 2 (SNMPv2), 237, 241–2
  version 3 (SNMPv3), 242–3
Singapore, digital libraries, 297
Site autonomy and heterogeneity, 134–6
Site graph algorithm, 151
Solaris real-time thread dispatcher, 63–73
Source Address, 222
Standard Generalized Markup Language (SGML), 188–9
Standards
  data encryption (DES), 227
  digital libraries, 267–8
  electronic information, 267–8
  Library of Congress, 287
Stanford University, 285–7
State parameters, 208–9
Steganography, 273
Strategy pattern, 87
STREAMS, 17
STRIPS, 321–2
Structural differences, 136
Summary schemas model (SSM), 125, 139, 144–6, 153
SunSoft IIOP. *See* IIOP
Synonym, 145
System transparency issues, 136–7

T

Taiwan, digital libraries, 297–8
TAO, 1, 3, 62, 64
  abstract factory pattern, 105
  Acceptor-Connector pattern, 95–6
  Active Object pattern, 99–100
  benefits of use of patterns, 112–13
  blackbox benchmarks, 66–7
  buffer management system, 31
  concurrency architecture, 72
  connection architecture, 72
  efficient and predictable memory management, 12
  efficient and predictable presentation layer, 12
  efficient and predictable real-time communication protocols and protocol engines, 11
  efficient and predictable request demultiplexing and dispatching, 11–12
  extensible software architecture, 82–113
  inter-ORB protocol engine, 18–19
  liabilities of use of patterns, 113
  off-line scheduling service, 41–50, 45
  on-line scheduling model, 39–41
  optimized ORB demultiplexing strategies, 27–9
  priority-based concurrency architecture, 20
  priority-based connection architecture, 21–2
  Reactor pattern, 92–3
  real-time I/O (RIO) subsystem, 17
  real-time scheduling service, 32–4
    and run-time scheduler, 17–18
  real-time vs. high-performance tradeoffs, 13
  relationships among patterns used in, 86
  Service Configurator pattern, 108–9
  strategy pattern, 103–4
  synopsis, 9
  Thread-Specific Storage pattern, 31, 101
  using TCP, 78–9
  whitebox benchmarks, 71–2
  wrapper facade pattern, 89
Task Control Architecture (TCA), 325
TCP, 180, 192, 220–2, 231, 243
  Sequence Number Prediction, 247
  session stealing, 231
  TAO using, 78–9
TCP/IP protocol, 180, 182, 192, 246
TCP SYN Flooding, 247
TELNET, 192, 193
Term indexing, 301

Textual document indexing, 301
Thread-specific storage pattern, 87, 100–2
Threats, 222–4, 228–9, 234–7, 243–6, 248–9
Trademark infringement, 271
Transaction management, 137–8, 146–58
Transaction processing, 141
  model, 147–9
Transmission Control Protocol. See TCP
Transmission File Protocol. See TCP
Transport Layer, 221, 222
Transport Layer Security (TLS), 245
  version 1 (TLSv1), 248
Trivial File Transfer Protocol (TFTP), 193
TULIP Project, 292–3
Two-phase commit (2PC), 150, 153
Two-phase locking (2PL), 152

U

Unicast key management, 238–9
Unicast routing, inter-domain, 229–32
Unicast traffic, 232
Uniform Resource Locators (URLs), 180, 207, 209
United Kingdom, digital libraries, 294
University of California at Berkeley, 280–1
University of California at Santa Barbara, 281–2
University of Illinois at Urbana-Champaign, 283–4
University of Michigan, 291–2
University of Michigan Digital Library (UMDL), 284–5
Unrepeatable read, 146
Upper-layer protocols, 224
User Datagram Protocol (UDP), 222
User-level locking overhead, 72–3
User Security Model, 242

V

Value-added networks (VANs), 245

Vector Field model, 341
Virtual communities, 215–16
V-locking
  algorithm, 161–5
  concurrency control, 158–65
VRML interface, 305

W

Web. *See* World Wide Web (WWW)
Whitebox benchmarks, 63, 67–73
Wide Area Information Systems (WAIS), 180
Wide area network (WAN), 182
Wide area wireless network, 127
Wireless LAN, 127
Wit project, 172
World Wide Web (WWW), 120, 179–218, 244, 306
  applications, 186
  behavior, 215
  characteristics, 183–4
  dynamic technologies, 194–210
  end user's perspective, 184–5
  historical perspective, 185–8
  social effect, 214–16
  success factors, 183–4
  survey data, 184–5
  underlying technologies, 188–95
  vs. Internet, 220
Wrapper facade pattern, 86, 88–90, 92

X

X.500 Directory Service, 240
X.509 certificate
  version 1 (X.509v1), 241
  version 3 (X.509v3), 240, 241, 247
XML, 190–2

Y

Yale University Project Open Book, 292

Contents of Volumes in This Series

Volume 21

The Web of Computing: Computer Technology as Social Organization
    ROB KLING AND WALT SCACCHI
Computer Design and Description Languages
    SUBRATA DASGUPTA
Microcomputers: Applications, Problems, and Promise
    ROBERT C. GAMMILL
Query Optimization in Distributed Data Base Systems
    GIOVANNI MARIA SACCO AND S. BING YAO
Computers in the World of Chemistry
    PETER LYKOS
Library Automation Systems and Networks
    JAMES E. RUSH

Volume 22

Legal Protection of Software: A Survey
    MICHAEL C. GEMIGNANI
Algorithms for Public Key Cryptosystems: Theory and Applications
    S. LAKSHMIVARAHAN
Software Engineering Environments
    ANTHONY I. WASSERMAN
Principles of Rule-Based Expert Systems
    BRUCE G. BUCHANAN AND RICHARD O. DUDA
Conceptual Representation of Medical Knowledge for Diagnosis by Computer: MDX and Related Systems
    B. CHANDRASEKARAN AND SANJAY MITTAL
Specification and Implementation of Abstract Data Types
    ALFS T. BERZTISS AND SATISH THATTE

Volume 23

Supercomputers and VLSI: The Effect of Large-Scale Integration on Computer Architecture
    LAWRENCE SNYDER
Information and Computation
    J. F. TRAUB AND H. WOZNIAKOWSKI
The Mass Impact of Videogame Technology
    THOMAS A. DEFANTI
Developments in Decision Support Systems
    ROBERT H. BONCZEK, CLYDE W. HOLSAPPLE, AND ANDREW B. WHINSTON
Digital Control Systems
    PETER DORATO AND DANIEL PETERSEN

International Developments in Information Privacy
  G. K. GUPTA
Parallel Sorting Algorithms
  S. LAKSHMIVARAHAN, SUDARSHAN K. DHALL, AND LESLIE L. MILLER

Volume 24

Software Effort Estimation and Productivity
  S. D. CONTE, H. E. DUNSMORE, AND V. Y. SHEN
Theoretical Issues Concerning Protection in Operating Systems
  MICHAEL A. HARRISON
Developments in Firmware Engineering
  SUBRATA DASGUPTA AND BRUCE D. SHRIVER
The Logic of Learning: A Basis for Pattern Recognition and for Improvement of Performance
  RANAN B. BANERJI
The Current State of Language Data Processing
  PAUL L. GARVIN
Advances in Information Retrieval: Where Is That /#*&@¢ Record?
  DONALD H. KRAFT
The Development of Computer Science Education
  WILLIAM F. ATCHISON

Volume 25

Accessing Knowledge through Natural Language
  NICK CERCONE AND GORDON MCCALLA
Design Analysis and Performance Evaluation Methodologies for Database Computers
  STEVEN A. DEMURJIAN, DAVID K. HSIAO, AND PAULA R. STRAWSER
Partitioning of Massive/Real-Time Programs for Parallel Processing
  I. LEE, N. PRYWES, AND B. SZYMANSKI
Computers in High-Energy Physics
  MICHAEL METCALF
Social Dimensions of Office Automation
  ABBE MOWSHOWITZ

Volume 26

The Explicit Support of Human Reasoning in Decision Support Systems
  AMITAVA DUTTA
Unary Processing
  W. J. POPPELBAUM, A. DOLLAS, J. B. GLICKMAN, AND C. O'TOOLE
Parallel Algorithms for Some Computational Problems
  ABHA MOITRA AND S. SITHARAMA IYENGAR
Multistage Interconnection Networks for Multiprocessor Systems
  S. C. KOTHARI
Fault-Tolerant Computing
  WING N. TOY
Techniques and Issues in Testing and Validation of VLSI Systems
  H. K. REGHBATI

Software Testing and Verification
    LEE J. WHITE
Issues in the Development of Large, Distributed, and Reliable Software
    C. V. RAMAMOORTHY, ATUL PRAKASH, VIJAY GARG, TSUNEO YAMAURA, AND ANUPAM BHIDE

Volume 27

Military Information Processing
    JAMES STARK DRAPER
Multidimensional Data Structures: Review and Outlook
    S. SITHARAMA IYENGAR, R. L. KASHYAP, V. K. VAISHNAVI, AND N. S. V. RAO
Distributed Data Allocation Strategies
    ALAN R. HEVNER AND ARUNA RAO
A Reference Model for Mass Storage Systems
    STEPHEN W. MILLER
Computers in the Health Sciences
    KEVIN C. O'KANE
Computer Vision
    AZRIEL ROSENFELD
Supercomputer Performance: The Theory, Practice, and Results
    OLAF M. LUBECK
Computer Science and Information Technology in the People's Republic of China: The Emergence of Connectivity
    JOHN H. MAIER

Volume 28

The Structure of Design Processes
    SUBRATA DASGUPTA
Fuzzy Sets and Their Applications to Artificial Intelligence
    ABRAHAM KANDEL AND MORDECHAY SCHNEIDER
Parallel Architecture for Database Systems
    A. R. HURSON, L. L. MILLER, S. H. PAKZAD, M. H. EICH, AND B. SHIRAZI
Optical and Optoelectronic Computing
    MIR MOJTABA MIRSALEHI, MUSTAFA A. G. ABUSHAGUR, AND H. JOHN CAULFIELD
Management Intelligence Systems
    MANFRED KOCHEN

Volume 29

Models of Multilevel Computer Security
    JONATHAN K. MILLEN
Evaluation, Description, and Invention: Paradigms for Human-Computer Interaction
    JOHN M. CARROLL
Protocol Engineering
    MING T. LIU
Computer Chess: Ten Years of Significant Progress
    MONROE NEWBORN
Soviet Computing in the 1980s
    RICHARD W. JUDY AND ROBERT W. CLOUGH

Volume 30

Specialized Parallel Architectures for Textual Databases
    A. R. HURSON, L. L. MILLER, S. H. PAKZAD, AND JIA-BING CHENG
Database Design and Performance
    MARK L. GILLENSON
Software Reliability
    ANTHONY IANNINO AND JOHN D. MUSA
Cryptography Based Data Security
    GEORGE J. DAVIDA AND YVO DESMEDT
Soviet Computing in the 1980s: A Survey of the Software and its Applications
    RICHARD W. JUDY AND ROBERT W. CLOUGH

Volume 31

Command and Control Information Systems Engineering: Progress and Prospects
    STEPHEN J. ANDRIOLE
Perceptual Models for Automatic Speech Recognition Systems
    RENATO DeMORI, MATHEW J. PALAKAL, AND PIERO COSI
Availability and Reliability Modeling for Computer Systems
    DAVID I. HEIMANN, NITIN MITTAL, AND KISHOR S. TRIVEDI
Molecular Computing
    MICHAEL CONRAD
Foundations of Information Science
    ANTHONY DEBONS

Volume 32

Computer-Aided Logic Synthesis for VLSI Chips
    SABURO MUROGA
Sensor-Driven Intelligent Robotics
    MOHAN M. TRIVEDI AND CHUXIN CHEN
Multidatabase Systems: An Advanced Concept in Handling Distributed Data
    A. R. HURSON AND M. W. BRIGHT
Models of the Mind and Machine: Information Flow and Control between Humans and Computers
    KENT L. NORMAN
Computerized Voting
    ROY G. SALTMAN

Volume 33

Reusable Software Components
    BRUCE W. WEIDE, WILLIAM F. OGDEN, AND STUART H. ZWEBEN
Object-Oriented Modeling and Discrete-Event Simulation
    BERNARD P. ZIEGLER
Human-Factors Issues in Dialog Design
    THIAGARAJAN PALANIVEL AND MARTIN HELANDER
Neurocomputing Formalisms for Computational Learning and Machine Intelligence
    S. GULATI, J. BARHEN, AND S. S. IYENGAR

Visualization in Scientific Computing
    THOMAS A. DEFANTI AND MAXINE D. BROWN

Volume 34

An Assessment and Analysis of Software Reuse
    TED J. BIGGERSTAFF
Multisensory Computer Vision
    N. NANDHAKUMAR AND J. K. AGGARWAL
Parallel Computer Architectures
    RALPH DUNCAN
Content-Addressable and Associative Memory
    LAWRENCE CHISVIN AND R. JAMES DUCKWORTH
Image Database Management
    WILLIAM I. GROSKY AND RAJIV MEHROTRA
Paradigmatic Influences on Information Systems Development Methodologies: Evolution and Conceptual Advances
    RUDY HIRSCHHEIM AND HEINZ K. KLEIN

Volume 35

Conceptual and Logical Design of Relational Databases
    S. B. NAVATHE AND G. PERNUL
Computational Approaches for Tactile Information Processing and Analysis
    HRISHIKESH P. GADAGKAR AND MOHAN M. TRIVEDI
Object-Oriented System Development Methods
    ALAN R. HEVNER
Reverse Engineering
    JAMES H. CROSS II, ELLIOT J. CHIKOFSKY, AND CHARLES H. MAY, JR.
Multiprocessing
    CHARLES J. FLECKENSTEIN, D. H. GILL, DAVID HEMMENDINGER, C. L. MCCREARY,
    JOHN D. MCGREGOR, ROY P. PARGAS, ARTHUR M. RIEHL, AND VIRGIL WALLENTINE
The Landscape of International Computing
    EDWARD M. ROCHE, SEYMOUR E. GOODMAN, AND HSINCHUN CHEN

Volume 36

Zero Defect Software: Cleanroom Engineering
    HARLAN D. MILLS
Role of Verification in the Software Specification Process
    MARVIN V. ZELKOWITZ
Computer Applications in Music Composition and Research
    GARY E. WITTLICH, ERIC J. ISAACSON, AND JEFFREY E. HASS
Artificial Neural Networks in Control Applications
    V. VEMURI
Developments in Uncertainty-Based Information
    GEORGE J. KLIR
Human Factors in Human–Computer System Design
    MARY CAROL DAY AND SUSAN J. BOYCE

Volume 37

Approaches to Automatic Programming
    CHARLES RICH AND RICHARD C. WATERS
Digital Signal Processing
    STEPHEN A. DYER AND BRIAN K. HARMS
Neural Networks for Pattern Recognition
    S. C. KOTHARI AND HEEKUCK OH
Experiments in Computational Heuristics and Their Lessons for Software and Knowledge Engineering
    JURG NIEVERGELT
High-Level Synthesis of Digital Circuits
    GIOVANNI DE MICHELI
Issues in Dataflow Computing
    BEN LEE AND A. R. HURSON
A Sociological History of the Neural Network Controversy
    MIKEL OLAZARAN

Volume 38

Database Security
    GÜNTHER PERNUL
Functional Representation and Causal Processes
    B. CHANDRASEKARAN
Computer-Based Medical Systems
    JOHN M. LONG
Algorithm-Specific Parallel Processing with Linear Processor Arrays
    JOSE A. B. FORTES, BENJAMIN W. WAH, WEIJA SHANG, AND KUMAR N. GANAPATHY
Information as a Commodity: Assessment of Market Value
    ABBE MOWSHOWITZ

Volume 39

Maintenance and Evolution of Software Products
    ANNELIESE VON MAYRHAUSER
Software Measurement: A Decision-Process Approach
    WARREN HARRISON
Active Databases: Concepts and Design Support
    THOMAS A. MUECK
Operating Systems Enhancements for Distributed Shared Memory
    VIRGINIA LO
The Social Design of Worklife with Computers and Networks: A Natural Systems Perspective
    ROB KLING AND TOM JEWETT

Volume 40

Program Understanding: Models and Experiments
    A. VON MAYRHAUSER AND A. M. VANS
Software Prototyping
    ALAN M. DAVIS

Rapid Prototyping of Microelectronic Systems
    APOSTOLOS DOLLAS AND J. D. STERLING BABCOCK
Cache Coherence in Multiprocessors: A Survey
    MAZIN S. YOUSIF, M. J. THAZHUTHAVEETIL, AND C. R. DAS
The Adequacy of Office Models
    CHANDRA S. AMARAVADI, JOEY F. GEORGE, OLIVIA R. LIU SHENG, AND JAY F. NUNAMAKER

Volume 41

Directions in Software Process Research
    H. DIETER ROMBACH AND MARTIN VERLAGE
The Experience Factory and Its Relationship to Other Quality Approaches
    VICTOR R. BASILI
CASE Adoption: A Process, Not an Event
    JOCK A. RADER
On the Necessary Conditions for the Composition of Integrated Software Engineering Environments
    DAVID J. CARNEY AND ALAN W. BROWN
Software Quality, Software Process, and Software Testing
    DICK HAMLET
Advances in Benchmarking Techniques: New Standards and Quantitative Metrics
    THOMAS CONTE AND WEN-MEI W. HWU
An Evolutionary Path for Transaction Processing Systems
    CARLTON PU, AVRAHAM LEFF, AND SHU-WEI, F. CHEN

Volume 42

Nonfunctional Requirements of Real-Time Systems
    TEREZA G. KIRNER AND ALAN M. DAVIS
A Review of Software Inspections
    ADAM PORTER, HARVEY SIY, AND LAWRENCE VOTTA
Advances in Software Reliability Engineering
    JOHN D. MUSA AND WILLA EHRLICH
Network Interconnection and Protocol Conversion
    MING T. LIU
A Universal Model of Legged Locomotion Gaits
    S. T. VENKATARAMAN

Volume 43

Program Slicing
    DAVID W. BINKLEY AND KEITH BRIAN GALLAGHER
Language Features for the Interconnection of Software Components
    RENATE MOTSCHNIG-PITRIK AND ROLAND T. MITTERMEIR
Using Model Checking to Analyze Requirements and Designs
    JOANNE ATLEE, MARSHA CHECHIK, AND JOHN GANNON
Information Technology and Productivity: A Review of the Literature
    ERIK BRYNJOLFSSON AND SHINKYU YANG
The Complexity of Problems
    WILLIAM GASARCH

3-D Computer Vision Using Structured Light: Design, Calibration, and Implementation Issues
  FRED W. DEPIERO AND MOHAN M. TRIVEDI

Volume 44

Managing the Risks in Information Systems and Technology (IT)
  ROBERT N. CHARETTE
Software Cost Estimation: A Review of Models, Process and Practice
  FIONA WALKERDEN AND ROSS JEFFERY
Experimentation in Software Engineering
  SHARI LAWRENCE PFLEEGER
Parallel Computer Construction Outside the United States
  RALPH DUNCAN
Control of Information Distribution and Access
  RALF HAUSER
Asynchronous Transfer Mode: An Engineering Network Standard for High Speed Communications
  RONALD J. VETTER
Communication Complexity
  EYAL KUSHILEVITZ

Volume 45

Control in Multi-threaded Information Systems
  PABLO A. STRAUB AND CARLOS A. HURTADO
Parallelization of DOALL and DOACROSS Loops—a Survey
  A. R. HURSON, JOFORD T. LIM, KRISHNA M. KAVI, AND BEN LEE
Programming Irregular Applications: Runtime Support, Compilation and Tools
  JOEL SALTZ, GAGAN AGRAWAL, CHIALIN CHANG, RAJA DAS, GUY EDJLALI, PAUL HAVLAK,
  YUAN-SHIN HWANG, BONGKI MOON, RAVI PONNUSAMY, SHAMIK SHARMA, ALAN SUSSMAN
  AND MUSTAFA UYSAL
Optimization Via Evolutionary Processes
  SRILATA RAMAN AND L. M. PATNAIK
Software Reliability and Readiness Assessment Based on the Non-homogeneous Poisson Process
  AMRIT L. GOEL AND KUNE-ZANG YANG
Computer-supported Cooperative Work and Groupware
  JONATHAN GRUDIN AND STEVEN E. POLTROCK
Technology and Schools
  GLEN L. BULL

Volume 46

Software Process Appraisal and Improvement: Models and Standards
  MARK C. PAULK
A Software Process Engineering Framework
  JYRKI KONTIO
Gaining Business Value from IT Investments
  PAMELA SIMMONS
Reliability Measurement, Analysis, and Improvement for Large Software Systems
  JEFF TIAN

Role-based Access Control
  RAVI SANDHU
Multithreaded Systems
  KRISHNA M. KAVI, BEN LEE AND ALLI R. HURSON
Coordination Models and Languages
  GEORGE A. PAPADOPOULOS AND FARHAD ARBAB
Multidisciplinary Problem Solving Environments for Computational Science
  ELIAS N. HOUSTIS, JOHN R. RICE AND NAREN RAMAKRISHNAN

Volume 47

Natural Language Processing: A Human–Computer Interaction Perspective
  BILL MANARIS
Cognitive Adaptive Computer Help (COACH): A Case Study
  EDWIN J. SELKER
Cellular Automata Models of Self-replicating Systems
  JAMES A. REGGIA, HUI-HSIEN CHOU, AND JASON D. LOHN
Ultrasound Visualization
  THOMAS R. NELSON
Patterns and System Development
  BRANDON GOLDFEDDER
High Performance Digital Video Servers: Storage and Retrieval of Compressed Scalable Video
  SEUNGYUP PAEK AND SHIH-FU CHANG
Software Acquisition: The Custom/Package and Insource/Outsource Dimensions
  PAUL NELSON, ABRAHAM SEIDMANN, AND WILLIAM RICHMOND

Volume 48

Architectures and Patterns for Developing High-performance, Real-time ORB Endsystems
  DOUGLAS C. SCHMIDT, DAVID L. LEVINE AND CHRIS CLEELAND
Heterogeneous Data Access in a Mobile Environment – Issues and Solutions
  J. B. LIM AND A. R. HURSON
The World Wide Web
  HAL BERGHEL AND DOUGLAS BLANK
Progress in Internet Security
  RANDALL J. ATKINSON AND J. ERIC KLINKER
Digital Libraries: Social Issues and Technological Advances
  HSINCHUN CHEN AND ANDREA L. HOUSTON
Architectures for Mobile Robot Control
  JULIO K. ROSENBLATT AND JAMES A. HENDLER

ISBN 0-12-012148-4